Praise for *Invisible Rulers*

"Renée DiResta is a superhero protecting reality from insanity. Her work and voice are indispensable. If humanity doesn't ruin its future through idiocy, DiResta will be one of the reasons why."

—Jaron Lanier, author of
Ten Arguments for Deleting Your Social Media Accounts Right Now

"In this compelling and beautifully written book, DiResta sheds fresh light and understanding on the greatest threat to social cohesion. If you care about securing a better future for generations to come, read this book, and work with others to implement DiResta's thoughtful recommendations."

—General H. R. McMaster, author of *Battlegrounds* and
At War with Ourselves

"Who decides what we pay attention to, whom we trust, and how we engage with each other? In *Invisible Rulers*, a unique and unusual work of observation and scholarship, DiResta provides the answer—and it is not reassuring. Among them are people who know how to game algorithms, people who want to sell advertising, or people who want to alter our politics, foreign authoritarians among them. DiResta shows how domestic trolls and foreign oligarchs now wield influence on a global scale, turning online trends into truth, and shaping our understanding of reality itself."

—Anne Applebaum, author of *Twilight of Democracy*

"No one understands this new world of information warfare, a world where the rumor mill and the propaganda machine work in tandem to distort reality, better than DiResta. She is the go-to person for everyone who wants to understand influence operations, from technologists to government officials. She sees things before others do. And more important, she knows what it takes to fight back."

—Bruce Schneier, author of *A Hacker's Mind*

INVISIBLE RULERS

The People Who
Turn Lies into Reality

Renée DiResta

PUBLICAFFAIRS

New York

PublicAffairs

Hachette Book Group

1290 Avenue of the Americas, New York, NY 10104

www.publicaffairsbooks.com

@Public_Affairs

Printed in the United States of America

First Edition: June 2024

Published by PublicAffairs, an imprint of Hachette Book Group, Inc. The PublicAffairs name and logo is a registered trademark of the Hachette Book Group.

The Hachette Speakers Bureau provides a wide range of authors for speaking events. To find out more, go to hachettespeakersbureau.com or email HachetteSpeakers@hbgusa.com.

PublicAffairs books may be purchased in bulk for business, educational, or promotional use. For more information, please contact your local bookseller or the Hachette Book Group Special Markets Department at special.markets@hbgusa.com.

The publisher is not responsible for websites (or their content) that are not owned by the publisher.

Library of Congress Control Number: 2024934465

ISBNs: 9781541703377 (hardcover), 9781541703391 (ebook)

LSC-C

Printing 3, 2024

To Justin, A., B., and C.

Contents

Introduction

Power, Influence, Lies, and Truth

IN LATE DECEMBER 2014, Patient Zero walked in through the park gates of the Happiest Place on Earth, kicking off what would come to be known as the Disneyland measles outbreak. Over the next month, more than 120 people in California fell ill, including a dozen infants. Nearly half of the infected weren't vaccinated. Dozens of the sick wound up hospitalized. The outbreak quickly spread to neighboring states, and by the end of the year, more than six hundred cases of measles were recorded across the country. It was a shockingly high number for a disease that had been declared eliminated in the United States fourteen years earlier.

I had no way of knowing, back then, that this incident would trigger one of the opening skirmishes in a war for power, influence, and reality itself—a conflict in which the ends justify any means, and one that has ripped America apart, threatened our very democracy, and consumed my own life for the past decade, leading to death threats, congressional subpoenas, lawsuits, and legal bills running into seven figures.

When the Disneyland outbreak started, I was the mom of a twelve-month-old. As it happened, just one month prior I'd been poring over a decade's worth of California school immunization statistics. The effort had been inspired by an unfortunate San Francisco parenting rite of passage: getting my kid onto preschool waiting lists before his first birthday. While pregnant, I'd joined a few mommy boards and quickly gotten fed up with the tendentious anti-vax threads that rehashed debunked nonsense. Links to the blogs of grifters selling homeopathic oils were presented as counterpoints to safety studies in medical journals. There was a whooping cough outbreak happening, even as celebrity pediatricians were telling their vaccine-hesitant clients that it was OK to "hide in the herd";[1] they knew the diseases were dangerous but assured these parents that *other* people were still vaccinating, so overall rates would keep the unvaccinated protected. I'd read about California schools with vaccination rates "lower than South Sudan,"[2] and I didn't want my son to wind up at one.

And so I found myself scrutinizing tables that showed the rates of "personal belief" exemptions—opt-outs justified not by any medical or even religious concern but by the simple desire to opt out. More than ten years of data from across the state showed an unmistakable trend over time: a steady decline in classroom vaccination rates.

It had been nearly twenty years since a fraudulent study by Andrew Wakefield asserted a link between vaccines and autism, instilling fear in a generation. Since then, study after study had confirmed the safety of the measles-mumps-rubella (MMR) vaccine, and the media had long since stopped giving airtime to the vaccine-autism conspiracy theory. And yet the trend suggested that a small but growing minority of the California public was increasingly skeptical of the safety of routine childhood shots. The opt-outs, meanwhile, driven primarily by fear instilled by bad information, didn't only impact the families of those who claimed them. They impacted everyone. They impacted other people's kids.

I wrote a quick blog post about my frustration: "How California's Terrible Vaccination Policy Puts Kids at Risk." Then I did something I'd never done before: I called my local state assembly representative to ask whether the policy might be changed.

When I made that first call in November 2014, the assemblyman's staffer said no: the anti-vaccine movement was a well-organized political force, and there was no appetite for a fight over school vaccine opt-outs. But when the Disneyland outbreak began, I called back, and the reaction I got was completely different: the outbreak had highlighted the extent to which anti-vaccine misinformation—increasingly visible on social media—had exacerbated hesitancy. The public was angry. The state senator from Sacramento, Dr. Richard Pan, happened to be a pediatrician, and he was introducing legislation to eliminate the personal-belief exemption in an effort to raise classroom vaccination rates (which would impact community coverage more broadly). The San Francisco staffer asked whether I might like to help support the legislation as a parent voice and suggested I call Senator Pan's office. So I did.

I had no idea what I was getting into.

The next few months would upend my understanding of politics, propaganda, and social movements, as I got a firsthand experience of how a new system of persuasion—influencers, algorithms, and crowds—was radically transforming what we paid attention to, whom we trusted, and how we engaged with each other. I went down the rabbit hole of the anti-vaccine movement, joining its groups, following its influencers, and spending hours each night looking at its memes, becoming an observer of what felt like an alternate reality...while simultaneously trying to grow a countermovement, in real time, to push back against all of it. It was obvious to me that this was a new battlefield, that the rules of engagement had changed. It was a war of memes, not facts. Winning was going to take more than quoting some vaccine safety statistics.

Dr. Pan's staffer had connected me with a handful of other moms who'd also called asking if they could be useful. They included a former senate staffer, a graphic designer, a professor who specialized in vaccine law, a nurse and longtime community organizer, a public relations pro, and a conservative activist accustomed to generating bipartisan consensus in the overwhelmingly blue state of California. I had a fair bit of quantitative analysis and data science experience from years on Wall Street and a solid understanding of social media from my then current gig in venture capital. Together, we had to figure out how to grow a pro-vaccine parental countermovement virtually overnight. So we set up a Facebook page and Twitter (now doing business as X) account under the name Vaccinate California. We wanted to make sure that people searching for information about the bill found us, so we started posting memes featuring cute kids (our own) with our logo, alongside arguments making the case for why school shots mattered.

A hashtag had begun to emerge around the number assigned to Senator Pan's bill: *#SB277*. From the start it was largely dominated by antivaccine activists, many of whom got nasty in the replies to any comment in support of the bill. Some were from California, but what quickly became apparent to those of us waging this war was that many were from out of state; anti-vaccine advocacy, it seemed, was a core part of their identity, and they'd been at this for a while. They deluged our Facebook posts and Twitter replies, accusing us of being pharma-paid baby killers. That was just the beginning of the attack.

Some dug through our backgrounds, families, and past jobs. Others found and posted our addresses on social media (a tactic known as *doxxing*). A few particularly delusional trolls took photos of my baby son that I'd shared on a personal tumblr and Facebook the prior Halloween and began reposting them to Twitter, accusing me of not really vaccinating him, being a devil worshiper (one possible interpretation of a Maleficent costume, I suppose), and other bizarre and creepy things. I set my personal social media accounts to private, but they'd already taken the photos they thought would be most exploitable. Anti-vax activists made videos calling us "medical fascists," splicing us into footage of Adolf Hitler leading rallies; on two occasions, they followed outspoken supporters of the bill down the streets of Sacramento, posting their photos and location to incite both online *and* offline harassment. They barraged the practice ratings of physicians on our side with one-star reviews and called to scream at their receptionists. It quickly became clear that cute kid memes were not going to be enough; this was going to be bare-knuckle-brawl politics. They wanted to intimidate us into simply bowing out of the fight.

The fight to pass the bill, which began in January 2015, turned out to be a six-month battle that left me deeply concerned about the growth and reach of the anti-vaccine movement. But what fascinated and alarmed me most was the mechanics of *how* the battle was fought, because I could tell even as it was happening that the tactics and dynamics were applicable to far more than one small political fight in California. There were bots and trolls, coordinated harassment brigades and doxxing, and Facebook pages run by God-knows-who. There were YouTube channels and secret Facebook groups with tens of thousands of members, dedicated to mobilizing online armies, gaming trending algorithms, and selectively editing videos to recruit new adherents. There were precision-targeted ad campaigns—including ours!—that focused on reaching handfuls of constituents in specific zip codes; Facebook's powerful targeting tools made them possible, though the company did little to verify who was running the campaigns and offered no easy way for audiences to know who was behind them. There were viral memes and commandeered hashtags. These were the tools—sometimes weapons—that by 2020 would be the norm for networked activism in an increasingly polarized America, but only five years prior were hardly known at all. It is sometimes easy to forget how rapidly our online world has changed.

It felt like I was seeing the future, while simultaneously participating in it: virality determined what people talked about, and virality was a function of how well influencers, algorithms, and crowds could make something capture the public's attention. Public opinion on any given issue would be shaped by content currents that flowed across high-speed, frictionless social networks that curated what their users saw and, increasingly, whom they connected with. The accuracy of the message, or whether it came from a credible source, was largely irrelevant. What mattered was whether the content captured user attention and generated engagement: whether it made audiences want to participate, by liking, sharing, or joining a group around whatever the cause happened to be. "Public opinion" no longer even seemed like the right phrase—it implied a need to persuade a mass group of people, a majority of society, even as that seemed increasingly impossible. The online world was rapidly devolving into factions.

Three points quickly became clear to me. First, the anti-vaccine opposition was well networked and really understood social media. Second, this relatively small group—most of whom sincerely believed that vaccines caused autism and the government was covering it up— had influence that belied its size. While the pro-vaccine position was still the dominant opinion in the "real world"—approximately 85 percent of kids in California were vaccinated—we were a very small minority in the online conversation. Third, public health officials and institutions absolutely did not understand the importance of the internet in shaping social movements...or community beliefs.

So, to understand how the opposition organized and attracted new members, I began to study their content and networks online. I wanted to understand who was influential in their community—what kind of rhetoric and content they used, what topics they talked about, how they engaged with the broader crowd of activists and persuaded them to act. I followed Robert F. Kennedy Jr. and Del Bigtree and the other propagandists for the movement, as well as the contrarian doctors who sold medical exemptions and "homeopathic vaccines" to the fearful. I observed the automated bots that incessantly posted anti-vaccine memes to the *#SB277* hashtag on Twitter, allowing the anti position to dominate share of voice in the conversation. I noticed that longtime die-hard "vaccine truthers"—the most conspiratorial members of the community, deeply convinced that the government and "Big Pharma" were colluding to cover up a link between vaccines and autism—had suddenly begun to conceal those deeply held beliefs and instead emphasize new talking points that refocused the conversation around "parental rights" and "medical freedom." School immunization requirements were government tyranny and an affront to "health choice," they claimed, as they began to reach out to libertarian and Tea Party activists to grow their movement. The anti-vaccine faction also, unfortunately, liberally relied on harassment: sending online brigades of angry activists from all over the world to barrage California legislators whom they saw as being on the fence or as having disrespected their movement; targeting doctors who testified in legislative hearings in favor of the bill with negative reviews and threats to staff; and doxxing ordinary parents advocating for *their own* "parental rights." It was certainly my first experience being doxxed and harassed for expressing a political point of view.

I began to write about these dynamics, posting on my little blog and on Twitter, sending notes to the California representatives considering the bill—many of whom were trying to figure out why they were being harassed and whether the overwhelming amount of anti-vaccine activism online meant that the public was, in fact, opposed to the bill. It was polling well among their constituents, they observed, but the social media conversation was overwhelmingly toxic. How could those two things be reconciled?

And that, it turned out, was one of the key challenges of my second point: there is an asymmetry of passion on social media. There is some scholarly debate about whether conspiracy theories are on the rise—they have always existed, after all, as we shall see—but in today's information environment, relatively small groups of true believers (a few thousand people) can leverage the tactics of networked digital activism to produce the kind of sensational content and attract the initial engagement that algorithms subsequently boost. Their zealotry, their constant posting and fervent commentary, gives the impression that they are far more numerous than in fact they are.

By contrast, the overwhelming majority of people in California—millions of us—vaccinated our children and then simply went on about our lives; we didn't get on social media to tweet or post about it. Vaccinate California had to figure out how to make people do just that. We had to pull the silent majority off the fence and into the public conversation. However, while we were slowly growing an audience willing to call their representatives and post about the importance of shots for school to Facebook friends, there were no obvious figureheads or influencers with massive audiences who could blast the messages out to their followers. Getting reach was difficult.

The anti-vaccine side had charismatic leaders who spoke like revivalist preachers, people like Robert F. Kennedy Jr. but also wellness gurus with large Instagram followings who produced beautiful lifestyle content (and occasionally argued that vaccines had no place in "authentic, holistic health"). They understood what resonated on social media; meanwhile, the pro-vaccine side got an occasional boost from the rare positive comment by a celebrity.

As we learned the ropes of online activism—building the plane while flying it—it also became clear that public health institutions were remarkably disinterested in what was happening on social media. Even as savvy conspiracists were expanding their movement (while we were just beginning to grow ours), authoritative institutions such as the Centers for Disease Control and Prevention (CDC) seemed completely flatfooted. They very obviously did not understand how social media worked or what got engagement; while the anti-vaxxers were going viral with slick YouTube content and emotional first-person testimonials about vaccines causing allergies (false), SIDS (false), and autism (false), scientists were posting statistics-heavy PDFs and blog posts to get accurate information out. The public health experts believed that the public would ultimately trust what they said because they were, after all, the authority figures—the people with PhDs and MDs. They believed that what happened on social media didn't matter. As a CDC employee put it to me at the time, "Those are just some people online."

Meanwhile, the Southern California crunchy moms who had long been the pillars of California's anti-vaccine movement were bringing entirely new groups—from the Tea Party to the Nation of Islam to the Church of Scientology and its celebrities—into the fold with their liberty rhetoric and social network outreach. Within a few years, this big tent of strange bedfellows would include local militias, sovereign citizens who believed the US government itself was illegitimate, and conspiracy theorists convinced that elected officials were secretly members of satanic pedophilic cabals. The growth of this movement and the recasting of public health interventions as government tyranny may have seemed fringe at the time, but it would have profound implications as the world fell into a global pandemic in 2020.

The pro-vaccine side did ultimately win passage of Senate Bill 277, and California moved to a medical-exemption-only policy for school immunizations. But the way that the fight had played out—the tactics for shaping public opinion, the actors involved, the influencer-algorithm-crowd interplay that drove virality and commanded attention, the harassment brigades—was a harbinger of a profound shift and more upheaval to come. The anti-vaccine movement's loss left its adherents more convinced than ever that they had to continue growing their numbers and dominating the online conversation. They began fund-raising on GoFundMe and canvassing wealthy donors, soliciting money for ad campaigns to drive people to their Facebook groups. They created networked state-level "Medical Freedom" pages committed to boosting each other's messaging and growing a movement. Meanwhile, Vaccinate California continued to exist, but as a side project—our volunteers had lives to get back to and kids to raise. Some were burned out by the toxicity. There was no obvious source of funding. No one was responsible for continuing to grow a pro-vaccine parent movement.

I was captivated by the tactical dynamics of what I'd just seen and participated in. Although I also had a full-time job and my baby son, I began to spend increasing amounts of time at night examining how influential figures grew their audiences on Twitter and Instagram, how information moved across networks of Facebook pages. I tracked how conspiratorial communities seemed to be cross-pollinating with each other through nudges from platform-recommendation algorithms.

As I would soon come to learn, others had begun to notice similar dynamics playing out around some pretty high-stakes issues. The Islamic State was growing a virtual caliphate. Fake news stories were increasingly going wildly viral. Russia, it seemed, was using something called the Internet Research Agency to create mass confusion and spread propaganda to advance the Kremlin's interests, particularly in Ukraine. It was also creating bots and fake accounts, taking the old Soviet Cold War strategy of "agents of influence"—people who tried to nudge public opinion in a direction that benefitted the cause or country on whose behalf they worked—into the virtual realm.

And yet, even as demonstrably adversarial actors gained a foothold on social networks, it was unclear whose responsibility it was to stop them. Tech platforms, which controlled the infrastructure upon which this was occurring, wanted to build products and make money. They didn't want to have to decide who was real or fake or how to balance user expression against harmful content and harassment campaigns. While a handful of people in government, academia, tech, and civil society saw the crisis coming, most did not take these early signs seriously. It was, after all, just some people online. It wasn't real life.

By 2015, we were already entering a world in which truth was determined by popularity, viral nonsense trended daily, and partisan polarization was actively exacerbated by armies of trolls, foreign and domestic. I felt that things were going off the rails: for example, because I'd been watching anti-vaccine videos, YouTube's recommendation engines began to suggest I might also be interested in chemtrails, flat Earth, and 9/11 conspiracy theories. The trending algorithms on Twitter could reliably be gamed with bots, and the trending feature on Facebook was promoting outright false articles. But perhaps most disturbingly, our social norms seemed to be resetting. Sensational and extreme ideas were increasingly visible, while speaking against them seemed to require spinning up a counterfaction capable of resisting personal harassment intended to push opponents out of the conversation. Ordinary people began to treat this as normal partisan behavior, even as we had more power than ever to shape public opinion by clicking on the "like" and "share" buttons, pushing outrageous stories into the feeds of friends and family. We could all increasingly retreat into online groups in which we saw only what we wanted to see, or what platform algorithms thought we wanted to see, and very little else.

In late December 2019—five years after the Disneyland measles outbreak started—Patient Zero walked out of the Huanan Seafood Market in Wuhan, kicking off what would come to be known as the COVID-19 global pandemic. Or so we thought. Four years after that, we would be debating whether he'd *really* walked out of the Wuhan Institute of Virology, and every single facet of a pandemic that killed over six million people—with over one million of them within the United States—would be a matter of irreconcilable debate contested by identitarian factions that could agree on only one thing: the others were lying to you.

The same California anti-vaccine groups and influencers that Vaccinate California had fought against in 2015 were early to pick up on the COVID story and played prominent roles. The pandemic that emerged four years after the Disneyland measles outbreak revealed the full extent to which the influencer-algorithm-crowd trinity—the new means of shaping public opinion—has reallocated power, transformed our understanding of the world, and impacted our capacity for collective action. A global rumor mill propelled theories about the vaccine's safety, efficacy, and toxicity to mass audiences, exposing the challenge of telling rumor from fact in the era of virality. Theories traveled far faster than facts could be known. Although the tropes were nearly identical to those that had long circulated about diseases and vaccines past, effective counter-speech was largely absent. Platforms—the curators and recommenders of stories—had to decide what to surface. COVID laid bare and accelerated the public's loss of trust in institutions, media, and authority figures.

Creating narratives is no longer solely the purview of elites. This power—for centuries, almost wholly dominated by media, institutions, and authorities—has been upended. Ordinary people can influence what their friends see, what their communities talk about, and what their country focuses on more easily than ever before. We are no longer the passive recipients of mass media messages. Instead, we all have the power to shape public opinion, to wield the tools that engender virality, to spread messages that reach and potentially influence millions. In this book I will investigate what that means.

Some of the change is positive: a proliferation of voices, an abundance of creativity, the formation of new communities that bring people together independent of geography. But there are also serious consequences. A new system of incentives has given rise to novel forms of propaganda and tools for manipulation. Shared reality has splintered into bespoke realities, shaped by recommendation engines that bring communities together, filled with content curated from the media and influencers that the community trusts. Very little bridges these divides. This has profound implications for solving collective problems or reaching the kind of consensus on which democracies depend.

This is *not* a book about social media. There are enough of those. Rather, my focus is on a profound transformation in the dynamics of power and influence, which have fundamentally shifted, and on how we, the citizens, can come to grips with a force that is altering our politics, our society, and our very relationship to reality. For sure, companies and governments must bear their burden of figuring out how to regulate this new space, and how to restore trust and shore up institutions, but we as citizens have a responsibility to understand these dynamics so we can build healthy norms and fight back. This is the task of a new civics.

Understanding the forces driving a revolution requires a theory. And so, in Part I we set forth a theory about how the new power dynamic works, examining how what we may see as discrete influencers, algorithms, and crowds have a combinatorial power that enables them to intersect and build on each other to create not only powerful social movements but bespoke realities. We'll delve into a menagerie of influencers, the modern opinion leaders who not only process news and information for their audiences but also work to shape public opinion directly by creating their own social media content for clout and profit. We'll look at the curation and recommender algorithms of social networks that decide what we see and shape what we create. We'll consider the public itself: the virtual crowds, factions, and fandoms that are now active participants in online rumor mills and propaganda machines. And we'll explore how the three members of this influencer-algorithm-crowd trinity influence and respond to one another, with platforms offering the capacity for attention and reach—influence-as-a-service—to creators, who produce content carefully tailored to both the algorithm and their niche audiences.

Part II then examines how the rise of this new system of influence has transformed politics, war, Great Power propaganda campaigns, your local government, and even your relationships with your friends and neighbors. It takes a clear-eyed look at the role of experts and institutions and why they are now so distrusted. And, rather unexpectedly, it tells the story of how studying this system and exposing its worst manifestations led to multiple congressional subpoenas and lawsuits for me personally—acts of political retaliation by elite lawmakers, political influencers, and niche propagandists angry at the academics who laid bare how the invisible rulers of a new communication ecosystem attempted to delegitimize a free and fair election.

Today, who controls the internet controls reality. We have all been given the capacity to influence. We all have the ability to persuade communities, amplify messages, create viral conspiracy theories, and instigate real-world protests. We have profound power but no commensurate responsibility. Very few of us have reckoned with what that power means.

*   *   *

Before delving into the why of the theory and the how of the way our society is being changed and undermined, let's first look at the way one person—let's call him "Guitar Guy"—descends step by seemingly inconsequential step down the rabbit hole. (While Guitar Guy is not modeled on any particular person and is admittedly drawn as a caricature, his journey illustrates the way that many have been drawn into bespoke realities.)

Guitar Guy is in his early forties and lives in a suburb of a midsize American city. He learned to play guitar as a kid, mostly through taking in-person classes, reading books, and making friends with others who jammed in the basement at the local music store. He had a band and toured for a bit. Today, he's a music teacher at a few local elementary and high schools and supplements his salary by teaching some private lessons as well.

When Guitar Guy was just starting out, he advertised his lessons with fliers posted in the local coffee shop and library. But as the internet took off, he started posting ads on Craigslist to reach potential new students and set up a blog on Blogger. The content was nothing fancy, just some tips on becoming a professional guitarist, funny stories about being a teacher, and discussion about shows he seen. Honestly, though, no one really read the blog, and he gradually abandoned it. However, through his writing, leaving comments on other people's blogs, and joining some message boards, he did manage to connect with other musicians, all over the world. That's the best part of the internet, he thinks; it's helped him meet others who share his passion for guitars and fingerstyle. In 2006, shortly after YouTube launched, he decided to create an account and began posting videos of himself playing in his living room at night.

In 2009, Guitar Guy joined Twitter, a "microblogging" platform that let him post 140-character bursts of thought. In 2011, he created an account on the then photo-sharing, now also video-sharing app Instagram (which would later be acquired by Facebook/Meta). In 2020, he joined TikTok, drawn by its effortless "duet" video stitching technology, which let him add his own riffs directly on top of videos posted by other musicians—asynchronous jam sessions facilitated by nothing more than an app...magic. He now regularly posted content to TikTok, Instagram, and YouTube, sometimes Facebook and Twitter too, and over the years he managed to attract something of a following: tens of thousands of guitar-loving people followed him on each platform.

Guitar Guy didn't aspire to be an influencer as he set up his accounts. Making money wasn't on his agenda. He was just a guy who wanted to post his art and chat about it with people who shared his interests. But it turned out he was pretty relatable, and people liked both him and his content. And, of course, the social media platforms made it so easy to get started: a laptop, a webcam, a good microphone, and a niche. He created a little setup in his garage and would go out to it for an hour each day after dinner to sit and play. At first he uploaded short videos and then checked back later to see what other people had to say about them. As social media platforms added new features—and as his audience grew—he got into livestreaming. He posted his streaming schedule to his YouTube profile—Monday, Thursday, Friday, 7 to 8 p.m. PT. His followers would get a little notification telling them to come watch his performances and demos. They could chat with him, and he would respond between songs. He could also cross-post the content—upload a copy of the same stream—to other platforms later on. He could make short clips of the best parts, creating his own little hit reel for platforms with audiences who preferred shorter videos.

Those hours spent livestreaming were some of the best of his week. He made real connections with fans who often felt like friends. He could say whatever was on his mind—even if it wasn't music related. He found a community and a culture. And the icing on the cake was that he was also making some extra money: his stream watchers could tip him, and he was earning some revenue from ads that ran before his videos played. He'd started getting approached for sponsorships by companies who wanted him to tout their pedals or straps; even a local brewery had reached out, hoping he'd talk about their beer on Instagram. Some of the companies offered a few thousand dollars for a post.

Then one night, as Guitar Guy was getting ready to do his biweekly YouTube livestream, he decided—quite innocently!—to discuss a roiling controversy in guitar land: rock idol Eric Clapton's latest comments about COVID vaccines. Clapton had described experiencing some personal side effects after getting the jab and appeared on conspiracy theorist YouTube channels claiming that the government and pharmaceutical companies were using mass hypnosis and subliminal messages to make the public consent to getting the shots.[3] That part was a bridge too far for Guitar Guy, but some of Clapton's other complaints—like refusing to perform at venues requiring his audience to show proof of vaccination— had kind of resonated. That argument, about freedom of choice, felt compelling. Guitar Guy had gotten vaccinated but didn't love the idea of mandates. Adults could decide if they wanted to risk getting sick in a bar. Musicians did have to earn a living, and those who didn't have social media, who relied solely on in-person gigs, were really struggling.

A lot of his friends, in fact, had a hard time making ends meet as the pandemic dragged on. He decided to chat with his audience about it, get their take. Maybe play Clapton's protest song.

As he started streaming, chatting about Clapton's arguments about hypnosis and lockdowns, he noticed a significant jump in the number of likes, comments, and reactions from his audience. A few were complaining, but others were cheering him on, using the "tipping" feature to drop him a few bucks in real time.

Hmm, he thought. This is interesting.

To keep the discussion flowing, hopefully maintaining the high rate of likes and comments (and tips!), Guitar Guy kept talking about the controversy, going into related stuff he'd seen on TikTok. He'd been on the fence about the boosters thing, he confessed, and influencers he followed, particularly some of the fitness people, were also hesitant. In fact, he added, some of them thought mRNA vaccines were quite dangerous. After all, we just didn't know enough about them—this was the first time the technology had been used on humans!

Guitar Guy had no medical credentials or scientific expertise, and neither did the fitness accounts he paid attention to and cited. Neither did Eric Clapton, for that matter. But his forty thousand fans were now hearing a perspective on vaccines from someone they had come to like and, more importantly, to trust. They could speak back to him, have a conversation about their own feelings on the matter—and he listened. Some shared the livestream with their friends: "Check this guy out, follow him, he's saying the kind of stuff you never hear on TV." Others tried to push back—"Oh come on, not you too with the conspiracy theories!"—but as debates got heated in the comment threads, they eventually gave up and just left.

The controversy Guitar Guy unwittingly kicked up, it turned out, was great for his engagement numbers, both during the livestream and after. A lot of people shared the video, and he got a bunch of new followers. He continued skirting controversy—he didn't want to get outright banned from the platforms, obviously, and he knew they had policies against vaccine misinformation. But it wasn't that hard to pivot ever so slightly to other controversial topics, culture war stuff that platforms didn't have policies against: parents' rights, LGBTQ commentary, gun control, abortion, even Big Tech's control of information. Being provocative kept the engagements rolling in and the follower counts climbing up. And the higher the count went, the better he did financially.

Guitar Guy now had a big decision to make. It didn't take a rocket scientist to figure out that engagement was highest when he was talking about controversial political topics and weird online theories—not guitars. His livestreams were now regularly getting reposted to other platforms, sometimes in hashtags that he honestly didn't love—conspiracy theory stuff that creeped him out a bit—but this still translated into high view counts and more income. The problem was that the right-wing and left-wing crowds each seem to be looking for stronger ideological commitment, probing in the comments to see if he really was "one of them." Truth be told, he'd never really been an ideologue, never fit neatly in one bucket, but he was feeling pressure to align more vocally with some online political faction.

He decided to keep leaning into controversy. His content shifted: instead of playing for most of the stream, he now played one or two songs and then talked, tying the lyrics into some outrageous thing that had happened that day.

Over the course of the next few weeks, his YouTube and Instagram follower counts spiked. He checked his YouTube channel analytics dashboard again and saw that a higher percentage of viewers were finding his videos from the platform's suggested videos.

Recommendation algorithms, perhaps noticing his sustained high engagement, were suggesting his content. More and more of his videos were getting high view counts, particularly ones where he was adding controversial—but not highly moderated!—keywords. And people were following him, but not the same kind of people who used to follow him. No, judging by the comments, he now had an increasingly large percentage of followers who knew him as the "guy who wasn't afraid to show some support for Eric Clapton" or "the guy who made the TikTok sea shanty about Big Tech censorship." He used to have a fairly nice fan community that wanted to talk about what was still his main love: guitars. But now he had a big and still-growing following—he'd just crossed 480,000 YouTube subscribers!—and those new folks were there for a reason. Sure, they liked music, but they were more likely to share the provocative stuff. If Guitar Guy wanted to keep his engagement rate up, he had to give them what they wanted.

The influence-as-a-service machine was humming: Guitar Guy was producing content, which recommender algorithms in turn boosted and made even more popular among highly specific audiences, delivering more followers and engagement (which equals money) to the creator, who in turn produced more content. As Guitar Guy produced highly engaging—and increasingly inflammatory—content in response to these incentives, his audience wasn't just getting larger; it was changing. It was being skewed away from the original community of guitar enthusiasts and toward those who came for the controversy. It had become pretty clear that they weren't there for a nuanced discussion of the topics he'd been posting and writing little ditties about. They wanted red meat.

Guitar Guy was actually a little bit concerned about continuing down this rabbit hole, which is what, deep down, he knew it was. Sure, he had some honest concerns about the COVID restrictions, the kind of stuff he talked about in his first few controversial videos, but his new followers were now regularly alluding to more far-out theories in the comments: Jeffrey Epstein, microchips, Bill Gates, the New World Order. He may have accidentally stumbled into becoming a culture war influencer, but these followers would spell out what staying in this new territory entailed. He was a bit worried. Would they turn around and attack *him* if he pushed back against the most extreme voices, tried to restore some sanity or nuance to the conversation? He was not wrong to be nervous: he was now beloved by a particular faction, and expressing views counter to their other politics very well might lead to his being harassed. But if he said something they wanted to hear, well…they'd give him unconditional support and would share his content far and wide, helping him to continue to grow his follower count—and his bank account.

You might be wondering, what happened to Guitar Guy's original audience. What must they be thinking? Have they fled his channel, or are they still watching?

Some dropped off after realizing that the vague conspiracizing was more than a passing thing. Some pushed back, trying to get at the nuance inherent in controversial culture war topics, but got fed up with constantly having to do battle with the influx of new supporters and left. But some simply listened. They too got into conversations with the new supporters. And they were not necessarily turned off by what Guitar Guy or the new community members had to say; some perhaps even found them persuasive.

It is possible that if you are reading this book, you have at some point in recent years asked yourself, "Is it just me or has everyone else lost their mind?" or "How did we get here?" It doesn't matter if you are conservative or progressive, because the phenomenon has affected people across the political spectrum.

The aim of this book is to guide you through the evolution of this carnival hall of mirrors, this world of echo chambers, grifters, and keyboard culture warriors, to explain just how we got here and how we might get out.

PART I

1

The Mill and the Machine

"There are invisible rulers who control the
destinies of millions."
—Edward Bernays, *Propaganda*

Anti-vaccine zealots dominating social media and reawakening the measles virus in Southern California. Prominent politicians inveighing against kids using litter boxes in their school bathrooms. A growing number of people—including at least one famous athlete[1]— avowing that the Earth is in fact flat, not round.[2] A man attacking the Speaker of the House's husband with a hammer—and his lawyer then arguing *the internet made him do it.*[3]

Occurrences like these—unsettling, divisive, and often at odds with common sense—seem to be happening with increasing frequency. And they are deeply entwined with *who* shapes public opinion and *how*— something that has shifted significantly over the past decade.

The age-old pursuit of shaping public opinion is how leaders, institutions, rebels, and reformers attempt to deliberately and strategically exert their influence on society. Their aim is to mold their audiences' attitudes, beliefs, or behaviors with regard to ideas, people, policies, and even social norms. The ultimate goal is to create consensus that advances their way of seeing the world . . . maybe to get a president elected or shift how people feel about a controversial topic. It can be a long, arduous, thorny process—and one with high stakes. Reaching consensus is how societies make decisions and move forward, and steering that process can transform the future.

Societies require consensus to function. Yet consensus today seems increasingly impossible. Polarizing topics are black-and-white and compromise unthinkable. Our political leadership is gridlocked. Our media

21

feels toxic. And social media seems like a gladiatorial arena, a mess of vitriol. The culture war is everywhere. Handwringing about "post-truth" and "misinformation" dominates the diagnoses of one media ecosystem, while sneers about "censorship" and "woke totalitarianism" are the focus of another. Many of us feel that something has gone horribly wrong. Maybe tech is to blame, maybe the unraveling of the social fabric more broadly. Either way, we feel we are no longer able to speak with friends and family or to trust institutions.

It increasingly seems like we don't live in the same reality. And that's because, in a very critical way, we don't. Consensus reality—our broad, shared understanding of what is real and true—has shattered, and we're experiencing a Cambrian explosion of subjective, bespoke realities.[4] A deluge of content, sorted by incentivized algorithms and shared instantaneously between aligned believers, has enabled us to immerse ourselves in environments tailored to our own beliefs and populated with our own preferred facts.

Who Says What to Whom

For centuries, people passed information to one another primarily through word of mouth. We still do, of course: talking with friends and family members, sharing stories, discussing the news, persuading them to our view about, say, which candidate to vote for. They, in turn, talk to other people, who do the same to others. The way that a message cascades through a community depends on how people are connected to each other—on who knows or talks to whom. That web of connections is a social network.

"Small talk" spreads through a social network: how the kids are doing at school, why I love or hate that new restaurant. Other times, though, a different kind of information spreads: important and ambiguous information, like speculation about a brewing conflict, an outbreak of a novel disease, or a scandal involving a local official. These are *rumors*, unofficial information circulating in society, which are powerful precisely because they sometimes—but only sometimes—turn out to be true.

Rumors take "raw, confused facts" and attempt to explain them, to posit a reality based on a small amount of evidence.[5] The community discusses the claims and tries to make sense of it all; the rumor is the consensus explanation they reach. If the facts are sparse, we rely on our imaginations to fill in the blanks, often drawing on community lore or popular tropes. We spread the rumor because we want to know the truth and want to participate in the community conversation—particularly when the facts involve an ambiguous or troubling incident with the potential to impact our lives.[6] The intent isn't to manipulate or even deliberately shape public opinion—rather, rumors spread because of the natural human tendency to share information, especially if it's intriguing or sensational. Yet the spreading whispers often do affect how individuals perceive events, sometimes introducing uncertainty and doubt—especially if the whispers conflict with the official story. We have a colloquial name for the way that rumors pass from person to person: the *rumor mill*.

The structure of a social network shapes how information or rumors spread: not all people are equally connected or persuasive. In a village nestled in, say, the north of England a thousand years ago, people would hear opinions and form perceptions based on conversations with their trusted friends and neighbors. But not everyone knows or regularly talks to the same people—and *who has access to whom* matters. The village gossip or pub owner might know everyone, while the blacksmith might only speak regularly with the small number of people he sees during the workday. The handful of highly connected, highly informed community members—those most equipped to make messages spread—have the potential to significantly impact the overall community's perception of what's happening in the world. The gossips will talk to twenty people each day and the blacksmith to only two or three (including the gossip). This means that a message or rumor can disperse across the town much faster if gossips get hold of it and decide it's interesting. They can curate, or select, the most interesting piece of info from among the many things they hear. If they decide to share something, it has the potential to cascade, first reaching the gossip's twenty connections, who then talk about it with their friends; then those people spread it to their friends, and so on. If one gossip talks to another gossip—another highly connected speaker—the information or rumor has the potential to move even faster and to reach an even wider audience. The best connected have the potential to shape public opinion by virtue of their reach.

There's an interesting dynamic that can arise when some individuals are far better connected than most: their opinions begin to seem like the majority opinion. If the village was surveyed and 85 percent believed that the pubs should close at 5 p.m., but the gossips' and pub owners' opinions fell within that other 15 percent, their minority viewpoint would likely seem like the prevailing opinion to everyone else in town. Most people would hear about the debate from them, with their spin on it. This *majority illusion* can trick you into believing that a minority opinion is the dominant consensus point of view overall, when it's really the viewpoint of the loudest or best-connected members of a community.[7]

Of course, the structure of the social network is only part of the story. The best-connected people may be popular because they're particularly charismatic or compelling storytellers: the gossips are good at capturing their audience's attention because they have an innate sense of what details to embellish, emphasize, or exclude. Their stories stir up emotions. A combination of being well connected *and* compelling increases the likelihood that people who hear the gossip's spin on a topic pass it along. It's probably far more interesting than the cold, hard facts.

Imagine a situation in which a few customers get sick after a night out at the King's Arms Pub. Were they served bad ale, or was there an outbreak of a disease? Who knows. If a few people who fell ill chatter, the incident might stay confined. But if a gossip who doesn't like Geoffrey, the pub owner, spins the events into a spicy, innuendo-laden rumor, the whole village will hear not only allegations of bad ale but the gripping tale of how Geoffrey didn't keep the pub clean because he was too busy dallying with the wife of the butcher. Geoffrey now has a situation to reckon with. From this example, we can see that the structure, speaker, and substance all play a role in shaping public opinion.

The rumor mill—unverified stories flowing across social networks, organically spread by interested people—has always existed in some form. How social networks are organized, and the fact that connections are not evenly distributed, shapes how information and messages spread from person to person. Access to community, and thus potential for influence, was long determined by in-person relationships.

Yet, while important, this system for shaping public opinion has, since the fifteenth-century invention of the printing press, competed with a more centralized alternative for receiving information: mass media.

Who has access to whom can shift dramatically when communication technologies rearrange connections between people, which means that the character or flavor of the information we receive shifts dramatically as well. What happens if everyone has access to newspapers, radios, television—the internet? When communication goes from one-to-one to one-to-many?

More information will reach people, including from those with whom they have no personal connections. And that's exactly what happened in a handful of pivotal transitions in history: an advance in communication technology changed the topology of human connections, creating new networks of influence by which small numbers of people could reach millions.

As with peer-to-peer chatter, mass media spreads plenty of benign and neutral information: the ups and downs of the stock market, a story about a tornado, an investigation of a corporate cover-up. Coverage that presents the basic facts, keeping the audience informed. But other times, media outlets spread information with an agenda: a nightly newscast that skews crime statistics or a front-page story that assails a political candidate with little cause. These stories often still contain facts—they're not complete fabrications—but they're spun so as to benefit a particular group that wants to move public consensus in a particular direction. This deliberate presentation of inflected information that attempts to further the agenda of those who create it is *propaganda*.[8] The collection of powerful individuals and outlets who participate in systematic attempts to shape perception comprise the *propaganda machine*.

Propaganda shapes public opinion not by simple persuasion but rather by manipulating perceptions and constructing favored narratives to guide our views. It deliberately and systematically frames issues, emphasizing certain aspects while downplaying others, with the intent of building a specific worldview or gaining support for an agenda. There is usually a core grain of truth; propaganda is rarely built on outright lies. It strategically uses collective myths, emotional stories, and existing fears to appeal to deeply held values and beliefs. Propaganda often argues that a particular consensus already exists (but has been suppressed) and relies on repetition to normalize even extreme ideas. The propaganda machine adopts the stylings of the rumor mill at times, particularly while smearing targeted individuals, institutions, or ideologies via innuendo-laden whisper campaigns that aim to discredit them—but this is deliberate, not spontaneous and organic.[9] Spread through mass media, propaganda can reach millions simultaneously.

In his 1928 book *Propaganda*, American social theorist and "father of public relations" Edward Bernays dubbed the people with the power to shape public opinion "invisible rulers." "There are invisible rulers who control the destinies of millions," he wrote. "It is not generally realized to what extent the words and actions of our most influential public men are dictated by the shrewd persons operating behind the scenes."[10]

Bernays wasn't referring to the *visible* rulers, like then US president Calvin Coolidge or the wildly popular 1920s American newspaper columnist Dorothy Dix. He was referring to the people behind the curtain: public relations experts, senior government aides, advertising executives, and propagandists with the know-how to shape the thoughts and behaviors of the public through messaging, psychological techniques, and the strategic presentation (or manipulation) of information. These were the individuals who wielded true influence—even over people like the president.

Bernays wasn't being hyperbolic. Often these invisible rulers had the ability to ignite significant social or political upheaval. Consider Wayne Wheeler, a contemporary of Coolidge and Dix with a lower profile, unknown to many—but whose propaganda as head of the Anti-Saloon League led to the passage of the Eighteenth Amendment and thirteen years of Prohibition. Wheeler specialized in working the media to create a perception of widespread support for his positions (even before that support had materialized), then parlaying this exaggerated perception into real pressure on elected officials.

Advertisers and marketing professionals, Bernays offered, were invisible rulers who specialized in making people feel compelled to buy something—whether a product or an idea. Their job was to create the circumstances and feelings that led to purchaser demand or public buy-in, and the best way to do this was to address people both as individuals and as members of a group.[11] Linking a group identity to a product or idea was immensely effective; Bernays himself worked to create the perception that bold, liberated women smoked cigarettes. The same approach could be applied to politics. People who advised sophisticated politicians, Bernays argued, needed to recognize that politics was also about creating demand; spectacle, not policy, was what mattered, and it could be engineered to sell the public on candidates just as with products or ideas. Although "the voice of the people expresses the mind of the people," Bernays pointed out, that mind was in fact made up for it by the leaders the public trusted—and therefore by the hidden individuals behind these leaders, who knew how to steer public opinion.[12]

Invisible rulers still possess these abilities, but there has been a dramatic shift in who—and nowadays what—they are.

The Infrastructure of Influence

In 1517, preacher and theologian Martin Luther posted a list of arguments challenging Catholic Church doctrine to the door of Castle Church in Wittenberg, Germany.[13] His "95 Theses," reprinted as pamphlets across Germany, triggered a religious reformation. The technology used to print them, the Gutenberg printing press, triggered a media revolution, ushering in the era of mass communication and introducing a significant increase in public literacy. Without the printing press, Luther's arguments about the church might have remained confined to his immediate locale or to his elite intellectual community of theologians and church authorities. Instead, they were translated and spread all over Europe, and the Protestant Reformation took off.[14]

Luther was a prolific writer, described by scholars as "pithy" and "a master communicator with a growing cult of personality."[15] He had a brand, producing recognizable and digestible content covering the most interesting topics of the day ("Whether One May Flee from a Deadly Plague," written in 1527), and far exceeded his Catholic opponents in popularity. He understood how to shape public opinion, writing in understandable language, with illustrations, for a common audience, taking doctrinal debate down to the level of ordinary people. In doing so, he managed to generate a degree of support "unprecedented among prior heresies."[16]

The Catholic Church's response to Luther's provocations was to excommunicate him in 1521 and to undertake a significant influence effort of its own over the next century. By that time, the Catholic Church was struggling with a crisis of authority as a religious revolt spread across Europe. It was in a position of defending both doctrine and continued reliance on the Latin language of the far smaller, elite, educated population.[17] The tension ushered in both a "pamphleteering war"—a battle for hearts and minds fought with paper booklets either praising or decrying certain religious opinions and leaders[18]—and a real shooting war: the devastating Thirty Years' War of 1618 to 1648.[19]

As the war raged, in 1622, Pope Gregory XV created the Sacra Congregatio de Propaganda Fide (Congregation for Propagation of the Faith), a body dedicated to coordinating missionary activity and ensuring the spread of the Catholic Church. Derived from the Latin word *propagare*, meaning to "spread" or to "propagate," *propaganda* was a term for a process, emphasizing not the substance of the message but rather the imperative to disseminate it.[20] In the *Inscrutabili divinae providentiae arcano* of June 1622, the pope exhorted his clergy to draw the public back to the one true faith—the one true reality—through the spread of persuasive information.

The Catholic Church ultimately did maintain its stature as a religious force and authority, but it was compelled to reform. The pamphlets enabled by Johannes Gutenberg's technology continued to proliferate, permanently transforming the flow of information. Although each individual missive had limited distribution, together they achieved a kind of micro-virality at times: the German word for the pamphlets was *flugschriften*, or "flying writings," which evoked the sense of speed. The new technology meant that anyone inclined to influence the public could stitch together some printed material to plead his case, reaching other villages perhaps via men on horseback, expanding the reach of a message beyond the confines of immediate geography and peer-to-peer village chatter.

The *flugschriften*, sold by peddlers and passed around the community, were full of subversive images, often mocking authority or certain groups of people.[21] The practice perhaps portended microblogging and memeing: an analog precursor to the viral self-published content we can all create and spread today. Viral news of dubious authenticity, scandalous stories, attacks on authority, inflammatory headlines—rumors and propaganda abounded. The style quickly spread beyond Europe. In the eighteenth century it was adopted by the American Founding Fathers, a group of men looking to influence a nascent but growing public.[22] They published flurries of fiery political pamphlets intended to persuade colonists to think a certain way about a Native American tribe or to unify behind a currency; some of the most famous, of course, were the Federalist Papers, which worked to shape public opinion around ratifying the Constitution of the United States.[23]

The printing press reshaped the rumor mill, coupling its decentralized, bottom-up, peer-to-peer nature with the beginnings of mass media. But this coupling wasn't permanent.

The heated battles of the pamphleteering wars fell away as the media began to centralize. By the 1700s, "broadsheet" newspapers, which covered and aggregated the stories (and rumors) relevant to a locale, gained in popularity. Like the pamphleteers, many of the earliest newspaper publishers were not constrained by a need for accuracy, focused as they were on opinion and often tied to political parties. However, gradually, reporting—previously a luxury paid for by businessmen interested in verifiable facts to inform their business decisions—became a core part of these publications, and journalism became a proper profession with ethics and best practices. By the 1830s, the public came to hold the expectation that print media should attempt to be accurate, and investigative journalism and reporting became the norm, although the business of sensationalism, fake news, and scare headlines did continue in the form of "yellow journalism" and the tabloid press.[24]

This evolution in journalism led to the emergence of a professional media class, which, rather than simply self-publishing rumors, attempted to pursue an understanding of the facts—injecting friction into haphazard speculation. More importantly, perhaps, the professionalization of news production led to significant centralization and another reshaping of the networks of information flows. It cost money to operate a newspaper; there were printing expenses and reporters' salaries to be paid. Now, too, there were standards. The people who controlled the newspapers served as information gatekeepers, determining what showed up in their publications. They set the agenda for what topics were covered, how stories were framed, what letters to the editor were published, and what was deemed newsworthy—or not. They controlled the technology by which information was disseminated, which gave them the power to shape public opinion.

The arc of print media—from pamphleteering to consolidated, professionalized journalism—is the first part of a story of democratized access to information, access to large audiences, and the capacity to profit from both. The tension between upstart rebels and authority, the understanding that sensationalism and spectacle are innately appealing (a reality of human nature), the recognition that trusted speakers matter, and the awareness that audience demand and business incentives drive what is covered (and how), all predate our current media environment by centuries.

As journalism and its relationship with the public evolved, governments and institutional participation evolved too. Officials and experts served as sources for journalists and in turn leveraged newspapers to strategically release information to the public. Some governments established their own official media outlets, known today as "state media." State media was funded by the state and often editorially controlled by it too.[25] These outlets might be pointed inward, at the citizenry, enabling the state to control the narrative within its borders. They might be outward facing, tasked with spreading official messages to foreign publics.

Sometimes the state concealed its ownership or control of newspapers, creating fake "front" media properties within the borders of other nations, which masqueraded as local news outlets. Other times, the state controlled individual journalists: agent-of-influence contributors who could write for unwitting outlets, capitalizing on reputation and audience trust while putting out stories that weren't quite what they seemed. Getting a message out was critical to amassing real-world power. Shaping public opinion mattered, and state propaganda was a means of making it happen.

The early operators of American state propaganda efforts felt this acutely. Bernays had worked during World War I for a US government public-influence effort known as the Committee on Public Information (CPI). Headed by journalist George Creel, the CPI aimed to generate support among Americans for World War I—to produce, as Creel put it, "not propaganda as the Germans defined it, but propaganda in the true sense of the word, meaning the 'propagation of faith.'"[26] In the organized strategic messaging campaigns of wartime, propaganda was a tool of *influence operations*—formalized efforts to weaken the resolve of the enemy or to create support and resilience on the home front. Bernays had come away from his work on the CPI convinced that crystallizing public opinion, shaping consensus via the strategic presentation of persuasive information, was in fact critical to democratic governance—even in peacetime. Much like the Catholic bishops, the twentieth-century heirs to the methods of the Propaganda Fide considered the propagation of messages a moral obligation, key to a successful democratic society. "The conscious and intelligent manipulation of the organized habits and opinions of the masses is an important element in democratic society," Bernays wrote in *Propaganda*.[27] He continued, "Those who manipulate this unseen mechanism of society constitute an invisible government which is the true ruling power of our country. We are governed, our minds are molded, our tastes formed, our ideas suggested, largely by men we have never heard of. This is a logical result of the way in which our democratic society is organized. Vast numbers of human beings must cooperate in this manner if they are to live together as a smoothly functioning society."

Today this sounds elitist, even borderline authoritarian. Propaganda as an ethical obligation? Indeed, by World War II, the term was becoming synonymous in the American mind not with propagating truth but with the manipulative messaging outputs of Nazis, fascists, and other malign forces. This was, in part, because Creel himself had worked to create that association to ensure that US audiences distrusted German media during World War I.[28] However, even as that perception shift occurred, the idea that *someone* had to ensure that busy people were properly informed, so that they might fully participate as citizens in an effective democratic process, remained strong. So too did the idea that government and institutions should actively work with the media to communicate accessible, accurate information to the masses.

The next two significant technological shifts that followed print media—radio and then TV—again reshaped information networks, access to audiences, and the capacity to influence and shape public opinion. Notably, these two shifts further centralized the control of media. Unlike printing pamphlets, producing radio or TV content required more expensive equipment, more expertise, and coveted broadcast licenses from governments.

Manufacturing the Consent of the Governed

These three technological advances—the printing press, the radio, and the television—changed the structures along which information moved, reshaping networks and reallocating power. Those who controlled the means of information dissemination became a distinct class of professional media elite with the power to shape public opinion and influence consensus reality. Even as the public's access to information increased, the power imbalance between the speaker and the audience grew. What the media elites decided to publish was largely what the public saw— even as the public relations pros, the partisan insiders, and the other invisible rulers jockeyed to ensure that their messages made it out. The public were primarily recipients—targets—of the messages.

The question of how to reckon with the implications of this power evolved over time. A contemporary and sometime mentor of Bernays, Walter Lippmann, journalist and founder of the *New Republic*, was also sympathetic to the idea that propaganda should play a role in shaping public opinion. Lippmann's book, *Public Opinion*, published in 1922, six years ahead of Bernays's *Propaganda*, argued that individuals operated in personal, subjective realities that he called "pseudo-environments," where they primarily, and quite rationally, paid attention to their own experiences, needs, and issues. Opposing groups in particular "live in the same world, but they think and feel in different ones," he wrote.[29] To bridge these gaps and to create the sort of informed public that the Founding Fathers considered requisite for democratic governance, Lippmann argued, meant that a well-functioning society needed experts, institutions, and centralized media working in tandem—needed a propaganda machine. This technocratic elite would determine appropriate courses of action for particular social and policy issues to facilitate the "manufacture of consent" of the governed. (Noam Chomsky would go on to make that phrase famous sixty years later.)

This process of persuasive influence—experts identifying solutions and presenting them to those in power, who then worked with the media to communicate them to the public—would create order out of chaos, both Lippmann and Bernays argued. It would eliminate the information distortions of our medieval village; it would bring people into a shared reality and generate the kind of social cohesion required for democratic consensus.

Of course, this presupposed a benevolent government of the honest.

The mass media ecosystem that enabled the propaganda machine, it turned out, would also undermine it—by revealing just how naive that assumption of benevolent honesty was. TV inadvertently exposed the complex relationship that had developed between government, institutions, and media gatekeepers and the public they supposedly served: people could observe, on their TV screens, stark differences between what was said at official press conferences and the footage the networks aired. This was particularly true in the coverage of the Vietnam War. Elites, it seemed, hadn't been showing us the capital-*T* Truth; they had been showing us their cut-up, spun version of the truth. The obvious discrepancies generated outrage, precipitating protests about the war itself and eroding trust in government. This also sharply reduced trust in mainstream broadcast media.[30]

The decline of confidence in "establishment" media channels inspired a resurgence of interest in independent, underground publications, including what were known as *zines* (short for *fan magazine*). These small, self-published print publications were produced by and for members of distinct communities: artists, activists, people with niche political beliefs.[31] One was a small antiwar outlet, begun in 1965, that called itself *The Fifth Estate*. The title was an allusion to the *Fourth Estate*, a term for the institution of journalism with roots in eighteenth-century British political theory.[32] The first three estates were those of the French ancien régime: the clergy, the aristocracy, and the commoners. That the press was the fourth reflected the gravity of its role as an independent force that could hold the others accountable. As the American people of the 1960s began to lose confidence in media, the phrase *Fifth Estate* came to refer to the independent voices that would hold media accountable. The independent outlets that sprang up to present a counterpoint to the dominant narratives about the Vietnam War were defiantly decentralized in the age of increasingly centralized and controlled media structures. They were, in a sense, a second coming of the *flugschriften*—a reversion to an unfiltered past that became popular among communities that had begun to feel that mass media were not reflecting their understanding of reality. Yet, much like their predecessor pamphlets, they spoke to niche audiences—capturing far less attention than the official narratives presented in mainstream print and broadcast media or press conferences.

The entrenched power of mass media, its massive reach and capacity for shaping opinion at a national level, and its role in the "manufacture of consent" of the governed became the focus of Noam Chomsky and Edward Herman's seminal 1988 *Manufacturing Consent*. Unlike Lippmann and Bernays, with their rosier view of propaganda, they argued that a system of incentives inherent in the mass media ecosystem skewed information to serve the media and the governing elite, not the public interest. While the agendas of official state-controlled media outlets were obvious, the propaganda that moved through mainstream, free channels was more insidious because the public was unaware of what was happening.

The system Chomsky and Herman identified had five underlying incentives, or "filters," which shaped its output: ownership, advertising, sourcing, catching flak, and ideological orthodoxy (anticommunism at the time). Ownership in the age of mass media (before the internet) was an expensive proposition: broadcast license fees, printing presses, studio equipment. As a result, a small and wealthy enclave came to own the ecosystem. They were incentivized not to disrupt their other investments and entanglements. (Would a newspaper owner who also held significant stock in a pharmaceutical company allow reporting on a new drug's dangerous side effects?) Advertising was the primary funding model for mass media, incentivizing the media both to placate advertisers and to attract the kind of audiences they wanted to reach. (If that same pharmaceutical company were a major advertiser, would a network run the risk of angering it by covering a story that portrayed the company negatively?)

The remaining three filters had less to do with money and more to do with relationships and psychology. Sourcing—or access to newsmakers— incentivized media to play nice with the powerful, lest they be denied a future scoop. Fear of catching flak like boycotts or lawsuits incentivized the media to avoid prickly topics or unpopular segments. And the human us-versus-them instinct—fear of other ideologies—incentivized the media to tell stories with "worthy" or "unworthy" victims. Nuance and complexity fell by the wayside.

These incentives, Chomsky and Herman argued, led the media to self-censor; to lie by omission; to prioritize the "right" narrative, not the accurate one; and ultimately to shape public opinion in a way that undermined—rather than bolstered—democratic society. In Chomsky and Herman's view, the propaganda machine was for mass manipulation, not mass education; for false consensus, not true consensus.

As the twentieth century came to a close, events suggested Chomsky and Herman's cynical take on the propaganda machine as a hegemonic tool was more accurate than their predecessors' idealism about it as a mechanism for creating an informed public. The Iraq War of the early 2000s, with its yellowcake uranium and "weapons of mass destruction" stories, reinforced the idea of the press and government as unreliable, even manipulative.[33] The public, meanwhile—the target—had little capacity for shaping messages through mass media and primarily made their voices heard by counterspeaking, protesting, writing letters to the editor, and voting.

The Mill Matters More?

And yet the view of the public as helpless naifs hopelessly misled by media liars also was not entirely accurate. There had been great interest throughout the twentieth century in understanding, to adapt a phrase from communications (and propaganda) theorist Harold Lasswell, "who says what to whom on which platform and to what effect."[34] The impact of propaganda on the outcome of World War II had been a matter of great concern to government leaders and academics alike; many felt deeply uncomfortable with it, even decades prior to Chomsky and Herman's treatise. Scholars and experts had assumed that exposure to messages on radio and TV influenced people—they certainly seemed to. Propaganda slogans became memes: "Loose lips sink ships." People do, indeed, think and feel a certain way as they move throughout the world; they obviously come to hold certain convictions. It certainly *appeared* that propaganda could persuade people or deepen their commitment to previously held beliefs.

But in the mid-1900s, some fascinating studies upended the idea that mass messaging to the public was effective in the way that government, media, and even some of the invisible rulers thought. Influence, it turned out, worked a bit differently than previously believed. Even in a time of nightly news programs and prolific radio content, human social networks and word-of-mouth interpretation still mattered—a lot.

In 1955, social science researchers Elihu Katz and Paul Lazarsfeld published *Personal Influence: The Part Played by People in the Flow of Mass Communications*, a book that challenged conventional wisdom about whether and how media influenced the public. The pair had been inspired to investigate the role of mass media in society, noting that both its supporters and its detractors shared a foundational belief that mass communication was wildly effective for changing hearts and minds. Supporters saw mass media as a new dawn for democracy, full of informed, enlightened participants; detractors saw radio and TV as "powerful weapons able to rubber-stamp ideas upon the minds of defenseless readers and listeners"[35] and argued that misleading propaganda had led the United States to enter World War I when it should have stayed out. Both camps assumed that people were being persuaded left and right by what they heard on the radio or saw on the television.

Yet an earlier study by Lazarsfeld, which looked at the formation of political opinions about candidates in the 1940 presidential election, had found that people who had changed their mind about whom to vote for in that contest reported that the greatest contributor to their opinion shift was other people—not the media coverage they consumed.[36] "The one source of influence that seemed to be far ahead of all the others in determining the way people made up their minds was personal influence," Katz and Lazarsfeld reflected.[37] The individual, they argued, needed to be studied both as "a communicator and as a relay point in the network of mass communications."[38]

Intrigued by this finding that individual contact was still the most influential factor in political decisionmaking despite mass media prevalence, Katz and Lazarsfeld set out to investigate the impact of mass media on opinion formation via a study conducted on a group of eight hundred seemingly influential women in Decatur, Illinois. The researchers observed this community and noted that the influential women processed the stories they heard in the media—whether reporting, persuasion, propaganda, or entertainment—and passed information on to their friends. As in our medieval village, some were more influential than others, and Katz and Lazarsfeld found that those individuals, whom they dubbed *opinion leaders*, were much more likely to report being influenced by the media themselves (even as they, too, also reported being influenced by friends).

Katz and Lazarsfeld's pivotal observation was that "ideas often seemed to flow *from* radio and print *to* opinion leaders and *from them* to the less active sections of the population."[39] They found that some of the women in Decatur were monitoring the media very closely, watching news broadcasts, listening to the radio, and then communicating their opinions on what was said in the media to the rest of their network of friends. These opinion leaders shared several attributes: they were personable and likable, were perceived as knowledgeable and competent, and were well connected. They served as information intermediaries, interpreters, who informed their community of things they'd found out and, in doing so, served as opinion shapers for a trusting audience.

Influence through media, it turned out, was not a "hypodermic process"[40]—people did not adopt new opinions as if by "injection" following the mere hearing of a claim on a mass media news broadcast. That idea, held by both supporters and detractors of mass media, was simply wrong. Rather, influence happened far more often by way of this process of intermediaries engaging directly with their communities.

Katz and Lazarsfeld called their model *two-step flow*. The work was revolutionary in the field of communications because it found that media, for all its reach and ability to span massive networks of people, did not appear to influence the public directly. Although a given radio program or magazine might reach audiences of millions, it did not seem to impact them all uniformly or necessarily at all.

Katz and Lazarsfeld found that individuals were still far more likely to be influenced by personal contacts: their friends, family members, neighbors, members of their religious community. Even in 1955, Katz and Lazarsfeld summarized their work as a *rediscovery*—the empirical rediscovery of the primary group as a critical force in shaping public opinion.[41] Even after all these seismic technological shifts and broadcast media advances and the formation of a propaganda machine with massive reach, people actually seemed to remain much more susceptible to that very old, original form of influence that powered the village network: messages from people they knew in real life. Communication technology changes around us, but human psychology remains largely the same.

The Mill and Machine Collide

Media is additive; it has never replaced these human connections. It has an impact of course: the women of Decatur were talking to their friends about things they heard on the radio, read in print, and saw in the movies. Bernays saw media as preeminent in molding the public mind, but he also recognized the power of individuals, particularly in their role as members of groups, as allies to be marshaled in the effort to shape consensus. He encouraged aspiring invisible rulers of public relations to find and turn opinion leaders into advocates for whatever product or idea they were promoting. Chomsky and Herman's work laid out how the media heavily determines what stories are covered—what content we and our opinion leaders have available to us as the foundational basis for discussion. But for the process of coming to consensus—of both individually and collectively deciding what is true or false, what opinions to hold, what policies to adopt—the influence of peers remains key.

Never has this been more apparent than over the past two decades, as social media platforms connected humans on a scale never seen before, redefining the meaning of *peer* and reallocating the capacity to influence the masses and shape public opinion. This technological transformation created communication structures that eliminated human gatekeepers from the process of curation, reducing the power of media elites. It gave rise to an entire new class of speaker—influencers—and reorganized broadcasting from one-to-many to many-to-many. Mobile phones with cameras reinforced the shift as they became ubiquitous; any protest, military conflict, crisis, or petty disagreement between two people could be recorded, uploaded, or livestreamed by anyone for anyone else to see. This kind of content, shared to social media platforms, turned algorithms and crowds into curators and distributors and highlighted that the world was vaster, richer, and more complex than what old-guard media had previously chosen to convey. Audiences became direct participants in shaping and disseminating narratives.

But this did not put an end to propaganda. Quite the contrary: it put the power to create it into everyone's hands.

The last revolution in communication technology caused the collision of the rumor mill and the propaganda machine. The rumor mill, that ever-turning wheel of speculation and innuendo, has long thrived on the human fascination with the unverified, the mysterious, and the tantalizingly possible. On the other hand, the propaganda machine is agenda driven, a calculated force, its humming machinery designed to strategically distribute carefully constructed narratives that sway opinions and manipulate emotions for the purposes of power or profit.

Now, as the propaganda machine and the rumor mill have violently smashed together like two ancient galaxies, something fiery and perilous has emerged. And what has emerged is still growing, even as we struggle to accurately define it.

These two distinct systems of influence—both of which shape consensus reality, yet are historically associated with different sources of power—have converged into one. The result fuses the reach of the propaganda machine with the norms and stylings of the rumor mill and harnesses the fervor of human curiosity while being guided by the invisible hands of those who seek control.

The propaganda machine refined narratives from the top down; it required control of communication technology, formerly the purview of political elites, governments, and mass media institutions. Now, a vast array of actors use the features and capabilities that platforms offer their users to influence public perception in service of their own agendas and to draw the audience into acts of direct participation.

The rumor mill was once a relatively local affair, associated with networks of neighbors and individuals. It spread unverified information, gossip, and speculation, thriving on the unquenchable thirst for the latest scoop, but stayed confined largely to those close by and paying attention. Now, it has transcended geographical boundaries; it is peer-to-peer but also global and vast. Gossip and speculation are seen by millions and then picked up by the propagandists of the new media ecosystem, who use the rumors to their own ends—because rumors, too, have the power to shift perception, mobilize groups, and challenge "official" narratives.

State actors, terrorists, ideologues, grassroots activists, and even ordinary people now compete against each other in a war of all against all to shape public opinion.

This collision, combined with social media's restructuring of human social networks, has enabled something far more dangerous than Lippmann's de facto pseudo-environments, something fundamentally at odds with consensus reality: it enables *bespoke realities.*

Bespoke realities are made for—and by—the individual. The collision of the propaganda machine and the rumor mill gave rise to a choose-your-own-adventure epistemology: some news outlet somewhere has written the story you want to believe; some influencer is touting the diet you want to live by or demonizing the group you also hate. Other people, wherever they may physically be, are visible on the internet expressing vocal support for each individual belief. Whereas consensus reality once required some deliberation with a broad swath of others, with a shared epistemology to bridge points of disagreement, bespoke reality comfortably supports a complete exit from that process. By selecting or manipulating information, experiences, or beliefs to align with personal preferences or biases, you can construct or curate a version of reality— one that can be tailored to fit whatever desires or agendas drive you. An algorithmic curator will helpfully reinforce your choices. This may lead to a subjective and distorted perception of the world. It may eventually result in a harsh confrontation with the laws of physics or biology. But in the day to day you may sit, comfortably ensconced, in the bespoke reality.

If the bespoke conflicts with the mainstream, the bespoke will win. Jon Askonas captured why in his essay "Reality Is Just a Game Now":

A real-world event occurs that seems important to you, so you pay attention. With primary sources at your fingertips, or reported by those you trust online, you develop a narrative about the facts and meaning of the event. But the consensus media narrative is directly opposed to the one you've developed. The more you investigate, the more cynical you become about the consensus narrative. Suddenly, the mendacity of the whole "mainstream" media enterprise is laid bare before your anger. You will never really trust consensus reality again.[42]

This splintering has profound implications. In the 1920s Lippmann was concerned about how to bind Americans into a common public, to create an ideal democracy.[43] He recognized the importance of people coming together to make decisions about critical matters of public interest and thought—as paternalistic as it may sound—that a shared narrative informed by expertise and authority could improve democratic governance. Lippmann's sparring partner on the topic, philosopher John Dewey, disagreed with his technocratic prescription—controlled narratives were wholly antidemocratic, he argued, reducing democracy to name only. Dewey believed that journalism alone, absent propaganda, could be enough. But each agreed on the need to bridge the pseudo-environments and ensure that people were operating in the same world, in service of the public interest.

Today, too, there are numerous critical matters of public interest. Some involve facets of reality that are wholly unconcerned with human consensus: a tornado does not care who believes in it. Neither does a contagious virus. "Tornado reality" is savagely indifferent to online rumors and the rantings of propagandists alike. Even as our confidence in experts, elites, and each other wanes, and as more individuals inhabit bespoke realities, challenges requiring collective solutions continue to mount.

However, in a world where no one possesses the moral authority to bridge the gaps in our factual understanding, we lose the ability to act collectively. Institutions that once contributed to our shared perception of the world, helping to bind it together—including through overarching national narratives—are in a state of decline. And yet, we seem to have given up on fixing them or rebuilding the bridges. Instead, targeting the legitimacy of institutions and leaders is fertile ground for modern propagandists who require a villain.

The art of manufacturing consent has undergone a remarkable transformation as the invisible rulers have changed. Gone are the days of a single, all-encompassing propaganda machine. Now, a symphony of influencers, algorithms, and crowds work tirelessly to construct intricate belief systems, not across society but within their respective niches. The once-feared "hegemonic system" that Chomsky cautioned against is increasingly a relic. It wasn't worthy of glorification or even restoration; it enabled colossal deceits and launched unjust wars.

But its replacement is even more formidable—and certainly not the "town square" of ethical journalism and deliberative debate that we hoped for.

2

If You Make It Trend,
You Make It True

Influencers, Algorithms, and Crowds

I N THE SUMMER OF 2020, as the world fretted its way through some of the worst days of the COVID-19 pandemic, the popular online furniture store Wayfair started selling something highly unusual: trafficked children.

That, at least, was the claim that exploded across a series of social media posts that popped up on Twitter, Facebook, TikTok, and YouTube—basically everywhere that mainstream Americans spent their online time. The argument: that product listings for certain industrial storage cabinets—costing up to $10,000 each and marketed with human names[1]—were in fact code for abducted children who shared the same name. Or possibly even had the abducted children inside them.

The bizarre accusations were soon generating millions of engagements on social media.[2] Posts appeared from as far afield as Turkey and Argentina, featuring pictures of girls who had been reported as missing—and even some who hadn't—next to images of extremely expensive cabinets and pillows that shared their first names.

"Y'all this Wayfair Human trafficking thing is crazy. Look at this, there are two pillows/shower curtains that are the exact same, but one is $100 and the other is $10K. The $10K one is named the same thing as a Black girl missing in Michigan," said one post on Twitter that was retweeted 70,000 times and liked 139,000 times.[3]

The viral rumor, which congealed under the hashtag *#SaveTheChildren*, turned angry very quickly. Threats were issued against the popular

Boston-based furniture company and its employees. Real-life children and teens, whom the internet hive mind had decided were victims of trafficking via filing cabinet, found themselves recording videos denying that they had even been abducted. Their efforts did not assuage the online mob. One eighteen-year-old was told that she was clearly being forced to make her denial by her captors. When she pushed back, again, she was criticized for her lack of gratitude to all the people trying to "save" her.[4]

Federal investigators and nongovernmental organizations running tiplines—people who investigate and combat actual human trafficking, as well as a child aid organization actually named Save the Children[5]—had to take time out from looking into real abductions to examine the slew of fake reports. Some made their own appeals on social media in attempts to quell the rumor, begging the public to please stop flooding their lines with calls about Wayfair.

The notion of young women stored in filing cabinets could be easily dismissed; as the Twitter trend gained mass attention, many observers roundly mocked it. The threats that accompanied the theory, however, had to be taken seriously. After all, in 2016, outlandish accusations that former secretary of state Hillary Clinton and a cabal of Democrats were running a child-trafficking ring out of the basement of a Washington, DC, pizzeria prompted a man to show up at the restaurant, armed with an AR-15 rifle and a revolver, to rescue them.[6] He fired at a locked door; luckily, no one was hurt. "The intel on this wasn't 100 percent," he said in an interview following his arrest, while emphasizing that his intent had been to help people.[7]

And yet, despite the fact that no children had been found, despite the fact that there was not even a basement in the building,[8] that theory—known as Pizzagate—did not dissipate.

Influencers who had gained large followings by concocting and promoting it, such as naval reservist turned right-wing conspiracy theorist Jack Posobiec, did not recant following the incident. They doubled down: the man with the AR-15 who showed up at Comet Pizza was a plant, a false flag, who went to make them look bad.[9] In the time since Pizzagate erupted into real-world violence, Posobiec's following has grown from 57,000 to 2.3 million on Twitter; he now has active followings on Rumble and right-wing alt-platforms, as well as myriad contributor relationships with right-wing media and advocacy organizations. Posobiec, as we will discuss later in this book in the context of his work pushing wild theories about an array of topics, is rarely constrained by facts. Yet, despite making immense profit from misleading claims and conspiracy theories, he presents himself as an ordinary person just there to help his audience break free of the lying mainstream media.

Similarly, the tens of thousands of people who coordinated in Facebook groups and Reddit communities to "investigate" Pizzagate did not disperse after the sheer impossibility of the claim was laid bare. Quite the contrary: many metamorphosed into adherents of the even broader cultlike conspiracy theorist community QAnon, which alleged that then president Donald J. Trump was secretly battling a Satanic cabal of pedophile globalists who were harvesting and drinking the blood of children.[10] In fact, the majority of people who initially pushed the claims about Wayfair's expensive industrial filing cabinets were QAnon adherents[11]—though many other virtual bystanders saw the conspiracy theory appear in their feeds and, perhaps intrigued, helped it spread by retweeting and sharing it. *Someone should look into this...*

How had this all happened?

It began when a middle-aged, blond Canadian woman with a YouTube channel and the online handle "Amazing Polly" wrote a tweet. On June 14, 2020, she posted a catalog page showing some standard, if pricey, Wayfair cabinets with the accompanying text: "My spidey senses are tingling. What's with these 'storage cabinets'? Extremely high prices, all listed with girls' names & identical units selling for different amounts."

Following Polly's post, the rumor percolated on Reddit, Facebook, and Instagram, gathering steam before going viral on July 10.[12] Her fellow QAnon "investigators" picked it up first, but it spread outside the community as online sleuths got to work finding pictures of kids who'd been reported as missing—including, at times, those who had been reported falsely or runaways who had since reunited with their families—making collages that put their photos, names, and details alongside Wayfair products with the same name.

The collages were made by ordinary people: they weren't influencers with hundreds of thousands of followers. Yet they too felt compelled to participate. Some were part of a community of "warriors" who prided themselves on discovering the secrets of elites and fighting a theoretical shadowy cabal of famous politicians who moonlighted as child traffickers, but as the rumor spread, it drew in others who were simply intrigued in the moment. Meanwhile, the content they created and shared as part of this mission to expose wrongdoing—all of the videos and tweets and posts that used the word *Wayfair* or included the *#SaveTheChildren* hashtag—were picked up by social media algorithms. The algorithms, in turn, saw the sudden high-velocity outpouring of interest in pricy filing cabinets as a signal to surface the theory to even more people.

And yet, understanding *how* it happened from a mechanical standpoint raises far more important questions. Why was an obscure woman in Canada, spewing obvious nonsense, able to whip up such a global frenzy? Why were so many otherwise rational adults willing to believe her?

The story of Amazing Polly's viral Wayfair moment is that of a simple process that happens many times a day: an influencer on the internet says a thing, and her many followers react. Algorithms boosts that collective signal, which makes more influencers, people, and media pay attention and participate as well. This straightforward process describes the dynamic not only of the Wayfair debacle but also of countless other rumors that propagate across social media many times a day.

People like Polly are transforming our politics, culture, and society. The power to shape public opinion—for centuries, the purview of invisible rulers within media, institutions, and positions of authority who had the capacity to define and disseminate messages—is no longer controlled from the top down. The new invisible rulers—influencers and algorithms supported by online crowds—excel at bringing information (along with a proliferation of rumors) to mass attention, from the bottom up. Underpinning this ecosystem is a new reality: if you make it trend, you make it true.

The Influencer

You have probably never heard of Amazing Polly; most people have not. But within the QAnon conspiracy community, she was an influencer, with eighty-eight thousand followers on Twitter around the time of the Wayfair debacle. Before YouTube and Twitter shut down her accounts a few months later, she'd reached 375,000 subscribers and 24.7 million video views on YouTube and 141,000 followers on Twitter.[13]

Polly is an avatar for the new cast of people wielding influence today. With her several hundred thousand followers, Polly had access to an audience comparable to a respectably sized local media outlet. But she was not media. She was an active participant in a very particular niche community, QAnon, and was perceived as a trustworthy person within that group. Her followers considered her interpretation of current events and online stories worth not only paying attention to but amplifying, even involving themselves in. Polly was influential within her niche, even if the broader American public had never heard of her. She was a conduit who interpreted media stories and real-world incidents for her audience, but she had the power to create and spread her own narratives as well. And on that day, her narrative reached millions.

A handful of seemingly arbitrary people on social platforms, "influencers," now have a significant impact on what the public talks about and what the news media cover on any given day—particularly when it comes to culture war politics. Influencers are the opinion leaders of the internet age. But instead of simply digesting what the media is saying for their community of friends, as the women of Decatur did, they drive the conversation, not only curating but also creating, with a healthy dose of support from online algorithms and audiences who share and comment on their content. This new system determines what goes viral, what gets attention, and what is then reported on by the media—in turn shaping public opinion, steering culture, and stoking political battles.

But what is an influencer, exactly?

The term came from marketers. Back in the early days of the internet, marketers serving corporate America discovered that certain charismatic people had a talent for connecting with niche audiences and persuading them to buy things.[14] The term *influential* and then *influencer*—meaning someone with a large following and a uniquely relatable presence—began to appear on marketing blogs to refer to these folks.[15] That charisma came not from being larger-than-life or famous—in other words, not a celebrity—but from being ordinary, albeit with a slightly charmed life (or the ability to make it seem so through selective editing). Aspirational, yet achievable. These captivating folks often had a particular skill, hobby, or interest that they were infectiously excited about—something that inspired them to take to the internet and share with the world.

The influencers, it seemed to the marketers, were people with the potential to shape the culture: what people listened to, what they bought, even what slang they used. This didn't necessarily mean that they could accomplish this feat writ large—influencers usually didn't have national name recognition—but that didn't matter. They were connecting with particular communities of people as they blogged, vlogged, and eventually Instagrammed and TikTok'd their everyday lives. And many companies wanted to reach those particular communities of people.

The elite among influencers possess the storytelling chops of a Madison Avenue ad exec, have the reach of a mass media TV anchor, and create the cozy, intimate feeling of a phone call with your best friend. Some promote products, using their clout to earn money—being an influencer can be a very lucrative career. Others, particularly since 2015, promote ideas and ideologies, delivering political commentary with the rhetorical adroitness of a master propagandist. Some influencers, strikingly, do both—purveying politics *and* products—because once an influencer has grown a sufficiently large audience, people will consume their posts not only on the niche interest they were originally known for but also on whatever topic they decide to weigh in on. A mom blogger, who got famous for her fun school lunch content, weighing in on Fed rate hikes? Why not.

How have these seemingly ordinary people on social media become profoundly effective at driving the conversation on some very unexpected topics: trafficked children, COVID vaccines, school curricula, police funding? The short answer is that influencers are masters of attracting attention and then using that attention to amass more influence.

Let's look at how this cycle came to be and how it works.

The early social internet—sometimes called Web 2.0—changed the media landscape, giving anyone with a dial-up connection free tools to blog, post photos, and make memes. The Age of the Creator began.

However, while the internet delivered free creation tools and blogs, a lot of the content that was created languished in obscure corners of the web. Everything was decentralized, spread out across millions of individual sites, with only some fairly primitive search engines to surface interesting items. This made it hard for people to find the content and hard for creators to grow an audience.

That changed in the mid-2000s as social networking companies gave their users even simpler on-platform tools for making content, encouraging them to type a one-sentence status or upload a photo of the kids. But more importantly, the platforms also put the tools to target and spread content into everyone's hands. The structure of communication was once again transformed.

Social media affordances—the features and capabilities that social media companies offer their users—democratized distribution. Hundreds of thousands of users joined the nascent platforms, hanging out first with their real-world friends and later with friends they made online. Now, with massive potential audiences all largely in one place, creating and sharing content felt meaningful—exhilarating even. Anyone could create and spread a message, whatever it happened to be. This new ecosystem overturned any conception of audiences as passive; they had now become active participants in both creation and dissemination.

Some early creators used these tools to share news, first on blogs and subsequently across all available social platforms. Journalist and professor Dan Gillmor referred to the new class of contributors as "citizen journalists."[16] Some participated in an ad hoc way, helping to write the first draft of history for a particular event by sharing their stories of being in a relevant place at a critical moment. Others established a more permanent presence and built up self-published news sites. These creators, the media-of-one, adopted the mantle of media through declaration and branding. Despite official-sounding newsy names, they were often run by one or two people from their living room—passion projects, at first, though some of them attracted significant followings and quickly professionalized. Ezra Klein, Andrew Sullivan, Brian Stelter, and Matt Drudge, for example, began as bloggers, gained acclaim, and then became high-profile journalists. Some pursued breaking stories within a particular niche area of expertise, such as a previous industry they'd worked in. Many, however, chose to focus not on breaking news—investigative journalism often requires significant resources—but on analysis and commentary, using the tools of social media to turn journalism, as Gillmor put it, into a conversation rather than a lecture. They would come to redefine the industry.

But alongside this (d)evolution in media came a unique offshoot in the evolutionary tree: individuals who used the same social media tools and strategies as the proliferating new-media entrepreneurs but positioned themselves quite deliberately as ordinary people.

These ordinary folks—like Polly or, perhaps most famously, the dance phenom Charli D'Amelio, a cheerful brunette from Connecticut with 151 million TikTok followers—didn't bother trying to construct some corporate or newsy brand identity and didn't declare themselves "citizen journalists." They just wanted to talk about the random interests they were most passionate about: the retiree who loved to discuss gardening; your kid's piano teacher, who, on the side, was super into knitting and cooking; a full-time barista with a secret passion for ecotravel.

They posted as themselves, using a casual, first-person, low-production style. And yet, despite being completely ordinary, some managed to amass huge audiences. These creators had the reach of mass media—passionate fandoms who shared and retweeted and reposted their content—but they were intriguing to audiences precisely because they didn't have a corporate media feel. Their ordinariness granted them a combination of authenticity and relatability: *I am just like you.* And while this "ordinariness" may become manicured over time, its origins are genuine.

Their audiences listened to what they had to say and, more importantly, kept coming back to hear more. Some influencers didn't even have particularly massive followings, but their opinions were respected enough that they could potentially drive their followers to form a positive opinion of a brand or try out a new product. Marketers encouraged their corporate clients to engage with this emerging force: to sponsor posts or to enable product placement. These elite content creators were a contemporary manifestation of Bernays's invisible rulers: people who understood psychological and emotional currents, who could unlock the motives behind a community's desires, who could create purchaser demand.[17] Because the influencers were members of the community themselves, marketers believed, they could convince people to buy things—and, as political forces began to take note, to believe things.

It turned out to be a bit more complicated than that: having a lot of followers didn't translate into having the power of persuasion, and influencers weren't magicians capable of manifesting trends out of nowhere.[18] But they were good at forging close and trusting relationships with their fans. They created an online experience truly designed for the social media age, in which the audience could participate by commenting and chatting back. Influencers joke around in the comments, often replying to followers individually. People genuinely feel that they know many of the influencers they follow. The influencers might live a million miles away, yet they are present. They are the antithesis of old media, which is aloof, one-way, talking *to* their audience. Instead, influencers talk *with* their audience.[19]

This also makes them distinct from celebrities, who are often anointed by the media and remain somewhat inaccessible. It's not always clear how or why the legacy media decide to anoint someone. Early in her rise to stardom, for example, Kim Kardashian was often described as "famous for being famous"—a concept articulated decades prior by Daniel Boorstin, a prominent American historian, author, and media theorist of the mid-twentieth century.[20] Many influencers seem to fit this characterization. Charli D'Amelio poked fun at it in one of her TikTok bios as she rose to stardom: "don't worry I don't get the hype either." She'd been an early adopter of TikTok when the app was still relatively new in the United States and was a talented dancer, but algorithmic alchemy played an undeniable role in her meteoric rise. Indeed, in addition to being engaged and available, influencers are distinct from celebrities in that they are often self-made; while the algorithm provides an assist (as we will discuss), they attract their early attention themselves by being good at social media. They control their own content, brand, and distribution. While influencers can certainly become celebrities—garnering movie cameos or guest spots on TV programs like D'Amelio's stint on *Dancing with the Stars*—that happens after they've been effective on their own.

But what makes an effective influencer? The opinion-leader ladies of Decatur were fellow members of a geographically constrained real-life community who were personable and attuned to the news around them. If everyone has access to the same tools, what sets some people apart, enabling them to amass influence in an increasingly virtual world?

Traits that endear people to others, such as charisma, attractiveness, humor, and a lively personality, are also key to an influencer's popularity. But beyond being relatable, they are highly attuned to their audience; as their following evolves, they balance authenticity with being appealing.[21] They know what social media trending and curation algorithms will reward—in fact, they spend a lot of time paying attention to that.

But first and foremost, the influencer is a storyteller—someone adept at creating twists, conflicts, heroes, villains, and all the other trappings of a good narrative.

Marketing is also about telling a story and creating context and an image around a product. So is public relations, as Bernays repeatedly emphasized. Therefore, it is unsurprising that corporate storytellers were the first to see the power of social media influencers. As social media gained more adopters in the late naughts, marketers developed the criteria of "reach, relevance, and resonance" for assessing what made particular influencers successful.[22]

Reach—how many people an influencer could, well, reach—measures an influencer's audience size, an important metric for determining how far a message might spread. How does an influencer get that reach, though? By creating and curating content that interests people—often within a particular niche to start. *Relevance* is about sharing information that a specific audience cares about. Certain influencers become top-of-mind for a particular topic: Jordan Ferney of Oh Happy Day for her whimsical, made-for-Instagram children's birthday parties, PewDiePie for gaming, Jeffrey Starr for makeup application videos (and, recently, raising yaks).[23] Even if not broadly known to the whole country (like a celebrity), the influencer is perceived as a compelling or authoritative speaker producing meaningful content for a particular niche.

Resonance is the creator's ability to make a message so compelling that people take action: buy a product, attend a rally for a cause, or even just share the creator's video. And this is where skill as a storyteller comes into play. Relevance assesses whether an influencer is posting about topics interesting to a particular audience, but resonance asks whether an influencer's posts are clicking with their audience emotionally, enticing followers and fans to spread the content and come back for more. Even influencers with low follower counts are useful if they have resonance and relevance within a distinct, tight-knit community.[24] They may have fewer followers, but they enjoy a trust and rapport that celebrity spokespeople don't have. Influencers know what stories are relevant to their audience because they're part of the same community. But knowing *how* to tell them—what tone to strike, what kind of rhetorical style to use, what memes and in-group language to drop to frame the news of the day, what will build trust or entice a share—sets some influencers apart because it helps them capture and keep attention. And if they delve into the political realm, the combination of trust and skill at storytelling gives influencers the power to sell something far more potent than products: they can sell ideologies.

The power to influence opinions lies with those who can most widely and effectively disseminate a message. This holds in all media environments and was even true in our old word-of-mouth English village. But platform tools for sharing have supercharged dissemination—and made it into something of a game.

The Algorithm

The spread of Amazing Polly's conspiracy theory about filing cabinets was aided and abetted by more than her folksy charisma and an impressionable audience. It was made possible by "the algorithm": the kingmaker of trends and influencers, the shaper of crowds, and an invisible ruler wrought from code.

"The algorithm" is not one thing, of course, though the term has become a shorthand for the important processes that curate, suggest, and rank content—rather opaquely—on social media platforms. Newsfeeds, recommendation systems, search engines—algorithms like these influence whom you know, what you see, what you post, how you feel, and even how you behave online (and off). They are often talked about in neutral terms, like a series of steps undertaken to solve a particular problem, computer code that simply processes user input or data.[25] But in reality, social media algorithms are anything but neutral. They are intensely shaped by platforms' primary business incentive: maximizing user engagement in service to advertising revenue. They are also, in conjunction with the terms of service and other policies, a manifestation of the values of the platform: what it will privilege, present, tolerate, or throttle.

Algorithmic system results on social media are often highly personalized. Social media companies are working to keep you on site (to see ads) or attempting to deliver results useful to you. You can see this personalization reflected in the results of search engines, like Google, which try to maximize relevance: searching for "bakery" in New York should return different results than searching in Paris. Features like the little predictive-text nudges of autocomplete also look to maximize relevance by suggesting refinements: typing in "cats" might prompt the user with "cats *movie*" or "cats *that don't shed.*"

Autocomplete suggestions offer a glimpse into the algorithm's understanding of aggregate user behavior—an immensely important part of how key social media algorithms work. The outputs are personalized, but the data sets are massive, and the platforms are mining for similarities across vast quantities of user information. If a whole lot of users near you or similar to you complete the query that you've begun with specific words, the autocomplete algorithm takes that into account and may be more likely to suggest them to you. Since the results are derived from data related to millions of searches, autocomplete is, in a sense, holding a mirror up to society. Occasionally what shows up in that mirror is uncomfortable, or worse: during the 2012 presidential campaign, autocomplete results included "Is Obama *a secret Muslim*" or offered up his middle name—"Hussein"—at a time when his birthplace and loyalties were the subject of many conspiratorial-media smears. Autocomplete reflected the extent to which those smears had people looking for answers. More recently, internet studies scholar Dr. Safiya Noble cataloged all the offensive suggestions that follow "Why are black women so..."[26] The autocomplete results are a nudge; the results that follow can take people in unexpected directions.[27]

All media environments have had a mechanism for shaping who is influential and determining, to some extent, what people see. In print, radio, and television, the curators were other people, the editorial gatekeepers, who decided what to cover on the news. With the advent of the internet, vast quantities of content on every conceivable topic could be found online, produced by whoever had a mind to post. Search engines became a critically important form of curation in a world with a growing glut of content. But autocomplete algorithms went one small step further, by adding a suggestion layer—the digital equivalent of a bookstore or library laying out a table of enticing content that a user hadn't gone looking for but couldn't resist.

Nudging people with things they hadn't gone looking for quickly became a foundational tool for Big Tech to engage its users.

Some of the first nudges social media algorithms presented to users were connections with other users. They began to shape whom we know, foundationally reorienting human social networks by connecting people who'd never met in real life and moving us from "friend graphs" to "interest graphs." This is, in fact, the phenomenon that birthed influencers: influencers become influencers in large part because algorithms recommend them. Charli D'Amelio didn't have a sleek PR firm or lavish marketing budget at her disposal when she started posting dance videos in May 2019.[28] But she did have engaging content and an algorithm incentivized to spread it—and her fifteenth post, on July 17, 2019, went viral as TikTok's curation algorithm promoted it.[29] She gained thousands of followers. And then, as she continued to post more dance videos, the TikTok algorithm, along with word of mouth, reliably grew her audience.

Consider algorithms like Facebook's People You May Know (PYMK) feature: a recommender system that proactively suggests potential friends, displaying the recommended profile's picture and name in a prominent spot on the website. Its goal is not only to link users who might know each other in real life but to connect friends of friends as well—because Facebook's growth team observed that knowing more people increased a user's time on site. Facebook's engineers estimated that typical users might have forty thousand friends of friends, while "power users" might have as many as eight hundred thousand.[30] Recommender algorithms work—on Facebook and elsewhere—by creating a sense of serendipity or curiosity and inspiring us to click. These algorithms succeed in connecting people at a massive scale and in a way that transcends geography—creating new social networks for content and opinions to traverse. They turned *friend* into a verb.

PYMK and similar connection-recommendation algorithms leverage any and all data at their disposal. Social media apps ask for access to your phone contacts so they can check the numbers against their registered users, then suggest that you friend or follow the matches. Other ways of connecting people include physical proximity—like if your phone's location capabilities show you and another individual are working at the same location or going to the same school at the same time.[31] This works decently well but at times reveals that the recommenders do not actually understand the social norms they simulate. Tech journalist Kashmir Hill conducted an investigation into one troubling incident in which PYMK algorithms recommended a therapist's patients to each other, presumably based on their mutual links to her (for example, having her practice's phone number in their phones).[32] Algorithms are optimized to achieve a particular objective; this means that if they aren't carefully thought through, they may have unintended consequences.

Facebook was originally built on the idea of "friends" and bidirectional relationships: you were friends with someone, and they were friends with you. It was, to a large extent, replicating real-world social networks in virtual space. But other platforms, such as Twitter, built their businesses and user experience around a "follower" model: you could follow a person on the platform and see their public posts even if the person had no idea you existed and didn't follow you back. You could follow people based on interests.

Algorithms that suggested people to follow based on their prominence or topical relevance helped unintentionally birth influencers simply by giving their accounts pride of place on a list. In January 2010, tech entrepreneur Anil Dash wrote a blog post describing his experience of being placed on Twitter's Suggested Users list, a feature that debuted in 2009. Dash noted he had eighteen thousand followers in October 2009. "If I'd have continued my normal rate of growth, I'd have about 25,000 followers today," he wrote, "but thanks to being on the list, I've got close to 300,000 followers."[33] Getting more followers begets yet more followers, as popular accounts are suggested more often. The Suggested Users recommender system was somewhat controversial even in 2009, as people recognized its power to consolidate influence online in ways that felt random, like the algorithm or platform owner putting his thumb on the scale; it felt decidedly different from how fame was earned offline, despite there also being a fair bit of randomness in how media anoint celebrities.[34]

Elon Musk, who bought Twitter in 2022, offers a more recent example. As of early 2023, following Elon Musk surfaces clusters of similar accounts that Twitter's algorithm thinks will interest the user: Marjorie Taylor Greene, Tesla, Jim Jordan, Leo Terrell, SpaceX, and Donald Trump Jr. Being put on the suggested followers list of the site's most famous user delivers benefits to the others pulled along for the ride; Marjorie Taylor Greene's and Jim Jordan's follower counts jumped by hundreds of thousands within a month.[35] It was an interesting glimpse into where Twitter's algorithms thought Musk was situated politically. And if you were to follow one of the suggested accounts, you would, in turn, see another wave of suggestions similar to *them*—perhaps more right-wing politicians or right-wing entertainers. The recommendation engine shapes networks of influence and amplification with potentially significant impacts.

Facebook, too, gradually began to connect people around interests. It did this in large part by beginning to recommend not only friends but groups, persistent communities set up around a topic—Backyard Chickens, Melanoma Warriors, My Baby Won't Sleep—in which people came together not around mutual connections but around interests. People formed deep friendships in these groups—which tended to increase time on site. This was good for the company.

And so, it set about reorienting users' social networks through recommender systems that promoted groups. In their simplest form, recommender systems suggest content based on expressed interests. Known as *content-based filtering*, that type of algorithm takes signals from what the user herself has done, such as watch a video about gardening, and then suggests more gardening content or communities. But as platforms amassed data from millions of users, recommender systems developed the capacity to elicit similarities *between* users, offering up suggestions derived not from what the target herself had done but from what people like her had done—a process called *collaborative filtering*. Watching a video about gardening might lead to suggestions for vegetarian cooking groups, perhaps, or jogging.

As social media algorithms sucked up and processed more and more data from user behavior—including around politics—and refashioned it into nudges, they proved to be extraordinarily accurate at suggesting things that people were interested in but also troublingly amoral. Between 2013 and 2015, signs began to emerge of an unintended consequence: algorithmic recommendation of deeply toxic communities. In 2014, for example, Twitter began to have something of a problem with the Syria- and Iraq-based terrorist group Islamic State (ISIS, or Daesh). ISIS recruiters and fanboys were present on the platform, using it as a tool of propaganda and influence, spreading their messages and growing their followings.[36] They were there to cheerlead for the ideology of their so-called virtual caliphate, and if you followed one account, the algorithm suggested more.

In 2016, Facebook's group recommendation engine had begun to suggest Pizzagate groups to users who were in other conspiracy-theory groups, such as pseudoscience communities focused on vaccines and chemtrails.[37] By early 2018, it had begun to suggest QAnon groups, long before QAnon (or Amazing Polly) became the subject of extensive media coverage, helping the nascent fringe theory to grow into an omnicon-spiracy, a singularity in which all manner of conspiracy theories melted together and appealed to far more adherents than any component part.[38] The recommendation engine was functioning as something of a con-spiracy theory correlation matrix: *You appreciate flat Earth content and believe NASA is lying to you, so you should definitely check out these people over here who believe pedophiles are drinking the blood of children in a pizza place and John F. Kennedy Jr. has returned.* This unintended consequence has persisted for years and appears across many topics; in May 2023, my team at the Stanford Internet Observatory discovered that following one account in a child-exploitation network on Instagram resulted in sug-gestions for more.[39] People looking for this kind of extremely illegal and very harmful content were being connected to each other not only by keywords or real-world relationships but by a recommender system that intuited they had mutual interests.

The collaborative filtering algorithm was doing precisely what it was designed to do: suggesting content or communities to people likely to be interested because of some underlying similarity to other people (in the case of the conspiracy correlation matrix, perhaps a shared distrust in government). To a large extent, these algorithms reflect existing hu-man preferences: birds of a feather flock together. And, indeed, PYMK and other recommender algorithms that arrange people into networks often generate communities of highly similar users (*high-homophily net-works*), a fact that has led to concern about echo chambers.

Some of these edge cases, however, went beyond echo chambers; the recommendation engines were pushing people into communities that were borderline, if not directly, harmful. By late 2018, QAnon was al-ready, in essence, a decentralized cult,[40] connected to several instances of violence as well as enough stories of terrible family impact to warrant a dedicated support group (called "QAnonCasualties").[41] On multiple occasions, anti-vaccine groups promoted by the algorithm saw members suffer child deaths after a misguided parent ignored sound medical advice in favor of suggestions from fellow members. One mother in the highly algorithmically recommended group Stop Mandatory Vaccination chose to skip Tamiflu after members warned her against Big Pharma's treatments and suggested she try elderberry or breastmilk, or put onions in her son's socks instead. He later died from the flu.[42] Another skipped the vitamin K shot that prevents newborn brain bleeds out of fear that it was a vaccine with toxic ingredients—a misconception widely spread within the group. At the time, search engines were also surfacing anti-vaccine blogs in response to searches for "vitamin K shot."[43] The algorithms work with what they have.

Although some academics, journalists, and activists (like me, at the time) wrote about these situations and urged a rethinking of recommender system ethics, platforms largely avoided action, though internally they were secretly beginning to have some concerns. In 2016, Facebook's internal research found that 64 percent of people who joined an extreme group did so by way of a recommendation and that the groups were, as Jeff Horwitz of the *Wall Street Journal* put it, "disproportionately influenced by a subset of hyperactive users."[44] In summer 2019, Facebook's internal research teams set up a persona account—a politically conservative mother named Carol—and found that within two days, she too was being pushed into groups dedicated to QAnon.[45] Broadly speaking, this is how people like Polly and her audience connected with each other, how the community grew, and how its influencers came to serve as centers of gravity for large numbers of people. And yet Facebook's leadership team largely ignored its own findings.

By 2020, concern had grown too large to ignore. In October of that year, ahead of the US presidential election, Facebook disabled group recommendations for all political and social issues[46] and also banned QAnon pages and groups.[47] However, although the platform eventually moderated, the groups simply reassembled elsewhere; by this point the social network connections were already made, the worldviews shaped, the friendships and fandoms solidified. People had been nudged into conspiracy theorist communities, sending them down rabbit holes into full-blown bespoke realities, for years. And as technology ethicist L. M. Sacasas puts it, "The worlds we now inhabit are digitized realms incapable by their nature and design of generating a broadly shared experience of reality. This can be lamented, if one is so inclined, but it cannot be undone."[48]

Algorithms shape not only whom we know but also what we see. After encouraging us to join groups and follow people, curation and feed-ranking algorithms select from among these (and similar) accounts to push content into our field of view.[49]

As social media turned everyone into content creators, platforms found themselves wrangling with the problem of a content glut. Early social media had largely relied on a reverse-chronological feed, with the most recent post at the top. Feed-ranking and curation algorithms instead filtered and sorted to try to determine what would be the most engaging, surfacing personalized content for any given user. These curation systems start with an inventory of all possible content on the platform available for the user to see—often the posts from influencers they follow, groups they're part of, or content similar to either.[50] Then they remove "borderline" (problematic) content[51]—things that bump up against the platform's moderation policies and are ineligible for curation (and, at times, for monetization); this is called being *deboosted*, *downranked*, or *demonetized*. From the posts that remain, the curation algorithm selects a subset of "candidate" posts with high likelihood of being relevant to the target user and then ranks them. That ranking process is where the platform guesses which of the relevant posts you're most likely to engage with, keeping you interested, on site, and able to see ads.[52]

Curation algorithms are critical to a platform's business—and an influencer's livelihood. Facebook's Feed, Twitter's For You timeline, and YouTube's right-side column of video thumbnails all strive to pick precisely the right posts to keep a specific user on site.[53] Indeed, on one of the fastest-growing social apps of the 2020s—TikTok—the For You Page (FYP) moved away from curation based on users' social graphs and toward curation primarily based on users' intuited interests. Seemingly arbitrary videos often become very popular. In a study of popular election-related content in 2022, my team noticed that many of the Tik-Tok videos with the most views were not those with obvious political hashtags (which might indicate people found them through search) or from accounts with big audiences (which might indicate organic reach).[54] Rather, they appeared to be videos that the FYP algorithm had decided should be amplified. It was, in fact, nearly impossible to find the most popular election videos through search because keywords weren't what mattered—trying to figure out what election-related content was most popular on TikTok in 2022 was like searching a dictionary for a word you don't know how to spell. Compounding the opaque nature of things, in January 2023 it emerged that some TikTok employees had access to a tool called the "heating" button, which enabled them to boost specific videos (across any content category). The button was purportedly used to entice influencers and brands into partnerships,[55] and "heated" video views were sometimes 1 to 2 percent of the daily total video views on the platform—an extraordinary number.[56]

Competing for attention in the ruthless online arena is incredibly challenging. For savvy or lucky influencers, the curation algorithm can be a kingmaker: content that is widely boosted to For You–type features on TikTok, Instagram, or Twitter or gets pushed by Facebook Watch or YouTube's autoplay can result in tens of thousands of views, tens of thousands of new followers, and potentially quite a lot of money. Influencers may prize authenticity, but those who turn social media into a career—or who use it to pursue clout and power—are also acutely aware of what the algorithms will reward. They constantly play what social media scholar Kelley Cotter called "the visibility game," testing creation strategies to see which consistently yield follower growth or higher engagement.[57] A 2023 *Wired* profile of one prominent talent manager for influencers, Ursus Magana, highlighted his personal slogan: "Influence the algorithm, not the audience."[58]

Influencers spend inordinate amounts of time chasing the whims of algorithms because their boost can be life changing. Consider the former pizza shop employee who posted a sixteen-second TikTok clip of herself playing a video game, received three million views, and now spends her time trying to make it as an influencer.[59] But an occasional algorithmic boost isn't enough—after all, influencers are in constant competition with others to capture attention. Their followers are following other influencers as well. The influencer's primary job is to grow an audience, a crowd of followers who will serve as eyeballs on the content as well as a secondary distribution machine. Reach significantly determines to what extent the influencer makes money or accrues power, so the temptation to pepper content with the kind of bait that the algorithms will boost to a niche is ever present.

Recommendation and curation algorithms, in other words, shape the very nature of content itself.

In 2020, during the COVID pandemic, Facebook's Watch tab began to push a curated feed of videos of attractive young women doing bizarre and often gross things with food: mixing punch in a toilet bowl or putting SpaghettiOs into pie crust. The content was the work of a group of creators tied to magician Rick Lax.[60] No matter what types of accounts you followed, it seemed, the Watch feature *really* wanted you to see videos from Rick Lax's network of creators; their aggregate view counts were in the hundreds of millions.

A short while later, the gross food videos seemed to disappear, and a new style of massively popular videos featuring the same women began to dominate Watch, but this time they were acting, pretending to be discovered having affairs. The spouse would come home, and for a full twelve minutes the video would show the clueless spouse getting *so close* to discovering the paramour as they ran around trying to hide in increasingly ridiculous ways. There were dozens of variants; sometimes the spouse coming home was a returning veteran! Judging from the comments, many Facebook users who had been pushed the content via the Watch recommender algorithm found it obnoxious. But they also often clearly watched to the end—waiting for a payoff that never came—and then left a peeved remark. The recommender system was doing what it was supposed to do: serving content that kept users watching. But it also felt a bit like things had gone off the rails; these videos so frequently dominated the Watch page that a colleague of mine, Ryan Butner, compared the situation to an invasive species proliferating and going haywire within an ecosystem, crowding out all other types of content. Cane toads taking over the Watch tab.

Intrigued, I took a closer look at the network behind these videos and found a cadre of creators and influencers all cross-promoting and linking to each other. The actors had their own Facebook pages, where they were posting the videos; some had a lot of followers, but many did not. Yet these videos had millions of views. The algorithmic Watch feed was clearly driving engagement.

As I looked at the data behind the videos, going back months, I noticed that Lax had progressively discovered a formula for content titles that seemed to have helped things along. The whole network of creators gradually began to use simple, shocking, curiosity-inspiring phrases as titles for their mini soap operas: "What he saw when he opened the door!" or "When she looked under the couch!" The engagement on titles in that format was through the roof. Lax had worked out the magic formula, creating content specifically designed to feed the algorithm; he and his friends were getting rich as a result.[61]

There's a famous saying from media theorist Marshall McLuhan: "The medium is the message." Different types of media—print, radio, television—created different types of experiences for audiences. The *structure* of the communication channels incentivized what *substance* moved across it. Media theorist Neil Postman put it another way in his book *Amusing Ourselves to Death*: "Form will determine the nature of content." Social media affordances shape what we all create and share. Influencers make content not for humans but for the intersection of humans and algorithms. We all do this, to some extent—even if we are primarily posting for a small group of friends, it has become second nature to think about the composition of a photo or the moment it captures as something to optimize for Instagram. Influencers define an "Instagram-worthy" aesthetic for engagement optimization, and then the rest of us unwittingly replicate it.

Top influencers understand how structure and substance are connected. They are experts at blending resonant rhetoric and content that also check the boxes on what the algorithm is inclined to boost. But there's a cat-and-mouse game in play: platforms conceal the details of what their algorithms are likely to reward because they know people will go to great lengths to engineer that algorithmic boost. And platforms notice when users start to not like, or get tired of, a particular thing and adjust their algorithms accordingly. So it was with Rick Lax: after a few months of extraordinary popularity, the Facebook Watch algorithm changed what it rewarded, and his meticulously constructed clickbait titles were rendered ineffective. Engagement plummeted. The algorithm giveth, and the algorithm taketh away.

Social media companies aren't oblivious to the fact that their business models intersect with influencers' business models in perverse ways. While some influencers, particularly the content creators who are primarily focused on broadcasting their lives, strive for broad appeal, the fastest path for many is to target a niche. For political influencers, as with the media-of-one, there is little incentive to be broadly appealing; generality is too vague to meaningfully target. The ever-present need to capture attention from a specific niche encourages the production of sensational, and at times even toxic, content. One internal report from Facebook was particularly revealing: "Our algorithms exploit the human brain's attraction to divisiveness," read a slide from a 2018 presentation. "If left unchecked," it warned, Facebook would feed users "more and more divisive content in an effort to gain user attention and increase time on the platform."[62]

There is no such thing as a "neutral" ranking or recommendation system. Every algorithmic curation system—even the reverse-chronological feed—is encoded with value judgments about what criteria are most important for determining what to place on users' screens. These value judgments create incentives for those who want to capture attention in pursuit of power, profit, or clout. Ranked feeds might promote sensationalism, but reverse-chronological feeds incentivize frequent posting.

Invisible, opaque algorithms play a significant role in deciding what gets attention and when. In tandem with influencers, they determine what people see, what they talk about, and what they create on any given day. They decide what will dominate millions of people's feeds on a Tuesday afternoon. They are the purveyors of community connection. They are also purveyors of overwrought drama and dubious stories with little substance, yet big potential to capture attention.

But there's a third part of the equation—of the new trinity of influence—that makes this system so powerful: online crowds.

The Crowd

Amazing Polly's saga wasn't limited to paranoid Twitter threads—*#SaveTheChildren* leapt offline, impacting people in very real, very disruptive ways. As the trend progressed, with more and more participants chiming in, law enforcement and child safety organizations were overrun with calls about the Wayfair conspiracy. Professionals had to plead with people to stop calling about the situation, because it distracted them from saving actual children.

Together, Polly the influencer and the platform algorithms convoked a frenzied crowd. But that crowd was no passive entity: it completed a feedback loop, reinforcing Polly's incentives and the algorithms' behavior. Working in tandem, the trinity had made a rumor go wildly viral that day, and concern for nonexistent trafficked children eclipsed the needs of real ones.

Groups of likeminded people have gathered and organized for centuries. Activism and grassroots organizing call attention to worthy causes and bring people together with a shared sense of mission. People join religious groups or organize into unions or political parties. Crowds come together spontaneously in protest against injustice, both online and off. But crowd activity can also go bad, souring into moral panics, mass delusions, and hysteria. Mob violence can have terrible consequences. From tulip bubbles to witch hunts, history is replete with examples of extraordinary popular delusions and the madness of crowds.[63]

Platforms have imbued crowds with new qualities.[64] They are no longer fleeting and local but persistent and global. They engage symbiotically with influencers but don't require a leader or physical space to assemble. Platform affordances empowered crowds; they are now active participants in chronicling history and shaping narratives.

Influencers are acutely aware of the power of the online crowds. The influencer can use targeted ads and paid boosts to help her work get seen by the right audience. But achieving mass viral distribution—getting something to trend—requires appealing to either the algorithm or the crowd, or both. Algorithms, as we saw with Rick Lax, can be fickle; a platform can change its feed-ranking weightings or content policies overnight and tank a creator's reach. Consistently resonating with a passionate, activist niche crowd, getting its members liking, sharing, subscribing, and reposting, is a lower-volatility approach to making money and achieving reach. Fans who feel passionately about a message may propagate an influencer's posts from YouTube to Facebook to Reddit to Mastodon, ensuring that the influencer's work is seen by audiences everywhere, even if they themselves aren't particularly active on a given platform. This approach, however, does still put some pressure on the influencer: they are inclined to continue to make content that the audience wants to see—or won't disagree with.

Large online crowds have the ability to drive mass awareness and trends at a global level. As they decide among themselves what to amplify, from among the various posts and aligned influencers they follow, they help influencers (and brands and political candidates) rapidly identify the memes and messages that truly resonate and capture public attention.

Individual platforms created distinctive features to encourage users to connect into groups, reordering social networks. Platform design and affordances then influenced how communities behaved. Facebook, as noted, heavily promoted groups via recommendation engines, nudging users to join them. On Twitter, groups were private, created by an owner who then invited members. They were very effective spaces for calling attention to whatever was happening on the platform: any given member could share a tweet into a group, and rest of the group could go interact with it. Sometimes this involved liking or retweeting something posted by a group member to boost engagement and help attract attention. However, Twitter groups were also useful for coordinating a brigade against an unfortunate tweeter or initiating a campaign to mass-report a particular post. Everyone has access to the same affordances; the difference in how they're used comes from community norms.

Twitter's design really offered the opportunity for emergent collective behavior, for spontaneous crowd formation, which carried with it the potential to suddenly devolve into a mob. If enough people saw even a completely earnest post—"I enjoy having coffee with my husband in our garden in the morning"[65]—it was guaranteed to be hideously offensive to some malcontent, who would feel absolutely compelled to let the original poster know (*Have you thought about how this sounds to people who don't have husbands?/gardens?/coffee?*). The quote-tweet feature let one user boost another's tweet while adding some commentary to it— while it was often used to support someone's post with just a bit of added opinion, it was equally effective as a tool for "dunking on," or mocking, the underlying post or user. Adding a hashtag, especially one that tied the post into a broader grievance narrative or gave a distinctive brand to the controversy (*#CoffeeGate*), made it discoverable to both algorithms and other people. Twitter's curation algorithms might process the proliferating number of posts as a sign that a lot of people were interested in a topic and push it out to more audiences.

Hashtags were an extraordinarily useful tool for making communities and topics discoverable: *#BlackTwitter, #ScienceTwitter, #Caturday*. But like any tool, they could be used as a weapon, and the way that they intersected with Trending Topics (a feature in which Twitter curates a semipersonalized list of hashtags popular in the moment) created incentives for conspiracy theorists, hyperpartisans, and brawlers to try to get rumors, propaganda, and harassment hashtags trending. Trending hashtags were prominently featured on a list, and the intrigue could pull in bystanders, who in turn might create their own posts or further amplify the ones in the hashtag. So it went with Amazing Polly, her crowd of supporters, and *#SaveTheChildren*.

In internet parlance, this process of many users sharing related content nearly simultaneously—which often leads to a broader algorithmic boost or featured promotion—is how something *goes viral*. The phrase, lifted from epidemiology, refers to how pathogens spread from person to person. But "it went viral" is a curiously passive phrase for a very active and participatory process. Things don't just "go viral"; we deliberately spread them.

The media often covers viral content as if it were caused by algorithms— particularly if it's a "borderline content" trend that a large group of people feel should have been moderated and downranked. But that framing strips the users of agency, and online crowds have more agency today than ever before. The algorithms provide lift and raise broader awareness, but virality is a collective behavior: each user makes a deliberate choice to post or retweet content because they find the post or messaging appealing, they believe in it, or they're outraged by it.

Facebook's design, unlike Twitter's, didn't lend itself to spontaneous crowds in active pursuit of heated frenzies of rage. The closed nature of Facebook groups and the privacy controls on the platform broadly, which allow people's posts to be visible only to friends or fellow group members, were useful for keeping people on site but not particularly effective for the roving bands of the outraged. Groups could certainly coordinate to target their enemies—indeed, the anti-vaccine groups did so liberally—but users had to hop off platform to carry out the mobbing in more conducive spaces, and that friction seemed to reduce the appeal. As a result of their closed nature, persistent communities on Facebook talked and shared opinions, coming to consensus in a more traditional, deliberative way. This produced communities with staying power, a deep trust between members, and a sense of permanence and long-term goals. Backyard Chickens and Melanoma Warriors were not populated by people trying to capture attention in the arena.

Facebook's Trending Topics feature, too, was focused on surfacing viral articles that many users were sharing and discussing—not wayward comments by hapless people. However, it nonetheless became a source of controversy, because committed financially and ideologically motivated groups began trying to game it. These manipulators encouraged members (or used fake "sockpuppet" accounts) to mass-share articles at the same time. In an effort to minimize the impact of gaming and reduce the reach of content mills monetizing clickbait headlines, Facebook added a layer of human editorial curation to the trends it displayed. However, a small but vocal cluster of right-wing influencers and their fans did not like this at all. Many of the clickbait sites produced right-wing hyperpartisan content, and when these were downranked and removed from trends, the company faced a litany of accusations of anticonservative bias from a faction of ideologically aligned users, right-wing influencers, and hyperpartisan media, who spun the situation into a tale of Facebook being biased against conservatives. (A faction is a combative and ideologically homogeneous subset of the larger crowd.)

The manufactured controversy—Trending Topicsgate—proved to be a watershed moment: Facebook responded to the complaints from prominent conservatives by firing its human curators, and the feature became an algorithmically mediated free-for-all,[66] which primarily communicated that working the referees ("ref-working") was an effective strategy for achieving a policy outcome favorable to one's interests. It also demonstrated conclusively that a faction could be riled up by the belief that their viewpoint was being unfairly suppressed, even if that was not actually the case.

After the human curators were fired, wild, fake viral news stories proliferated—demonstrably untrue stories such as "Pope Francis shocks world, endorses Donald Trump for president"[67] or "Breaking: Fox News Exposes Traitor Megyn Kelly, Kicks Her Out for Backing Hillary."[68] Facebook would eventually kill the feature entirely; it is now, in 2024, trying to reintroduce it on its Twitter-competitor, Threads. But at that point, both the formula for capturing mass attention via platform affordances and the value of loudly complaining had been uncovered; Pandora's box was open.

At their best, groups on Facebook help people from all over the world find community; there are support groups for rare diseases, fan groups for specific artists, and spaces for activists to connect as they solve humanitarian challenges. However, the most extreme groups on Facebook became echo chambers that actively fostered distrust of any expert, influencer, or media not of the tribe. QAnon would not have existed as it does today without Facebook's inadvertent algorithmic recruitment, plus its tools for sustained connection on a massive platform where users already spent a lot of time. At its worst, Twitter made mobs—and Facebook grew cults.

Mobs and cults, each subsets of crowds, require fuel to sustain their outrage or paranoia or mythology—to sustain their bespoke reality. Without new kindling, they risk burning out. And on today's internet, there's no shortage of fuel, due to a media practice with origins forty years before Twitter or Facebook even existed.

In the previous century, TV broadcasters had to confront something of a novel problem: technology had transformed the length of the news cycle. No longer were news organizations limited by just one publication per day or per week—they could broadcast all day, every day. And as the number of stations and channels increased, they competed for stories that would attract listeners and viewers. This incentivized somewhat sensational coverage: stories of dubious newsworthiness might be published solely because of their potential to capture and hold attention. "Electronic media cannot bear to suffer a pause of more than five seconds; a pause of thirty seconds of dead airtime seems interminable," mused Daniel Boorstin.[69]

Media's "solution" to this challenge extended beyond merely covering the sensational—it led to the creation of content for content's sake and the elevation of people who were famous for being famous. Media manufactured "important" moments that captured public attention but were in fact meaningless. These supposedly newsworthy moments were only so *because* they were covered on the news. Boorstin dubbed them *pseudo-events* in one of his most seminal books, 1962's *The Image: A Guide to Pseudo-events in America*. Pseudo-events are "synthetic" media moments, events that exist solely to be reported on: a senator's anodyne press conference on the steps of Capitol Hill or a ribbon cutting ceremony for a business under new ownership.

Bernays, writing long before television, had in fact instructed invisible rulers to manufacture news from nothing in service of public relations (propaganda). Facts that the invisible ruler wished to call attention to could be presented as news; ideas could be developed into events so that they too could claim attention as news. "The public relations counsel, therefore, is a creator of news for whatever medium he chooses to transmit his ideas. It is his duty to create news no matter what the medium which broadcasts this news," he argued.[70] Once created, interesting news could theoretically spread across whatever channels already held the public's attention.

Boorstin, forty years later, recognized the effect of the strategy: "The power to make a reportable event is thus the power to make experience."[71] Pseudo-events were produced in response to media incentives, but they had an impact on the audience. The public was, in good faith, consuming what had been sold to them as "news." They watched with the intent of becoming informed, and yet their attention was being pointed at nonsense. They were not entirely innocent—Boorstin believed that many people wanted to be fooled—but ultimately he directed the majority of his ire at the media outlets selling a false vision of reality to the public.

Sixty years later, the power to create pseudo-events has been democratized along with every other aspect of media. Influencers are masters of attention capture; it is their business. And today they can create pseudo-events of a caliber beyond Boorstin's wildest dreams, enticing a crowd to spend time watching them unbox a lipstick or recount on TikTok the latest manufactured controversy on Twitter about, for example, whether a dad who made his child figure out how to open a can of beans with a manual can opener was abusive—a real battle that trended on Twitter for nearly half a day.[72]

The things on social media that pass as significant moments of mass attention capture—two celebrities angrily @ing each other; a corporation tweeting a banal apology for a previous poorly worded tweet; "The Jews," which trended on Twitter in May 2023[73]—would, in a media era past, have been nonstories or relegated to explicitly sensational outlets like tabloids. Today they reach an audience, draw them in as participants, and dominate the daily conversation—but they remain ersatz at their core. They have lost even the pretense of being "news" and more often serve as a socially acceptable vehicle for outrage. And today the audience is no longer a passive consumer but an active participant.

Pseudo-events may differ depending on which faction a user belongs to—anti-vax, pro-choice, transit activist, QAnon. Within their online community, your neighbor or your sister may well be blind with rage about an obscure topic mentioned in an ephemeral tweet that you'll never see. And yet, it is completely real to them: if you make it trend, you make it true.

Social media's pseudo-events are especially potent because they're not confined to that realm—they can and do jump to mass media too.

I remember waking up one morning in January 2019, opening Twitter, and seeing an extraordinary amount of outrage in my feed about a situation that seemed to have transpired in Washington, DC, between a teenage boy in a MAGA hat and a Native American Omaha Nation elder with a drum. The moment, captured on video, seemed to show a smirking, disrespectful boy getting in the face of the elder, creating a disruption at a protest at the Lincoln Memorial. The video was pretty clearly on track to become a big deal; a lot of very prominent media people, activists, and left-leaning verified influencers with large followings were tweeting about it. Some were pretty nasty: the kid has a "punchable face," one reporter commented. As I watched the viral video clip, I did feel inclined to believe that the kid was a jerk; I didn't feel inclined to tweet about it, however, because after years of watching trending outrage content, I've also come to believe that there's little upside to offering my personal take. Selective edits and crops of videos can reframe a moment, and what you see isn't always what it seems.

Indeed, as the day went on, longer video clips of the situation emerged—including one showing the native elder approaching the boy, not the other way around. Right-wing media accounts and large-audience right-wing influencers went nuts—here again, they said, was mainstream media getting it wrong, yet more evidence of anticonservative bias against a kid in a MAGA hat. Antimedia commentary trended on Twitter.

The next day, still more video emerged—uncut, nearly two hours long—in which it became clear that a third party that hadn't appeared in either of the earlier two outrage cycles had also played a major role in events.[74] A small group of Black Hebrew Israelites had been off to the side, yelling at the MAGA boy and his friends, harassing them as well as other passersby. The Native American elder had stepped in between the two groups, but he gave conflicting accounts as to what his motivations had been, saying alternately that he was trying to diffuse tensions and yet simultaneously implying that the boys had been the instigators (a claim not borne out by the long video). As I watched the longer video, it seemed clear to me that the boys had not provoked the encounter at all . . . but the influencers and media I'd seen tweeting about the incident in the early hours of the viral video were not talking about it anymore.

As things had unfolded, for me and probably many others, it felt nearly impossible to figure out what sources were reliable and what the most accurate summary of events actually was. Points of view seemed split along predictable factional-partisan lines. The boy in the hat eventually sued several mainstream media outlets for defamation; several suits were dismissed, but some outlets chose to settle.

The point of this example is not to litigate the specifics of this one event or even to describe the challenge of figuring out what really happened. Rather, it's to highlight that for multiple days, many thousands of people on the internet, hundreds of influencers, and then numerous media articles dissected this extremely small moment of tension, something that, I would argue, never needed to be an online moment at all. Nothing had really happened. No one was injured. No one had to fixate on these people or go dig through their lives to find out who they *really* were. Three groups of people had a short disagreement, a few moments of real-life tension. What resulted was a pseudo-event, a spectacle, something that influencers called attention to and media covered in ways framed to appeal to their particular audiences.[75] Depending on whom you followed, you heard about it at a different time, saw it described in very different ways, and heard that the "other side" was a bunch of liars, manipulators, and villains. Depending on which influencers and outlets you trusted, you formed a particular view of events, who was right or wrong in the situation, and what their online punishment should be.

Social media's curation algorithms, particularly trending topics, push these pseudo-events and manufactroversies into the fields of those who have previously engaged with similar types of content—bait dangled at those mostly likely to take it. While I would argue that this mess was bad for everyone involved, it was great for platform engagement and influencer engagement, and the online crowds got some excitement out of a morning of righteous indignation.

The pseudo-events, now highly participatory, are not always so fraught. The mass media are not always quite so directly involved. Indeed, cultural divides between the two ecosystems are often visible: mainstream media's coverage may gawk and marvel at the absurdity of an online moment (*In other news, crackpots on TikTok are saying...*) or write think pieces about what it all means. But that distinction is less important than the fact that, through its coverage, the bait of the day nonetheless makes it to the nightly news, reaching a new and more diverse audience of millions. Social media hands off the baton to its "predecessor," mass media, and mass media hands it back—these two ecosystems are not separate and distinct but rather form two parts of a larger whole.

The Trinity

The influencer, algorithm, and crowd are distinct, but their incentives are inseparable. The influencer is always aware of the algorithm and the crowd because they determine her reach and revenue; the algorithms boost relevant influencers to keep the crowd on site, steering the attention of the latter and the output of the former; the crowd members volunteer to be nudged and monetized but in exchange find community, entertainment, and camaraderie—including with prominent figures who can call attention to things they care about.

Bernays's concept of invisible rulers from the 1920s finds resonance in the realm of modern influencers. Influencers are opinion leaders with the power to influence what people believe or buy and the capacity to shape sentiment and norms within their niche. They innately understand how to connect with others in a digital age, developing intimate trusted relationships with their followers, yet are also capable of achieving reach commensurate with mass media.

The algorithms, which emerged with and shaped this media ecosystem, are also invisible rulers. Created and controlled by private companies, they determine what content is shown to potentially billions of users, effectively guiding not only their online experiences but reshaping communities and norms in ways that have significant real-world impact. Algorithms shape the flow of information and influence the narratives that users encounter. By tailoring content based on user preferences and engagement patterns, they not only reinforce existing beliefs but nudge users in sometimes terrifying directions. This selective exposure to information can reinforce biases and shape users' perceptions in ways akin to the invisible rulers' influence over public opinion.

And then there is the audience—traditionally, the target subject to the influence of invisible rulers. Indeed, the crowd's behaviors, decisions, and preferences are increasingly shaped by the curated content its members consume and the algorithmically mediated interactions they have. And yet the sense of shared identity and the camaraderie fostered within these digital spaces lead to collective behavior and the formation of online factions in which they actively participate. The members of the crowd influence not only each other but the influencer. Social media users have become both the targets and the agents of influence, blurring the line between the invisible rulers and their subjects.

QAnon influencers and adherents like Polly are fond of a saying: "We are the media now." By this they mean that they set the agenda for what the public talks about. This is a bit of an exaggeration, but only a bit. Within each niche, the influencer-algorithm-crowd trinity shapes consensus and defines the beliefs of *their* public.

This trinity thrives on the proliferation of attention-capturing pseudo-events; sensationalism, spectacle, and tribalism are rewarded and reinforced. The environment is tailor-made for spreading rumors far and fast and for reinforcing connections and ideology *within* niches— not bridging *across* them. Influence is local to small networks, centered around influencers or within partisan factions or the bespoke realities of growing conspiracist communities. There is little common ground between the niches; one online faction often does not even see something that is outraging another, unless it erupts into a fight between them.

Not all influencers covet pseudo-events or factional brawls. Some just want to post about gardening or astronomy, and damn the clout or money. But incentivized influencers like Polly, particularly those focused on politics, are many. And their role is dynamic: projecting accessibility despite power, building trust while inflaming emotions, and seeking new ways to monetize—all the focus of our next chapter.

3

Gurus, Besties, and Propagandists

How Influencers Shape Culture, Politics, and Society

KHABY LAME, A SENEGALESE Italian twentysomething, was laid off from a factory job early in the COVID pandemic.[1] He took to Tik-Tok with his newfound free time, making videos mocking *other* videos, often in the "life hack" and "thirst trap" genres.[2] His "everyman" facial expressions as he watches someone, say, use a knife to peel a banana are relatable and funny. Sometimes compared to Charlie Chaplin, as of December 2023 he has the most followed account on TikTok, with 162 million followers.

Candace Owens, a conservative commentator and firebrand, is hard to miss online: you may spot her on Twitter (over 4 million followers), on Instagram (4.6 million followers), or in countless podcasts and videos. She may be championing Kanye West, questioning the motives of Black Lives Matter activists, or exhorting young women to appreciate their natural beauty (and stop wearing yoga pants in public).[3]

Then there's MrBeast (real name Jimmy Donaldson), a YouTube star with 183 million subscribers who got his start creating outlandish stunt-challenge videos and is now the most extremely online philanthropist in the world.[4] He matches boundless creativity with bottomless pockets to orchestrate not only jaw-dropping feats but also acts of kindness such as supporting medical care for amputees.[5]

Keffals is the streaming name of Clara Sorrenti. She got her start broadcasting herself playing video games on Twitch, though her content became more political as trans rights became the subject not only of online factional battles but of legislative efforts in Texas. Keffals has a comparatively smaller following but a strong niche appeal with a younger audience disinterested in cable TV news, appreciative of a fresh, often underrepresented perspective, and eager to troll mutual ideological opponents.[6]

If you're over twenty-five, you may never have heard of Khaby or Keffals and the rest, but these folks—and people who use social media as they do—are the most important force shaping culture, entertainment, and, increasingly, politics today.

Khaby Lame, MrBeast, Candace Owens, and Keffals are influencers. And they achieved their level of success partly through creativity and partly through skill at leveraging platform affordances for creation and reach: the instant publishing, liking, and retweeting tools that TikTok, YouTube, and others provide.

These platforms offer "influence-as-a-service," the same way Google and Microsoft provide office productivity tools as "software-as-a-service." It's a turnkey model: influence-as-a-service packages up the tools of creation and dissemination, audience access, and dashboards of metrics—everything necessary to amass reach, capture attention, and parlay them into power and profit.

But it's not just the technology. Successful influencers are also remarkably talented at connecting with their audiences on a human level, which is what makes them resonant and sticky. People love them. Dedicated followers not only watch or read their content but spread it, remix it, and get chatty in the comments. The influencers develop relationships and, in aggregate, amass fandoms—or factions.

"Invisible rulers" may seem an odd way to describe influencers—after all, they're highly conspicuous, brazenly seeking followers and dominating our feeds. But while the influencer herself is visible, her influence often is not. We may still see Sean Hannity or the anchors of *Good Morning America* as the de facto power brokers, but people, especially those under twenty-five, are increasingly taking cues from unexpected taste-makers like Keffals, Candace Owens, MrBeast, and Khaby Lame.

What Is Influence?

The internet teems with influencers, but *influence* is a surprisingly hard concept to define. Plenty of information flows past us every day; our minds aren't immediately changed simply because something hits our radar. Some of the information we encounter comes from people and sources with whom we already share beliefs and perspectives—while they might be reinforcing or echoing our opinions, that's not the same thing as shaping or influencing them.[7] Many academic definitions of influence therefore focus on *effect*: "Influence is a way of having an effect on the attitudes and opinions of others," wrote Talcott Parsons, one of the most prominent figures in twentieth-century sociology, in 1963. He emphasized that the person trying to influence others was acting intentionally and that the effect could be not only to cause a change in attitude or opinion, but also to prevent one.[8]

But figuring out what actually has an effect—what really changes attitudes or shapes opinions—is very, very difficult. Why did hundreds of thousands of people suddenly decide that a perfectly respectable furniture company was secretly involved in online child trafficking? How did millions come to be involved in QAnon in the first place? How does anyone decide to become part of any activist social movement, for that matter? We're constantly bombarded by messages and information and nudges, by way of the media, social media, and our social circles. Apps and advertisers battle for our attention, sending pings to our ever-present phones. News is everywhere, and there's a never-ending stream of content for us to dip into. How does influence actually work?

Social psychologist Dorwin Cartwright studied how influence impacted group and organizational dynamics and moved across social networks decades before Facebook and Twitter were even an idea. In 1965, he boiled influence down to a succinct idea: an agent does something to a target that results in a change in the target.[9] Maybe the target adopts a new opinion or takes an action.

Some influential figures—a celebrity such as Taylor Swift—may influence audiences just by being who they are. Others, however, are quite intentional, driven by age-old motivations of power, money, and clout in pursuit of a particular outcome. A salesperson wants to persuade a prospective customer to buy a car, while a political candidate wants to entice voters to vote for her. Influence is a means to an end.

Online influencers share these same motivations: Some simultaneously earn a living while also seeking to change the crowd's mind about an issue or to galvanize action, like Keffals does with trans rights. Others seek economic gains: MrBeast is on the cusp of becoming a billionaire, and there are dozens of YouTube videos dissecting his success in an effort to replicate it.[10] And still others, like Amazing Polly, are rewarded by the likes, attention, and sense of status within their (QAnon) community.

Cartwright pointed out that influence was based in large part on *access*: the agent has to be connected to a person somehow in order to "do something" to him or her. The means of exerting influence might vary: it could take the form of reward and punishment, direct physical power, or shaping opinion. All of these means are still pertinent today, though their manifestations have changed.

In Cartwright's time, access often involved knowing someone in "real life"—people in the same community or with common friends or family members influenced each other. But the access could also be more removed: authority figures (a senator, the president, the pope) were not directly connected to the average person, yet might be a significant presence nonetheless as their words and actions were conveyed through the media.

Social media has exponentially expanded the notion of access, and knowing someone online can result in as strong a bond as a physical connection. Influencers have significant reach and access to audiences within their own follower communities; you might not know MrBeast personally, but his relatability and constant presence in your feed create a sense of connection, of some sort of relationship. They also have reach and access across communities, by virtue of crowds sharing or algorithms pushing content.[11] You might not know who Keffals is, but her hashtags and ideas might cascade from her community into yours.

This increased ease of access has transformed Cartwright's potential means of influence in unexpected ways. The potential for "reward and punishment" has expanded; influencers and online mobs are now quite adept at threatening their targets' livelihoods through collective campaigns to get people "canceled." Consider Justine Sacco, not at all a public figure, who in 2013 tweeted a tasteless joke about AIDS shortly before boarding a flight to South Africa. By the time her plane touched down, a journalist had shared the tweet, *#HasJustineLandedYet* had become a top trend globally, and Sacco's reputation and career had been destroyed.[12] There have since been many far more deliberate efforts in which online culture warlords and angry factions demand a target be punished—often, fired—for a "bad" opinion, a distasteful comment, or even something mundane but willfully misinterpreted.

The dynamics of online mobs have also led people to think quite differently about "direct physical power" and the risk it poses as a tool of retaliation against speech. Online rage has led to threats to election officials, to public health workers during COVID, and to school board officials around curriculum debates. It has occasionally translated into late-night protests outside random doctors' homes, people being followed to their cars after community council meetings, and even scattered physical violence. The implied, and sometimes realized, threats have led to widespread resignations of targeted groups. There is no longer any real line between online and offline, no comfortable "in real life" designation that separates online influence and offline impact. The virtual world's norms threaten to spill over into the real, and that can be extremely frightening. It might have been hard to pin down which specific post sent a man over the edge to rescue children he thought were being harmed in the basement of a pizza shop, but being immersed in that bespoke reality had an undeniable effect—it resulted in his going to the shop and firing a gun.

It's that third mechanism of influence Cartwright described—the capacity to shape opinion—that has most significantly transformed in the age of influencers, algorithms, and online crowds, and it will be our focus. The propaganda machine and the rumor mill, formerly largely distinct means of shaping public opinion, have collided; now competition for attention and audience happens on social media, where access to nearly anyone in the world is just a click away. There are new agents, albeit with fairly old motivations, enabled by new means of connecting to targets.

Who are the targets? Anyone and everyone. You. Me. Your neighbor. Yet, as Cartwright pointed out in 1965, the person being influenced in some situations is the agent in others[13]—and today the online audience itself has extraordinary capacity for shaping public opinion, actively participating in creating messages and spreading them. Indeed, in some of the examples we will explore, a random person from within the crowd makes a claim, which is then boosted by an influencer, gets picked up by an algorithm, and winds up the focus of the nightly news on cable television. Having influence is a path to power or profit, or both, and today that path is open to virtually anyone.

There is an important caveat, however, that Cartwright emphasized: the target's attitude toward the agent matters. If the target rejects the authority or legitimacy—or the expertise—of the agent, the agent won't be able to exert much influence. But influencers enjoy the trust of their followers. They are liked by their followers. They may not actually possess the expertise that Walter Lippmann in *Public Opinion* believed was so important to democratic society, but their followers feel that they do (a topic we'll cover more in Chapter 7). In other words, they have access to their audience, a means of influencing them, motivation for doing so, and a high likelihood that their message will be well received, or at least considered. And that's because the influencer, while distinct from the crowd in some ways, is very deeply part of it—just like the women of Decatur in the twentieth century and just like Amazing Polly today.

The Influencer Emerges from the Crowd

Influencers often start out as members of a community. Before Keffals had fifty thousand Twitch followers, she was an adolescent playing Team Fortress 2. And before Candace Owens was a marquee name in the conservative movement, she was one in a chorus of voices attempting to raise awareness about the disproportionate online harassment that women face.[14] But their unique talent for telling stories that capture their audiences' attention, and their understanding and leveraging of the affordances of social media, turned them into centers of gravity.

Influencers are differentiated by a larger—sometimes much larger—number of followers than other members of their community. Their content is both relevant and resonant, inspiring the crowd to boost it. A flywheel effect then kicks in: once the influencer starts to amass a following, their popularity is further reinforced as the ever-growing audience shares their content to their own networks. More and more attention goes to those who manage to accrue some. In fact, many social media platforms have what industry people call the 90/9/1 problem: 90 percent of the participants are simply lurkers, 9 percent participate a little, and 1 percent participate very heavily.[15] Influencers, who are part of that 1 percent of regular content producers, have far more engaged audiences than others on the platform, which means that they have a disproportionate impact on information flows.

However, despite their larger followings, the fact that they emerge from the crowd means that they continue to be seen as fellow members of the crowd. Their audiences view them as authentic, believable, and accessible—even if others don't. They also post as themselves; this makes them distinct both from the media-of-one outlets that social media also enabled and from larger-than-life celebrities.

Instead, they're fellow participants in a shared identity—a fellow mom, a fellow gamer, a fellow Christian conservative, a fellow privacy activist. Sometimes the shared identity is demographic, but it can also be a mutual passion for some particular interest. The influencer comes to be seen as representative of that identity. Indeed, people who are not part of a particular community but are interested in understanding its position on a debate or issue will often check an influencer's commentary to get a sense of the prevailing opinion of the group they seem to represent.[16] (This does not always yield accurate results; remember the story of majority illusion plaguing the English village in Chapter 1.)

Influencers spend a lot of their time on social media, not just talking *to* but *with* their audiences. They engage like people, not media. MrBeast may have over twenty million followers on Twitter, but he still @ replies to fans with emojis and quick comments. Media outlets convey a message; influencers have conversations. They read what their audiences say, or tag them in, and then decide what to riff on or amplify. That combination of creation, curation, and chatter makes them feel accessible.

But, perhaps most importantly, influencers manage to occupy a liminal space in which they are simultaneously elite, in terms of what they can accomplish and the power they wield, and not elite, because they're perceived as *one of us*. This is particularly critical, as we'll discuss, in the political arena.

The value of being *of the crowd* is hard to overstate. It gives influencers an innate knowledge of the language to use, the memes to reference, and the tone to take to make their audience react in whatever way they're going for. They are fluent in the in-group language and lore of their niche, which gives them the ability to immediately react to whatever is going on in the world and frame it for their audience—to create the story.

The influencer is often both the storyteller and the story itself. As storytellers, influencers use the same techniques as screenwriters, novelists, and playwrights: familiarity, novelty, and repetition. All stories are made up of familiar building blocks. There are setting or plot tropes, like the Isolated Cabin in the Woods at Night and character archetypes like the Quirky Best Friend. These familiar elements bring an immediate sense of recognition for the audience, setting the stage and signaling that you're about to see a horror movie or a romantic comedy. They help the audience feel familiar with the broad strokes of the narrative to come. But a good storyteller avoids being completely formulaic—and that is where novelty comes in. Plot twist!—the damsel in the cabin is actually perfectly capable of fending off the slasher; the quirky best friend has chemistry with the lead's love interest. The novel detail makes the audience sit up and take notice. Finally, the repetition of key motifs, symbols, or phrases—both within one story and over time—reinforces the important message.

Influencers' content on social media—especially where political propaganda, rumors, or conspiracy theories are concerned—is no different. They have their tropes and archetypes: the claims they make repeatedly, the villains and heroes they recurringly highlight, weaving them into a cinematic universe. Knowingly saying, for example, "Soros" or "Koch" conveys instantaneous meaning to their audience. The individual rumors or claims they promote have the requisite element of novelty: the hacked voting machines were compromised... by sneaky election officials, or by Central Intelligence Agency supercomputers, or by Russians, or by Italian satellites (these are real stories, as we will discuss in Chapter 5).[17] And they leverage repetition: sharing and sharing and sharing similar types of stories to reinforce an impression that the world operates in a certain way. Over time, as we'll see, repeating particular claims can increase the audience's perception that they're true.[18]

Influencers are good at producing content that evokes emotion, because they're creating for people *just like them*. They intimately understand what kind of rhetoric, memes, and narratives will get a rise out of their audience. They're writing multiseason dramas that keep their fans not only coming back for more but amplifying what they put out. Influencers like Owens and Keffals and MrBeast are part of a new generation of highly skilled storytellers, who know how to use tropes, how to create a sensational twist, and how to leverage any new feature that a platform comes up with to their advantage.

Influencers' combination of storytelling acumen, understanding how to work the structures of social media, clicking with an audience around a mutual passion, and reacting quickly and fluently to the fast-moving world of information on social media grants them an important power: they become aggregators and curators of the beliefs of the crowd.

Contagion, The Discourse, and Vibe Shifts

How influencers curate and move information is just as important as what they create. Their posts shape what's in their audiences' feeds, both directly and through related "You Might Like" content that algorithms helpfully serve up. What influencers decide to talk about, or amplify, can have a huge effect on what—or whom—*everyone* seems to be talking about. This manifests as what the extremely online call *The Discourse* and *vibe shifts*.

There is another epidemiological metaphor, besides virality, used to describe how information spreads online: *contagion* refers to how an idea or rumor is passed from person to person. Simply hearing an idea does not mean that it will "infect" or find a home in the mind of the recipient. But the influencer is in a unique position when it comes to information contagion: a piece of content is more likely to achieve significant reach if someone with a large engaged following pushes it out to thousands of people.[19] The influencer becomes something of a curator and a gate-keeper for what goes viral, because they have a higher capacity to kick off cascades. They're a tipping point in the rumor mill: if they choose to boost something, it can become a subject of mass online conversation—like Far Right agitator Jack Posobiec promoting the baseless claim, which first emerged on relatively obscure Far Right message boards, that Democratic National Committee employee Seth Rich had been murdered by the Clintons.[20] Alternatively, if influencers ignore it, a claim often stays confined to low-level chatter.

How do influencers decide what to boost? They, too, are bombarded with information and posts from the people they follow. But they often have a well-cultivated understanding for what stories will work within their community and strong internal relevancy engines—gut instincts—that help them quickly see how a real-world event can be connected to a broader narrative that their audience already understands. And they pay close attention to their engagement metrics—they know exactly how much pickup they get when they share certain types of memes or talk about particular topics.

Sometimes the decision to boost something is an easy call: it's familiar to the audience already. They'll intuitively understand how to react to it. And react they will, spreading the message along. This simple contagion—the spread of already-familiar, well-accepted opinions—is an easy win for the influencer.

Other times, however, the influencer will see something novel that may make followers sit up and share (earning the influencer a clout boost), but which is a little outside the norm, something like a new technology—maybe a cryptocurrency—or a fringe political idea. There's a bit of potential risk to the influencer's reputation if they start promoting it.

Pulling a novel claim or idea from ambient chatter and moving it into the awareness of their broader audience can be a dangerous move—influencers stake some of their credibility on that call. In simple contagion, an influencer's decision to spread a message is low stakes because the thing is already normalized—they're boosting its reach but are primarily amplifying a message rather than introducing an influential new idea. This doesn't mean the idea is normalized *everywhere*—a conspiracy theory that is widely believed within a faction is low stakes for one of its influencers to propagate but still a big reputational risk for a "normal" person. But when considering novel ideas, the influencer will have to see an emerging claim multiple times, from different people, before deciding it's worth spreading themselves. During this time, incentivized members of the crowd who already hold the belief (or have adopted the novel technology) may egg them on, tagging them in posts about it, encouraging them to read up on it, prodding them to share, before the influencer finally decides that jumping on the bandwagon makes sense for them.[21]

This process of novel ideas moving from the periphery of a social network to the center is known as *complex contagion*; understanding how it works offers insights into who influences whom and helps explain how certain ideas or behaviors become widespread. Influencers serve not only as conduits for ideas but as gatekeepers, waiting to get sufficient signal before moving an idea from the fringe to the center of the conversation via their boost. They may begin by using language like "big if true" as a hedge, introducing an idea to their followers while not fully staking their reputation on it—this gives them an out if raising awareness does not translate to community acceptance. But once an influencer has chosen to associate themselves with a particular viewpoint, meme, or even crazy conspiracy theory and has seen indications of acceptance through engagement, they will often repeat it—and, as discussed, the repetition is a form of reinforcement for the community.[22]

Influencers thus help drive The Discourse[23]—a slang term for heated debates or obsessive discussion of a particular niche social or political issue—by deciding what to amplify and how to frame it (or meme it). While members of the niche crowd often care deeply about the issue, those outside the community may find it somewhat ridiculous and a ripe opportunity for mockery; The Discourse generally involves both types of participants. Hot takes are abundant. With their larger-than-average reach, influencers can shape the way that their followers repeatedly see an issue framed, in both how and how often they talk about a particular topic. They can make something seem important (*We are going to talk about policing*) and then help create and propagate the memes that a community begins to use to describe it (*#DefundThePolice*).

What people talk about and how creates opportunities for influencers with a particular sense of the zeitgeist to rise. Think about it as an ecology: the online ecosystem lends itself at a particular moment to particular species, which thrive and in turn reshape their environment. As the ecosystem evolves, in tandem with the offline world, some influencers (or influencer archetypes) adapt and continue to shape the conversation and public opinion; some wane in popularity and come to feel like relics of an internet past; new ones emerge that meet the moment, either through innate talent or because they can read the room and tailor their content to fit the mood. The early optimistic online influencers created very different content and set a very different tone than those who became ascendent during the mid-2010s, as harassment mobs became potent and visible and norms of behavior changed.

Transformations in the overall atmosphere, energy, or mood of a person, group, or environment—*vibe shifts*—are remarkably real in online spaces. More importantly, they intersect heavily with social, economic, and political dynamics in the offline world. Is crime rising or falling? There are, of course, real-world statistics that can answer this, but the vibes matter a lot for shaping public opinion online—which also translates to offline organizing or voting. Are more people being shot by police officers? Is inflation destroying the economy? Is America on the verge of civil war? The perception shaped in online communities, the collective mood and sense of the issue, is often more important than any actual facts.

Influencers can introduce new ideas, push a new meme, or change the tone in which they talk about something, contributing to a sense for the audience that things have changed.[24] This can reset the culture of a community, changing norms not only online but in the real world as well, for better but also for worse. A positive vibe shift can yield feelings of joy, inspiration, and motivation. A negative one can lead to a sense of unease or of being under threat.

In their roles as creators, curators, and gatekeepers, influencers make a meaningful impact on how their audience feels and thinks; they can harness attention and direct the energy of their audience—at times, both online and off. Importantly, because of that liminal space they inhabit—as both elite wielders of power and "one of us"—influencers serve as mediators between the propaganda machine and the rumor mill. They have the power to pull things up from the chatter of the crowd and amplify them. Media pays attention to influencers, covering what they and their followers talk about as an online-interest story.

This makes influencers pivotal figures in "trading up the chain"—getting a sometimes dubious idea from a social media niche to mass awareness on broadcast media.[25] *Was* Seth Rich murdered by the Clintons? Fox News anchors Lou Dobbs and Sean Hannity, in fact, asked just that question.[26] In prior information environments, the ability to pull an idea from the fringe to mass awareness used to take a lot of time; now this strategy—beloved by propagandists—occurs seemingly daily in the major news cycle, sometimes multiple times per day.

And, of course, influencers serve the needs of the propaganda machine in the other direction as well: in their role as opinion leaders, they curate from the glut of media coverage and then frame and interpret it for their audiences. Both top-down and bottom-up narrative creation happens across media and social media today, and the influencer sits in the middle of the action.

Despite their similar origins, shared skill sets, and access to the same tools, however, influencers can vary wildly in their presentation and intentions—comprising a cast of archetypes as diverse as exotic animals in a menagerie.

The Influencer Menagerie

Describing the persuasive power of influencers by referencing their follower count (nano, micro, mega) or their niche topic area (gaming, cooking, fashion) misses important ways they establish resonance: how they present themselves, what rhetorical style they take, which particular roles they play in The Discourse.[27]

We can better understand influencers through the types of information product or relationship they sell or what audience need they attempt to satisfy. While my menagerie of frequently encountered influencer archetypes is by no means comprehensive—in fact, it's intended to be tropey, in keeping with our discussion above—you will likely recognize many.

There are the *Entertainers*, who produce videos, images, podcasts, and other content focused on a topic of interest. There are many different categories: photographers, dancers, writers, cooks, ASMRtists, cultural commentators. They want to entertain their audience, to make them laugh or cry. MrBeast is an Entertainer, trading in videos that mix comedy with tenderness. So is Khaby Lame.

The *Explainers* produce content on a topic in which they have deep expertise. They may be experts or academics or simply passionate hobbyists, and they want to share their depth of knowledge and help their audiences make sense of the world. Some prioritize being useful: the relatable mom offering five ways to get chewing gum out of the carpet. Whatever your problem, someone on YouTube has made a video about how to solve it.

Influencers like the *Bestie* make themselves, not a topic, the focus of their posts. You're there to get to know *them*. They largely stick to personal commentary—sometimes it gets political, but everything is presented in a way that reinforces a trusted friendship with their followers. A lot of younger influencers on TikTok will simultaneously share a new makeup product while talking about a date they went on or their opinion on some social issue. They create a sense of intimacy by sharing (and often monetizing) their lives; it's like reality TV, but in short snippets and with more actual reality. Charli D'Amelio's TikToks, for example, grant viewers a "candid" glimpse of her coffee habits, her dressing room, her hangouts with friends.

Idols share and monetize their lives as well, but they offer something aspirational, not accessible: a larger-than-life bravado, glamor, excitement.

The audience is there to be voyeurs into a truly fabulous life. Idols mimic the stylings of celebrities; each Instagram post could be straight out of a glossy magazine. The main difference is that they control their own content, and having the "day job" of the celebrity—for example, being an actor or musician, which in turn confers fame—is no longer required. They are the epitome of Daniel Boorstin's "famous for being famous" characterization. Why do you know who they are? An algorithm decided you should.

Then there are the *Gurus*. In a complex, chaotic, and confusing world, secular Gurus are a growing force: they are going to help you. Think of Tim Ferris, exhorting his two million Twitter followers to sleep this many hours, eat this superfood, and use that psychedelic drug—success, wealth, and health can be yours in just four hours a week. This is not the drop-in type of information the Explainer imparts; it's a guide for a lifestyle. As with their legacy offline counterparts, charisma is more important than being on epistemologically solid ground; one can simply wave a hand and dismiss the expertise of others—particularly *the establishment*.[28] The expert consensus is wrong, and if it is right, it is right for the wrong reasons; iconoclasm is central to the Guru's appeal. Grievance is a common undertone: the establishment has conspired to suppress their genius and keep the truth from the people. Their expertise is rarely confined to one topic; they have a grand unified theory of the universe and the prescience of Cassandra. A wellness Guru who Instagrams beautiful smoothies also presents herself as an authoritative source of knowledge about 5G technology. The audience may follow for one kind of content but will be taken on a journey through the rest. The Guru is a lucrative position of influence—there are many opportunities to sell what their followers "need," both informationally and in the form of products. More importantly, however, the Guru meets an emotional need. The world is in turmoil; there is a crushing glut of information; norms are in flux. The Guru offers not only soothing simplification but tangible actions that her followers can take to feel better.[29] They can empower themselves, reclaim their agency, make an impact in the world.

As COVID-19 took hold in 2020, there was a notable convergence of wellness Gurus and the QAnon conspiracy theory, which highlights the complex ways in which influencers help propagate narratives across diverse online communities.[30] Initially, wellness influencers, particularly on Instagram, had attracted followers who were seeking guidance on physical and mental health, drawn to the holistic lifestyles and alternative therapies the influencers discussed. Many—including the wellness influencers themselves—distrusted mainstream medical experts following bad personal experiences. That distrust of the establishment, rooted in real experience, was, for some influencers, easily extended to other topics. The pathway became somewhat familiar: descriptions of a nagging feeling that things were not as they seemed, followed by a decision to dig into another type of purported government coverup. For the women, particularly mothers, real concern about sex trafficking motivated their search for "the truth." As the Guru herself became convinced, the popular wellness language and beautiful Instagram aesthetic was used to convey fringe beliefs; QAnon theories became interspersed with their usual content about clean living and nutritious baby food.[31] The audience often participated quite directly; while some unfollowed, disgusted with the turn toward conspiracy theorizing, others suggested even more outlandish things for the influencer to look into to continue their mutual "awakening."

Following a Guru as she spreads "forbidden knowledge"—things *they* don't want you to know—offers the thrill of uncovering hidden truths. People experience a sense of excitement or hope rather than the disillusionment of their prior experience.[32] *Conspirituality*, as this blend of wellness and conspiracy theorizing came to be called, gave people a sense of power and control over their lives and the world around them,[33] even as some came to be immersed in very cultlike bespoke realities.

The Entertainers, Explainers, Idols, and Gurus of the menagerie might talk about politics occasionally or boost causes they care about. But there are species of influencer who are *explicitly* political, who significantly drive the political discourse, and they will be our focus through much of the rest of this book.

Influencers who are first and foremost partisans—whose content primarily focuses on endorsing a political position, cause, or candidate[34] or who grow their audience around partisan political identity—are a growing force. They play the role of opinion leader, curating content and serving as an avatar for what it means to be a "good" Republican, Democrat, libertarian, neoliberal, socialist, and so forth. Some have deep connections to political elites, such as elected officials and party insiders in positions of power, and come to serve as modern propagandists. Others are good at galvanizing the crowd to action. While they exist on a spectrum with activists, political influencers are not quite the same: they wield their influence to shape political narratives and public opinion, but prioritize the cultivation of their personal brand. Activists, by contrast, are more focused on direct engagement with lawmakers, community mobilization, and action-oriented advocacy to bring about social or political change. While a particular activist may become the face of an issue—like Greta Thunberg for climate change or Chris Rufo for critical race theory—activists keep the focus primarily on the cause, not themselves. They may leverage propaganda, but they are primarily building a movement toward a goal, not an audience for their personal brand.[35]

Among the political influencer archetypes are the *Generals*—like right-wing provocateur Ali Alexander (whom we will discuss in Chapter 5)—who keep the faction riled up. They are effective at mobilizing factions to act, both online and in the physical world. They fashion themselves as heroes fighting for a cause, and their active interaction with the group offers followers a chance for recognition. They may not actually achieve much—some are just the political version of famous for being famous—but they present themselves as being in the trenches with the crowd. However, their fight is often primarily rhetorical. As we will see, this kind of political influence does not necessarily translate to leadership or accountability if something goes wrong or violence erupts.

The *Reflexive Contrarians* are also quite adept at rallying the factions, often with a healthy dose of conspiracism. They are the Explainers of a mirror world who capitalize on novelty: everything you know is wrong, and they are going to tell you why. You think you know about this historical event, but you were miseducated. You think that the outbreak of

Zika was caused by a mosquito, but in reality *they* were behind it. The Reflexive Contrarians sell counterfeits in the marketplace of ideas. They understand the rumor mill and the tropes that activate it and are adept at the rhetorical stylings used by merchants of doubt in eras past: they're "just asking questions," letting insinuation and innuendo do the heavy lifting.[36] It's good to ask questions, after all—*Why isn't mainstream media talking about this? The media lie. Authorities lie. That other political party lies.* The universal rejection of an idea by mainstream experts is a ringing endorsement in the mirror world. The Reflexive Contrarians have evolved the paranoid style in American politics: some of their most viral criticisms of elites focus less on tangibles, such as their tax policies, and more on whether or not they are baby-eating pedophiles.[37]

The *Propagandists*, as they were in the age of mass media, are tightly aligned with a power center or political party. They produce content and work in alignment with politicians and leaders who hold real power. As in media eras past, their content serves to advance the ideological aims of the faction. Today, however, the new Propagandists present as charismatic individuals, not prominent mass media or shadowy public relations figures. These influencers are often closely aligned with hyperpartisan media, sometimes taking contributor roles at such outlets, but they remain their own brand. Perhaps most importantly, the new Propagandists develop deep ties to audiences as *accessible individuals*. They are simultaneously trusted opinion leaders—chatting about their interests, hobbies, the latest article they read—and invisible rulers. It's a potent mix: they are idol, friend, comrade, and persuader.

Because people still largely associate propaganda with "media," and political influencers present as individuals, they manage to achieve the reach of media while being perceived as somehow exempt from its incentives. In reality, they may well be true believers of an ideology, but they also benefit financially. Candace Owens, with her unique blend of conservative talking points and lifestyle advice, is a signature Propagandist: magnetic, dogmatic. She got her start producing her own content, was picked up by conservative activist organization Turning Point USA, and eventually became a regular voice on the partisan news site the *Daily Wire* until the site parted ways with her over antisemitic commentary. Throughout, she has maintained her own brand.

There is a particular undertone to the content of many prominent political influencers, one which draws in audiences and is potent for growing factions of the like-minded. And so, finally, there are the *Perpetually Aggrieved*, who are also *professionally* aggrieved. They amass significant clout and massive audiences by channeling the real rage felt by a niche public and exacerbating it to create nihilism and more rage—which they sometimes direct at specific political enemies. The Perpetually Aggrieved have a solid understanding of how platform algorithms drive amplification and a nuanced understanding of how to avoid moderation. Being dinged by the algorithm for inappropriate posts can have long-lasting repercussions for visibility and revenue, so many become vocal opponents of platform content moderation and "free speech absolutists" who work to sway policy in ways favorable to their content. Ironically, these influencers often experience *less* moderation than ordinary users. Platforms are often hesitant to moderate the most inflammatory and prominent political influencers because their audiences and their aligned political elites will become enraged. There's a threshold at which influencers become too big to cancel.

The Perpetually Aggrieved have a way with words and memes and a knack for the sort of personalized online dunks that can instantly turn targets into the "Main Character" of the day online. (One astute Twitter user pointed out that each day there is one Main Character on Twitter. "The goal is to never be it.")[38] They are chroniclers of the last days of morality and the fall of empire, articulating and creating a center of gravity around a sense of injustice felt by many across the political spectrum. Their ability to tap into this very real sense of injustice—which does not exist in a vacuum—is what makes them so resonant. Brace Belden, for example, is a left-wing provocateur who first gained fame chronicling the Syrian civil war on Twitter from the conflict's frontlines.[39] Today Belden hosts the *TrueAnon* podcast, which rigorously covers sex offender financier Jeffrey Epstein's very real crimes—but also leverages them to argue that nearly all institutions are hopelessly corrupt and virtually all elites have the most nefarious of intentions.[40]

Painting with a broad brush is as old as time, and a grain of truth or real justifiable outrage is what makes this kind of content potent: Mass media often *doesn't* cover the powerful as forcefully as they should. There *is* injustice in the world. Highlighting and channeling outrage is critical to the political process, and influencers are very well positioned to do just that. But, as we will discuss in Chapter 8, the unique superpower of some political influencers is an ability to channel that sense of grievance, turning aggrieved factions into online mobs who attack their perceived enemies both online and off.

Clicks, Clout, Capture, and Cash

All of these influencers, from the Entertainers to the Perpetually Aggrieved, are driven by their desire to have some kind of effect on their target audience. They're also responding to various incentives—including financial. Influencers are looking to earn money and clout—and, particularly in the political sphere, to amass power.

Influencers compete for their audiences' time, which means that many hop from topic to topic. They generally maintain the same tone—some are sentient fortune cookies, others are rhetorical bomb throwers—and the same degree of confidence, even as they weigh in on everything from the latest celebrity gossip to attempted Russian coups to imploding submarines.[41] This competition, however, leads many to present their opinions in increasingly extreme ways—they have to, in order to grab attention from both algorithms and human followers that reward moral righteousness, provocative claims, and outrageous rhetoric.

As writer Helen Lewis put it while describing online gurus, "The internet is built to enable extremophiles."[42] She highlighted Maajid Nawaz as one example. Nawaz hopscotched from membership in a political Islamist group (during which he was imprisoned in Egypt), to antiextremism activist and advisor to the UK government (at one point falsely accused of being anti-Muslim by the Southern Poverty Law Center),[43] to heterodox intellectual, attempted-politician (he was not elected), and talk radio host. He lost his radio host position in January 2022 after nearly a year of recurring conspiracy theorizing: he'd opined that COVID-19 lockdowns were a "global fraud" perpetuated by the Chinese Communist Party, propagated some truly outlandish claims about the 2020 US presidential election, and repeatedly argued that various world events were connected to a "New World Order."[44]

In response to his contract ending, Nawaz started a Substack newsletter, *Radical Media*, and encouraged his followers to subscribe, saying that it was now his family's source of income. Nawaz's livelihood, in other words, was now being provided directly by an audience interested in Maajid Nawaz, Investigator of Conspiracies. As one astute analyst of social media dynamics summarized the situation, "Instead of performing real investigation, he [Nawaz] is now merely playing the role of investigator for his audience, a role that requires drama rather than diligence, and which can lead only to his audience's desired conclusions."[45]

Nawaz also became quite vocal about how media and Facebook were silencing him (Facebook had labeled some of his posts); the Wrongly Censored Truth-Teller is a popular and highly monetizable figure today. He currently has 509,800 followers on Twitter and tens of thousands of subscribers on Substack. During the week of a submarine imploding while taking people to view the *Titanic* and Russian oligarch Yevgeny Prigozhin marching a mercenary army on Moscow, Nawaz simply declared both events to be scams, willfully boosted by mass media.[46]

Feminist writer Naomi Klein has beautifully described this process of influencers and audiences mutually shaping each other, using the case of Naomi Wolf, Klein's self-described "doppelganger" and another prominent extremophile who fell deeply into the mirror world of COVID-19 conspiracy theories: "By claiming to possess some secret piece of knowledge that she alone had uncovered, and by claiming she was being terribly persecuted by daring to share it, she was able to insert herself in the middle of countless trending cultural conversations. Where there was heat, there was her."[47] Although most on the outside see descent into a bespoke reality as a fall, the influencers who go down this path still get engagement and influence people. They are still doing what they set out to do: capturing attention, accruing clout, and earning a living.

Influencers of all stripes—even the most dignified—can feel the allure of producing sensational content and capturing audience engagement. I've been lucky enough to get to know a few top-notch science and health creators with millions of followers. They're truly passionate about their work and bubble over with enthusiasm while describing their projects. They are motivated by a deep sense of mission: to teach the world cool things about science and to serve as educators and communicators who make complex concepts accessible and entertaining. They are extraordinarily creative, and they work very, very hard.

They will also tell you that sometimes it's audiences who do the capturing. Influencers are acutely aware of their engagement metrics, because creating content is their livelihood. It is a struggle, sometimes, to remain true to their vision and eschew putting out spicier takes or clickbait titles that they don't love but which they know will get that extra algorithmic lift. This is the realm of audience capture[48]—a feedback loop in which creators produce content their audiences will approve of and gradually begin to internalize it themselves (the fate of Guitar Guy in this book's introduction). That feedback loop spins and spins and can drive a content creator into a particular niche that's difficult to escape, taking them in a completely inauthentic or extreme direction. They are aware that they'd have to continue producing more and more sensational content to keep earning a living, because the audiences looking for outrage and conspiracy content are hard to keep satisfied—if they get a sense that the creator isn't fully aligned with their ideology, they will depart for something more extreme or someone else willing to reinforce their beliefs. This is how an influencer who starts off as an Explainer talking about some anodyne topic—wellness, cooking, yoga—becomes a Reflexive Contrarian ranter going on about GMO crop cover-ups, if it gets them a lot more views.

As these influencers find the community that takes them seriously and even financially supports them, they change, becoming ever more what their audience seems to want them to be.[49] It's sometimes hard to tell, as an outsider, whether they've had a genuine conversion or are driven more by financial incentives than deeply held beliefs. Ultimately, their fans will make the call, and they will succeed or fail.

Audience capture happens as a result of influencers' desire to grow their following. They want to grow their audience, because large audiences enable them to earn more money, accrue more power, and get more clout. These things, too, are related. As Naomi Klein put it, "Clout is the values-free currency of the always-online age—both a substitute for hard cash as well as a conduit to it."[50]

In fact, many people who have followed influencers or been active users of social media for years still don't understand how the people whose content they see every day get paid—and, in some cases, get extraordinarily rich—by posting online. Influencers, even those with followings nearly as large as broadcasters, style themselves differently than media, emphasizing their ordinariness, relatability, and authenticity. Because they seem like ordinary people, even those who understand that media incentives shape coverage—including those most concerned about "corporate media"!—rarely stop to wonder about how influencers' incentives are shaping what they post or talk about.

Influencers make money in several ways. Some have their own domains and use their social media profiles and content to direct people to visit their websites. They can monetize site traffic with ads or simply sell "merch" (branded products), like Charli D'Amelio's hoodies, T-shirts, or tote bags ("i hope we have just the right collection of product to create your vibe," she writes invitingly).[51] Some platforms, like Instagram, enable merch selling right in the app. Influencers can also monetize their social media channels and content directly. When MrBeast posts a video to YouTube, YouTube shows one or two short ads before the video plays. MrBeast gets part of this revenue from YouTube. The more people who watch the content, the more money the creator earns as the platforms share the ad revenue. About nine months after Elon Musk purchased Twitter, he introduced a similar model to the platform: the Creator Ads Revenue Sharing program.[52] Twitter began giving certain influencers—initially, right-wing political influencers that Elon Musk regularly engaged with—a percentage of the advertising profits generated by their content. The lucky few in the pilot tweeted screenshots showing monthly incomes of between $1,000 and $20,000.[53] The program was eventually opened to more users, and many of the payouts began to decline.

And then, of course, there are highly sought-after sponsorships. Influencer marketing is now a fairly established strategy for brands, who recognize that these opinion leaders, trusted by their audiences, have the power to shape culture and drive purchasing decisions.[54] They "sponsor" posts with influencers who speak to audiences that *they* care about. A young mom, posting photos of her messy-but-adorable children on Instagram, sponsored by Tide. A teenage girl, doing a mascara tutorial on YouTube, backed by Maybelline. You get the idea. Subtle product placement and word-of-mouth endorsements were a novel change from slickly produced ads and celebrity spokespeople. A big brand might pay $10,000 to a decent-sized influencer for a two-minute sponsorship pitch at the start of a video and offer the creator a revenue-sharing affiliate link—a code to give viewers or readers that lets the brand track how many new customers click through and purchase the product. The company can see how many sales the influencer delivers while also letting the influencer earn a cut of the profit. It's very low lift for a creator, who is then also still able to monetize the rest of the video with ads. *Collabs*— cobranded collections with prominent brands—are another way to generate buzz.

Companies pursue influencers in part because audiences report thinking highly of them. One recent study by Pew Research Center found that three in ten adult social media users have purchased something after seeing an influencer post about it.[55] I've certainly bought meal kits and kids' toys promoted by mom influencers on multiple occasions. Edelman's 2022 Trust Barometer reported that 67 percent of respondents changed their lifestyle in the last six months because of an influencer they followed, such as by starting a new hobby, trying a new beauty style, or supporting a cause. It also found that 58 percent who followed influencers reported trusting what they said about brands even when they were paid.[56]

A large audience can equal a lot of money; in 2019, brands were paying upward of $50,000 to top influencers to make videos promoting their products—or slamming their rivals' goods.[57] Those with truly incredible reach, like Khaby Lame, were reportedly able to command $350,000 for a post in 2022.[58] The Top 50 Creators on the Forbes 2022 Influencer List—which featured Charli D'Amelio right up at the top—have a combined 1.9 billion followers and in aggregate made $570 million.[59]

Contributor relationships are another avenue; some prominent political influencers produce their own content but move in and out of relationships with niche media outlets. One such political influencer is Steven Crowder, the right-wing provocateur of YouTube and Rumble. In January 2023, Crowder published a YouTube video of himself, outraged, accusing conservative media outlet the *Daily Wire* of offering him a "slave contract." The deal would, in his telling, gag him and prevent him from speaking the truth to his audience. But Crowder's adversarial rhetoric and the attention his allegations attracted inadvertently revealed a much different reality. The "slave contract" simply compelled him to create content that wouldn't be demonetized—as he had been on several occasions—and it would have netted him $50 million.[60] Being a political provocateur can be quite lucrative.

These are the cream of the crop, of course, but there is a very long tail of nano-influencers who make much less, yet still pull in respectable livings or supplements to their income. Influencer marketing platforms that connected massive brands like Clarins and Nike to databases of influencers sprung up in the mid- to late 2010s and still operate today.

And yet, talking about the financial perks—and the incentives they create—is a tightrope walk for influencers who want to project authenticity. The wellness influencer getting a cut from the essential oils she's touting prefers to keep the focus on how she's teaching her fans to live their most natural, best lives. The seemingly amateur political vlogger is just sharing his thoughts, though his monetized YouTube channel brings in revenue per view, incentivizing him to make the most attention-grabbing videos possible.

Dark Monetization

Laurence Scott's history of the influencer "from Shakespeare to Insta-gram," published in the *New Yorker*, noted the emerging power—and danger—of influencers in 2019. Writing during the days of the Donald Trump presidency and Robert Mueller's report, Scott observed, "It's no accident that the term [*influencer*] has entered the lexicon at the same moment that influence of a different sort has become a geopolitical weapon of unprecedented proportions. The social-media influencer has an eerie double in the hacker who covertly shapes political discourse."[61]

The methods that Scott describes for marketing—like influencers' murky commercial relationships with brands and politicians—echo Ber-nays's argument that invisible rulers create demand for everything from shoes to candidates. It is not a surprise to most people today that political candidates reach out to high-follower influencers, seeking promotion to their niche audiences. Indeed, during the 2016 election cycle, the Trump and Bernie Sanders campaigns engaged heavily with social media influ-encers to help with messaging and capturing attention.[62] One strategy was to use influencers and their crowds to help get things trending and inform media coverage. The efforts were largely invisible; outreach hap-pened via text messages and direct messaging groups. Then, in the 2020 Democratic Party primary, Michael Bloomberg paid Instagram influenc-ers to publish tongue-in-cheek posts in support of his campaign.[63] The effort was funny, and there was no attempt to conceal it, but it prompted questions about how audiences would know, going forward, whether a political post was sponsored (since influencers are not always the best at disclosure).

Databases similar to the influencer marketing platforms mentioned above also exist for political efforts. In July 2022 I received an interest-ing phone call from Ben Wofford, a reporter at *Wired*. He was looking into a Virginia-based marketing firm called Urban Legend, which en-abled influencers to sign up and participate in paid political advertising campaigns. Urban Legend's website made no secret of the fact that the firm saw political advocacy as a natural fit for influencers who wanted to earn some money off their audiences while calling attention to a cause or policy they supported. "Meet the Lobbyist Next Door," Ben titled his eventual article.[64]

Urban Legend staff combed the Internet looking for the "right" influencers who enjoyed resonance and trust within a particular niche. Reach was secondary, subordinate to the influencers' understanding of how to communicate with their audiences. Interested influencers identified by the team could sign up with Urban Legend and were given access to look over client campaigns—clients ranged from labor union SEIU to the conservative Heritage Foundation and the National Republican Senate Committee—that they could participate in. Influencers interested in a campaign received a brief detailing the key points they had to make and an action they'd ask their followers to take: like a page, sign a petition, and so forth. To track their conversions, Urban Legend gave each influencer a unique link with a special tracking code that connected the action to the influencer's specific post. (Social media companies and the Federal Trade Commission [FTC] require that this affiliate marketing be disclosed, but no one is responsible for enforcement.)

Ben had uncovered a particular URL format, known as a shortener, that made it possible to find posts specifically tied to Urban Legend campaigns. He'd gone looking at some of the posts that bore the special affiliate URL code but didn't disclose it. He was interested in tracking down more and was curious about how this operation compared to other affiliate efforts. Was this new for politics? Should it be regulated?

I'd seen affiliate campaigns before, often undisclosed. For a while they were popular with health pseudoscience communities. Ty and Charline Bollinger produced one quack webinar series, titled *The Truth About Cancer*, and amassed millions of followers and views by encouraging other pseudoscience pages to boost their content and paying them affiliate fees. The Bollingers followed on this success with a subsequent webinar series, *The Truth About Vaccines*. The pages that shared it, including those of prominent anti-vaccine leaders like Robert F. Kennedy Jr.'s Children's Health Defense foundation, made it sound like they were genuinely enthusiastic. Maybe they were. But they also didn't disclose that they were getting paid, sometimes a lot, to boost the content. One affiliate participant reported income of $240,000.[65] The sharer's audiences, meanwhile, were paying the Bollingers for the content.

After chatting with Ben, I pulled up a tool called Crowdtangle, which Facebook makes available to journalists and researchers who want to search public Facebook posts for particular types of data. I searched for the unique URL shortener that Urban Legend had used, and up came hundreds of posts by very famous political influencers, media figures, and elites. Benny Johnson of right-wing media property Newsmax had posted a Twitter thread culminating in a petition to support pilots against vaccine mandates that cumulatively received over 24,600 likes and 7,900 retweets. Diamond & Silk, the pro-Trump influencer sisters who were frequent guests at his rallies, had posted several campaigns to their Facebook page. Dan Scavino. Laura Ingraham. Donald Trump Jr. posted numerous exhortations: join the "war against CRT," tell Democrats to secure the border, protect parental rights in schools, all positions that he likely authentically holds. But there was no indication to his followers that in these cases he was positioned to profit from sharing those URLs. Indeed, some of the links posted by the influencers percolated around the internet as their followers shared them along, unwittingly helping the influencer earn even more money in a kind of information cascade pyramid scheme, while making none themselves. The political Left, of course, participates as well; the Democratic Association of Secretaries of State was on Urban Legend's public client list, and a handful of left-leaning institutions and influencers appeared among those sharing the links on Facebook.

Influence, activism, and profit are increasingly intertwined. The line between authentic enthusiasm versus paid promotion blurs the line between content and propaganda. It's not subterfuge per se—but when online presence is monetizable, truth/untruth and interest/disinterest lie along a spectrum. The influencer may genuinely believe what he's saying but is also benefiting financially or gathering more attention (which increases future monetization potential). The influencer is therefore incentivized to promote the causes that their followers will respond positively to, even if they themselves are not true believers.[66] What matters is that the *audience* believes they are being authentic.

Urban Legend is just one of many companies and political organizations shaping (and responding to) the incentives of the present communication ecosystem. In 2021 researchers found that groups like Turning Point USA and Prager University (both conservative) and The 99 Problems (liberal) were funding what amounted to political ads masquerading as organic content on TikTok,[67] despite TikTok's avowed ban on political ads. And in 2023, the *Texas Tribune* published an exposé about Influenceable LLC, "a fledgling company...that recruits young, conservative social media figures to promote political campaigns and films without disclosing their business relationship."[68]

There's very little transparency around the money flowing through the influencer ecosystem. From a basic consumer-protection point of view, this is not good: when we see a video touting, say, a pair of headphones, we should know whether the praise is real enthusiasm or a compensated testimonial. If the content is political—calls to sign a petition or call your representative about some prescription drug bill—it's even more important to understand if the position is paid for by a political action committee or a company.

This is not, of course, a new challenge; celebrities have endorsed products for centuries.[69] And, indeed, in 2009, as influencer marketing began to boom, the FTC created what was described as the "mommy-blogger" rule (blogs started by mom influencers were a big deal at the time): any blogger receiving any form of compensation from a company the blogger was reviewing had to disclose it "clearly and conspicuously."[70] This was, interestingly, distinct from rules for celebrities: in 2012 an FTC commissioner argued, "Everybody understands that a celebrity is not going to be in an ad for a product unless they're paid to do that."[71] However, even as influencer marketing continued to grow, the rule didn't involve any plan for finding rule breakers (short of responding to news exposés of egregious violations or searching for potentially harmful products such as medicine).[72] Since there was minimal enforcement, and it fell to influencers to proactively disclose, most simply did not.[73] In the decade since, the FTC has issued updated disclosure guidance for social media influencers several times,[74] but still doesn't seem to be doing much enforcement.[75] And so, it was not much of a surprise to see the political influencers of Urban Legend not being transparent either. However, as more and more of our political discourse happens on platforms built for commerce and powered by advertising, the blending of personal expression and commercial and political speech is at the forefront of legal and regulatory debates.[76]

From Five Filters to Four Fire Emoji

Sponsorships, ad revenue sharing, and—in the case of political influencers—even dark money schemes are all prevalent online today. But joining their ranks more recently is another monetization option that sidesteps the transparency issue entirely: subscriptions.

Subscriptions are hardly a novel idea: newspapers and magazines have relied on them since the nineteenth century. But grafting that model onto the modern influencer ecosystem is a new—and wildly profitable—development. Today, adult performers on OnlyFans and pop culture pundits on Patreon can earn comfortable salaries from their content, even if it reaches a relatively small audience. Substack newsletters—featuring everything from salad recipes to economics commentary to 9/11 truther content (classified under "education")—are a burgeoning outlet for creators. An influencer with an audience of just two thousand, each paying $5 a month, can bring in around $100,000 per year (Substack currently takes a 10 percent cut; OnlyFans takes 20 percent).

Whatever the kink—from nudes to recipes to conspiracy theories—consumers can find their niche, sponsor it, and share its output across the internet.[77]

Subscription models, particularly on Substack, have been especially fruitful for the media-of-one figures we mentioned earlier: individuals who brand themselves not as influencers but as journalists of the Fifth Estate. Using social media infrastructure, a lone pundit can operate with the veneer of a traditional newsroom: slick branding, daily newsletters, and other affordances. Of course, the trappings of a traditional newsroom—fact-checkers, discerning editors, ethics policies—are absent. Since social media platforms reduce the cost of providing commentary but not the costs of investigative journalism, these outlets are primarily editorial pages, staffed with one voice and absent the rest of the newspaper. Their creators, however, deeply understand that making content for a niche offers a path to attention, revenue, and clout.

The media-of-one figures who focus on politics and the culture wars regularly position themselves as anti–Big Media; as intrepid Davids battling entrenched Goliaths like network news stations and newspapers of record. This is not an accidental strategy; it is one that Bernays described in his book *Crystallizing Public Opinion*, which preceded *Propaganda* and describes instruments and techniques for molding the public mind. Invisible rulers, he argues, are most effective when they discredit not only a specific idea but also the authority that promulgates it. "The council on public relations," Bernays writes, "after examination of the sources of established beliefs, must either discredit the old authorities or create new authorities by making articulate a mass opinion against the old belief or in favor of the new."[78] Foundationally undermining the trust and legitimacy of the old authorities opens the door not only for one new idea but for whatever the newly trusted emergent authorities want to convey going forward.

And while David versus Goliath makes for a neat narrative, it's also deeply untruthful. Media-of-one Glenn Greenwald reportedly earned around $2 million from Substack each year;[79] a staff editor at the *New York Times* can expect to make about $100,000 annually. (And Substack was just one of Greenwald's revenue streams; he also has a Rumble channel with 450,000 followers, a YouTube channel, and in 2023 migrated his print audience to Locals, Rumble's Substack competitor.)[80] The new independent media, the Fifth Estate, may wish to represent themselves as anti-elite, but they are in fact simply a *new* elite, dominating a new system of shaping public opinion.

Media-of-one figures are still beholden to incentives. They remain at the mercy of Noam Chomsky's five filters, just slightly updated for the digital age. For example, patronage may depend on patrons, not advertisers. Yet, deviate from what the patrons want, and you lose subscribers—and money. Double down on what they want—embrace the audience capture—and the till remains full. There is little incentive to create content for everyone—catering to a distinct niche that will boost and promote you makes more economic sense. Meanwhile, the "flak" that Chomsky-era media once feared is now coveted. Patrons love drama, and so every political newsletter, every scoop, is encouraged to be explosive and combative. In fact, Substack initially recruited creators to its platform based on how engaged their followings were on Twitter, ranking them on a scale of between one and four "fire emojis."[81]

The other filters have been reoriented as well. Sourcing concerns are less about appeasing the powerful and more about platforming those who reinforce patrons' worldviews. Constellations of ideologically similar creators guest on each other's podcasts or cross-post on each other's Substacks. And fear of the other—the worthy versus the unworthy victim—remains a potent filter but is now incredibly granular. It's no longer the United States versus the Communists; the "unworthy" party is the mom down the street who has different political opinions about charter schools.

The negative effects of these incentives are self-evident; just like Chomsky's original five filters, the contemporary incentives breed manipulation and misdirection. But rather than creating a single filtered picture of reality, this system enables a galaxy of bespoke realities.

In the 1920s, Walter Lippmann and John Dewey worried about the dangers of irreconcilably fractured publics and stressed the need for a shared understanding of the world. A century later, that objective seems impossible. The public fractures further every day, "coming together" only to assail each other in factional warfare. And while the propaganda machine of mass media was indeed manipulative, it is hard to see what we have now as objectively better. Relentless online propaganda, now at the niche level, entrenches people within bespoke realities, diminishing the chance of bridging perspectives and reaching consensus.

Although influencers are still closely associated with dance videos, e-commerce, and marketing, their role in shaping public opinion—especially around politics—is outsized. Influencers can harness attention, radiate trust, evoke emotion, and direct energy—all to great effect. They capitalize on atmospheric vibes and intuitions, giving people the right evidence to substantiate what they feel intuitively.

Influencers may present themselves as the every(wo)man: Khaby Lame, MrBeast, Candace Owens, and Keffals appear to be just like us, broadcasting from their living rooms and posting goofy memes. Or they present themselves as plucky Davids: Glenn Greenwald appears to run on moxie alone.

But by all measures of influence that matter, they are Goliaths. Influencers are very much a new elite, born of the present information age. They shape the culture not through older establishment power centers, like universities or media, but by forging a new space.

In his *New Yorker* piece, Laurence Scott aptly summarizes both species of influencer, the apolitical and political: "Both flourish in our increasingly networked world, in which digital influence is sharply double-edged—a salable commodity and a threat to democracy, a commercial dream and a political nightmare."

4

The Crowd

Contagion, Consensus, and the
Power of the Collective

"An illusion shared by everyone becomes
a reality."
—ERICH FROMM

YOU'VE PROBABLY SEEN IT: a flock of starlings pulsing in the evening
sky, swirling this way and that, feinting right, veering left. The flock
gets denser, then sparser; it moves faster, then slower; it flies in a beautiful, chaotic concert, as if guided by a secret rhythm.

The flock moves this way not due to an intentional determination
to get from its starting point to a landing place but because of a strange
quirk of biology: each bird sees, on average, the seven birds nearest it and
adjusts its own behavior in response.[1] If its nearest neighbors move left, it
tends left; if they dive right, then it usually dives right as well. The bird
does not know the flock's ultimate destination and can make no radical
change to the whole. But each of these birds' small alterations, when
occurring in rapid sequence, shifts the course of the whole, creating mesmerizing patterns. We cannot quite understand it, but we are awed by it.
It is a logic that emerges from—is an embodiment of—the network of
potentially thousands of birds. The behavior is determined by the structure of the network, which shapes the behavior of the network, which
shapes the structure, and so on.[2]

This undulating dance—called a *murmuration*—occurs as information cascades across the flock. Looking only at what any one individual is
doing misses the full scope of what is happening. This kind of beautiful,
synchronized movement of the whole out of the aggregate actions of its

parts is known in biology as *collective* or *emergent behavior*. It's seen in fish, ants, and bees and is, in fact, also a perfect metaphor for the behavior of flocks—or crowds—of people online.

Particularly where trending topics are concerned.

Collective behavior happens when individual members of the flock take cues from each other; there is no deliberate, intentional leader setting an agenda.[3] Computational biologists and computer scientists who study collective behavior describe what's happening in a starling murmuration as "the rapid transmission of local behavioral response to neighbors."[4] Each bird, bee, or fish has the capacity to influence the behavior of its neighbors even though it's not consciously aware that it's doing so.

The idea of groups having more power than the sum of their parts and individuals collectively influencing each other appears in human social psychology as well. While we may now be extremely online users of modern technology, our brains remain the same. Indeed, the notion of *crowd psychology* predates the internet by centuries. Chapter 2 touched on some of the good and the bad manifestations of this: social movements, moral panics, witch hunts.

Social platforms transformed our old networks, reorganizing us into new flocks formed around interests and identities, but they gained traction due to our age-old desire for connection with like-minded people. Information still passes from person to person, as with the rumor mill of old. But now it passes at unprecedented scale and speed and—most importantly—guided by algorithmic nudges that shape what is seen, by whom, and when. Platform design decisions transformed crowds in terms of their organization, what they paid attention to, and by what means they could communicate their message and reach others. Curation algorithms, for example, choose what content or users appear in your feed; the algorithm determines the seven birds, and you react. Design decisions now play a huge role in determining whether groups online are going to behave like civil communities or mobs—and yet, at the same time, the participants in the crowd also have agency.

The internet is where reality is made. You might think that sounds dramatic or absurd—the world existed prior to the internet and is governed by the laws of physics. A tornado will destroy your house whether you choose to believe it's real or not. But for many other topics, determinations of what is "real," "true," or "accurate" come about by way of *social consensus*. People come together in groups to evaluate rumors, stories, experiences, and information and decide the truth of a matter, so perception shapes reality. Our perception of what's happening around us today is significantly informed by what we see online. Many people get their news,[5] spend their time, and come together to discuss the issues of the day on the internet, particularly social media. And of course, what happens online doesn't stay online.

The digital crowd is the third part of the influencer-algorithm-crowd trinity. It's composed of ordinary people, the vast majority of whom aren't trying to be influencers. In past media environments the crowd was often relegated to the role of "the audience"—the recipient of narratives. But today's online crowds are extraordinarily influential participants; the flocks that career around the social web both feed the algorithms and influence the influencers. Crowds are key to virality—they can turn a wayward comment by a random person into the focus of a mob, and they can shape consensus or create a perception of majority opinion simply by making certain stories trend.

Angry Birds

In May 2020, the United States was teeming with crowds as millions of Americans gathered to condemn police brutality following the murder of George Floyd. Most of these gatherings were peaceful demonstrations in both big cities and small towns. Some of these gatherings were chaotic mobs that left destruction in their wake: looted stores, burning cars. And some of these gatherings were strictly online: digital debates about race, law enforcement, and the roiling American landscape.

David Shor participated in those digital debates—and the crowd took notice.

At the time, Shor—about thirty years old—was a data scientist and political analyst at Civis Analytics, a data science firm. He had earned accolades in his field, playing an important role building voting forecast models for Barack Obama's second presidential campaign.[6] But he was by no means a public figure. Yet.

On the morning of May 28, 2020, amid the protests and just months before a presidential election, Shor tweeted an observation about how the two might intersect. "Post-MLK-assasination [*sic*] race riots reduced Democratic vote share in surrounding counties by 2%, which was enough to tip the 1968 election to Nixon," he wrote. "Non-violent protests *increase* Dem vote, mainly by encouraging warm elite discourse and media coverage."[7]

The tweet cited research from a political scientist at an Ivy League university and featured a thumbnail image packed with text and a busy-looking graph. It was exactly the type of tweet you would expect from a data scientist working in politics amid protests and an election.

But Shor's tweet didn't reach a few colleagues and then fade into oblivion. Instead, a handful of left-wing influencers seized on the tweet, suggesting it wasn't simply an observation about the country's race issue but rather a manifestation of it. "Go to Minneapolis and fill the protesters in about your findings. Be sure to video it for our viewing pleasure," responded Benjamin Dixon, a political podcast host and prolific tweeter.[8]

A couple of hours later, Ari Trujillo Wesler, the creator of an organizing app for progressives, joined the conversation: "Minimizing black grief and rage to 'bad campaign tactic for the Democrats' is bullshit most days, but this week is absolutely cruel," she tweeted. Wesler also tweeted at Shor's boss, alerting his manager to the perceived "anti-blackness."[9]

Shor's tweet wasn't quite viral—to this day it has only around five hundred quote tweets—but it was enough to stir up a crowd of angry progressive tweeters, who reprimanded Shor for an alleged lack of grace or, worse, outright racism. That crowd elicited an earnest apology tweet from Shor, but the damage was done: Shor had assumed the dreaded role of Twitter Main Character. In the following days, he was dismissed from his job at Civis Analytics.[10]

Then the crowd went into overdrive.

Chatter on Twitter about Shor's firing spilled over into traditional media, bringing the saga to an exponentially larger audience. "Stop Firing the Innocent," read an op-ed headline in *The Atlantic*, written by author and political scientist Yascha Mounk.[11] "The Still-Vital Case for Liberalism in a Radical Age" was the title of columnist Jonathan Chait's essay in *New York Magazine*.[12] The media coverage likely contributed to Shor being ejected from a progressive email list,[13] which fueled more press coverage and podcast segments, which fueled more tweets. To crowds on the political right and in the center (and even some on the left), Shor was a martyr—an innocent casualty of "cancel culture." To crowds on the left, Shor remained villainous, an exemplar of tone-deaf white America weighing in on racial justice.

By July, the saga was culture war canon—significant enough to warrant an entire explainer article on the news website *Vox*.[14] Writers across the political spectrum debated whether or not this was an example of "cancel culture"—and, of course, whether cancel culture even exists. Murmurations on Twitter had transformed an unremarkable tweet by a young data scientist into the very center of The Discourse.

There is, perhaps, no clearer illustration of the importance of online crowds than the fact that media today report on the mere existence of fleeting online trends. In prior broadcast and print media ecosystems, the public gathered to discuss the events or ideas that talking heads debated on the nightly news. These days, "some people online are talking about David Shor's tweet" is newsworthy. Trending moments on Twitter are overwhelmingly pseudo-events—Main Character–driven kerfuffles that are forgotten, sometimes within hours, as the next thing moves in to take its place. But in that moment the entirety of some faction is tenaciously fixated on a thing, absolutely mad with outrage. Indeed, within some of the most vitriolic echo chambers, this happens with such intensity and frequency that pseudo-events string together into a full-on bespoke reality: an unending stream of rumors, fabrications, and manufactured controversies capture attention, reinforcing and further entrenching the beliefs of the already convinced.[15] Meanwhile, those outside the faction are wholly unaware of the tempest.

Affordances for Activism

Digital crowds are so potent largely because of the tools that platforms give them, which enable them to assemble effortlessly, to spread information instantaneously, and to achieve nearly global reach. Facebook, Twitter, and others have built tools—and multi-billion-dollar businesses—that expertly facilitate the primal human urge for community.[16]

This became abundantly clear by the early to mid-2010s, when a series of events dispelled the notion that social media platforms were simple places for posting about a sandwich or checking in on your cousin's latest party pictures. They were also, it turned out, places for activism, influence, and power. Committed activists used them to topple regimes: the collective behavior of ordinary Egyptians seeing a Facebook invitation to protest in Tahrir Square in 2011 eventually took down a government.[17] Activists across the political spectrum in the United States took careful note. More malign forces did as well: Islamic State (ISIS) terrorists began to use crowds of online sympathizers on Twitter to boost their recruitment efforts and share their content, glorifying physical attacks and inspiring copycats. And, unbeknownst to most at the time, governments had begun to participate surreptitiously: by the time of the US elections in 2016, Russia had been running fake accounts and bots for nearly two years, not only creating and disseminating the messages it thought would best serve its own interests but turning crowds of real Americans into unwitting accomplices. The platforms were useful, in large part, because everyone was on them, and everyone was targetable.

The tools that facilitate these crowds—and the consequent revolutions, mustering of armies, and election meddling—are algorithmic in nature. In Chapter 2, we discussed the algorithms that nudge people into joining groups or following influencers, even if those users never proactively search for the person or term. These algorithms are always gathering data to refine their suggestions: if the user responds by clicking, the algorithm has learned that the person—and more importantly, others like them—might be receptive to similar things.

This algorithmic entanglement happens outside the view of the members of the crowd. But platforms have given their users other algorithmic tools to leverage actively and consciously: features for liking, sharing, and commenting.[18] Every scroll or hover communicates back to platform algorithms whether a user is interested in something, but liking, sharing, and commenting convey a *strong* signal—the person has taken time to engage and amplify. Indeed, sometimes a like alone is all it takes for a platform to push that piece of content into the feed of the user's friends or followers.

Through these tools, even people who aren't trying to become influencers have the power to influence. Ordinary people spread messages among their own social networks every day. Each discrete action, each like or share, doesn't matter very much at the individual level. But when there is some momentum, when many users share the same news URL or meme or hashtag at the same time, platform algorithms then push it out to an even broader crowd of people who are likely to be interested.

The principle is simple: information moves faster when many people are connected to many other people. In situations where huge influencers have millions of followers, but those followers are not connected directly to each other, the message travels only so far.[19] This one-to-many connection is how broadcasting works on radio or television. But many-to-many connections, decentralized across millions of nodes, enable truly mass dissemination.

The potential for virality depends on the substance and tone of the content, of course, too—no one shares boring material. But the structure is key, and so are the affordances that the platforms give the crowd. On Twitter or Facebook, if there are lots of committed sharers or likers, something can spread easily. If high-follower-count influencers with significant reach get involved, things can move farther and faster. The content won't necessarily hop across communities, but it will capture attention within the one that is riled up about it. Instagram and YouTube, by contrast, don't have on-platform sharing functions, so virality doesn't happen in quite the same way. But tons of attention to a particular hashtag or searches for a specific phrase might make it show up as a topic of interest, and a lot of views all at once might result in the platform featuring a video or image on a main landing page. And, of course, it's very easy to repost an Instagram meme or YouTube video to Twitter or Facebook.

These affordances are part of the reason digital crowds wield such tremendous power today. People move things from one platform to another, from one community to another, relatively effortlessly. Stories move from the bottom up—mass media is not the only agenda setter. But the power given to us by new computer software at times intersects in unexpected ways with old human software—our psychology.

Open or Closed: The Behavior of Online Crowds

In 1960, Nobel Prize–winning writer Elias Canetti, a Bulgarian-born Jew who fled Austria as the Nazis took power, published a book on crowd psychology called *Crowds and Power*. Despite long predating the internet, Canetti's work, like that of Walter Lippmann and Edward Bernays, remains a useful contribution toward understanding human behavior even as it now manifests in a different landscape.

Canetti defined four attributes he believed are universal to crowds across history, from ancient tribes to the roiling masses of the French Revolution to the disaffected citizens of the Weimar Republic. First, the crowd always wants to grow. Second, within the crowd there is equality: all members stand on equal footing, and previous divisions of race, class, or other characteristics are temporarily erased. Third, the crowd loves density: there can be no component parts, just the singular crowd. And fourth, the crowd needs a direction: a shared objective to unite and propel members to act in the common interest. The direction is essential for the crowd's existence. While crowds have culture, symbolism, and ritual, this shared goal is what keeps them from disintegrating. As Canetti put it, "A crowd exists so long as it has an unattained goal."[20]

Much like Noam Chomsky's five filters, Canetti's four attributes are still relevant today, but with adjustments to account for the virtual nature of gathering. Online crowds still want to grow and are now unhindered by physical restraints. Online crowds still have surface equality, though internecine fighting and accusations of doctrinal impurity are not uncommon; power struggles sometimes result in highly visible schisms. Online crowds still love density, and our digital accounts can be packed together more easily than our physical bodies; there's always room for one more Twitter handle or hashtag. And as for direction, well, the shared mission is easier than ever to create given the steady supply of Main Characters and tweet-length hot takes.[21] Common enemies and scintillating commentary are abundant and accessible.

Perhaps the most relevant part of Canetti's book today is his theory about why some groups of people—members of churches and the like—come together, often in large numbers, yet remain relatively peaceful, while other large groups come together more spontaneously and are far more likely to turn violent.

He called the first group *closed crowds* and the latter *open crowds*. Closed crowds, he wrote, like churches, Rotary Clubs, and community groups, all have persistent members. They are people who share a common worldview, identity, or purpose and tend to form strong ties over time. There is a set time and place for meetings, an organizational structure. Sure, some closed crowds, including cults and extremist groups, actively dislike "out group" people. But closed crowds, overall, are largely neutral—in fact, they often evolve into institutions.

Open crowds, Canetti wrote, have no such persistence or clearly articulated reason for existing. They are far more spontaneous, emerging out of some kind of disruption and then rapidly growing by drawing people in with an almost gravitational force. The open crowd, Canetti argued, often assembles in response to an outrage. It does not dissipate until there is some sort of release, which is often chaotic or violent.

The theory of open and closed crowds maps neatly onto the dynamics of different social media platforms in the present day. The persistent community groups of Facebook, Discord, and WhatsApp lead to deep relationships and places for strategizing and discussing content with the like-minded. These platforms produce closed crowds. They can still become extreme or even generate violence, but the members know each other, and there is a persistence to their bond. Twitter, meanwhile, operates like an arena—a virtual Roman Colosseum where toxic, highly visible battles are fought within hashtags, and mobs of thousands tweet at (or about) just one or two people, seething with rage as even more by-standers look on.[22] The platform produces open crowds. Anyone drawn to the energy can immediately jump in.

An early example of these chaotic, open-crowd battles was a 2014–2015 episode dubbed "Gamergate."[23] The drama had started off as a niche fight: some gamers, mostly male, got angry at (and about) women in the video game industry campaigning to reduce what they saw as sexism and misogyny in game design (female characters with skimpy clothes and exaggerated breasts and the like). These opponents of the effort felt that "political correctness" was ruining video games. There was simulta-neously some conspiracy theorizing about how several prominent women in gaming had become prominent in the first place—one woman was accused by her boyfriend of cheating on him and sleeping with a reporter for a gaming website in exchange for better reviews (the reporter had not reviewed any of her games; the ex-boyfriend later blamed the insinuation on a typographical error).

Some gamers saw the rumor about sleeping with reviewers as evi-dence of manipulative behavior; they harassed the target and others who waded into the controversy, framing their outrage as being about "ethics in video game journalism" and as part of a fight to preserve the gamer identity. The other side, including those who joined in to defend the women who were targeted, argued that this was a social justice issue.

What might once have been a personal fight between a handful of people connected to a specific precipitating incident instead ballooned into a massive harassment campaign tied up with a seething online cul-ture war about feminism.

Some of the early gamer-identity combatants expended significant effort in trying to sway public opinion to their side. A vitriolic subset, however, organized targeted harassment campaigns on the message board 4chan. The goal of their behavior, which included posting private information, hacked nude photos, home addresses, and threats, was to intimidate their targets and drive people out of the conversation entirely. Some fled their homes. Even just tweeting an opinion about Gamergate, as a bystander who happened to see the hashtag, might lead to significant harassment as the mob coordinated to brigade others. Hyperpartisan media, such as Breitbart, began to cover the events—its then executive chairman Steve Bannon later described how instructional Gamergate was, how he'd learned the art of factional activation from watching how its most vicious trolls behaved and realized the potential of online armies in political fights.[24] Eventually, mainstream media began to write explainers, describing the "online culture war" and its intersection with offline issues.[25]

While Canetti's framing remains relevant, the nature of open and closed crowds has evolved. Twitter's design creates an opportunity for emergent collective behavior in which bystanders *everywhere* can instantly jump right into open crowds and start brawling. Yet Twitter's crowds lack the peak and then dissipation that Canetti described. In the real world, statues are toppled, and protests come to an end; alternately, hatred and violence can be mitigated by looking into the eyes of the target and recognizing their humanity.

But online harassment, brigading, and dogpiling have no similar catharsis. There is no physical requirement to disperse and no achievement indicating that things have come to an end. Instead, there is a perpetual state of simmering outrage or vitriol, ready to boil over at an opportune provocation; Gamergate itself lasted for months.[26] As members grew tired of brigading one person or raging against some idea, they simply grasped at the next. And participants in the mobs are often further emboldened by the cloak of online anonymity. There are no consequences for the behavior and minimal potential for de-escalation short of the platform suppressing a trend or suspending accounts of the worst participants—cold comfort, as new members of the crowd will be online again a few hours later to continue the fighting, and still more will appear to complain about "censorship."

The power of closed crowds has evolved as well. The recommendation engines' proclivity for connecting the like-minded on platforms like Facebook led to the formation of millions of insular crowds who congregated within persistent virtual gathering places, often built up deep trust between members, and shared long-term goals. Some oriented around a shared political identity, forming persistent places for communion among fellow travelers. The most partisan and extreme groups became echo chambers, where members distrusted outsiders, and opposing viewpoints rarely made it in (unless they were shared to be mocked). They were a small percentage of the groups overall, but they had significant disruptive impact. The proliferation of potential communities and crowds to participate in enabled users to choose their own adventure.

These new dynamics of open and closed crowds have distorted our perception of opinions, events, and even norms. Groups that felt themselves underrepresented in mainstream media conversations—sometimes marginalized or small communities but also conspiracy theorists—realized that by dominating the online discourse they could own *share of voice* (a marketing term referencing the percentage of media representing the opinion of your company or side in a political campaign compared to that of your competitor). By coordinating in a group chat or Facebook group to come together in a strategic manner on Twitter, activists could ensure that people looking for information about a controversy or debate would see their opinions. If they had few ethical scruples, harassment tactics could be used to discourage the other side from participating at all. A small group could manufacture the appearance of being the majority, in fact, if their opposition didn't consider the online battlefield equally important or was sufficiently intimidated.

The anti-vaccine movement, for example—while growing—is still relatively small. Recent surveys suggest that those opposed are estimated at approximately 15 percent of the US population,[27] even as the view appears to be a majority perspective based on social media vibes. Similarly, polling shows that only 18 percent of Americans support defunding the police,[28] but that position often seems quite mainstream on Twitter and other platforms. Yet a small, committed group can game (or more effectively use) a social platform to make their viewpoint seem dominant. A combination of effective networked crowds and compelling influencers means that some of us now perceive minority opinions as the majority viewpoint, outliers as the norm, and embellishments as facts—illusions that happen because the actual majority is silent, not active on the platform, or not creating the kind of content that platform algorithms are curating. Most people do not tweet about their children getting vaccinated and having no side effects; the child gets the routine immunization, nothing happens, and they just go about their day. There are online groups dedicated to spreading the "truth" about a flat Earth—but not a round Earth.

The Political Factions

Recognition of the power of online crowds to shape perception and galvanize action led to a proliferation of online factions specifically dedicated to fighting about politics and policies. In the mid-2010s, emojis became very popular, and Twitter users increasingly began to include emojis, hashtags, and keywords in their usernames and bios to prominently signal their political identity or allegiance.[29] The Pepe the Frog meme—a leering cartoon frog popular on alt-right message boards—was distilled down into the frog emoji (🐸); many Gamergate trolls began to use it, as did a growing community of young Donald Trump supporters.[30] Hillary Clinton's supporters were slower to embrace Twitter battles, but eventually adopted the blue wave emoji (🌊), which stuck for Democratic activists in subsequent elections even as Trump fans moved to American flags. Emoji-in-bio was a quick signal of allegiance, much as warring bands might have used coats of arms on their shields in eras past. By the late 2010s, emoji-delimited factions oriented around causes or ideology had proliferated: the rose of the democratic socialists, the meridian globe of neoliberals, the bike of public transit activists, the avocado of activists calling on their cities to build more housing (adopted after an executive made an ill-considered comment that young people couldn't afford to buy homes because they spent too much money on avocado toast).[31] And, alongside the factions, were fandoms: the bee for fans of Beyoncé, the purple heart for the die-hard fans of the K-pop band BTS. Each flock engaged with the others, at times in unexpected ways.

This was precisely the case in 2020, when one San Francisco activist tried to generate a viral moment for his political campaign—and ended up sparking something entirely different.[32]

Shahid Buttar, a self-described Democratic Socialist, was challenging Nancy Pelosi for her seat in the House of Representatives. One Sunday morning that July, a message appeared in a Discord server (a group chat room) named "Bernie or Vest," a reference to Senator Bernie Sanders and France's "Yellow Vest" protest movement—both of which are popular with young left-wing Americans. The server was home to a couple thousand of the rose-in-bio Democratic Socialist activists. The message contained an image of Buttar and asked the members of the server to participate in a social media campaign to boost his candidacy and attract public attention. The goal was to get the hashtag *#PelosiMustGo* to the top of the Trending Topics list, in hopes of calling attention to a long-shot candidacy that the media had largely ignored. The author of the request included a list of criteria that would make the curation algorithm more likely to push out the individual posts and less likely to penalize the group for trying to game it.

At 11:57 a.m., a Twitter user with a modest seventeen hundred followers jumped the gun on the planned 12 p.m. start time for the campaign: "*#PelosiMustGo*," they tweeted. Buttar himself posted promptly at noon: "Why do you think *#PelosiMustGo*?" he asked his 113,000 followers.[33] His tweet inspired several hundred replies and retweets, some encouraging him, others questioning him, others mocking him. More of his followers began to join.

#PelosiMustGo moved up Twitter's rankings, elbowing aside other topics that were trending at that moment: AR-15s, a golf tournament, Trump's pardons, and Education Secretary Betsy DeVos. As it reached number seven on the Trending list, GOP congressional candidate (and QAnon supporter) DeAnna Lorraine—who herself had run against Pelosi—noticed the hashtag and tweeted her own contribution to her then 330,000 followers. She and Buttar disagreed on nearly everything—except that *#PelosiMustGo*.

What happened next was fascinating.

Within three minutes of her post, the hashtag—until then largely confined to the Democratic Socialist faction—began rippling through the right-wing followers of Lorraine. A second faction had entered the campaign! The conspiracy brokers of the QAnon Twitter faction quickly got in the game, appending *#PelosiMustGo* to their own addled posts about Wayfair and child trafficking (this was mere weeks after Amazing Polly's viral hashtag). Pelosi supporters—the blue wave emoji-in-bio crew—also materialized, tweeting in an effort to reframe the hashtag in a positive light: "*#PelosiMustGo* straight to the White House and take over the presidency!"

Forty-five minutes after Buttar's first tweet, Jack Posobiec—the Far Right Pizzagate agitator and ideological polar opposite of Shahid Buttar—picked up the hashtag. His contribution was a banal observation: "*#PelosiMustGo* is now #6 trending." He himself did not even know why it was trending. But his post was enough for his followers to understand the role they were to play. His flock liked his post sixteen thousand times and replied or retweeted it thousands more. They added their own color to the conversation—*#DemocraticCriminalNetwork*, *#PlantationDemocrats*, *#PuppetRegime*—and propelled the hashtag fully into the national political conversation. The trend hit number one. Mission accomplished.

Hyperpartisan conservative media outlet the *Daily Wire* pulled the trend from social media into the broader media universe, reporting on what some people on the internet were saying, noting the hashtag's popularity, and quoting some of its most successful left-wing contributions while studiously avoiding any mention of the right-wing faction's involvement in getting it there. In their telling, the outpouring was wholly reflective of a massive left-wing revolt against Nancy Pelosi.[34]

Most of the hundreds of thousands of Twitter users who saw that hashtag trend never knew that *#PelosiMustGo* began because someone gave marching orders in a private Discord channel. The hashtag hit their field of view, and they reacted. They likely assumed that some sizable number of Americans somewhere were spontaneously tweeting against the then Speaker of the House—and clicked on the trend because they were curious about why.

The visible online factions, battling under their emoji banners, are having an impact. Sociologist Chris Bail, head of the Polarization Lab at Duke University, conducts interviews with social media users who become passionate participants in online political factions. They describe these online political fights as attacks on their identity. Seeing opposing views does not inspire careful reflection of the underlying policy or idea—it feels like a personal affront. Some report that the highly visible presence of opposing factions led them to become more entrenched in their own political identity—to study talking points so that they might fight online more effectively. They also described the experience of online conflict as interactive; unlike when passively seeing something on the TV news, they could search for terms, find the latest factional battle, and immediately jump in. "There was a war going on, and [they] had to choose a side," recounts Bail, describing the experience of one liberal woman.[35]

People initially come to participate in online crowds because of a mix of algorithmic nudging and personal interest. Being part of a political faction can be fulfilling—there's a cause and a mission. Fighting a common "enemy" creates camaraderie and a sense of belonging. It can also be fun. But participation in factions may lead to entrenchment, more extreme beliefs, or stronger and more belligerent partisanship. The groups that we're part of are fundamental to our sense of self; being a persistent factional warrior becomes part of a person's identity.[36]

Crowds, Cults, and Extremes

Social networks transformed not only how crowds of people convene and behave but how people within crowds influence one another. In Chapter 3, we discussed the phenomenon of audience capture—when an influencer shapes their content and opinions to fit the mold of what their audience wants. A similar phenomenon can trap crowds too, creating *social capture* as members reinforce each other's point of view, and diversity of opinions becomes increasingly scarce.

We decide what information is correct by considering what others think is correct (consensus reality). We also determine what behaviors are correct to the degree that we see those around us performing them.[37]

Members of groups tend to reinforce each other's views, often moving each other toward a more extreme point than where they started.[38] Factions appear to coalesce around the opinions of the most forceful members, and those who hold differing opinions—maybe more moderate—don't express them for fear of being ostracized.[39] Since beliefs are shaped collectively, new information that conflicts with the group identity or comes from someone with an "outside" identity can simply be rejected; this is one reason that partisans easily dismiss fact-checking if it comes from the "other side."[40]

This also happens with group norms and behaviors; people try to conform to the norms associated with their identity, which may also drift toward the more extreme over time. Psychologists have found that norms are followed more strictly if there's tension with an opposing group[41]—you don't consort with the other side while you're at war!—and in the gladiatorial arena of social media, there is always tension.

The identity of an online faction should ideally reflect their positive beliefs—the things they stand for—but some instead come to be defined oppositionally. The phrase "owning the libs" or "triggering the libs" is a meme that captures the driving motivation of some right-wing factions. It's a joke, but a revealing one: without liberals as an antithesis, the faction loses cohesion. Indeed, this is one reason why right-wing alt-platforms are slow to see significant adoption: there are no libs around to own. It is more fun to stay on a platform with an opposing crowd.

Loudly railing against an enemy gets engagement.[42] As members post and tweet during factional battles, the most extreme voices usually get the most attention; because of the way platforms are designed and how algorithms surface content, they appear to represent the opinion of the whole group. So the most extreme views from one side end up visibly clashing with the most extreme views from the other side. People with more moderate or nuanced views might get harassed, or self-censor, or not even be seen in the discussion...or they might express opinions far stronger than the ones they actually hold in order to fit in.

Performing an identity and achieving uniform opinions within a group is not the same thing as reaching consensus. It's not a process of evaluating facts, deliberating, taking in a diverse set of opinions, and forming a view of the world. Unfortunately, the incentives to go through that deliberative process are not the ones that drive the influencer-algorithm-crowd system.

Rather, the system tends to reward content that generates strong reactions and aligns with prevailing opinions. People within the faction who are particularly good at mocking collective enemies or ideological dissenters get recognition from their peers; their clout within the group increases. And when mockery, hostility, and nastiness are not only normalized but incentivized, people will deliver. Marxist writer Freddie deBoer described the dynamics well in a critique of an online pro-housing movement (which he broadly supports), though the problem is not specific to any one faction: "Social incentives cut in favor of nastiness and extremity and against nuance and bridge-building, so the forums gradually become ugly places that are hostile to dissent and celebrate excessive expressions of the group's orthodoxies precisely because they're excessive."[43]

Social media is impacting social cohesion. The networked crowd allows for the exchange of information, facilitates social influence, and—depending on who is influential—has an impact on norms.[44] Social media crowds offer us echo chambers but also echolocation.[45] People look for a sense of belonging and understanding of social rules not just by being part of a group but by gauging how groups align with or oppose each other. They try to navigate what opinions are popular, often using engagement as an indicator.

Influencers are like beacons for this navigation process. They draw attention, embody popular opinions, and then rally the group toward collective action.

Men of Words and Men of Action: The Influencers and the Crowds

People we admire and find persuasive, particularly those we find relatable, tend to have more influence on us. This is especially true for issues we consider significant or in situations we see as threatening.[46]

One of Canetti's contemporaries was author and philosopher Eric Hoffer, who in 1951 published *The True Believer*. The book studies the members of crowds in mass movements—persistent, large groups united by a fervent and often fanatical devotion to a common cause or ideology. The true believer of the title is someone who becomes deeply committed to the movement's ideals because it offers the potential for escape from the dissatisfaction he feels in his life. Indeed, one of Hoffer's chief points, hotly debated by some, is that mass movements and their component parts (i.e., people) are essentially interchangeable regardless of ideology, which explains why people may flip from one movement to another that is seemingly the opposite in its core beliefs. This is because, he argues, mass movements appeal to the same types of people: "All movements, however different in doctrine and aspiration, draw their early adherents from the same types of humanity; they all appeal to the same types of mind."[47]

The behaviors and emotions of the true believers, Hoffer explained, add up to define the overarching behavior of the movement. Its traits can be either negative (discontent, paranoia) or positive (an honest desire for constructive change), but objective reality becomes less important as the movement becomes the primary source of hope for the future. Any point that threatens that hope is ignored or actively rejected. Dogma permeates the movements—there is one truth, one goal—and any available tools, including propaganda and coercion, are permissible to sustain it.

Shared values and goals hold movements together, Hoffer writes, but nothing is quite so strong as a shared enemy: "Mass movements can rise and spread without belief in a god, but never without a belief in a devil."[48] Hatred of another group, he argued, "is the most accessible and comprehensive of all unifying agents." This remained true as mass movements moved online, as was evident, in sometimes amusing ways, even in the earliest days of the internet. In the mid-1990s, for example, as public adoption of the internet was taking off, the open-source software movement was at its peak. What bound the motley collection of contributors together was partially a commitment to collaboration and better software—and partially a loathing of Bill Gates and Microsoft. "If you cared about Linux on the desktop, there was a big list of jobs to do," remarked technology writer and critic Clay Shirky in a 2003 keynote address at the O'Reilly Emerging Technology Conference. "But you could always instead get a conversation going about Microsoft and Bill Gates...Nothing causes a group to galvanize like an external enemy."[49]

People who become active participants in online movements and factions feel called to action. At a time when many people feel powerless and rudderless in their offline lives or disconnected from their communities—the isolation of the COVID-19 pandemic exacerbated this—online communities offer meaning. Recall Amazing Polly, who galvanized thousands of people to post about Wayfair's secret side business selling children. The participants in the *#SaveTheChildren* hashtag sincerely believed that they were helping children held hostage by Wayfair—or even, more simply, that they were helping raise awareness of the evil that is child trafficking. QAnon movement adherents believe that their "research" into Q's cryptic posts will uncover mysteries, expose hidden truths, and, in doing so, hopefully lead to consequences for those whom they deem evil.

Today's online audiences are not mere passive recipients of information from influencers. Members of online factions sort themselves into particular roles suited to their temperaments and talents. Studies of online extremist movements describe a variety of ways that the crowd collectively works toward capturing attention and growing its numbers, even absent deliberate coordination.[50] Some accounts act as solicitors, or recruiters, drawing others to the movement; ISIS accounts, for example, targeted disaffected young men and women, promising them friendship, comradeship, and glory.

Some create content that educates observers about the group's theories or claims, intellectualizing it and often pointing people to relevant discussions on other platforms or message boards. There is often a fear that some platform will decide that the group is no longer welcome, and so creating redundancy and a place to preserve group knowledge is important. Many highly factional crowds, as well as extremist groups ranging from white nationalists to ISIS to QAnon, maintain propaganda websites or wikis that define terms and convey group lore that is often below the radar of media explainers.

Then there are the shitposting agitators, whose accounts primarily focus on rage and inciting anger. These often attract the attention of algorithms looking for highly emotionally engaging content or draw members of other factions into fighting about some hashtag or meme.

Meanwhile, much of this activity is observed by a second tier of crowd members: sympathizers, or "fanboys," who support the movement more passively, perhaps retweeting and amplifying or even just quietly liking the content. They are often disseminators, not creators, but their actions can potentially trigger trending algorithms or provide enough engagement to boost a tweet or post to wider curation by platform algorithms.

Researchers who study the ways all these different members of the crowd interact note that the educators and solicitors were influential in getting the other members to spread content about the group, but the agitators were often more active in spreading content that people would think of as "fake news" or information that was deliberately false but highly engaging.[51]

When it comes to classifying members of the crowd, Hoffer's seventy-year-old analysis once again proves salient. The same characters are also discernible in *The True Believer*. Hoffer identified the "men of words": those who seed the initial ideas of a movement and lay the groundwork for a mass of true believers. The success of a movement depends on discrediting the prevailing order and institutions and familiarizing the potential of the new—as Bernays described, the work of the invisible rulers. The men of words might be novelists or muckraking journalists or propagandists—or, today, firebrand influencers—and they craft the doctrines and slogans of the new faith as they create the demand.[52] Then come Hoffer's Fanatics, the disenchanted and angry chaos agents willing to believe the unbelievable, who spread the word and generate the gravitational pull of the early crowd. Today, Fanatics may be a more polite name for shitposters, the more nihilistic foot soldiers of the faction. Finally come the "men of action"—those who step up to helm the movement, who hoist the oriflamme and eventually build the power structures necessary to crystallize the vision. Think Donald Trump.

The leaders who rise to steer the true believers, Hoffer explained, are characterized by audacity and joy in defiance; by brazen disregard for consistency; by delight in symbols and spectacles; and by deep understanding of human nature, like the craving for communion.[53]

Canetti's dynamics and Hoffer's archetypes are easier to spot today because social media have enabled them to proliferate. Content production and dissemination is free and easily available for the men of words; dangling bait for the crowds has never been easier—all it takes is a hashtag. Fanatics are legion, loitering on Twitter or within Discord servers. And men of action are watching eagerly, quick to capitalize on the latest "belief."

The concept of individuals and crowds taking action has always been integral to propaganda. French philosopher Jacques Ellul, writing about propaganda in 1962, argued that it seeks not to change minds but to stir people to action. "Action makes propaganda's effect irreversible," he wrote. "He who acts in obedience to propaganda can never go back...He is obliged to continue to advance in the direction indicated by propaganda, for action demands more action...He is forced to accept the new milieu and the new friends propaganda makes for him."[54] Ellul likely had Vichy collaborators in mind when he penned these words, but he might as well have been talking about QAnon supporters or any other die-hard, always-online faction.

Perpetually online crowds are the new normal—and their evolution is powerfully transformative. Movements that might have grown over time as they built up an infrastructure for organizing can now spring up overnight. This velocity change carries new challenges—while online crowds are adept at capturing attention and sometimes achieving an objective or two, they are also often fragile and conflict ridden, lacking the organizational depth or capacity to achieve meaningful change. They may struggle to build alternatives rather than simply tearing things down.[55] But they nonetheless offer the potential to galvanize nonviolent movements for justice and human rights.

The Online Crowd and Consequences

We have focused heavily on political crowds and warring factions, but the power of online crowds is broad. In January 2021, anyone who was still naive enough to believe that online crowds don't have bearing on the offline world was quickly disabused of the notion. No, this isn't a reference to the events of January 6 at the US Capitol—we'll talk about that in the next chapter.

This is the story of stonks: an extraordinary series of events involving online crowds, their murmurations, and billions of real-world dollars.

The online forum Reddit has traditionally been a place for people with shared interests to gather and discuss movies, sports, celebrities, board games, current affairs, or any number of other topics. Reddit's groups, known as *subreddits*, can range from ordinary (spaces for people to chat about the latest blockbusters) to the truly unconventional (like r/BirdsWithArms, where members post pictures of birds with arms photo-shopped onto them).

While debates can get heated among enthusiasts of this movie or that game, the chats are usually fairly innocuous. But in January 2021, a small group of mom-and-pop investors posting in r/wallstreetbets (tagline: "Like 4chan found a Bloomberg terminal") decided to take on powerful hedge funds that were trying to short-sell the struggling video game company GameStop. By the time they were done, the group—most of whom only interacted on the subreddit—had gutted one of the most successful hedge funds in the world.

Why did they do it? It was partly out of nostalgia for GameStop, which had been a major chain store in the 1990s, before video games were easily downloaded direct to consoles, and was now trying to move into the online market. And it was also meant to stick it to the man, to thwart the greedy capitalists who, like sharks, had sensed the weakness of the flailing video game company and were shorting its stock for a quick buck.

Whatever the exact motivation, the movement started with a sim-ple meme: a crudely drawn man in a business suit standing next to a stock trading board with an orange arrow shooting upward and the word *stonks* written on it. The versatile meme had been around for years and was often used to mock experts who gave bad financial takes, to poke fun at people making bad financial decisions, or to express disdain for the unnecessary complexity or surrealism of modern financial markets.[56] The funny misspelling of *stocks* was, of course, deliberate. In this incarnation, it became a rallying cry. Wall Street hedge fund traders had long mocked small-time retail investors as blundering bumpkins, but now the crowd was gearing up to take them on.

The hedge funds knew GameStop was in trouble and were trying to short it—that is, borrowing the company's stock at one price, selling it (in massive quantities), and buying it back on the cheap before returning the borrowed shares. In effect, they were betting that they could drive the price down, since other people who held the stock might see the momentum and try to get out of their own shares as well. In the unlikely event their market research was wrong and the stock for some reason went up, they would be on the hook for billions.

The small-time traders on Reddit decided that they were going to stop them. They started buying up modest quantities of GameStop shares online, using investing apps like the appropriately named Robinhood. There was no actual planning—just a sudden, almost spontaneous move to buy GameStop shares and stymie the corporate raiders. As word of what was happening spread, it started trending on Twitter and other social media, where other day traders joined in, and a chorus of digital onlookers cheered them on.

Even Elon Musk, an extremely online billionaire with a complicated relationship to market manipulation, added his voice—a single-word tweet reading "Gamestonk!"[57] It was seen as a rallying cry for the masses, further fueling the fire. The stock price spiked immediately following Musk's contribution.[58]

Before the short squeeze began, GameStop shares were trading at around $19. As r/wallstreetbets users weighed in, it approached nearly $500 per share at its peak.[59] The big investors were facing a catastrophe. Robinhood and other brokerages eventually suspended trading, citing insufficient funds to cover investors' stock. This outraged the crowd, which saw it as an effort to protect the hedge funds.[60] Robinhood chatter popped up across social media platforms as people darkly speculated about its motives.

By then it was too late for hedge funds like Melvin Capital, which had started the month of January 2021 worth more than $12 billion and saw more than half of its value wiped out by the collective hijinks of the Reddit users. Its founder, Wall Street star investor Steve Plotkin, later quietly announced he was shuttering his fund.

The rout was complete.

The Power of Murmurations

It was not just short-selling hedge funds that were wiped out, of course; many of the people in the crowd who were drawn to the momentum and excitement bought near the top and lost significantly. There were plausible market-fundamentals angles at the core of the GameStop trade, but millions of observers and participants were sucked in primarily by the David versus Goliath story—the highly relatable narrative of nihilism, retribution, and lulz.[61] Narratives have always had the power to move markets—the tulip bubble occurred prior to the invention of radio—but social media has transformed the way that incentivized crowds parlay online narratives into real-world economic events.[62]

This bottom-up social network amplification chain—this human murmuration—is incredibly powerful. It can surface civil rights violations, spark protest movements, move markets, and help the public follow breaking events, whether traditional media choose to participate or not. But it's also how a daily parade of rumors, pseudo-events, and conspiracy theories are made to trend: *#Ivermectin*, *#SaveTheChildren*, *#StopTheSteal*, *#TheJews*. Although they are the target of invisible rulers, monetized by influencers and platforms alike, the power of the crowd in shaping perception today is profound.

This is the new normal; each day there are new hashtags that suck in tens of thousands of people, capturing attention and also sparking factional vitriol. Momentarily viral narratives swell up and then recede like waves. The specifics are often forgotten, but the rage, the tribalism, is further reinforced with each new battle. Whether organic or contrived, these moments are propelled by influencers, amplified by online crowds, and curated and pushed out to specific factions by algorithms that reward engagement with yet more engagement. A giant web of interconnected users, each with an agenda, shouting at one another to pay attention.

What you see in your online crowd or in your bespoke reality is often wholly different from what is rippling through others'. There is consensus and cohesion within the crowds but often not across them. Every crowd proclaims itself *the* public, while it is merely *a* public.

It is a good thing that we are no longer restricted to hearing the voices and opinions approved by institutions or filtered by media elites. But the fractured system that has replaced its predecessor is hardly an improvement: a maelstrom of viral hashtags competing for attention, hopping from community to community, amplified by crowds of true believers for whom sharing and retweeting are akin to religious ritual. Each individual act of clicking or resharing may not feel like impactful, but in the aggregate those acts shape conversations, beliefs, realities.[63]

Influencers, algorithms, and crowds are increasingly defining reality. And America's political and civic norms have not yet adjusted to these conditions. We may not be entirely sure why something popped up in our feed, but that doesn't obviate the nagging feeling that we should pay attention. We are now surrounded, at all times, by urgency; by demands to question elections, howl about censorship—and even storm capitals.

PART II

5

Propagating the Big Lie

A LI ALEXANDER ENTERED AMERICAN politics around 2007, working as an unremarkable campaign staffer on John McCain's failed presidential bid. Twelve years later, he rose to national prominence when, campaigning for Donald Trump's 2020 reelection, he helped popularize a now infamous slogan, "Stop the Steal," as the rallying cry of a political movement.[1]

Alexander's transformation can be viewed on one level as an individual one: the journey of a provocateur troll who grew increasingly unhinged in his rhetoric, accusing a Democratic representative of marrying her brother, then questioning Kamala Harris's blackness, and finally calling for coups both at home and abroad.[2]

But his transformation is also representative of a larger change—a paradigm shift in the political landscape, resulting from the smashing together of the rumor mill and the propaganda machine. Although the McCain and Trump campaigns were both run by Republicans and separated by little more than a decade, they were wildly dissimilar. McCain viewed traditional media as essential allies; Trump viewed them as bitter enemies.[3] McCain struggled to gain traction on then nascent social media; Trump was Twitter's most famous user.[4] McCain's campaign reportedly chastised Alexander when he entertained the notion of voter fraud; Trump's campaign made the allegation of it their centerpiece.[5]

Alexander's story, and that of the 2020 election more broadly, is one of influencers, algorithms, and the crowds around them operating in concert to make bespoke realities—and history. It's the story of propaganda and rumors swirling together, compounding, and—tragically—undermining the 237-year tradition of peaceful transfer of power.

But how did it happen? Depending on the political party you align with and the media you follow, you may have heard the president and his inner circle—longtime political operatives like Rudy Giuliani and Roger Stone—pushing allegations of fraud.[6] Or you may have seen those claims covered (or fact-checked) by large broadcast media outlets. But this top-down, elite-driven propaganda machine was only half the story. The online rumor mill simultaneously operated in overdrive throughout the 2020 campaign as the *new* elite—the political influencers and their aligned factions—boosted story after story that purportedly provided evidence of the president's claims. Some participants were true believers, while others knew better. They were united by one common purpose: to repeat the narrative so many times that it became a reality.

They achieved that purpose. A complex system of small lies and rumors snowballed into the vast conspiracy theory known simply as "the Steal." And the result was real-world violence.

February 2020

The first factional skirmishes of the 2020 election happened on the left. The emoji-in-bio political factions proliferated as the Democratic primaries got underway: the bee for Kamala Harris's "*#KHive*," a hibiscus flower for supporters of Hawaii native Tulsi Gabbard, and the long-standing rose of Bernie Sanders–supporting Democratic Socialists.[7] Interestingly, while moderates such as Joe Biden and Pete Buttigieg had plenty of supporters, they did not have prominent emoji-branded fandoms; the center seems less inclined to visibly activate on social media platforms.

Yet the first contest—the Iowa caucus on February 3, 2020—was unexpectedly won by Buttigieg, the former mayor of South Bend, Indiana, with Bernie Sanders coming in a close second. Perhaps because he had a far less visible social media fandom than more progressive challengers, Mayor Pete's win was incomprehensible to some of the more passionate progressive influencers; surely if he was popular, they would have noticed that on social media? Despite the fact that Senator Sanders did not dispute the result himself, a highly visible portion of his faction of supporters began conspiracy theorizing about its legitimacy. The local Iowa Democratic Party, it turned out, had hired a contractor, Shadow Inc. (the conspiracy theories write themselves), to build a new vote-counting app for $63,000 with a two-month turnaround.[8] Not enough money, not enough time. On caucus day, it didn't work. Results were delayed as caucus organizers reverted to a manual tally.

Rather than presuming incompetence, the rose-in-bio faction leapt to malice. They alleged a plot to steal the primary from Bernie, just like Hillary Clinton and the Democratic National Committee had purportedly done in 2016.[9] Verified Sanders-supporting "blue-check" influencers, high-profile journalists, and politicians participated in the rumor mill, implying that the Iowa Democratic Party was stalling because it was unhappy with a Sanders win, that local party loyalists had in fact rigged results for Buttigieg, or that Buttigieg had somehow engineered the situation.[10] Supporters of other candidates wondered if Russia had been involved—absent any evidence.[11] *#MayorCheat* (rhymes with Pete) trended.[12]

As the debacle unfolded, some of the more conspiracy-minded settled on a scapegoat: Robby Mook, Hillary Clinton's 2016 campaign manager. Mook's name began to trend on Twitter, with tens of thousands of tweets darkly speculating about his role in the Shadow Inc. app (he had none).[13] These insinuations, too, were retweeted by high-profile influencers and journalists,[14] increasing their reach. Mook himself tweeted a denial, but as usually happens, his rebuttal got less attention than the theories; the engagement it did generate consisted primarily of further attacks.[15] This intraparty fight, meanwhile, was noticed by prominent Republican influencers: Turning Point USA founder Charlie Kirk, other Make America Great Again (MAGA) faction activists, and right-wing media boosted both the conspiracy theories and the more accurate stories about general incompetence.

While it's impossible to determine the identity of every rose-in-bio or MAGA tweeter whose engagement propelled Robby Mook into the villainous Main Character role that evening, the conversation appeared to be overwhelmingly driven by real, authentic, domestic influencers and passionate online factions. This wasn't a problem of "foreign interference" or "Russian bots," despite some of the online chatter: this time the conspiracy theorizing was coming from inside the house.

As I watched the fight unfolding in Twitter's Trending Topics feature that night, it occurred to me once again that terms like *misinformation* and *disinformation*—which media tended to use to describe moments like this—weren't quite right. The right was opportunistically amplifying the chaos unraveling their opponents, of course, but on the left the trends were driven by what seemed to be genuine, heartfelt rage and sincere belief in the claims. People were trying to make sense of the world in the moment, even as the facts couldn't yet be known. And yet, there was something alarming about how quickly the rumor mill had leapt to the assumption of malice, pulling out the "Man Behind the Curtain" trope and implying a deliberate effort to try to steal the Iowa caucus from the rightful winner. The online crowds were direct participants, digging around to find evidence that Mook was duplicitous, as political influencers poured gasoline on the trend. Other people, including Buttigieg's supporters, tried to counter the claims, but that too primarily perpetuated the trend. Sensationalism and conspiracy theorizing had become the norm.

A similar event had played out quite differently eight years prior. In 2012, before Twitter and Facebook had become gladiatorial arenas for warring political factions, Mitt Romney had been declared the victor in the Iowa caucus during the Republican primary. However, after amended counting, the victor flipped to Rick Santorum. And yet archives of Facebook posts and media coverage turn up very few allegations of malice or wild conspiracy theories about how Republican Party insiders were trying to rig the caucus. There was still plenty of partisan media in 2012—talk radio and cable news influencers and a growing social media ecosystem. But in the eight-year period between the Iowa caucuses of 2012 and 2020, something significant changed. Influencers, algorithms, and crowds had created new norms.

April 2020

The factional infighting in the Democratic races, however, was nothing compared to what would soon emerge in the campaign between primary victor Joe Biden and incumbent Donald Trump. Although the online rumor mill had churned with various theories propagated by the Democratic factions, the wild allegations of "rigging" were not amplified by the candidates themselves. When left-leaning mass media covered claims of fraud, they did so overwhelmingly to debunk them.

But in April 2020, as the United States was largely under lockdown for the COVID-19 pandemic, President Trump began to criticize mail-in ballots. They would lead to fraud, he argued. "Mail ballots—they cheat. OK? People cheat," he said in a press conference. "There's a lot of dishonesty going along with mail-in voting."[16] The claim became a drumbeat, restated again and again, for months, in press conferences and on social media.

There had been occasional incidents of ballot fraud in past elections, which offered a grain of truth to point at. But there was no evidence of significant or systematic fraud associated with mail-in ballots; Trump's own voter integrity commission examining the 2016 election had found no significant fraud,[17] and Trump himself had previously voted by mail.[18]

No matter: mail-in ballots were now a partisan grievance. Right-wing media began to write about them. Right-wing influencers began to talk about them. The partisan propaganda machine was in play, framing the topic for its audience.[19]

The belief that American elections were unfair, while not novel (see *Bush v. Gore*), had gained in prominence since 2016.[20] Trump and his supporters, in fact, had spent the last few weeks of the 2016 campaign declaring that the race would be stolen from him—a narrative that the storied Russian trolls had eagerly boosted, looking to delegitimize the election ahead of Trump's assumed loss.[21] When he unexpectedly won, groups of vocal Clinton supporters (and Clinton herself) became convinced that the victory was due to an assist from fake news on social media or from Russia.[22] Suspicions of Russian meddling snowballed into a series of investigations, which found little evidence of collusion[23] but incontrovertible evidence of interference;[24] the whole mess was munged together under the term *Russiagate*, and consensus on what had happened split along political-identity lines.[25] Now, in 2020, rumblings of stolen elections had begun again—originated by Trump, the sitting president of the United States.

The question was, What to do about it?

The Big Tech platforms did not want a repeat of the post-2016 hearings and investigations into how they'd failed to defend free and fair elections. Since 2017, they'd debuted new content moderation policies around election integrity. They'd developed policies specific to hacked materials (if, for example, Russian military intelligence again dumped a cache of one candidate's emails).[26] Facebook also laid out an overall enforcement rubric—"remove, reduce, and inform"—describing a collection of interventions, the most severe of which involved the removal of posts or accounts.[27] "Reduce" throttled distribution via algorithmic downranking, pushing content into user feeds less frequently. "Inform" involved attaching a pop-up notice or label to a post to add context and alert the viewer that the content had been fact-checked or might be disputed. Other platforms used different terminologies, but their toolkits were largely the same.

The platforms had also developed "coordinated inauthentic behavior" policies—rules to prevent, for example, fake Texas secessionists located in Saint Petersburg from piggybacking on or disrupting the political expression of *real* Texas secessionists. In 2018, most reasonable people agreed that interference in politics by foreign trolls was a bad thing. And so, Facebook, Twitter, and Google had built up integrity teams that had gotten quite adept at taking down networks of inauthentic accounts tied to foreign governments all over the world. They communicated with relevant government leaders and agencies worldwide about some of these findings and delivered briefings to media. The tech platforms had also begun to run "war rooms" during major global elections—America was not the only target.[28]

But inauthentic foreign actors weren't the sole problem. There had been several instances[29] of *domestic* groups using manipulative, inauthentic tactics as well: in 2016, the frog-in-bio pro-Trump faction used automated "bot armies" to dominate Twitter's Trending Topics lists and shape the conversation.[30] That same year, a prominent pro-Trump troll propagandist, Douglass Mackey, spread a meme encouraging Clinton voters to text their votes or vote on different days; he was found guilty of voter suppression in 2023. Thousands, it seemed from the legal filings, had been tricked.[31] At Mackey's trial, another pseudonymous troll, "Microchip," testified about the broader effort, including work to salaciously reframe the Clinton campaign's hacked emails—the foundation of Pizzagate. There was nothing particularly surprising or sinister among the emails, Microchip noted, though at the time he'd posted thousands of messages suggesting otherwise: "My talent is to make things weird and strange, so there is controversy." When a prosecutor asked whether he had believed what he'd posted, Microchip didn't hesitate: "No," he said. "And I didn't care."[32]

In late 2017, several different groups on the political left ran fake Facebook pages pretending to be right-wing media outlets in the special election for an Alabama Senate seat.[33] I knew of one such effort, run by a company I later worked for, which had created Facebook pages that looked on the surface to be made by center-right Alabamans but in reality were run by outsiders.[34] When the story about the efforts broke a year later, Facebook suspended the accounts of those responsible for the fake pages.[35]

By this point, however, the sense had taken hold that politics on social media was going to be the Wild West. Online manipulation became part and parcel of brass-knuckles politics; some party politicos and activists speculated aloud about whether they were at a disadvantage if they were *not* using all of the tactics that social media made possible.[36] And so it was unsurprising to see similar efforts appear again in 2020. A contractor named Rally Forge, working on behalf of Charlie Kirk's pro-Trump right-wing youth group Turning Point Action, was exposed for running hundreds of Facebook, Twitter, and Instagram commenter accounts that masqueraded as a grassroots conservative groundswell.[37] The accounts, some run by teenagers, played down COVID-19 and cast aspersions on the integrity of mail-in ballots—echoing the president's talking point.[38]

A different network, of nearly thirteen hundred domains masquerading as local news[39] (owned by activist Brian Timpone),[40] got in the game as well: the "Milwaukee City Wire" made false allegations about Milwaukee having more votes than registered voters. This story was picked up by Sean Hannity[41] and then shared by Governor Scott Walker, laundering the propaganda from blog to media to social media.[42]

By this point, both foreign and domestic trolls, influencers, and crowds had mastered the art of propagating "unfair election" allegations. Platforms were hustling to address this phenomenon and crafting policies specific to election-related content—but to their dismay, the trolls had by then also mastered the art of "unfair moderation" allegations.

The "Censorship" Pretext

Right-wing elites and media had claimed for years that Big Tech content moderation policies were biased against conservatives—recall Facebook's Trending Topicsgate in 2016. The chorus increased as platforms began to take a more proactive approach to moderation to reduce harassment and hate speech. Over time, removing, reducing, and informing all became the target of a deliberate, strategic reframing campaign to brand any content moderation—even the mere addition of a fact-check label—as "censorship." *Who are platforms to be the arbiters of truth or to determine what is hate speech? What about the First Amendment?* went the arguments. Alternative social media companies like Gab, Rumble, and Parler had emerged by this point, catering to MAGA audiences with rhetoric declaring their commitment to free speech.[43]

There is, of course, no legal requirement for a private company to adhere to the First Amendment, though all of the major social media platforms generally, and rightly, attempted to balance moderation and free expression. The value is important—we should want to maximize it! And yet, the design of the social media ecosystem had changed the dynamics of rumors and propaganda, lies and counterspeech so significantly. To thread this needle, in 2018 my colleague Aza Raskin at the Center for Humane Technology and I broached a way of thinking about the distinction between hosting and promoting content: "Freedom of speech, not freedom of reach."[44] Platforms should ensure that users could express themselves, but there was no right to algorithmic amplification. Decisions about what to suggest and what to curate were a function of complicated trade-offs made by companies with a business incentive to keep as many customers as possible happy, at a global scale. While it was important to be transparent about their policy enforcement, platforms did have their own right to moderate and curate. They might decide to host, for example, an alternative-remedy cancer group that touted juice fasts, but that didn't mean they were obligated to actively promote and recommend it to others.

There are real debates to be had about how platforms moderate and rightful concerns about unaccountable private power setting the rules of democratic debate on global communication platforms.[45] But the framing battle to redefine all content moderation—even labeling an article—as "censorship" is purely a political ploy.

Howling "censorship"—a word with bad moral connotations—has become a favored tactic for working the refs. Painting the entire endeavor of content moderation as morally reprehensible or illegitimate makes even nuanced policies suspect and reframes those who violate them as victims of tyranny. It positions private-company business decisions to maximize a positive user experience as the equivalent of authoritarian governments deliberately suppressing viewpoints (ironically, authoritarian leaders *do* try to force platforms to silence dissidents). The word *censorship* has become a thought-terminating cliché. One need simply levy the accusation to put the accused on the defensive.

All that said, however, there was no demonstrable or quantitative evidence that platforms were actually ideologically biased against conservatives.[46] Studies consistently found the opposite: that conservative viewpoints tended to dominate social media.[47] An independent audit of Facebook uncovered no evidence of systematic anticonservative bias.[48] The Trump reelection campaign's actions did not suggest a deep belief that they were censored; it spent more money on Facebook ads than any of Trump's Democratic rivals even while criticizing the company.[49] Peer-reviewed research conducted by Twitter found that the political Right enjoyed higher amplification compared to the political Left in six out of the seven countries examined.[50] Yet the perception of right-wing censorship persists among American Republicans, with 90 percent believing that social media sites censored their political views as the 2020 presidential campaign entered its peak.[51]

Right-wing influencers and hyperpartisan media also enjoyed a significant advantage over the academic experts painstakingly evaluating bias data: they could simply ignore any inconvenient facts and yell. Any moderation action against right-coded figures or media—even if accidental and immediately reversed—could be framed for the MAGA online faction as further evidence that *Big Tech hates you*, riling up the crowd for a viral social media moment. The result was a burgeoning class of Perpetually Aggrieved influencers and media-of-one persecution profiteers, each with hundreds of thousands to millions of followers, beloved by the recommendation engine and often heavily monetized across multiple platforms, wailing incessantly about how the elites, mainstream media, and Big Tech were silencing them—and, by extension, you.[52]

Trump, in fact, had played up this narrative in 2019, soliciting stories via a web form from ordinary people who thought they'd been censored by Big Tech[53] (nothing appears to have come of the effort) and hosting a gathering at the White House for "censored" influencers.[54]

One of those who attended the influencer forum was Ali Alexander, then thirty-five years old. Alexander had increased his profile since Trump's 2016 election victory by stoking online conspiracy theories and building ties to established figures in Trump's sphere, such as conspiracy theorists Alex Jones and Laura Loomer, as well as Roger Stone, a former Richard Nixon advisor who had made a name as a "dirty trickster" for the right. Alexander had also cultivated support from more extreme figures in the Republican congressional caucus such as Representatives Mo Brooks of Alabama and Paul Gosar of Arizona. And he appeared to have some clout with tech leaders; then Twitter CEO Jack Dorsey had asked his opinion on whether or not to ban Alex Jones.[55]

Alexander had first gained prominence among those who followed the shenanigans of online political discourse when he accused the Somali-born Democratic representative from Minneapolis, Ilhan Omar, of marrying her brother. He went on to denounce then presidential candidate Kamala Harris for not being an "American Black" because her father had been born in Jamaica.[56] That earned him a coveted retweet from Don Jr., Trump's son; though later undone, it nonetheless helped to cement Alexander as a rising star of the Far Right ecosphere at the time. He was a talented influencer, acutely aware of the power of trolling and online vibes; in his own words, he was an "interpreter of energy for this period."[57] But he would only shoot to national celebrity—and infamy—as one of the key organizers of the "Stop the Steal" rally on January 6, 2021.

May 2020

The moderation aggrievement cycle truly took off in May 2020 with yet another Trump tweet about mail-in voting, "There is NO WAY (ZERO!) that Mail-In Ballots will be anything less than substantially fraudulent."[58] On the surface, it was just one more post in a litany of repetitive claims to establish and reinforce the pretext that if Trump lost, fraud was to blame. Once again, the fact-checkers got to work.

This time, however, Twitter's moderation team chose to apply the "inform" option to the president's post and labeled the tweet with a link to a fact-check declaring the claim "unsubstantiated."[59]

The decision was incendiary. Republican political leaders, media, and influencers exploded. Trump raged over the label in a subsequent pair of tweets: "@Twitter is now interfering in the 2020 Presidential Election. They are saying my statement on Mail-In Ballots, which will lead to massive corruption and fraud, is incorrect, based on fact-checking by Fake News CNN and the Amazon Washington Post…Twitter is completely stifling FREE SPEECH, and I, as President, will not allow it to happen!"[60] The post hadn't been taken down. It was fully visible. But it had been contextualized—using the counterspeech of a label. Two days later, Trump signed an executive order[61] calling for the regulation of social media companies that attempt to censor or engage in "political conduct," stating, "One egregious example is when they try to silence views that they disagree with by selectively applying a 'fact check.' "[62] (Biden revoked Trump's order the following year.)[63]

The platforms chose to expand their election integrity policies ahead of the 2020 race because—both in- and outside the United States—the propaganda of election delegitimization presents a risk to democracy.[64] Delegitimization matters because it rejects the meaning and authority of democratic processes, institutions, and officials, hollowing them out and incapacitating them over time.[65] This is distinct from healthy skepticism or mistrust of a specific politician or policy or evidence-based concern about an election outcome. Delegitimization rejects reasoned inquiry in favor of demeaning, undermining, and threatening or making baseless, conspiratorial accusations about its targets. The problem is not as simple as a losing candidate declaring himself the *real* victor and inciting political violence. Delegitimization has a cumulative impact, eroding belief in both the value of elections and the rightful authority of the government.[66] There had already been a demonstrable and growing deluge of lies, dirty tricks, viral rumors, and influence operations happening on platforms globally, particularly around elections. Doing nothing would have been unethical.

Despite the stated policies, the largest influencers—and the president himself—were treated with kid gloves. They had massive followings, and if their posts were moderated or their accounts banned, they and their factions could air their aggrievement loudly on other platforms, often going viral in the process. And so the sitting president and his surrogates, aligned media, and top political influencers began to tell crowds of his supporters—online, on television and radio, and in print—that the election was going to be stolen from them—over six months prior to Election Day. The leader of the free world, with his 80.2 million Twitter and 29 million Facebook followers, began his 2020 reelection campaign by undermining the very democracy he wanted to represent.

It was in this environment that the Election Integrity Partnership (EIP) began its work.

July 2020

By the summer of 2020, efforts to preemptively delegitimize the election had become almost formulaic: Trump would catastrophize—absent any evidence—about rigged elections, often on Twitter. The claims were covered across the media ecosystem: Fox News and other right-wing media discussed the allegations, while mainstream media debunked or contextualized them. Influencers and prominent figures would share the resulting stories with their audiences.[67] But something else was happening as well: ordinary Trump supporters had begun to proffer "evidence" to support the theme—things they observed happening around them, now interpreted in the context of voter fraud. A decidedly bottom-up process had begun: rumors advanced by members of the faction, based on little more than a photo and an assumption, snowballed from the bottom to the top, as influencers, media-of-one figures, hyperpartisan media, and sometimes Trump himself boosted them.

It seemed clear that social media would be the main front in something more akin to a sustained information war than a normal presidential campaign. The American public was going to be barraged with messages from both authentic networked activists and also malign actors. Who was responsible for determining the difference, and what was the appropriate response?

Some political factions had dedicated themselves to creating the kinds of networks necessary to move information in the modern communication ecosystem: influencers with hundreds of thousands of followers and crowds in the millions; media-of-one creators and hyperpartisan-aligned outlets that could turn tweets into content for subsequent rounds of viral sharing, across all platforms; a deep understanding of how to move a claim not only from the top down (from elites to the public) but from the bottom up. They understood the dynamics of both the propaganda machine and the rumor mill and had strategies for each.

State and local election officials, fact-checkers, and those tasked with trying to counter misleading viral stories about the integrity of the election did not.

It reminded me of my experience with the fight over the California vaccine bill in 2015: the people with the most accurate information were still on the periphery. They could communicate with mass media or publish a fact-check, but there was not much of a strategy for networked communication or rapid response. And it wasn't clear whether the audience would trust what they had to say.

Recognizing this challenge, a handful of student research assistants at the Stanford Internet Observatory approached our director, Alex Stamos, about the lack of support for election officials dealing with viral claims and disinformation. This led Alex to propose a joint effort with other research institutions to observe public social media conversations about voting and election integrity, with the goal of trying to triage what was starting to spread rapidly. That way, counterspeakers could quickly respond to burgeoning rumors.

The students had interned at the Department of Homeland Security's Cybersecurity and Infrastructure Security Agency (CISA), where they had worked on the services that the federal agency was providing to the roughly ten thousand local and state authorities who actually run elections in the United States. While communication lines on direct cyberattacks against election systems were open, they recognized that there was little in the way of communication between social media researchers, who could see when stories were getting lift, and state and local government officials tasked with ensuring free and fair elections. State and local officials had a difficult time determining what was worth responding to. They found it hard to tell whether something was likely to go viral or was just a post by a random guy with six followers who was wrong on the internet; small cases were better ignored to avoid inadvertently amplifying a lie with a correction. If a correction was needed, however, getting it out quickly mattered quite a bit.

Disinformation campaigns by hostile state actors were also a significant source of concern; investigating evidence of foreign manipulation had to happen during the campaign, not after. Tech companies would have to be included, since this would all be playing out on their infrastructures; they'd stated clearly that they would be on the lookout for foreign trolls and violations of their election integrity policies, but having another pair of eyes on their effort was important.

The government was, of course, undertaking its own independent efforts: CISA, run at the time by Trump appointee Chris Krebs, announced a plan for a Rumor Control website that would put out official clarifications of stories that attracted national attention.[68] The Federal Bureau of Investigation's Foreign Influence Task Force, established in 2017 by Trump appointee Christopher Wray, and the State Department's Global Engagement Center, tasked with countering foreign propaganda campaigns, were responsible for assessing state actor shenanigans. Adjacent to those efforts, the Elections Infrastructure Information Sharing and Analysis Center, a nonprofit group of state and local election officials from all parties and spanning all fifty states, had been established in 2018 to share information around cybersecurity and other threats to elections; addressing misinformation about election procedures and voting fell under their remit as well.[69]

There were many different stakeholders trying to ensure a free and fair election, but everyone was largely working in silos. Tech and government discussed threats, and there were communities of researchers within civil society and academia who occasionally collaborated, but there had as yet been no attempt at a nonpartisan, networked response in which entities good at detection collaborated with those adept at rapidly countering misleading claims. Politicians, tech companies, and academics had been talking about a "whole of society effort" to mitigate online election manipulation for years by the time the 2020 campaign kicked off. Now, the Election Integrity Partnership was going to try to create one.

Our team at Stanford Internet Observatory had studied narrative dynamics and disinformation campaigns in several non-US elections already. We regularly identified and examined inauthentic networks and state propaganda campaigns, publishing research and briefing the media, Congress, and relevant agencies about our findings. The other three core members of the EIP had similarly deep experience: the University of Washington's Center for an Informed Public was expert in how rumors spread during crises; Graphika, a company of "internet cartographers," specialized in online network analysis; and the Digital Forensic Research Lab of the Atlantic Council (a nonpartisan think tank) had years of experience investigating the mechanics of state actor and violent extremist manipulation campaigns globally.

Beyond the inner circle, we set up a tip line for outside partners, which included civil society organizations like the NAACP and AARP.[70] We reached out to the Democratic National Committee and the Republican National Committee (the latter never responded). And we set up basic "ticketing" infrastructure using a commercially available tool called Jira to keep track of what kinds of narratives were appearing and going viral, not only for the purposes of rapid response but so that we could do a comprehensive academic study of 2020 election narratives after the fact.

Most importantly, the Election Integrity Partnership scoped our work solely around false and misleading claims related to voting, including those that attempted to delegitimize the election; we had no interest in following every fib that one candidate told about another. Politicians lie; leave that stuff to the fact-checkers. We cared about understanding viral narratives that might impact people's right to vote or shape public opinion about the legitimacy of the election itself.

As it turned out, there was no shortage of those.

September 2020

The sitting president of the United States didn't just lay the groundwork for allegations of a stolen election months before voting began—his campaign also conscripted an "Army for Trump" to watch for shenanigans and provide "evidence" of his claims. Mail-in ballots loomed large. Allegations began to pop up about found mail, destroyed mail, lost mail, dumped mail, and, of course, forged or fake ballots. The rumor mill diligently worked whatever it could generate, no matter how flimsy, into the broader frame of the massive steal.

On September 23, for example, a couple of trays of mail were found in a ditch in Grenville, Wisconsin. Local media reported accurately on the story, noting the presence of three trays of mail that included some absentee ballots.[71] However, the story was quickly picked up by Jim Hoft, founder of the hyperpartisan conspiracist outlet Gateway Pundit. In his hands, the facts turned into dog whistles: "Democrats are stealing the 2020 election. Two trays of US mail were discovered in a ditch near Greenville, a rural area north of Appleton, Wisconsin. According to local officials the mail included mail-in ballots. The USPS unions support Joe Biden."[72]

The flimsy innuendo did its job—Hoft's story went viral on Twitter as political influencers like Turning Point's Charlie Kirk shared it to their millions of followers, who in turn amplified it themselves.[73] A few days after the viral moment, Wisconsin election officials clarified that the mail had not included any Wisconsin absentee ballots; months later, in February, further investigation revealed that a disgruntled postal worker had been responsible and that seven Minnesota ballots were returned to the state and processed.[74]

In another instance, a person took a photograph of ballot envelopes in a dumpster in Sonoma, California, and reached out to dozens of influencers, including one named Elijah Shaffer, who was working at the time for Glenn Beck's right-wing media outlet TheBlaze. "SHOCKING: 1,000+ mail-in ballots found in a dumpster in California," Shaffer tweeted. "They were allegedly discovered in the Republic Services of Sonoma County central landfill. The zip code '94928' on the ballots matches the county. These are original photos sent to me. Big if true."[75]

It was not true. Nonetheless, within hours after Shaffer posted, the Gateway Pundit wrote the theory into a news story: "EXCLUSIVE: California Man Finds THOUSANDS of Unopened Ballots in Garbage Dumpster—Workers Quickly Try to Cover Them Up—We are working to verify."[76] The first paragraph of the article contained the ever-present phrase "big if true." Other right-wing influencers and QAnon influencers began to retweet Shaffer's tweet and share the Gateway Pundit's article; eventually Donald Trump Jr., who had 5.7 million followers at the time, boosted the theory.[77] It went massively viral.

Local election officials tried to clarify that the mail in the dumpster consisted of old envelopes from the 2018 election that had been disposed of in accordance with the law.[78] It may not surprise you to learn that their tweet got a fraction of the attention—a few hundred likes and retweets. Gateway Pundit appended its headline in response—"County Says Returned Ballots from 2018?"—but then added a sentence undermining the effort to correct the record: "The county says the ballots were already opened. You can judge for yourself."[79] Everything is just a matter of opinion.

The most remarkable thing about the myriad "Waylaid Ballots" stories was how formulaic, how tropey, they actually were. The rumor mill sometimes directly repurposed old content and images, using them to imply that a new Waylaid Ballot event had just happened or had happened in a new place. The political influencers and hyperpartisan media exaggerated the facts or used innuendo to concoct a villain even if there was absolutely no justification. The crowd shared each rumor with professions of outrage, tagging in political influencers, fueling the algorithm. If the claim got enough attention or did a particularly good job of advancing the drumbeat of pervasive, perpetual fraud, huge influencers, like the president's sons, his inner circle, or the president himself, might also get involved. The effect of that potent formula—familiarity, novelty, and repetition—managed to create the perception that a handful of disparate events were frequent, connected occurrences. After all, where there's smoke, there's fire. The repetitive drumbeat of rumors about ballots reinforced Trump's framing that mail-in voting was bad and created a perception that any individual anomaly was part of a sinister plot to steal the election.

In each case of an actual misplaced or destroyed ballot, local media diligently pursued follow-up investigations; none revealed politically motivated fraud. However, the influencers and hyperpartisan media that boosted the rumors didn't promote the findings of those investigations. "Big if true!"—but not worth clarifying if proven false. By the time the facts were out, incentivized propagandists had already redirected the audience to the next outrage.

As the 2020 campaign progressed, hostile state actors *were* still in the mix, pretending to be Americans: Russia and China created some fake accounts and spammy propaganda. Actors linked to Iran ran a rather bold anti-Trump effort pretending to be the Proud Boys and sent emails threatening registered Democrats with violence if they didn't change their registration and vote for Trump; the Election Integrity Partnership worked on this investigation after receiving a tip from a group whose members were threatened. The intent of the Iranian effort, perhaps, was to get press coverage that reflected poorly on Trump supporters.[80] But, in all of these operations, the engagement was comparatively very low. While foreign interference remains a serious concern, the accounts that truly made claims go viral were the real American influencers and their factions, leveraging the mill and the machine.

Rumors Versus Misinformation Versus Propaganda

Armies of fact-checkers from PolitiFact, the *Washington Post*, the *New York Times*, and other publications worked hard to try to correct the record about viral rumors. But their contextualization of the stories primarily as mis- or disinformation misdiagnosed what was happening.

So let's pause the retelling of 2020 to address semantics. Again, rumors are not the same thing as misinformation. Where misinformation is false or misleading, rumors are unverified and ambiguous—the truth isn't yet known. Participants in the rumor mill share (and contribute to) a story that is evolving; the rumors that go viral are salient and seem plausible to the community.[81] Sharing them is a form of social participation.[82]

This distinction between rumors and misinformation may sound like some niche academic terminological debate, but here's why it matters: fact-checking efforts focus on correcting the record around very specific claims. A fact-checker may take nearly forty-eight hours to research and post. That's a lifetime in the age of social media, and the people sharing the rumor have long since arrived at some consensus about what happened. Political influencers, hyperpartisan media, and the faction have already cocreated a reality. The fact-checkers, meanwhile, are outsiders, often distrusted, from a different media universe. By the time their version of events is released, the invisible rulers have moved on.

Rumors are better managed with a rapid response that explains what is known, transparently acknowledges what is presently unknowable, and gives frequent updates—as CISA's Rumor Control website and local election officials' tweets and posts tried to do during the 2020 election.[83] Ideally, the person pushing back on the rumor is also trusted by the community—a local journalist, perhaps, or a local government, community, or religious leader.

But trust is the element in shortest supply. The rumor mill has always been an alternative to the official narrative, and rumors are most potent when people harbor suspicions about whether government, institutions, or media are telling the truth. Even though Trump was the head of the US government, many of his supporters saw him as outside it—fighting the Deep State, at war with the bureaucracies—and therefore trustworthy, while his own appointees were viewed with suspicion. Aligned political influencers—fellow members of the faction!—were seen as trustworthy. Institutions, mainstream media, and others on social media were not. It should not be surprising that in this time of low trust and high polarization, we are awash in viral rumors.

The influencer, as noted in Chapter 3, participates in both *simple contagion*, spreading basic, already-accepted ideas, and in the reputationally riskier *complex contagion* of bringing new theories from the periphery to the masses.[84] In the MAGA faction, the idea of a massive steal was not remotely risky—it was widely accepted. Political influencers amplified fraud and theft claims over and over again during the 2020 election campaign. When they did advance something riskier, it was by way of "just asking questions," with "big if true!" caveats, which offered a reputation-preserving way to participate even while advancing outlandish ideas.[85] While this manipulative rhetorical distancing is not new, it often goes unrecognized—especially when the rumor confirms preexisting biases.[86]

This problem is compounded by the incentives for influencers and crowds to spread rumors today. They offer the sharer an opportunity to look important and in the know, to grab attention in the factional conversation by dropping something shocking or sensational. The influencer has the power to decide, with a few clicks, whether a rumor about destroyed ballots will get a much wider audience or a mere handful of people will sit around discussing it in a lonely thread. And, of course, trading in rumors and outrage can also pay handsomely: it can drive people to a media-of-one outlet's article, or YouTube stream, or monetized podcast to learn the salacious details. The bombast and innuendo of Charlie Kirk has earned Turning Point USA millions and millions of dollars—many of which end up in Kirk's pocket, according to an investigation by the Associated Press.[87]

Members of a crowd are also incentivized to be part of the rumor mill. People gain clout within their communities by being the person who uncovered a connection or found the hidden "evidence" that retroactively fulfills the criteria of a popular allegation.[88] During Election 2020, ordinary people regularly tagged prominent influencers in their posts theorizing about suitcases outside polling places or envelopes in dumpsters. It was not uncommon to see users with MAGA-emoji-laden profiles that proudly listed the political influencers who followed or retweeted them: "RT'd by @donaldtrumpjr and @charliekirk11." People have always spread rumors to compare their thinking to that of others, to persuade or influence their communities, or just to feel the pride of being the person with the novel, shocking, or plain-old-fun gossip. The psychology of rumors hasn't changed; it's the technology for spreading them that has.

And, of course, once something is gaining some attention, hyperpartisan media is incentivized to cover what some people online are saying: "Maidengate Scandal Breaks: Democrats Allegedly Registered Women Under Their Previous Names," read one headline, giving oxygen to yet another Ali Alexander conspiracy theory.[89] The article then rambled on,

> A resourceful American using the Twitter handle SomeBitchIKnow has uncovered what appears to be one of the ways that fake votes were harvested in the 2020 election when she discovered that her mother's vote had been cast under here [sic] maiden name. Posting her discovery using #MaidenGate she spurred other women to check their ballot status under their maiden names at previous addresses and what happened next appears to have uncovered one of the ways that fake mail-in ballots for Joe Biden were harvested and counted.

The sentences in articles like this are couched in innuendo and insinuation. The headline focuses on the claim, which is often softened in the article with qualifiers like "allegedly" or "appears to have." This is the art of propaganda that goes into solidifying a rumor, introducing the claims to people who may have missed the moment on social media. It provides monetizable content for the hyperpartisan media, and people who go on to share the article may give the controversy a second bout of attention.

Some of the claims that spread in the 2020 election were demonstrable misinformation: elections are not held on Wednesdays, the dates of primaries are not a matter of subjective opinion, and Sharpie markers are actually just fine for plenty of ballots. But much of what went viral were rumors, insinuations about overwhelming conspiracies. These ricocheted between the mill and the machine with impressive velocity, solidifying further into "fact" with each repetition.

November 3, 2020: Election Day

Election Day began within this environment of pervasive mistrust. It was a hectic twenty-four hours for the Election Integrity Partnership: allegations of voting irregularities proliferated on social media across all platforms. Some were statements of frustration: people complaining about lines and machines, as we all tend to do. But the ones that tended to go viral were from people who had a bad experience with voting—a machine didn't read their ballot—and leapt to conspiracy as the explanation: *The poll worker in Maricopa County, Arizona, was giving Sharpie markers to Trump voters deliberately so the machine wouldn't tally the vote!*[90]

The theory about Sharpie markers, in fact, became one of the most viral rumors that day. The "Sharpiegate" conspiracy theory, as it came to be called, claimed that the use of Sharpie permanent markers by voters in Maricopa County invalidated their ballots. People who spread the theory alleged that election officials intentionally provided Sharpies to Trump supporters, knowing that the ink would not be properly read by the voting machines and would lead to their votes being discounted. Interestingly, conversations on platforms like Parler—in which nearly everyone was a like-minded Trump supporter—were fairly reasonable and initially skeptical of conspiracy theories as the rumors began; as EIP analysts saw these threads, we wondered if the fact that these folks didn't anticipate nasty attacks from other factions on the largely homogenous network put them in a more deliberative frame of mind. Some Trump voters even argued against the conspiracy theory, noting that the Sharpies had worked just fine for them. But as the rumor snowballed on other platforms, like Facebook and Twitter, the angrier voices prevailed.

Election officials and experts quickly debunked the conspiracy theory. Maricopa County officials publicly announced that Sharpies were, in fact, the preferred writing instrument for their voting system.[91] They emphasized that all properly marked ballots, regardless of the writing utensil used, were processed and included in the final vote count. But as always, their efforts at clarification did not get nearly as much attention as the initial rumors.

Fox News unexpectedly called Arizona for Joe Biden at 11:20 p.m. Eastern Time[92] on November 3, 2020, effectively calling the election. Three hours later[93] President Trump made a speech claiming victory nonetheless.[94] Mainstream media outlets interrupted the broadcast to point out that the president's claims were not legitimate—an unprecedented moment. Far Right broadcast outlets such as the One America News Network (OANN) and Newsmax, however, and the online machine of hyperpartisan media and influencers began alleging an outright *steal*. In the bespoke reality of those who had been immersed in fraud propaganda and rumors for months, Trump's prediction had come true.

Both MAGA influencers and the right-wing media machine kicked into overdrive, flooding the zone with possible explanations for how the loss—the steal!—had occurred. A voting machine company, Dominion, became a bogeyman, accused of flipping votes.[95] Steve Bannon hosted a guest who went on about a Central Intelligence Agency supercomputer changing votes in favor of Biden. Even those who did not make explicit allegations became merchants of doubt: Tucker Carlson, who privately texted his producer mocking the Dominion theory, gave an on-air master class in innuendo and insinuation. "We don't know how many votes were stolen on Tuesday night. We don't know anything about the software that many say was rigged. We don't know. We ought to find out." Sean Hannity, Maria Bartiromo, and other prominent anchors took a similar tack.[96]

Since the call had been made in Arizona, many theories of theft focused heavily on the Sharpie markers of Maricopa County. *#Sharpiegate* and *#StopTheSteal* exploded. By the next day, November 4, *#Sharpiegate* was continuing to build, amplified by right-wing influencers like Charlie Kirk, Dinesh D'Souza, and Steven Crowder. Local media and election officials in swing states like Pennsylvania and Michigan tried to stem the spread of panic by posting fact-checking articles about the use of Sharpies in their regions. But by that night, the outrage had shifted offline. Protesters gathered outside the Maricopa County Recorder's Office, waving signs, Sharpies, and, in some cases, firearms. The event was livestreamed for those following along in other states. The next night, a group of protesters returned and were met by Alex Jones, who added to the chaos by shouting his own wider-ranging conspiracies through a megaphone.[97]

November 2020

Election Day receded, but its drama did not. Now the social media companies had to decide how to handle this postelection unrest and whether to implement the "Break the Glass" measures (Facebook's term) they'd come up with during scenario planning exercises about election violence.[98] Break the Glass measures had been deployed before—for example, in advance of an election in Myanmar. Facebook limited reshared content and replaced it in the feed with more content from friends; the intervention reduced viral inflammatory posts and hoax photos.[99] Similarly, for the United States 2020 presidential election, the measures were designed to downrank content related to the election, including debunked claims about voting and fraud, and the distribution of live videos related to the election—an effort to balance preserving free expression with minimizing the risk of political violence. However, because of the distinctly one-sided nature of the claims, the policies also presented an optics challenge: the overwhelming majority of people violating them were supporters of President Trump. Taking action in response required a series of hard calls.

First, there was the question of the election misinformation itself, which had become centralized around one party's most prominent elites and influencers as they worked aggressively to delegitimize the election they'd lost. Fox News and other outlets reported stories of "irregularities" alleged to have occurred on Dominion machines. (The subsequent defamation lawsuit was settled for hundreds of millions of dollars; it revealed text messages showing that several famous pundits who were airing the theory publicly were at the same time privately dismissing it.)[100]

Meanwhile, Ali Alexander was on Twitter and its erstwhile video livestreaming app Periscope pushing the *#MaidenGate* conspiracy theory.[101] Steve Bannon's *War Room* podcast continued promoting the supercomputer conspiracy theory.[102] It sounds insane, but this theory—known as "Hammer and Scorecard," after the names of the alleged supercomputer and its supposed election-rigging software—and others like it were also aggressively promoted by none other than Rudy Giuliani and presidential advisor Sydney Powell, including in official lawsuits trying to, in their words, "stop the steal."[103] That phrase, coined by Roger Stone and made a rallying cry by influencers like Ali Alexander, was no longer simply an online hashtag. It was repeated, everywhere, in top-down propaganda from the president's most elite insiders.

Despite the outrageous implausibility of the theories, platform leaders were afraid of looking politically biased; they were fully aware that it would be easy for sympathetic congressmen and right-wing media to spin any content moderation as yet another example of purported anti-conservative bias: *Big Tech hates you and your values.* Or, alternately, *Big Tech hates free speech.* There had been one particularly notable incident during the 2020 campaign in which Twitter made a terrible moderation call on a story that Republican elites cared a lot about—and that turned out to be true. On October 14, 2020, the *New York Post* had reported on a laptop it had obtained, belonging to Hunter Biden, full of sensational images of drug use and nudity.[104] Other media outlets, including Fox News, were hesitant to report on the story without the ability to verify the material; the specter of Russian hack and leak operations, with forged documents mixed with real ones, loomed large.[105] The social media platforms, which were on high alert for a repeat performance by Russian intelligence and had "hacked materials" policies, had to decide how to moderate.

Facebook chose to "reduce" the story, limiting its distribution for a few hours while waiting for validation of the facts (EIP did not look at this incident, as it was out of scope; I personally thought this was a reasonable call).[106] Twitter, however, chose to block not only sharing of the photos from the laptop—which contained a lot of graphic nudes—but the link to the *Post*'s reporting as well, including in private direct messages between users.[107] Even after Jack Dorsey, then Twitter's CEO, apologized for the call and lifted the ban,[108] it became the canonical example that right-wing influencers could point to where "big if true!" had, in fact, been true. The suppression of a news story became emblematic of Big Tech censorship and overreach for right-leaning audiences, eventually becoming the centerpiece of exactly what the platforms had feared: a congressional inquiry by a highly partisan committee angry about content moderation.

As the unrest continued, new moderation concerns emerged. Facebook Groups, that tool of closed crowds, had become the de facto infrastructure for *#StopTheSteal* organizing. Several groups that popped up in the immediate aftermath of election night grew very large, very quickly: one had amassed more than three hundred thousand members in a twenty-four-hour time frame, with over a million more waiting to join.[109] Facebook implemented an array of Break the Glass policies: posts into groups that were frequent rule violators now required group administrator approval; users looking to share election-related content had to click through notices pointing them to reputable information sources; posts classified as having a high potential to incite violence were reduced in the feed; content from groups ineligible for recommendations was reduced in the feed.[110] It also began to take down certain large *#StopTheSteal* groups advocating for violent retribution, such as hanging the purported thieves (election officials) for treason.[111] Internal research from Facebook, leaked in 2021, documented the issue: "Stop the Steal movement was propagated by a small core of individuals coordinating to send thousands of invitations to Stop the Steal Facebook groups"—a form of growth hacking—"often using multiple accounts to do so—itself a violation of the platform's terms of service," one report read.[112] Yet the company took action against only a small fraction of the activity. A whistle-blowing former employee, Frances Haugen, released an internal after-action assessment titled "Stop the Steal and Patriot Party: The Growth and Mitigation of an Adversarial Harmful Movement" that detailed Facebook's missteps: "Because we were looking at each entity individually, rather than as a cohesive movement, we were only able to take down individual Groups and Pages once they exceeded a violation threshold," the report explains. "After the Capitol Insurrection and a wave of Storm the Capitol events across the country, we realized that the individual delegitimizing Groups, Pages, and slogans did constitute a cohesive movement."[113]

Another one of Haugen's leaked documents reveals the internal metrics that informed Facebook's decision: quantitative assessments of the percentages of hate, violence, incitement, slurs, white supremacist phrasing, militarized social movement terms, QAnon terms, and election delegitimization content within the posts of a given group. "Growth hacking may not always be bad," the mitigation assessment report reads, noting that "a democratic movement, a movement seeking human rights, or an advertising movement, may all employ legitimate techniques to grow their audience quickly. However, when the growth is mixed with the signals of harm we described above, this rapid growth indicates the spread of harm, and may indicate *coordinated harm*."[114]

Rather unsurprisingly, the report name-checks Ali Alexander. As *BuzzFeed* summarized, "Alexander, an early promoter of 'Stop the Steal' as a slogan, 'was able to elude detection and enforcement with careful selection of words, and by relying on disappearing stories'" (an ephemeral content feature in which posts disappear after a fixed period). "We also observed [Alexander] formally organizing with others to spread the term ['Stop the Steal'], including with other users who had ties to militias."[115]

In a since-deleted clip on Periscope, Alexander—who had started his political career working on John McCain's 2008 presidential run—highlighted his collaboration with GOP representatives Andy Biggs, Mo Brooks, and Paul Gosar. "We four schemed up [ways] of putting maximum pressure on Congress while they were voting," he said. That plan aimed to "change the hearts and minds of Republicans who were in that body, hearing our roar loud from outside."[116]

But even if Facebook was more aggressive in defusing *#StopTheSteal*, social media had begun to decentralize. The *human* social networks, assembled through People You May Know and recommendation algorithms and real-world friendships so long ago, simply reconstituted themselves on other platforms that were less likely to moderate them. Indeed, as Facebook took down the large *#StopTheSteal* groups, they reassembled in channels on Telegram—a platform that largely will not moderate—and even popped back up again on Facebook itself under different names (the Whac-A-Mole problem of content moderation).[117]

Then came a lull. In late November 2020, the threat, it seemed, had begun to wane. As the immediate threat of unrest passed, platforms shed their Break the Glass measures and returned to normal operations—for a time, anyway.

December 2020

EIP spent the months between the election and the insurrection reviewing the most viral rumors: the myriad ballot controversies, Sharpiegate, Dominion, MaidenGate, and Hammer and Scorecard, among others. As we studied the data in detail, what emerged was that a fairly small number of influencers were repeatedly successful at transmuting rumors of fraud into a massively viral propaganda campaign spanning media and social media. In addition to Trump's inner circle (such as Donald Jr. and Eric Trump), twenty or so "repeat spreaders" kept appearing in data archives chronicling the most viral rumors.[118] These were the modern-day propagandists, it seemed, with a unique talent for framing things *just so* for their highly active followers. Gateway Pundit and Mark Levin, media-of-one (or two). Charlie Kirk and Tom Fitton, longtime hyperpartisan power players. Jack Posobiec, of *#PelosiMustGo* and *#Pizzagate* fame. Extremely online shitposters like "Catturd2," as well as QAnon influencers like "prayingmedic." Between them, they had tens of millions of followers, a remarkable reach.[119]

It was clear that from the earliest days of the election, President Trump and his influencer entourage—alongside Republican officials, media-of-one figures, and hyperpartisan outlets like the Gateway Pundit—had undertaken a sustained effort to relentlessly assault the credibility of the American electoral system. The extent to which it was coordinated is unclear; in certain instances, videos and messaging were posted independently by core players at almost exactly the same time.[120] What matters more, perhaps, is that explicit coordination was no longer required.

The online factions driving The Discourse know what they're supposed to do when a sensational claim or pseudo-event drops: ideologically aligned influencers amplify the message; the crowd shares the content across platforms, propagating it alongside the algorithm; other influencers join in to offer their take, continuing to harness the outrage; and the cycle continues, until hopefully the claim trends, which can be parlayed into broadcast and print coverage. If something about the content or the trend violates platform terms of service and gets downranked, removed, or labeled, the influencers and the faction cry censorship—and may get a second-order trend about that as well.

Interestingly, however, the Right seemed to be much more effective at operating this kind of machine. While it would be nice to diffuse smears accusing us of left-wing academic bias by saying that the American political Left also did this—"both sides!"—the scale was not even close. There was an undeniable asymmetry in the rumors that went wildly viral during Election 2020: of the top 150 "repeat spreader" accounts, only 11 appeared to be Biden supporters.[121] And among those on the right, just a few dozen invisible rulers played an outsized role in helping major rumors to go viral.

The finding that right-wing "repeat spreaders" were involved in key viral false election rumors and that they had a powerful effect in shaping (or at least steering) public opinion in the 2020 election was not a shocking revelation for anyone paying attention. If you were on social media and followed primarily left-leaning or mainstream media, you might have encountered only the wildest rumors when they trended or were fact-checked. But if you were following a handful of the repeat spreader accounts, you would have been barraged by their content, transported into a bespoke reality in which the election was being seized.

The Right and the Left have different online norms and cultures, but they also have evolved a different digital media ecosystem. Many of the now prominent right-wing political influencers and media-of-one figures prioritized Facebook, Twitter, and YouTube from the beginning. A 2018 book titled *Network Propaganda*[122] by three prominent Harvard researchers traced the evolution of right-wing media, noting that by 2016, it already functioned very much like a closed system, with Fox News at the center overall and Breitbart having dominance on social media. Competition among the other outlets led to a steady ratcheting up of intensity of content in an effort to grab audience attention. This cycle led to the production of increasingly more sensational claims, innuendo, and insinuation, on broadcast as well as social media. Rumors about voting and election legitimacy did, of course, pop up on the left as well, as they have in elections past; the *Network Propaganda* authors note that what is shared on social media tends to be hyperpartisan on the left as well. In 2020, left-wing election rumors often involved theories of imminent right-wing violence, such as unverified allegations that spread on TikTok claiming that the Proud Boys were planning to show up to the polls to suppress or intimidate Black or queer voters. There were rumors that the US Postal Service, run by a Trump appointee, was going to slow down mail and take mailboxes out of circulation. But rumors and misinformation were unambiguously far more prevalent on the right, which has for years invested in an extensive propaganda ecosystem, spanning media, social media, and alt-platforms and supported by influencers.[123]

When the authors of *Network Propaganda* turned their attention to the 2020 election, looking at some of the same ballot accusations that we'd examined during EIP, they described the efforts to delegitimize mail-in voting as a disinformation campaign, highlighting the role that right-wing elites and the media propaganda machine played in perpetuating the claims.[124] Our work offered a look at the other side: the rumor mill provided bottom-up support, enabling the stories to ping-pong from one sphere to the other, despite the absence of any concrete evidence of widespread fraud or wrongdoing. Elites, and most prominently the president himself, created the frame of the "rigged election," setting an expectation of fraud among pro-Trump audiences.[125] The rumor mill generated "evidence" as the crowds of supporters worked to fulfill that expectation. Elites worked the new evidence into the overarching fraud narrative, reinforcing the "rigged" frame with each new story. Conspiracy theorizing is a collaborative endeavor: a group of true believers and accompanying questioners try to make sense of the world. Rumors are similarly collaborative and improvisational. Just like a melody passed back and forth by jazz musicians, these stories have a certain structure and purpose but are shaped through spontaneity and participation.[126] This has always been true, but there is now a technological infrastructure that propels the rumors and theories squarely into the view of not only the online audience but the elites in the propaganda machine who then continue to leverage them, picking up the melody and taking it further.

In the story of the Sonoma ballots, journalists at hyperpartisan media outlets initiated a rumor based on reader-supplied photographs, initially believing they had evidence of ballot fraud. However, when the facts emerged, they did not unambiguously recant. Instead they cast doubt on the correction and moved their audiences along.

In Sharpiegate, after encouraging supporters to keep close watch at the polls to uncover voter fraud, the Trump campaign helped to elevate the conspiracy theory generated from the anecdotal evidence. Again, local election officials' attempts at clarification were rejected and ignored—some influencers even reframed the clarifications as part of the plot.

In MaidenGate, Trump supporters saw the claims of a random woman online telling them what they wanted to hear—that there was a clear mechanism by which voter fraud was happening—and began to search for evidence to corroborate the theory. With the help of the mobilizing capabilities of Ali Alexander and the *#StopTheSteal* organizers, they made these rumors go viral. They never produced any hard evidence, however, to support their claims.

Meanwhile, election officials who had the actual facts about voting machines, Sharpie markers, and ballot drop boxes, especially at the state and local levels, were simply unable to break through. And when they spoke up, they were often harassed or threatened. Indeed, well into 2022, election deniers were still directing significant vitriol at the people who had studied, or tried to counter, the Big Lie.[127] One prominent allegation was that the Election Integrity Partnership had deliberately "targeted" these conservatives because of their beliefs. This was nonsense, of course, but the performative aggrievement played very well among the Far Right factions on Twitter.[128]

Social media companies did try to moderate this morass: they removed some posts, reduced others, and put labels on many more. They tried to adapt their policies to new and emerging claims and tactics. But enforcement was often irregular and ad hoc, which further fed resentment.[129]

Two months later, when the crowd gathered outside the Capitol on January 6, "Stop the steal!" was what they screamed.

January 6, 2021

On the morning of January 6, 2021, three distinct but overlapping online communities congealed in the real world, forming one angry crowd at the Capitol: QAnon believers, militia members, and ordinary Trump supporters. QAnon and the militia folks had been planning various actions in chat rooms and on message boards since Trump's loss. When he tweeted on December 19 that there would be a "big protest" in Washington on January 6—"be there, will be wild!"—rhetoric began to heat up. Twitter's Safety Policy team noted an escalation in violent language, and Discord shut down a server (a type of chat room) that began "coordinated planning."[130]

Groups like the Proud Boys had been banned from mainstream social media as far back as 2018. QAnon had been officially kicked off Facebook in October 2020, under the company's Dangerous Organizations policy. Some of the more vitriolic influencers from these communities had lost their mainstream accounts as well. As a result, several prominent Far Right influencers, such as longtime social media troll "Baked Alaska" Gionnet, were livestreaming the action in front of the Capitol on a collection of alt-platforms promising minimal moderation,[131] which had been steadily growing in popularity. In these places people who had been deplatformed on major sites could post threads speculating about whether to use "gallows or guillotines" or debate what kind of zip ties might best subdue congressmen.[132]

But the last group of the three is perhaps the most interesting: a large crowd of generally law-abiding people had come into town to express their support for the president. On that day, however, they broke through a security perimeter, attacked police, stormed the Capitol, vandalized the building, stole from the offices, and, in some cases, threatened representatives and called for the hanging of the vice president. Anti-Defamation League director Jonathan Greenblatt, who studies extremism, wrote that "79% of those arrested had no explicit connection to extremist groups. This suggests that a significant number of seemingly ordinary Americans decided that mob violence was an appropriate response to the election results."[133]

What convinced the ordinary people to join the mob?

Several factors lead groups toward extreme beliefs over time: members are largely like-minded; out-groups are demonized; individual members can see themselves in relation to more extreme members, which opens the door to become more radical; and dissenters can easily leave the group rather than fight to change norms or beliefs.[134] Some features on social media platforms inadvertently support these factors. Social media often facilitate "high-homophily" communities[135] (including via recommender systems), and it's easy for people to see just how many more followers and likes a more extreme member of the community may be getting with their rhetoric. This creates an incentive, for some, to become more extreme so as to garner some of that attention and clout for themselves.[136] Meanwhile, it's also easier for those who become uncomfortable to exit an online group—leaving, after all, only takes a click.

Over the months of the campaign, millions of nonextremists had come to hold the belief that the election would be stolen—and then, that it *had* been stolen. The president himself, whom they trusted and admired, asked for their help. His rhetoric at the rally was inflammatory. There was energy and excitement in the crowd at that moment and a shared belief in the righteousness of their cause.[137] As those who came planning for violence began their action, the energy cascaded through the crowd, which had been mobilized for action by influencers and elites not only at the rally but for months prior.[138]

One of the key influencers whipping up enthusiasm for the rally was the ubiquitous Ali Alexander. On December 7, 2020, he tweeted that he would "give [his] life for this fight." That message was highlighted by the Arizona Republican Party, who quote-tweeted, "He is. Are you?"[139]

Using a variety of social platforms, as well as live speeches in front of gatherings of Trump supporters, Alexander worked to inspire the crowd he hoped would attend his "Stop the Steal Rally." On December 23, a post attributed to him on Parler warned, "If D.C. escalates...so do we." A week later, he implicitly threatened a Washington hotel that had announced it would close to the public during the rally. "Let me just tell the media right now: if something bad happens to the Hotel Harrington, don't ask me to denounce it. I'm not taking your call. If something bad happens to the Hotel Harrington because they violated the civil rights, I'll call it karma."[140]

Directing his wrath at Congress, should it certify Biden's legitimate victory, Alexander cited the size of the crowd he expected to show up on the Mall that day. "Everyone can imagine what me and 500,000 others will do to that building," he wrote on Twitter. But he added, "We're going to convince them not to certify the vote on January 6 by marching hundreds of thousands, if not millions, of patriots, to sit their butts in D.C. and close that city down, right?"[141] He also noted, ominously, that those "patriots" might have to "explore options" if their sit-in proved unsuccessful.

And then, after months of hearing from influencers, right-wing media, and the sitting president—and after months of discussing the claims with the like-minded online—when the crowds converged at the Capitol, they chanted Ali Alexander's hashtag, under which the rumors had congealed: "Stop the Steal."

Notably, however, even as the normies stormed the building, many of the prominent influencers who had served as agitators earlier in the day or as speakers at one of the two rallies stayed a safe distance from the violence—and from accountability. Alexander bravely livestreamed from a rooftop several blocks away once the violence began.

At around 4:30 p.m., roughly two hours after the rioters stormed the Capitol, he posted a since-deleted video of himself overlooking the crowd, claiming it was peaceful and praising those who didn't go inside, but also noting, "I don't disavow this. I do not denounce this."[142]

Two days later, as the enormity of what they had done began to dawn on some of the participants, Alexander posted another video. "I didn't incite anything," he insisted. "I didn't do anything." He also used the growing backlash as an opportunity to fund-raise from his followers, saying that he was in hiding and needed $2,000 a day to pay for bodyguards and other expenses.

Oddly, he also appeared to claim he was being targeted by supernatural forces. "Witches and wiccans are putting hexes and curses on us," he said. But even as he tried to distance himself from actual participation in the attack, he could not resist defending it. "I do believe we own that US Capitol," he said. "So I'm not apologizing for nothing."[143]

I was watching a different livestream on January 6, 2021—one by Russian state media outlet RT, which subsequently covered the events with considerable glee. I felt frustrated; there had been ongoing academic debates about whether propaganda worked, whether rumors mattered, whether "fake news" had an effect, and whether online content could truly precipitate offline action. We debated whether media or social media bore "more" responsibility, as if those systems were still distinct. Yet here were crowds of people screaming the online slogan "Stop the Steal" and smashing Capitol building windows. It certainly suggested that what happened online did, indeed, matter offline—online vitriol wasn't just performative. Maybe just a small number of people had been sucked into the most divergent bespoke realities—but that small number of people had succeeded in making a spectacle certain to impact American politics for decades to come.

There were many influencers like Alexander who'd spent the months of the 2020 campaign continuously riling up the online crowds with one rumor after another, turning to ever more outlandish claims and explanations for how "the steal" had supposedly been carried out. The apex of this stream of lies, smears, and innuendo was a riot at the Capitol—an attempt to prevent the certification of the 2020 election for the victor, Joe Biden. And within forty-eight hours after a horrified nation watched the violence unfold, the rumor mill and propaganda machine would be at it again: It was *antifa* that had breached the building. The Deep State had planted hundreds of agitators in the crowd! Tucker Carlson, whose private text messages later revealed a full awareness that the fraud allegations were lies even as he'd entertained them, referenced the mysterious "they" in his evening monologue: "We got to this sad, chaotic day for a reason. It is not your fault; it is their fault."[144]

January 2021

After January 6, the major tech platforms found themselves breaking glass again: shutting down groups, downranking content, blocking hashtags, and removing accounts and posts that contained vaguely threatening language. On January 10, Ali Alexander was banned from Twitter, Venmo, Cash App, and PayPal—cutting him off not only from his audience but from his main methods of online fund-raising. The next day, Facebook and Instagram both banned him too.

Another very notable user was moderated in the days after January 6 as well: the leader of the free world. On January 8, 2021, Trump lost his Twitter, Facebook, and YouTube accounts (his suspensions were lifted in 2023). On January 12, approximately seventy thousand QAnon accounts were booted off Twitter. Facebook's News Feed curation algorithm was refocused to curate nonnews stories: the platform temporarily took its users back to the baby announcements and wedding photos of the olden days—the sort of content unlikely to spark political violence.

Moderation is a series of value judgments made by people who are trying to apply existing policies to make the best possible decision in the moment. Were the suspensions the right calls? It's hard to say; how should a platform enforce its policies if a sitting world leader decides to incite violence? Analysis of who got moderated suggested, to me, that policy enforcement was rather backward. Prominent accounts appeared to have misleading content labeled more frequently, which made sense. However, small accounts seemed far more likely to be taken down than powerful influencers with political clout whom platforms feared. But it was precisely the large accounts that had the actual power to incite, to make online rhetoric cause offline harm, because they had followers willing to listen to them. With great power comes great responsibility—and enforcement should reflect that.

As Facebook and Twitter culled some of the moderately sized repeat spreaders, however, these accounts moved to less moderated, conservative-aligned alt-platforms like Parler, free-for-all broadcast channels like Telegram, or encrypted group chat apps like Signal and WhatsApp, where they continued to grow their audiences. Only now, they branded themselves as martyrs who'd been victims of anticonservative censorship. (Several years later, in 2023, Elon Musk would give them "amnesty"—inviting tens of thousands of accounts back to Twitter after he purchased the company.)

In the days following January 6, there was an influx of new users on the alt-platforms. Some were left-wing trolls there to antagonize Trump supporters following the insurrection. The majority, however, were there because they anticipated that mainstream social media platforms might crack down on them too. It was a migration for the true believers: the connections were already present, the beliefs already entrenched, and these cozier spaces enabled the bespoke realities to flourish undisturbed. Amazon and Apple cracked down on one alt-platform, Parler, that had been used to coordinate the insurrection because they did not want to host unmoderated violent content.[145] This, too, was a very polarizing decision. People across the political spectrum were alarmed that an infrastructure provider could take down a whole platform.

Content moderation is a thankless, never-ending game of Whac-A-Mole. In the case of election misinformation or rumors, the reality is that the largest influencers can simply reconstitute their communities elsewhere. Hyperpartisan media, podcasts, and livestreams find a place to thrive. While social media have created an infrastructure for the propaganda machine and rumor mill, demand for the content (and the social connections surrounding it) mean that no one platform's moderation policies can make it go away or wrench people out of bespoke realities.

January 8, 2023: Brazil

The bespoke reality in which Trump had won and actual reality in which the votes had clearly gone in the other direction came into violent contact on January 6, 2021. The propaganda machine primed the audience to believe that the election would imminently be stolen from them, and the rumor mill produced "evidence," amassing photos of everything from discarded ballot envelopes to hapless poll workers. Influencers mediated between the two, serving as opinion leaders for content coming from the top and producing their own, which in turn was picked up by crowds, algorithms, and often eventually media. The effort spanned the entirety of the social media environment as claims were discussed on both mainstream and alternative social media platforms, on message boards and Telegram channels. Rather than the public discussing what the media reported, the media often reported on the online chatter: *People on the internet are saying…*

Following the Trump presidency, a number of Trump acolytes turned their attention to Brazil. Supporters of the outgoing Far Right president Jair Bolsonaro—a former army officer dubbed "the Tropical Trump" for his pandemic tirades against masks and allegations of election fraud—were denouncing the October election of leftist Luiz Inacio Lula da Silva, more commonly known as Lula, and calling for a military intervention.

Bolsonaro's Far Right supporters used Facebook, Instagram, and Telegram to broadcast their calls for action, while using the encrypted chat app WhatsApp for more detailed planning. Former Trump advisor Steve Bannon coined the phrase "Brazilian Spring" while protesters wielded signs in English saying "*#BrazilWasStolen*." Ali Alexander went onto social media to effectively argue in favor of a military coup to overturn the election, saying, "Military can step in. This is why they're rewriting the Electoral Count Act. We were legal Jan 6th. Military in Brazil would be legal now."[146]

On January 8, the massed crowds that had gathered to camp out in the capital, Brasília, rose up and stormed the presidential palace, the congress, and the supreme court, smashing windows, vandalizing statues and artwork, and occupying official offices. Ali Alexander once again remarked on the situation from afar, this time posting to Truth Social: "I do NOT denounce unannounced impromptu Capitol tours by the people." A day later, he was reinstated to Twitter as part of billionaire tech entrepreneur and self-declared "free-speech absolutist" Elon Musk's amnesty program for previously banned users.

However, there was a key difference between January 8, 2023, in Brazil and January 6, 2021, in the United States. On January 8, 2023, Lula had already been sworn in. And Bolsonaro was ensconced in a friend's Miami home, sleeping in a child's Minions-themed bedroom. The resulting riot, therefore, was more of an inchoate rage than a serious effort to stop the transfer of power, and the police dispersed the throngs in the days that followed.

These perpetual outrage machines—and the fact that so many people leap instantly to the assumption of malice or the creation of a conspiracy theory when their preferred political outcome doesn't materialize—should scare us. While rumors may feel compelling in the moment, where the US election is concerned, the claims have consistently been found to be false, even nonsensical, when dispassionately investigated. The 2020 election has now been litigated in at least sixty-three court cases, and none has found evidence supporting a "steal."[147] Text messages from right-wing media elites reveal full awareness that Trump lost. And yet certain factions remain firmly rooted in bespoke realities; although the percentage of Republicans who believe that the election was stolen peaked in January 2021, it has remained above 50 percent through 2023.[148] Elected officials such as House Republican Jim Jordan, who voted not to certify the election, began to pander to that base by targeting the people who *studied* the Big Lie.[149] His effort reframed work examining the viral narratives underlying Stop the Steal—including the work of the Election Integrity Partnership—as a plot that had somehow *suppressed* these viral claims. This was nonsense, but as we will discuss in Chapter 8, the performative aggrievement played very well among the Far Right factions on social media, and the investigations and lawsuits took a significant toll.[150]

As for Ali Alexander, in June 2022 he testified for three hours in front of a federal grand jury looking into the January 6 attack and gave

US House's January 6 Committee all of his communications with Roger Stone from the day of the riots. He was briefly involved in the proto-presidential campaign of Kanye "Ye" West in early 2023 but was then caught up in a scandal related to inappropriate solicitation of personal imagery. Amid the internecine squabbling among Far Right factions vying for Trump's attention in the wake of the defeat, and with social media mostly shunning him after the scandal, Alexander largely receded from public view. But his contribution to the election delegitimization canon—"Stop the Steal"—is indelible.

6

Agents of Influence

It began with a picture of a dead horse.

"Another poor animal ☹," the Instagram poster noted, adding the hashtags "*#ColumbianChemicals #NewOrlean*." What seemed like a typo in the name of the famous Louisiana city would prove significant much later.

It was September 11, 2014, the thirteenth anniversary of the attacks on the World Trade Center and the Pentagon. And, as on every September 11 since 2001, residents of the United States were more on edge than they were on other days. Each anniversary brought with it trepidation about a copycat taking advantage of the day's somber significance to launch a new attack.

And so audiences reacted with some alarm as ominous posts suddenly began appearing on several social media platforms. The hashtag *#ColumbianChemicals*, referring to a black carbon factory in Centerville, Louisiana, began to appear alongside other hashtags like *#chemicalaccidentLouisiana* and *#DeadHorse*, seeming to suggest that something had gone horribly wrong. The proliferating tweets referencing *#ColumbianChemicals* were implying that there had been an explosion—and a possible leak of dangerous chemicals—at the factory. Some accounts promoting the hashtag were tagging prominent American politicians to make them take notice: "@PatrickBuchanan 'Patrick, is this really ISIS who is responsible for *#ColumbianChemicals*? Tell @Obama that we should bomb Iraq!'"[1] Other accounts linked to YouTube videos showing smoke and explosions or doctored screenshots of a website with "CNN" in the URL and a "Breaking News" caption alerting the world to the explosion.[2]

The content wasn't limited to accounts posting into social media hashtags. There were also clones of local news websites that covered the situation. Some local residents reported receiving text messages alerting them to an explosion in the area. A Wikipedia page describing the supposed incident materialized, and a Facebook page called "Louisiana News" posted an article about what had purportedly occurred; the page had been created sometime in August 2014 and by September 11 had amassed over six thousand likes.[3] A video appeared on YouTube showing footage of the Islamic State (ISIS) claiming responsibility for the attack; the Facebook page made note of the claims, and the video was cited on the Wikipedia page.

Meanwhile, baffled Columbian Chemicals executives posted a press release refuting the claims and text messages: there had been no explosion. And local reporters found no evidence of any dead horses or billowing smoke in the vicinity of the plant.

Yet, on social media, the conversation continued. Social media researchers noted nearly one thousand distinct participants talking about the supposed event.[4] And then the chatter gradually muted and fizzled, as online conversations tend to do.

No one scanning their screens on Twitter that day knew what had actually happened. The event was deemed a "hoax"; we weren't yet applying the vocabulary of propaganda eras past, like "disinformation campaign," to describe online manipulation. There was no immediately obvious attribution; some people speculated that perhaps the fabricated explosion story was retaliation for a business dispute, intended to harm the company's reputation. But baked in to how this particular incident was faked, and how the rumor materialized online, was an ever-so-slight clue—something that would prove to foreshadow an insidious new arena of politics and electioneering in America. Some of the posts used curious grammar: the typo "New Orlean" in some tweets, which was a rough transliteration of the city's name in Russian. A few social media researchers wondered if the hoax had been a Russian effort.[5]

It would be another nine months before *New York Times* investigative journalist Adrian Chen would attribute the hoax to the instigators behind it.[6] It was the work of the Internet Research Agency (IRA), a "troll farm" seemingly owned by a man named Yevgeny Prigozhin, an oligarch with close ties to both Vladimir Putin and entities useful for Kremlin operations ranging from the informational (the propaganda outlet Federal News Agency) to the kinetic (the private military company Wagner Group).[7] Prigozhin would go on to become far more famous and notorious for running a multiyear operation targeting American citizens with disinformation and propaganda during the 2016 US presidential election,[8] for his extensive involvement in the 2022 Russian invasion of Ukraine,[9] and finally for marching Wagner troops into Russia in an act of mutiny and then dying in an "aviation incident" two months to the day later.[10] The Columbian Chemicals hoax, it turned out, was one of the first salvos in a rapidly evolving Great Power information war that the United States wasn't fully aware it was fighting.

And it took the form of an online rumor. The propaganda machine and the rumor mill had merged, not only for ordinary people but for nation-states as well.

A New Shade of Gray

Governments have run propaganda campaigns for centuries. Sometimes they aim to influence the government's own citizens: recall that Edward Bernays got his start as a propagandist for the Creel Commission in World War I, selling the war to the American public.[11] Democracies throughout history have wrestled with establishing appropriate directives for how the government should work to persuade the public, trying to draw lines between persuasion or public service content and propaganda. Following World War II, Congress passed the Smith-Mundt Act—formally known as the US Information and Education Exchange Act of 1948—significantly limiting the United States in propagandizing to its own citizens while permitting it to peddle propaganda internationally. By the 1940s, many democratic nations had created state-funded outlets, such as Voice of America (1942) and the British Broadcasting Corporation

(BBC) (1922). There was a spectrum of entanglement: Some outlets enjoyed editorial independence even if their funding came primarily from the government. Some countries established restrictions for state media engagement with domestic publics. Others did not.

Authoritarian regimes did not wrestle quite so much with the ethics of propagandizing to their own citizens. Establishing leaders as demigods, building cults of personality, and aggressively promoting the party line are long-established authoritarian strategies carried out through controlled media. The leaders who leverage such campaigns deliberately point the messaging apparatus of the state inward, using it to reinforce ideology and slogans to keep their publics in line. They often also work to limit the presence of outside information, restricting access to or banning outlets and channels from abroad.

In the information ecosystems of earlier eras, it took significant resources to amass a media apparatus suitable for running propaganda campaigns. Broadcast technology was not cheap. However, given the importance of persuading (or controlling) one's own citizens and the value of propagandizing to citizens of rival nations, many powerful countries invested in building up the resources necessary to spread their messages far and wide. As new communication mediums emerged and technologies evolved, state actors quickly incorporated them into comprehensive propaganda strategies. Every emerging technology with the potential to reach large audiences was loosed onto the playing field. Radio, for example, created the opportunity to reach massive numbers of people at once, without the heavier lift of distributing print content.[12] Indeed, "modern" propaganda, Jacques Ellul argued in the 1960s, would not have been possible without the technological advances of mass media.[13]

State propaganda was often conducted in overt and attributable ways: demonstrably state-affiliated media properties, or *white propaganda*, were clearly the voice of the government, and there was no question about the agenda of the messenger. But there have always been more covert efforts in the mix as well. Military theorists and propaganda scholars use the metaphor of the monochromatic spectrum to describe attributability: *gray* meant that the source of the message was concealed enough to offer plausible deniability (funding or personnel ties between the outlet and government might be found with some digging), while *black* referred to content or outlets that were actively misattributed. Black propaganda outlets, sometimes also called *front media*, were designed to look wholly independent of the state. They were deliberately positioned as if they belonged to someone else entirely—and sometimes even as if they belonged to the target of their messaging. This active misattribution strategy tacitly acknowledged that people are more inclined to trust particular speakers, such as members of their own communities or local media; thus, front outlets masqueraded as messengers that would be well received to increase their persuasive power.[14]

The propaganda machine has long been a deliberate, strategic, top-down system; media and government (sometimes synonymous) played a significant role in what was communicated to the public. With each technological shift—from print, to radio, to TV—governments worked to maintain control of the information environment, and propaganda adapted to fit what the new medium made possible (while still leveraging older distribution channels as well).

And then the internet arrived.

By 2012 the world understood that social networks, particularly Twitter, YouTube, and Facebook, were profoundly powerful tools, giving ordinary people significant influence and reach. Scholars described a battle for perception between the elites who controlled broadcast media and the activists who used digital media: people could learn more about what was *really going on* through images and commentary online, particularly in countries where the government largely controlled TV and radio.[15] Messaging platforms for convening and inspiring online crowds to act in the "real world" could topple regimes. The Arab Spring in 2010 and 2011 became emblematic of the real-world power shifts that networked activism could achieve.[16] Authoritarian governments had taken notice, and so had US leaders. Alec Ross, a technology advisor in the Barack Obama administration, observed from his experience working in the White House, "I think the Internet is the single most disruptive force for the sovereign nation-state since the concept was founded with the 1648 Treaty of Westphalia."[17] Ever-larger audiences became chronically connected to a burgeoning collection of social media platforms; influencers, algorithms, and crowds as we know them today took shape; and we entered the age of *computational* propaganda.[18]

Early Efforts

Activists and crowds of ordinary people indeed had more power than ever before, but formidable, well-resourced governments certainly did not simply give up. Governments around the world began to realize the power of the new bottom-up system of influence—and, as in all technological shifts past, set about incorporating it into their own propaganda strategies. Strategies already used on broadcast media were tweaked for the new infrastructure.

In the United States, the Pentagon began to maintain overt, attributable propaganda websites, Facebook pages, and Twitter accounts in 2008 through a program called the Trans-Regional Web Initiative (TRWI).[19] Military combatant commands, at the time largely focused on counterterrorism, used them to communicate US views to locals in the regions where the military operated. These sites, which did contain language declaring who was behind them, were a natural technological evolution from pamphlets, news articles, and radio broadcasts.

State media from other countries began to go online as well, taking advantage of the opportunity to cheaply reach large audiences: Russian state media outlet RT established a presence on YouTube and was particularly adept at recognizing the lift it could get from algorithms inclined toward the sensational. Some of the earliest RT YouTube content, beloved by the recommendation engine, was disaster porn such as footage of amusement park ride collapses and tsunamis—the kind of content that users would engage with, reinforcing to the algorithm that RT content should be suggested to others.[20] As far back as 2009, some of China's flagship state media properties had established Facebook pages, using jaw-dropping images of landscapes and cute pictures of pandas in their audience-growth strategies.[21] By 2023, several Chinese state media outlet Facebook pages had hundreds of millions of followers—reaching the publics of other countries even as the Chinese Communist Party (CCP) prevented China's own citizens from accessing Facebook. Governments primarily still used social media as a broadcasting tool: posting content but not engaging with the audience. Still, platforms delivered significant potential for new reach, particularly because paid ads made it possible to target posts at specific audiences worldwide.

Even as the propaganda outlets of other states came online, however, the US Congress decided in 2013 to cut funding for the TRWI as its impact was unclear. Was anyone reading the messaging on the ten or so websites producing the content? Engaging with the accounts? The effort was something of a mixed bag. And so Congress terminated the contract.[22]

In a rather remarkable turn of events, multiple laid-off US contractors who'd worked on the program were quickly picked up ... by Russian state media outlet Sputnik. The division between Congress and the Department of Defense (DoD) on the importance of modern information operations played out in the media: "What seems to be clear is that the anti–status quo powers in the world today—Russia, China, Iran, and the Islamic State—know the value of information warfare and invest heavily in it," former Voice of America director and DoD information strategy advisor Robert W. Reilly commented in 2016, reporting on the former US contractors' move to Sputnik.[23] "It's a powerful illustration of who takes information warfare strategy seriously and who doesn't." One of the employees, who rose to a leadership role at Sputnik, argued that the decision to work elsewhere was a matter of not patriotism but rather simple economic self-interest. (Years later, in 2017, websites that shared technical indicators with the TRWI came back online; the Pentagon, it seemed, had decided to try again.)[24]

By 2015, "white propaganda" online had become the purview of not only states but also insurgent groups and terrorist organizations. Social media helped capture audiences' attention by pulling them directly into the action. ISIS, a radical Islamist terrorist organization operating primarily in Iraq and Syria, was particularly good at recognizing how to capitalize on online amplifiers. It had begun to amass a following and a recruiting operation on Twitter as it worked to position itself as a caliphate, a force to be reckoned with. The propaganda was not subtle or in any way concealed: the prominent black flag iconography throughout was instantly recognizable to anyone who saw it. Photos glorified fighters as they rode in convoys on the backs of pickups, bearing potent weapons. Terrible videos showed beheadings and other atrocities to instill fear and awe. Recruitment videos that looked like video game promo reels trolled the global powers, pointing to US coalition losses on the battlefield while entreating young men to come join the victorious side. The content was, essentially, brand-building—another example of the fine line between propaganda and public relations. It told a very old story: join us in this righteous cause, and we will give you meaning, comradeship, and glory. But it was uniquely "online": the jihadi brides posted like any other lifestyle influencer, sharing photos of themselves in black chadors next to rugged fighters and new babies, as the fighters tweeted selfies in which they fired guns, prayed, and even cuddled kittens.[25] Recruiters reached out to digital fans, directing them to secret chat rooms to continue the radicalization process.

ISIS's online content appealed to individuals, often disaffected twentysomethings who felt they had very little else going for them. The propaganda spoke to a deep human need to belong, to have a mission. On multiple occasions, ordinary people, inspired by what they saw, declared allegiance to ISIS in social media posts and went off to commit atrocities—creating "propaganda of the deed"[26] that the terrorists used to generate more attention and further recruitment.

Even though they ran print magazines and a radio station, ISIS focused heavily on social media propaganda. The passionate online faction—the few thousand highly active accounts working to amplify ISIS's messages[27]—used social media as it was designed to be used. Twitter's algorithms inadvertently helped ISIS along, suggesting jihadi accounts via "who to follow" recommendations, even as Twitter hemmed and hawed about how to handle the approximately forty-five thousand to ninety thousand accounts linked to the group.[28] ISIS made regular use of automated bots to aid in its distribution, and the black flag iconography was pervasive—both tactics that were easily discoverable with moderation technology. But *whether* to moderate was the question for some time: "One man's terrorist is another man's freedom fighter," said an anonymous executive in 2014,[29] noting that Twitter had long permitted political dissidents with extreme views. If Twitter were to moderate ISIS, would that open the door to the expectation that it would moderate other groups or define who was a terrorist and who was not? Facebook, meanwhile, banned the group as part of a comprehensive antiterrorism policy.[30]

After several incidents, including the terrible and tragic beheading of US journalist James Foley, Twitter began to reevaluate its policy and took down some of the accounts—leading ISIS to issue death threats against executives at the company.[31] Yet ISIS accounts were still easily visible in November 2015; after the Bataclan massacre, in which ISIS killed 130 people at a concert venue and stadium in Paris, fanboys celebrated on Twitter.[32]

ISIS illustrated, once again, that propaganda could have an effect in the "real world": women *were* responding to the influencer content of the jihadi brides and heading off to Syria;[33] disaffected young men *were* pledging allegiance to ISIS and then committing acts of terrorism. The appeal did not have to be widespread to have profound repercussions. The US government, meanwhile—still primarily accustomed to broadcast messaging—was both limited and not particularly adept in the social media space.[34] State Department bureaucrats began tweeting earnest messages at teenagers and twentysomethings—"Think Again, Turn Away"—but it was unclear if they were dissuading anyone who found ISIS content appealing.[35] The digital-native ISIS fanboys, steeped in internet culture and having an innate sense of what actually went viral, eviscerated this messaging with memes—which were increasingly becoming the preferred form of propaganda for the extremely online.[36]

I had followed the rise of ISIS's propaganda machine, enthralled and horrified by their ability to co-opt social media platforms like Twitter. This was shortly after I'd spent months deeply studying anti-vaccine networks and narratives. Here was another distinct community, I thought, that was having far more success capturing attention online than their real-world numbers would have predicted. Then the two things unexpectedly came together: I was invited to participate in a 2015 United States Digital Service project, working with the State Department to assess both ISIS's social media presence and the US government's response. It was fascinating work spanning both network analysis (how the messages spread) and brand analysis (what ISIS was trying to portray). I often thought of Adrian Chen's article on the Russian trolls—"The Agency"—which had stuck with me. If political activists and terrorist organizations alike had devised ways to use these systems to enhance their reach and power, surely adversarial nation states like Russia and China had as well. If they were running bot accounts, who was looking for them? Surely they would be doing it more covertly. What *was* the appropriate response? The US government countertrolling terrorists didn't seem to be particularly effective, but it was also unclear how the social media companies would come down on addressing the problem... or whether they should be making such important strategic decisions on their own.

Social media researchers working on the ISIS challenge began to lay out early visions for a path forward that might prevent the unwanted censorship of dissidents while limiting the reach of violent extremists: moderation had to be transparent so that the public could understand why users were being suspended. Given the tendency of accounts to "respawn" when platforms paid attention to other issues, moderation had to be consistent. There had to be recognition that platforms should not be the single authority for dealing with the issue; governments should collaborate, and input from activists worldwide should be taken into account.[37] And yet, takedown requests from governments were also a potential source of concern and should be handled very carefully. These early principles were broached by both platform teams and outside researchers, but often separately and with little discussion between them.

The State Propaganda Machine Co-opts the Rumor Mill

The internet, and then social media, expanded propaganda in terms of who could produce it, what channels it appeared on, and what style it adopted. Now that state actors had access to both broadcast and social media, they enjoyed new capabilities: overt broadcast (i.e., white propaganda on television) expanded its messaging channels into overt social media (white propaganda on Facebook). Covert broadcast—front media outlets—also expanded into creating online websites. But the new capacity of "covert social" changed the game for states interested in manipulating adversary publics outside their borders, inspiring new strategies useful not only for persuasion and activation but also for distraction and disorientation.[38]

There is a rich history of black propaganda, or disinformation, campaigns leveraging fake personas and front media to persuade or demotivate adversaries. This type of campaign also evolved with the technology of the times. In 1941, for example, Winston Churchill created a black propaganda team to target Germany, led by Denis Delmer, who'd worked as a German-language broadcaster for the BBC. They worked to create perceptions of military campaigns going poorly and tension on the German home front (stories about wives of deployed soldiers sleeping with Nazi officials), mixing the propaganda with popular music and cover-appropriate rants about the evil Brits. One operative working on behalf of the British effort, German exile and writer Peter Seckelmann, took on the persona of "Der Chef" (the chief), a disgruntled but committed Nazi officer who delivered lurid nightly broadcasts expressing outrage at the lazy and compromised Nazi military leaders who were failing Adolf Hitler—failing *the cause*. Der Chef used explicit, graphic language to describe their duplicity; stories of sexual depravity and egregious behavior abounded, alongside persona-appropriate criticism of the enemy (Churchill, in this case, was condemned as a "drunken old cigar-smoking Jew"). Delmer called it "propaganda by pornography." Aiming low and creating something sensational and shocking, he knew, would ensure attention: "I took an enormous amount of trouble over the Chef's erotica and devoted many hours of patient research to finding ever new forms of sexual depravity to attribute to our victims in the Hitler machine."[39] Der Chef was one character among many; other personas were a bit more professionally news-like. While it has always been difficult to measure the effects of propaganda campaigns, British assessments at the time suggested an "ever-widening audience," and interviews with U-boat prisoners found that German servicemen had been listening.[40]

Human nature has largely held constant in the intervening eighty years: sensationalism still sells, and algorithmic incentives make its dissemination ever easier. Social media's unique affordances, however, revolutionized black propaganda and disinformation campaigns, making persona accounts and front media properties significantly easier to run.[41] It became effortless to simultaneously conceal one's identity and connect directly to targets on social media by way of ads, audience building, and one-on-one chats. State actors have long leveraged fake personas in broadcast and print outlets, with made-up journalists authoring or laundering propaganda from one outlet to the next. But it was extremely risky, costly, and difficult for state actors to participate directly in peer-to-peer chatter networks (like those in Decatur) that more directly influence group opinion; they would have to find ways to become part of the community, and the potential reach was too limited to justify the effort in most circumstances.

Some governments, including those of the United States, China, and Russia, attempted to achieve deep influence within targeted communities via covert operations involving *agents of influence*: people with ties to a community the state wished to target, recruited to surreptitiously advance its aims.[42] Sometimes agents of influence are paid; often they are ideologically aligned. Generally they enjoy a high degree of credibility and usually enough visibility to be useful for shaping public opinion—be they artists, academics, journalists, or government officials. Another covert influence operation strategy was to infiltrate dissident groups or protest movements, including directly via spies, but this was a risky and time-consuming process. One mistake could undermine the whole dangerous and extremely costly operation.

But the culture shift brought about by social-networking platforms made it both easy and normal to make new online-only friendships and chat for hours without ever seeing the other person's face. Joining Facebook groups and Discord servers for activism and participating in direct messaging channels with people whose real names we may not even know are common online behaviors. There's an old saying from a *New Yorker* cartoon of a dog at a keyboard drawn during the days when anonymous chat groups were just becoming popular: "On the Internet, no one knows you're a dog."[43] Social media made anonymous friendships normal. They made it easy to be whoever you wanted to be. And it was free! Now the propagandist could participate very directly in shaping public opinion, speaking as a fellow member of the community from a seat at a desk an ocean away. Trolls run by foreign governments could in effect drive the rumor mill, offering a whole new set of opportunities both for steering consensus reality and for tearing it down.

From Russia with Likes

In 2018, two and a half years after the work examining ISIS propaganda, the bipartisan leadership of the Senate Select Committee on Intelligence (SSCI) asked me to gather a team to examine a large data set of the IRA's activities from 2014 to 2018. The data had been turned over to SSCI by Alphabet, Facebook, and Twitter; the companies had attributed the accounts to Russia and estimated that over a hundred million users had seen the content.[44] The data set included both paid and organic content from the IRA's Facebook pages, YouTube channels, and Instagram and Twitter accounts, as well as engagement counts and some metadata. Using the data provided by the platforms as a jumping off point and adding in lists of accounts published by Reddit and tumblr, my team quickly found additional IRA presence across the internet—on websites, in comment sections, and even on Pinterest, the game Pokémon Go, and the Far Right alt-platform Gab.

In its early days the Internet Research Agency ran a few more Twitter campaigns similar to *#ColumbianChemicals*. One, which involved a rumor about poisoned turkeys from Walmart, was posted on a message board on Thanksgiving 2015; it, too, was backstopped with a fake Wikipedia page and fabricated news coverage.[45] However, once again, the hoax claims were outlandishly sensational, and the accounts hadn't built up any credibility. Accounts springing up to talk about dead horses and poisoned turkeys, with no prior history and few followers, were not particularly persuasive—they might be able to temporarily capture attention and cause confusion, but they did not have nearly the kind of reach or resonance that authentic participants in a conversation could have. Their potential for impact was limited. Thus, by late 2015 the Russian trolls had evolved their strategy: they prioritized creating distinct personas with very specific identities, building up followers, and connecting with a community. Since American communities on the internet had already sorted into identity-based and partisan factions, the IRA found itself in the convenient position of primarily throwing gasoline on already-lighted fires.

Much of the media coverage of the IRA effort focused on its election shenanigans. But the broader story of how they operated reveals quite a lot about how adept propagandists can leverage internet culture by performing an identity and building up relationships and clout within an online faction over time—even via simple actions such as inserting fake persona accounts into viral-hashtag games or trying to catch the attention of influencers with a well-timed, quippy reply.[46]

The Russian interference effort was happening at the same time as the State Department's rather lame efforts to tweet at ISIS and shortly after Congress cut military spending on overt propaganda. But the IRA was staffed by twentysomethings familiar with meme culture who recognized that identity was foundational to influence on the internet and that segments of the American public were already living in factional bespoke realities. Memes and in-group language didn't replace the long-form narrative propaganda of front media or overt state messaging, but they were a critical addition—with potential for far more direct impact.

On each platform, the trolls presented themselves as members of the American communities they targeted. The propagandists behind the accounts were not infallible geniuses—indeed, in the early days they occasionally slipped into the uncanny valley as they mimicked, for example, American slang in ways that were just not quite right. They extensively targeted Black audiences and attempted to infiltrate their online communities,[47] but their inaccurate use of African American Vernacular English at times raised red flags.[48] However, the data set revealed that Russian trolls continuously adapted: they hired people who had a better command of the English language but also began to simply plagiarize from the vast ecosystem of vitriolic American trolls across the political spectrum. They cribbed memes from partisan activist groups like Charlie Kirk's Turning Point USA, a right-wing network for college conservatives, replacing the Turning Point logo with logos for their front media meme accounts (with names like "Army of Jesus" and "Angry Eagle.")[49] They cribbed material from a feminist T-shirt shop for their "Being Liberal" account. Why invent the voice of a feminist from New York when you could pull from her content directly?

The IRA's personas performed somewhat stereotypical identities: belligerent Texas secessionists, bitter descendants of Confederate soldiers, sanctimonious feminists, Black women interested in hair, leftist activists with mixed feelings about America, downtrodden veterans, Christians obsessed with Donald Trump. Their profiles described their politics and interests and included hashtags to signal belonging to relevant factions. While some of the content was cheesy, several of the troll account operators had a knack for resonance: Twitter persona "WokeLouisa," a "progressive Black woman deeply concerned about social justice," played her role so convincingly that Twitter CEO Jack Dorsey retweeted her, amplifying her messages to his millions of followers.[50] Pro–Second Amendment activist personas were retweeted by right-wing influencers such as Dinesh D'Souza.[51] Major American media outlets inadvertently embedded IRA troll posts as exemplars of man-on-the-street—"someone on the internet is saying"—commentary in their coverage of online conversations. Some of the accounts on Instagram, Facebook, and Twitter managed to accrue hundreds of thousands of followers; overall, the effort generated hundreds of millions of likes, shares, reposts, and other engagements across all social platforms.[52]

As I pored over hundreds of thousands of memes and posts that had appeared on Facebook and Instagram, I was struck by how well the people running them—outsiders—tapped into facets of the American experience that were barely visible to me as an insider. Over thirty distinct accounts purported to belong to Black Americans, split into a range of focus areas: pride, beauty, Baptist faith, liberation theology, Black excellence, and Pan-African spirituality.[53] Right-leaning accounts offered an array of options from flags-and-plains Reaganite patriotic content to the nihilistically ironic memes of the alt-right. There were highly specific identities; one account focused on life with an incarcerated spouse. And the posts—and ads soliciting new followers—were always written as if the author shared the identity of the target audience:

"Let's be real. Our hair is always political."

"Power to the People! We have to grow up, we have to wise up. We don't have any other choice this time but boycott the election. This time we choose between two racists. No one represents Black people."

"Do you support Trump? Wanna *#MakeAmericaGreatAgain*? Wanna see your kid on our account? Take pictures, make videos, send them to us via DM or tag *#KIDS4TRUMP* and we'll make a patriotic team of young Trump supporters here!"[54]

After speaking as members of the community, reinforcing pride in a shared identity over time, the Russian trolls then deftly cast those identities in opposition to each other. If there was a central theme, a question asked repeatedly, it might be best summarized as, Who is a real American? or Who is America for? Trolls pretending to be American veterans wondered why politicians were spending money on Muslim refugees. Meanwhile, on their fake Muslim accounts, they wondered aloud why Americans hated Muslims so much that they would turn away refugee women and children fleeing conflict zones (in wars caused by American aggression). Fake southern personas expressed deep pride in ancestors who had fought for the Confederacy, then attacked the positions of the Black Lives Matter accounts (run by other trolls) and argued that Americans were trying to "rewrite history" by tearing down Confederate monuments. The efforts spilled off the internet and into American cities and towns at times: for example, the trolls worked to galvanize distinct audiences to protest, and counterprotest, at the site of a Confederate monument in Stone Mountain, Georgia.[55] The audiences of a pro-Muslim and pro–Texas Secession Facebook page were each convinced, by people

sitting at desks in Russia, to attend a single rally in downtown Houston—
to support Islamic culture or to fight against the growing presence of
Islam in Texas—and when they showed up, police had to separate the
crowds.[56] The IRA regularly made efforts to recruit protest attendees to
send in video and photos, which they could mine for future posts.

And then, of course, in addition to the propaganda, there were the
rumors: in one remarkable example, the Russian IRA trolls worked to
boost social media chatter discussing right-wing media allegations about
the murder of Seth Rich, a Democratic National Committee staffer.
Rich, you will recall from Chapter 3, was the subject of Jack Posobiec's
conspiratorial rumors and subsequent misleading coverage on Fox News.
Their insinuations that his murder was payback for Rich's leaking DNC
emails were remarkably helpful to Russia's trolls...since those emails
had actually been hacked and leaked by Russian military intelligence.

Media coverage of the IRA effort to "sow social division" often focused on the divisive trolling in the Twitter arena. But this oversimplifies
the strategy that the IRA pursued within the closed crowds it brought
together on Facebook and Instagram: the methodical, painstaking work of
community building and creating content to engender community around
pride in a distinct identity, then leveraging that entrenchment to denigrate
other identities. IRA trolls were speaking to and exploiting the factions.

Propaganda, in most people's minds, is a strategy for persuasion. But
within each faction, users tend to already have similar beliefs; the IRA
created spaces for those who were already convinced and called on them
to be more vocal. The goal of propaganda targeting a faction today is to
activate it. The IRA data sets showed that the trolls only rarely made an
effort to change minds. Two topics stood out as exceptions: they tried
to shape Americans' opinions about the Syrian War—a matter of great
interest to Russia.[57] Most American factions did not have particularly
strong opinions about the war. Most Americans really didn't pay attention to it. But the Russian trolls made an effort to explain to Black communities that the United States should get out of the war because Flint,
Michigan, didn't have clean water—the United States should concentrate
on fixing its problems at home. They made anti-imperialist arguments to

the pro–Bernie Sanders, feminist, Muslim, and liberal audiences. On the right-wing pages, they argued that American involvement in the war would generate more damned refugees. They understood what arguments would resonate with which faction of America.

The other persuasion effort involved a series of posts that aimed to galvanize voters in the Republican Party to support a particular primary candidate. No, not Donald Trump—Rand Paul. After Paul flopped in early primaries, they refocused on Trump, working to mock Marco Rubio and to drive Ted Cruz's supporters to Trump: "Texas supports Donald Trump, not Ted Cruz. We know that many Texans support Ted Cruz as he is kind of Texan (born in Canada by Irish-Italian mother and Cuban father) and his ideas kind of attract many people of Texas. 'Kind of.' Sorry, Ted, Trump is everything you are not…Vote for Trump y'all."[58]

Full-Spectrum Propaganda: A Global Challenge

Russia remains the specter that has captured the imagination of the public (and academics) when it comes to influence operations. Although the impact of its troll factory efforts is not as profound as many on the left believe, it is prolific and brazen and invests significant time and resources in strategic manipulation. The Kremlin achieved an early, and deep, understanding of the mill-machine dynamic.

Russia is only one of many state actors worldwide that recognized what social media made possible. Creating persona accounts and front media properties online is now a standard playbook around the world. The most well-resourced states incorporated social media propaganda into their existing broadcast and print capabilities, creating a full-spectrum propaganda capacity: overt to covert strategies, deployed across both broadcast and social media channels, often in very integrated ways.[59] Social media didn't replace their other messaging efforts—it was additive. The full-spectrum approach let propagandists reinforce messaging across different mediums. They could use social media profiles and ad-targeting tools to push state-aligned or front media to whatever niche audience the state wanted to reach: young people on TikTok, right-wing American audiences on Truth Social, people who watch RT, or all of them at once.[60]

But more importantly, by using a combination of broadcast and social media channels, a state actor can run strategies beyond persuasion or activation. Creating confusion and distraction is easier than ever. The Chinese Communist Party, for example, is no stranger to using social platforms to its advantage—its "50 Cent Party" of paid commenters, who pseudonymously post "grassroots" commentary on Chinese social internet spaces, has been a long-standing participant in domestic social media conversations. Members of this cadre primarily use high-volume covert activity on social media forums to distract Chinese citizens from scandalous or inconvenient topics, pushing unfavorable threads or content out of public view by redirecting the attention of Chinese "netizens" to other matters.[61]

This redirection strategy is more challenging to execute on American social media platforms, where content moderation algorithms on platforms like Twitter quickly downrank spammy accounts doing high-volume posting. The dynamics of the online rumor mill, however, enable a different strategy: proliferate rumors within a trending hashtag to make it too difficult to know what really happened. Flood the zone with potential explanations for an event. Which story is actually reality? Who knows!

Russia used this strategy early on, in 2014, as it tried to wiggle out of accountability for shooting down a passenger airliner (MH17) in a conflict zone[62] (using fake accounts to suggest that *some people were saying* that there had *really* been a bomb on board) and for poisoning an ex-spy on British soil in March 2018.[63] Explanations proliferated, some given by state media, others by anonymous accounts. Then state media could report on the allegations of the anon accounts, and the anon accounts could in turn share the state media coverage.

Saudi Arabia took note: after operatives linked to the country's government murdered journalist Jamal Khashoggi in October 2018, an army of social media accounts offered overlapping and conflicting narratives, from denying the murder, to claiming it occurred elsewhere, to attacking Khashoggi's character.[64] (The kingdom's online trolls had also harassed him, incessantly, while he was alive; Saudi Arabia's interest in

Twitter extended to buying an ownership stake[65] and also surreptitiously placing a mole as an employee at the company to track dissidents.)[66]

In the age of full-spectrum propaganda, an online rumor can be quickly bolstered by articles written by state-controlled outlets. Fake personas can boost engagement on real, official government social media accounts—like those of diplomats who are "just asking questions."[67] As Peter Pomerantzev, a journalist who chronicled the rise of this strategy, put it, "Nothing is true and everything is possible."[68] The effect is disorienting.

The strategies are not always well executed. In 2019, a large protest movement took shape in Hong Kong; protesters were initially rallying against a new, strict bill related to extradition, though the movement expanded to have a broader pro-democracy focus. During a clash with policemen, one of the protesters was shot in the eye with a beanbag round by the police—images and footage traveled around the world instantly, and she became an icon.[69] The protests now had a human face—an extraordinarily potent turn—and other protesters began to wear gauze over their eyes in solidarity, generating more international coverage. The CCP responded with a barrage of activity to get their version of events into the mix, using a combination of what appeared to be real pro-CCP posters (who hopped over the Great Firewall to post on Twitter) and a flood of fake personas. These accounts began to reply to prominent Western media and other Twitter accounts that expressed support for the Hong Kong protesters, trying to cast doubt on reality with alternative explanations.[70] The protester's own comrades had shot her by accident, some state media outlets claimed; other accounts argued it was all a false flag to make China look bad. The deflection tactics were similar to the Russian and Saudi efforts.

Unlike Russia's trolls, however, the Chinese fake-persona accounts showed no indication that anyone had invested time in making them look plausible. Chinese state-linked accounts in the influence-operations data sets I've worked with most often have usernames consisting of a generic Western first name followed by a bunch of numbers: Sarah12513593402 suddenly has very strong opinions about Hong Kong protesters. Accounts often appear to have been compromised at some point, possibly purchased; they used to be fans of British pop bands but now care a lot about Chinese politics.

Meanwhile, even as clusters of fly-by-night fake accounts pop into hashtags and are quickly taken down, real Chinese Ministry of Foreign Affairs officials and other diplomats—known as the "Wolf Warriors"—mix things up using their own authentic, verified social media accounts, aggressively amplifying conspiracy theories, bad press, and controversies about their ideological enemies while stridently defending the CCP party line.[71] These are the authentic, overt voices of the state—yet they in turn get engagement from the networks of fake accounts.[72] Overt and covert tactics are deployed in concert.

Meanwhile, even as these attention brawls happen in the arena, China's overt state media outlets, some of which have amassed over one hundred million followers on their Facebook pages (some real, some likely fake),[73] calmly and consistently post pro-China stories featuring beautiful images and videos of Chinese culture, and run ads to target this content at audiences around the world.

While much of the media coverage of influence operations in the United States focuses primarily on Russia, China, and Iran interfering in American electoral politics, this is a global issue. The Middle East is a hotbed of influence operations; regional rivalries play out as social media propaganda wars. In 2021, my colleagues and I looked at forty-six operations that originated in Middle Eastern countries from August 2018 to March 2021. Iran targets Saudi Arabia and Egypt—but also Morocco, Senegal, and Sudan, among others. Saudi Arabia, Egypt, and the United Arab Emirates (UAE) target Iran, Yemen, Libya, and Qatar.[74] Some of the content in these regional operations is old-fashioned persuasion propaganda in which a country boosts itself and denigrates its rivals, now enhanced by the use of fake social media personas pretending to be citizens of the targeted country. These supposed "men on the street" argue in favor of some local politician or policy favorable to the country secretly running the influence operation, sharing content from a combination of real and front media expressing the same point of view. They tout how great a particular regime is: Iran stands up against neocolonialism for the oppressed people of the region; the Supreme Leader's wisdom and devoutness is a stabilizing force for the region. Saudi Arabia, in its own propaganda, positions itself as an ally to the West, as domestically successful and far more stable than Iran. The UAE positions itself as worldly, a global power player; personas made to look like European and Australian tourists praise the country for its hospitality and beauty.

As more state actors take advantage of social media, their propaganda is taking on a new patina; as in past media environments, the structure influences the substance. ISIS terrorists created content that looked like video game promos in 2014; members of Yevgeny Prigozhin's private military company, Wagner Group, created TikTok video clips of themselves shooting things, set to soundtracks of Russian black metal bands, to appeal to recruits as the 2022 war with Ukraine began.[75] Unaffiliated fan accounts made tribute videos glorifying the group. Ukraine, meanwhile, proved extraordinarily adept both at making memes (some engineered by the government, others produced by cadres of digital volunteers in Telegram channels)[76] and also at putting its leaders forward in livestreamed, personal, and engaging videos posted to social media platforms. They captured the attention of a global audience.[77] Both the attacker and the defender in the conflict prioritized creating material that audiences would boost and share, incorporating bystanders into the propaganda war.

While some content put out by official accounts clearly has a political objective—and people share to signal support for one side or another—this digital conscription is often very subtle. To galvanize the rumor mill—to turn ordinary people into unwitting propagators of state messaging—state propagandists have adopted the rhetoric of conspiracy theorists: *Some people on the internet are saying . . .* When Russia invaded Ukraine, for example, it leveraged conspiracy theories plucked from the dregs of American social media to advance allegations of "bioweapons labs" in Ukraine, which Ukraine was purportedly operating in cahoots with the DoD. This theory, first popularized on Twitter by American QAnon influencer "WarClandestine," was leveraged by Russian state media to serve as pretext for the invasion—Russia had to shut the labs down!—after other pretexts (such as the supposed need to "denazify" Ukraine) failed to generate popular support.[78] China promptly picked up and boosted Russia's bioweapons conspiracy theories, complaining about the involvement of the United States. "US owes world an explanation on bio-labs," admonished Chinese state media outlet *Global Times*, implying, shamelessly, that the labs were working on bat coronavirus samples at the time of the COVID-19 outbreak.[79] The Wolf Warriors tweeted complicated infographics purportedly exposing the "US' BIO-WEB."[80] The rhetoric was virtually indistinguishable from the run-of-the-mill conspiracy theorizing that regularly powers the rumor mill: "What is the U.S. hiding in the biolabs discovered in Ukraine?"[81] Indeed, remarkably, the question was echoed on Fox News by anchor Tucker Carlson.[82]

Hacked documents later revealed a bilateral agreement between Russia and China, signed in July 2021, to cooperate on news coverage and propaganda narratives.[83]

When it comes to actually executing these influence operations, professional PR and media firms—those original invisible rulers—are often behind the wheel. Regional firms that successfully manage the social media accounts of real individuals also run fake networks on the government's behalf. Indeed, an international industry has emerged: the governments of Honduras and Guatemala allegedly contracted with a US- and Venezuela-based firm to target their internal rivals.[84] One Israeli firm boasted to undercover reporters about being involved in more than thirty election "black ops" efforts.[85]

The State and the Crowd

State actors don't rely solely on fake personas when leveraging the rumor mill. The current ruling party of India, the Bharatiya Janata Party (BJP), blends bots with an organization of real supporters; authentic participants in pro-BJP WhatsApp groups work collectively to make things trend on popular platforms.[86] Some of the support is real grassroots activism. However, the BJP also relies on micro-influencers paid to praise the government and target its rivals, blending propaganda and rumors with a significant helping of harassment.[87] The "information yoddhas" (warriors), organized into thousands of regional cells, introduce content into the WhatsApp groups that real participants organically spread; at times, rumors have led to mob violence.[88] Other Indian parties, such as the Indian National Congress, have leveraged a mix of authentic and inauthentic tactics in their own efforts against the BJP.[89] The parties recognize that a narrative coming from trusted sources—for example, a friend-of-a-friend story forwarded by your aunt—is often more persuasive than something from a newscaster.[90]

Because WhatsApp is encrypted, it's difficult for Meta (which owns it) to respond to manipulation tactics as it does on Facebook or Instagram—the crowd is less visible. It has tried limiting the number of people in the groups and the number of times messages can be forwarded to avoid the spread of viral, decontextualized rumors. Civil society has created fact-checking initiatives whereby individuals can voluntarily flag content to a fact-checking team that will publish a quick blog post explaining the situation. Of course, as in the United States, the audience must be receptive to the fact-check. Bespoke realities are not limited to the United States.

Much like the ref-working domestic activists, state actors become unhappy when platform responses interfere in their interactions with useful crowds. Efforts to disrupt manipulation networks in India, for example, have seen platforms threatened with state retaliation. Jack Dorsey, former CEO of Twitter, asserted that Prime Minister Narendra Modi's government had gone so far as to threaten to shut down tech companies' in-country operations and raid the homes of their employees if tech companies did not moderate in accordance with the ruling party's demands; the Indian government denied his claims.[91] There have also been allegations that Meta has treated political accounts in India with kid gloves.[92]

Exposing influence operations can generate a lot of performative indignation and sometimes an aggressive response from those who ran or benefited from the campaigns. The responses include smear campaigns against the independent researchers involved (numerous state-controlled media outlets have written unflatteringly about Stanford Internet Observatory!). There are threats, sometimes implied, of legal or physical retribution—particularly if a researcher or tech company employee has family members who live within a country that is the subject of a take-down. Fear of retribution against family sometimes deters researchers with the deepest cultural knowledge or language skills from investigating disinformation campaigns by those governments or putting their names on their publications.

The Mass Production of Unreality

Influence operations happen on a constantly evolving playing field: every new platform becomes a target that propagandists can exploit as its user base grows. Any emerging technology that helps people create or share content transforms what's possible. When, for example, generative adversarial networks (GANs)—a type of AI that can be used to generate human faces[93]—began to produce images of people on par with those in stock photos, manipulators quickly incorporated the technology into their playbooks, using them as profile pictures for fake accounts.[94] Stock photos and stolen pictures of real people had been relatively easy for disinformation researchers to detect: a quick Google image search could surface the original, which was a red flag that a profile was not what it claimed to be. GAN-generated faces eliminated that easy tell.

Yet the "photos" of people who did not actually exist were not entirely undetectable. The eyes, noses, and mouths produced this way were located within specific regions of the photo. The AI also often screwed up details like teeth, ears, and the border between hair and background. Things that humans expect to be symmetric—collars, earrings, pupils— often weren't. The GAN-created pictures included dozens of tiny give-aways that enabled researchers to say with a high degree of confidence that a profile picture was likely AI generated—the new technology came with its own red flags.

After 2018, disinformation researchers began to see these fakes every-where, sometimes used by state actors in propaganda campaigns, other times leveraged by spammy companies trying to make connections for outbound sales.[95] As fake faces became more common, even on platforms like LinkedIn, social media platforms began to invest in technology to detect them.[96] Media wrote explainers to help the public recognize the signs. But even as tech companies gained the upper hand and much of the public became versed in the identifiers of fakery, generative AI using a different type of technology—generative pretrained transformers (GPTs)—became more widely democratized.

In 2020, OpenAI released GPT-3, a text generator that works by predicting the next word in a sentence with remarkable sophistication.[97] At the time, I was studying the long-form propaganda that Russian military intelligence (the GRU) had written for its front media outlets manipulating the conversation around the Syrian war.[98] The effort had been detected in part because the GRU's fake journalists plagiarized content—including from their own fake colleagues![99] As I simultaneously spent time in the summer of 2020 reading Russian propaganda and exploring the potential of GPT-3, it occurred to me that the technology would enable a propagandist to easily avoid the detection traps that had ensnared the fake journalists whose output I was reading. It could quickly and inexpensively produce original content, replicating the style and tone of any given community down to the in-group language and slang.[100] There would be no need to plagiarize anymore. The "copypasta" repetition and the little uncanny-valley malapropisms and misplaced punctuation we'd used as signals in detecting state actor disinformation campaigns were likely to disappear.

The technology democratized quickly with the launch of ChatGPT. Widely available text-to-image generation quickly followed: if you can describe an object or a scene, AI diffusion models like Stable Diffusion and MidJourney will draw the picture you're imagining in vivid detail. These tools, too, had early "tells"—just as the GAN-generated faces often had botched teeth and weird pupils, AI-generated pictures of people frequently included extra fingers. But within a few months, that tell was largely eliminated. It is now easy to create photorealistic images of people who do not exist, in places that do not exist, depicting events that never happened. It's possible to create audio of things that were never said, even in the voices of ordinary people. Video is on its way to being equally accessible. In other words, it's possible to mass-produce unreality.

Generative AI technologies are powerful and very useful for many applications. As with many technologies, this means that there are also malicious applications. After a few interactions with GPT-3, it became obvious that generative text tools, which produced writing indistinguishable from that created by people, would also be transformative for propagandists, simultaneously increasing the quality and quantity of their output while reducing the cost to produce it.[101] Large language models have the potential to make automated social media bots useful again, by powering chatbots responsive to users who try to interact with them.[102] Synthetic video clips, AI-generated images, or fake "leaked audio" can be used as the underpinnings of sensational viral stories. Technology evolves, and trolls adapt.

On the morning of May 22, 2023, someone on Twitter posted a photo of a black cloud of smoke and a building with the caption "Large Explosion Near the Pentagon." It went viral and caused a brief dip in the stock market.[103] This wasn't the first hoax on Twitter to create ripples in financial markets. But this time the image was AI generated. Investigative reporters found that the first account to post the content was a purported "news" account—it had "news" in its username, at least—that had paid to receive a blue check (account verification) on Twitter.[104] The account had previously posted QAnon content and sometimes pro-Putin commentary.[105] Other accounts involved in spreading the faked image included imposters piggybacking on the brand of reputable news outlets ("BloombergFeed," which had no affiliation with Bloomberg) as well as the Russian state media outlet RT and antiestablishment blog *Zero Hedge*. Interestingly, the building in the image didn't actually look like the Pentagon. The physics of the fence posts and building pillars were simply wrong. But some people found it persuasive, so they shared and reacted to it. The stock market blip was likely the result of trading algorithms lazily reading Twitter. But the scenario reminded me of *#ColumbianChemicals* and how much easier technology has made it to create hoaxes today.

Social media democratized content *dissemination*, making it possible for anyone and everyone to share a message, target an audience, and grow a community. Generative AI takes the cost of content *creation* to zero. The

206 | INVISIBLE RULERS

technology promises incredible benefits for the majority of the honest, authentic people in the world who use it. Society is unlikely to collapse under a proliferation of AI-generated manipulation campaigns simply because the tech exists; audiences must trust the messenger and believe the content is real for it to be influential. But it is likely that we will see these kinds of hoaxes increase in the near term, even as platforms begin to implement tools to check for watermarks or other signs of content authenticity. Influencers, particularly those with large followings, will become targets as manipulators try to convince them to share synthetic media to their large audiences.

Generative AI enables us to manufacture unreality: to produce images from worlds that don't exist, audio that speakers never said, and videos of events that didn't happen—the kind of magic that was formerly the purview of big movie studios or people with deep technological training or artistic skill. But another consequence of this technological revolution is even more important to understand: the *liar's dividend*, in which awareness of the existence of the technology enables a person to cast doubt on things that are real.[106] That leaked audio of real, hot-mic comments the politician wishes they hadn't said? Just dismiss it. *It wasn't me; it was AI generated.*

This is not merely theoretical. On October 7, 2023, a terrible act of terrorism happened in Israel: militants from Hamas massacred over eleven hundred Israeli civilians at a music festival and in dozens of locations near the Israel-Gaza border. Some of the militants, who were themselves killed, had worn GoPro cameras.[107] Footage from these cameras, as well as from the first responders who arrived on the scenes, flooded social media, appearing first on alternative platforms like Telegram before being picked up by users and shared elsewhere. Twitter influencers, some of whom were chasing clout (or profit from the monetization program that Elon Musk had started), made sensational and inflammatory claims and shared atrocity footage—including, unfortunately, from completely different atrocities that had happened long ago in other places.[108] The world was transfixed and searching for information, but it had become very difficult to know what was true on the platform that had previously been the best source of real-time information in a crisis.

As the horror of what had happened on October 7 was revealed, a handful of news outlets reported word-of-mouth rumors about a high number (forty) of beheaded infant victims. President Joe Biden commented on the claims, though it was unclear whether he'd personally seen the evidence or it had been relayed to him by advisors. Later that evening, an administration official told CNN that Biden had *not* personally seen pictures or confirmed reports of infants beheaded by Hamas, clarifying that the president's remarks were referring to public comments from media outlets and Israeli officials.[109] Media and fact-checkers subsequently sought to uncover the truth about the scope and means of death, even as highly polarized pro-Israel and pro-Palestine influencers and factions battled on social media about whether the allegation was all Israeli military propaganda.[110] As with the Russian invasion of Ukraine in February 2022, the fog of war made it difficult to know what was happening; rumors flew before the facts were known.

However, the Hamas attack and Israel's subsequent military response also became the first major conflict to play out in the era of democratized generative AI. Millions of people knew that highly realistic fake content could be created by machines. And so, people began to dismiss *real* atrocities as AI-generated fakes. When the government of Israel released photos of several murdered infants, some influencers ran the images—which were partially blurred in spots—through AI image detectors, at least one of which was fooled by the blurs and declared the images to be generated by AI. People who distrusted the Israeli government latched on to the false positive; some accused Prime Minister Benjamin Netanyahu of fabricating images of murdered children.[111] As the conflict continued, AI-generated images repeatedly went viral, *and* real images were dismissed as AI. Anything that was inconvenient to one side or another could be dismissed as a fake by an incentivized faction.

The combination of easily generated fake content and the suspicion that anything might be fake allows people to choose what they want to believe. Unreality—and its specter—will continue to compound our splintering into bespoke realities.[112] Although technological detection of generated content will continue to improve, it will never be a perfect solution. The problem is once again not solely technological—it's very much an issue of what sources and content audiences trust.

The Regulatory Arbitrage of Content Moderation

In the decade since *#ColumbianChemicals* happened on September 11, 2014, state actors have taken full advantage of the collision of the propaganda machine and the rumor mill. While many state-run influence operations (at least, the ones we find) often do not appear to be particularly impactful (some are), we nonetheless see sustained creativity and ingenuity from state actors as they incorporate new platforms, features, and technologies into their operations. It's a cat-and-mouse game, with the role of the cat primarily played by the tech companies.

In the years since late 2017, as governments, people, and platforms became aware of the details of the IRA's expansive covert social effort, tech platforms scrambled to address the situation. Facebook began to disclose information about the accounts behind ads on the platform and to require people running political ads to confirm their identity.[113] Facebook pages began to display the location of the page administrators and previous names of the page. The platforms established integrity teams staffed with dedicated employees to find and take down networks of fake accounts before they grew into something impactful, and a new policy area emerged: "coordinated inauthentic behavior." Networks of accounts came down if platforms determined that they were "inauthentic"—if, for example, the people behind the accounts were pretending to be something they weren't or were using multiple accounts in concert to manipulate engagement.[114]

The Russian troll factory employees in Saint Petersburg were saying many of the same things as authentic Texas secessionists or Black Hebrew Israelites, but their accounts came down because they, or the tricks they used to amplify their messages (such as automated bots), were not what they seemed on the surface. Platforms released public reports and made data sets available to researchers, like my team, who then did independent analyses and provided even more context and transparency to the public.

Friction in the gears didn't make manipulative state propagandists go home, but it did force them to update their tactics. To try to get around identity checks they could use virtual private networks, or hire people who had gotten verified, or buy old accounts. To bypass integrity teams and their investigations, they could hop to less moderated platforms or to new ones that were just becoming popular and hadn't yet staffed up defensive efforts. Rather than creating fake journalist personas, they could simply hire unwitting real people to write for online front media outlets.

As influence operations have evolved, the job of dealing with them has fallen largely to the social media companies. It is (rightfully) very difficult for a democratic government to write regulations for content policies because of the speech and expression implications. However, very few people want to spend time within a free-for-all of unreality, propaganda, and manipulation. Therefore, even as regulation has been sporadic, platforms have put in place synthetic media policies and announced watermarking initiatives as techniques like generative AI have become widely available. Google recently announced it would also leverage its image search tool to alert users to AI-generated images.[115]

In business and finance, *regulatory arbitrage* is the practice of exploiting differences in regulations across regions to gain a competitive advantage or reduce costs. There's regulatory arbitrage in content moderation too: bad actors increasingly set up shop on the platforms least equipped, or least likely, to moderate them away.[116] If Facebook is watching closely for fake accounts trying to manipulate the conversation around an American election, well, there's always Gettr, Truth Social, Gab, and even Telegram, which host relevant audiences and have made a commitment to little, if any, moderation. They have a right to set their terms of service. But their choice not to have integrity teams means that state-linked accounts taken down by the big platforms often remain active on anti- or minimal-moderation platforms.[117]

One memorable example that we saw after the Russian invasion of Ukraine was a fan page for popular US musician Kid Rock on Truth Social that suddenly had a lot to say about the war.[118] While the alt-platforms often have much smaller audiences, the fake Russia-linked

Kid Rock account managed to achieve a few breakout successes as its content was reposted by its audience to other, more mainstream social media platforms. Donald Trump Jr., for example, reposted one of the alt-platform fake–Kid Rock memes to Instagram.[119] These accounts may not get massive engagement or reach, but they can propagandize to niche audiences relatively undisturbed.

Telegram, not widely popular in the United States but huge in other countries, has long made clear that it has no intention of investigating who is behind even the most seemingly manipulative channels. It makes no effort to moderate disinformation campaigns, although it did respond to EU sanctions on Russian state media outlets and, in a limited way, to Apple and Google app store requests to restrict access to Hamas channels.[120] Given the platform's hands-off policy, it was unsurprising to see many manipulation campaigns related to Russia's invasion of Ukraine emerge from, and go viral on, Telegram. One notable example was the devastating claim that victims of a war crime in which Russia bombed a maternity hospital in Mariupol, injuring or killing multiple pregnant women, were really "crisis actresses" hired by Ukraine.[121] That bit of propaganda was quickly snuffed out on Twitter and Facebook, which took down state media and official Russian embassy tweets lying about the women and put up fact-check labels on related posts as quickly as possible.[122] However, the blitz of lies captured attention on Telegram, spread on the web, and even managed to temporarily trip up Google Search: for a few hours after the claim went viral, searching for the name of one of the young mothers who survived returned links to state media outlets smearing her.

Does It Work? Does It Matter?

These state-run influence operations affect the people whose lives they upend and the communities they target and mislead. Whether the state actor behind them is targeting its own citizens or those of a rival nation, the campaigns are manipulative and wrong.

Given these implications, we should not rely solely on tech companies to investigate what's happening; nor should we accept their findings without further verification. After 2018, academics, media, civil society, and tech platforms began to work more collaboratively to investigate state-sponsored influence operations.[123]

However, those outside the platforms can only see so much. Uncanny content, similarities in posting patterns, AI-generated profile pictures, and ties to past networks or domains are interesting signals, but not enough to concretely attribute a campaign to a state actor. A meaningful attribution has to be based on more than circumstantial evidence. This is why academic researchers often reach out to representatives of the social platforms after gathering initial intel about a seemingly inauthentic network; tech companies have visibility into far more data, including data related to devices used by the account or where accounts may be logging in from. For several years following the discovery of the Internet Research Agency's efforts to manipulate American society, tech companies shared findings with those who provided the initial tip and subsequently made data sets and a takedown report available to the public. But as of 2023, several tech companies have begun to walk these collaborations back as communication between platforms and researchers has reframed by bad-faith actors as some sort of conspiracy to suppress certain voices or political beliefs.[124]

In reality, these collaborations enable everyone to better understand disinformation campaigns and ensure that state power is checked. Transparency is key to making sure the public understands how duplicitous campaigns work.

Propagandists don't simply stop running influence operations after a network is discovered and attributed; there are rarely significant consequences for being caught. The state may lose most of its fake accounts, but they will inevitably eventually respawn. As long as targeted communities are reachable and the benefits of the operation outweigh the costs of running it, this Whac-A-Mole game will continue.

Not all state-run operations are resounding successes. Many flop. But not disrupting the network—simply not imposing any costs on manipulators—means that they will continue to grow.

State-sponsored disinformation and propaganda campaigns today don't need to reach a large audience or persuade entire societies—or even majorities of people—to think a certain way. In a world of splintered publics, such campaigns can target and activate specific factions. They can use the existing rumor mill and real online crowds to unwittingly propagate state-aligned messages[125] or even nonsense conspiracy theories like Pizzagate. It is enough, sometimes, to crystallize and exacerbate existing distrust and to entrench people further within bespoke realities.

Indeed, domestic media, domestic influencers, and crowds of real activists remain the invisible rulers running the show, as state actors piggyback and exploit existing dynamics. As the United States experienced protests and racial unrest in the summer of 2020, Russia, China, and Iran were very much in the mix to exploit the real grievances: Russian propaganda outlets, some easily attributable, some gray propaganda, produced content to amp up unrest at every opportunity.[126] Some of the outlets supported the left-leaning protesters calling for an end to policing; some supported the right-leaning pro-police perspective. China and Iran frequently weighed in as well, proclaiming the failure of democracy.[127] But these state-linked efforts are usually most effective at exacerbating something that's already happening: juicing a rumor mill or laundering narratives through propaganda channels. They don't have even close to the kind of impact that authentic influencers within a community can have. And this is, in fact, one reason why state actors have increasingly begun trying to simply hire influencers[128]—often surreptitiously—to produce content on topics ranging from mundane cultural commentary (China paying people to say nice things about the 2022 Winter Olympics)[129] to war propaganda (Russia paying creators on TikTok to spread Kremlin talking points).[130]

We should be able to hold two things in our heads simultaneously. First, nation-states have enthusiastically adopted social media as another channel in a full-spectrum propaganda strategy. They have adapted "agents of influence" strategies to the virtual world—recruiting unwitting journalists and influencers and infiltrating communities. This is happening globally: invisible rulers worldwide want the power to shape public opinion—to topple adversary governments or parties, disrupt societies, and move markets. Authoritarian governments in particular, which block Western social media platforms and work to prevent their citizens from organizing, aggressively take advantage of the free-expression affordances conferred by the internet and Western laws to manipulate the citizens of their adversaries, undermining their trust in foundational democratic processes and manipulating consensus. Democracies are more vulnerable to these types of attacks because our commitment to free expression leaves us inclined to permit content—unless we are absolutely certain that it is coming from an outsider—that explicitly undermines our leaders, institutions, and social cohesion; that exacerbates distrust; and that uses outright lies and conspiracy theories to do it.[131]

Second, the mere *effort* of state actors does not mean that state actors are *effective*. Overreacting to their efforts by elevating them to the stuff of legend actually serves the propagandists' aims.[132] Underestimating the threat of foreign influence can enable adversaries to flourish. But exaggerating the threat risks undermining public trust in the information ecosystem and fostering the sort of paranoia in which anyone you disagree with online can simply be dismissed as a Russian troll.[133]

Yevgeny Prigozhin invested in sending his company's trolls on trips around the United States to get a firsthand sense of what drove American communities.[134] Very few other efforts have put forth that kind of initiative. The well-informed mercenaries got good click-through rates on their ads; their targeting was on point. Some of the Americans who followed the accounts joined in-the-streets protests set up by the trolls, promoted their content, and occasionally chatted with them on Messenger. However, even though the IRA persona accounts amassed hundreds of thousands of followers, researchers still debate whether they affected the United States in any material way.[135] An agent had done something to a target, but was it influential?

It's highly unlikely that the IRA effort swung the election. Their political content was a small fraction of election-related content, even within the specific factions. The hack-and-leak operation by the GRU—the leaking of Clinton campaign chairman John Podesta's emails, among others, did demonstrably shift the *national* political conversation. The first email dump helped redirect national attention away from the "Grab 'Em by the Pussy" *Access Hollywood* tape (and the announcement earlier the same day that Russia was believed to have hacked the DNC).[136] But the GRU hack had another lasting societal impact: Podesta's emails about ordering food were the inspiration for the Pizzagate conspiracy, the precursor to QAnon, and the Russian trolls were right there to boost both. They gave domestic American faction members an assist as they fell into a bespoke reality in which Hillary Clinton and Podesta were running a pedophile ring out of the basement of a pizza place that had no basement. And, of course, eventually a man showed up with a gun.

Russia and the IRA took advantage of our own internecine fighting. Foreign actors might have been accelerants—but Americans provide the kindling.

Pandemic Propaganda

Four years after the 2016 election, the emergence of COVID-19 and a new pandemic-inflected reality created an explosion of mis- and disinformation, fueling the rumor mill and triggering expansive efforts by propaganda machines worldwide. The pandemic became the primary concern of almost every nation on the planet; few topics in our age have commanded and sustained public attention around the world simultaneously or provided such a wealth of opportunities for every conceivable actor, from activists to world leaders, to shape narratives in service to their own interests and incentives.[137]

Many state actors worked inwardly. As the disease spread within Iran's borders, Ayatollah Ali Khamenei rather quickly blamed the United States in internal state media, alleging that the virus had been "specifically built for Iran using the genetic data of Iranians."[138] Some worked both inwardly and outwardly, taking advantage of a chance to undermine their rivals. Saudi Arabia's state media, which broadcasts regionally, talked up the kingdom's internal successes, emphasizing its low death rate and high testing capacity while highlighting Iran's and Qatar's struggles and incompetence.[139] Saudi state media amplified the regional rumor mill, covering the "news" that Houthi rebels in Yemen were killing people diagnosed with coronavirus to stop its spread; the rumor spread so widely in Yemen that the Houthi leaders took the unusual step of issuing a statement, despite largely imposing a communication blackout about COVID within their community.[140] Russia's state media outlets RT and Sputnik pushed out English-language articles criticizing the pandemic response of Western governments, alleging that they were overreacting to the threat of the disease and unfairly infringing upon freedoms. Other RT articles, meanwhile, unabashedly praised China's handling of the pandemic and touted the success of China's and Russia's own lockdowns.[141] The audacity of this contradiction did not seem to trouble the audiences sharing the content.

But no state actor was quite so compelled to influence public opinion, both inside and outside its borders, as China.[142] Indeed, the country's nine-member task force for managing the COVID-19 response included the CCP's policy czar for ideology and propaganda and the director of its Central Propaganda Department.[143]

The COVID-19 pandemic began in Wuhan, China. That is an indisputable fact, though questions of lab leak versus natural origin persist. Yet the CCP quickly began a full-spectrum propaganda campaign to muddy the waters about the disease as it began to spread. It aggressively suppressed facts domestically: even as stories of what local media called "Wuhan pneumonia" emerged, they were downplayed. Doctor Li Wenliang—one of the earliest physicians to sound the alarm on Chinese social media—was detained on January 3, 2020, and forced to sign a letter stating that he'd made "false comments." On February 7, 2020, he died of COVID; the disease was indisputably a dangerous epidemic by that point, so state media simply reframed Li Wenliang as a hero, and his earlier detention went unmentioned.

China's overt English-language propaganda outlets also began touting President Xi Jinping's great successes in their coverage, which they shared to their Facebook pages: stories of hospitals built in two weeks and protective medical gear and aid sent to affected countries. They paid for Facebook post promotions to increase their distribution to audiences worldwide.[144] They boosted YouTube creators who made positive, and possibly paid, content about China's handling of the novel coronavirus.[145]

Meanwhile, outspoken government officials—including the Wolf Warriors—began to aggressively dispute that the virus had even originated in China. They pulled conspiracy theorist chatter up from the bowels of social media, "just asking questions" about whether COVID-19 had actually been brought to China by American athletes there for the World Military Games.[146] "Some netizens were saying" that the United States was responsible and that Fort Detrick was involved, and the theory deserved to be heard! Zhao Lijian, a foreign ministry official, alleged a vast US Centers for Disease Control and Prevention (CDC) cover-up: "CDC was caught on the spot. When did patient zero begin in US? How many people are infected? What are the names of the hospitals? It might be US army who brought the epidemic to Wuhan. Be transparent! Make public your data! US owe us an explanation!"[147]

Several of the anti-imperialist and anti-American Twitter factions ate it up, as did conspiracy theorists who felt gratified that their "truths" were being recognized. Indeed, as the allegations spread on social media, even the Chinese state media outlets, which had clearly and repeatedly acknowledged the disease's origin in Wuhan in their early posts, began to soften those prior statements and to speculate. Yes, they'd thought that the disease had come from Wuhan, but now there were simply too many unknowns to make a call! If a new narrative played well with crowds on the internet, well, history could be subtly rewritten.

Conspiracy theories about external threats have long offered state actors an opportunity to unite their citizens against a purported tyrannical secret elite that is trying to harm them; the government can position itself as the defender of the people. Tinfoil-hat diplomacy on social media is an effective, if unfortunate, update for the modern era: it captures attention and creates us-against-them conflicts that factional audiences on social media will amplify. The goal is the same, but the tactics have changed.[148]

Of course, Zhao's astonishing success as speaker of bold "truths" on Twitter did not appear to be entirely authentic. While he indeed received thousands of likes and retweets on his posts, social media researchers observed inauthentic networks of bot accounts following and retweeting

Zhao on multiple occasions.[149] And as subsequent Facebook and Twitter data would show, China also created front media properties and tens of thousands of fake accounts designed to look like ordinary people to attack the United States' and Hong Kong's pandemic response while touting China's.[150] The effort did not get much engagement, but the operators were demonstrably committed to churning out hundreds of sham accounts and comments per day.

The proliferation of all these alternate-universe theories ultimately led to information brinksmanship between President Donald Trump and the CCP: the Trump administration requested that the United Nations Security Council issue a statement verifying that the virus originated in China.[151] The proliferation of efforts to shape the narrative on social media triggered another response as well: the social media companies began prominently labeling the accounts of state media outlets and government-linked accounts worldwide—including China's Wolf Warriors.[152] Naturally, there was great gnashing of teeth about being so labeled: it was censorship, the state propagandists vigorously protested.

For the next few years, state actors worldwide would deploy their propaganda resources toward shaping the narrative on pandemic issues. But state actors were just one player among many.

7

Viruses, Vaccines, and Virality

O N MAY 4, 2020, a video on YouTube revealed the terrifying truth about the novel coronavirus that had recently arrived on America's shores: world leaders were letting it run free and suppressing known cures in order to make the public sick and fearful so that they might be mass-vaccinated later. The whistle-blower in the video had been persecuted for nearly a decade after crossing one of the evil men behind the conspiracy, a scientist who'd risen to the highest levels of government power by crushing those who opposed him: Dr. Anthony Fauci.

The time for silence was over and Dr. Judy Mikovits was naming names.

In the twenty-six-minute video, Mikovits's sympathetic interviewer, Mikki Willis—a filmmaker with salt-and-pepper hair and a soothing voice—draws out her harrowing tale of Big Pharma minions retaliating against "one of the most accomplished scientists of her generation," suppressing her research and even throwing her in jail. He insinuates that the revelations will put her life in danger—but brave Dr. Mikovits refuses to be intimidated.

After a convoluted personal story about Fauci stealing her research, establishing Mikovits's bona fides as a scientific martyr, come the claims about the pandemic. They tumble out, rapid-fire: this was not a naturally occurring virus; hospitals were being paid to say that deaths were due to COVID-19; flu vaccines contain coronaviruses, increasing COVID-19 susceptibility; Italy's flu vaccine exacerbated than country's pandemic crisis; effective treatments like hydroxychloroquine were being kept from the public; miracle treatments for autism were also being kept from the public; masks activate latent "coronavirus expressions" people might be carrying, making them sick.[1] *They*—authority figures, including Fauci—were trying to keep these truths from the public. Even beach closures were part of the plot: *they* knew that healing microbes in the ocean were a defense against coronavirus.

It wasn't a pandemic. It was planned. It was a "plandemic."

Willis released this first installment of what would become his *Plandemic* series on May 4, posting it to Facebook with a warning: *it will be censored*. People must help evade the platform censors, he said, by downloading and sharing the film themselves to ensure that its truths saw the light of day. With this call to action, Willis rallied his audience to become digital warriors in a battle against the elites and Big Tech. "We are the ones we've been waiting for," he wrote.

Plandemic hopped from the anti-vaccine echo chamber, where it had launched, into communities receptive to its tropes. It quickly spread within wellness groups (already distrustful of institutional medicine) and QAnon conspiracy communities (who already hated Fauci and believed COVID was part of a plot to control humanity). It hopped into MAGA spaces and then to other political crowds like the "Reopen" groups that were upset about lockdowns. It cascaded across the internet as those who found it persuasive, or at least a compelling curiosity, shared it with the myriad groups they enjoyed online: communities focused on sailing, corgis, gardening, music, church, all of the ordinary interests that people talk about with friends. These later sharers weren't anti-vaccine; they just saw something that resonated enough to warrant showing their friends. The conspiratorial anti-vaccine tropes were a novelty for those unfamiliar with the pseudoscience canon, and they were delivered by a very sympathetic archetype: the underdog, standing up to the powerful to tell her story.

The video spread like wildfire, responding to signals from both algorithms and crowds. It got over eight million views before social media companies began playing Whac-A-Mole to take it down.[2] But even as they tried, committed factions diligently reposted the *Plandemic* video to "censorship-resistant" video-sharing sites like Rumble and BitChute

(YouTube competitors popular with right-wing audiences), then shared those new links to mainstream social platforms—just as Willis had asked.

Even though the content was overwhelmingly a bunch of nonsense.[3]

As sharers and platforms battled it out, fact-checkers got to work trying to explain the facts behind the blizzard of wild claims. Mikovits, a longtime speaker on the anti-vaccine conference circuit, had pushed conspiracy theories about vaccines and autism for over a decade, and scientists from multiple fields stepped up to talk about her chronic unreliability. She'd been arrested for alleged theft of data and property from the lab she worked at in November 2011.[4] (Charges were later dropped.) Her most prominent paper, which claimed that mouse retroviruses in contaminated vaccines caused chronic fatigue syndrome, had been retracted in December 2011[5] by the journal that published it—an academic disgrace—but she responded by doubling down further on its claims.[6] Anthony Fauci had been the director of the National Institute of Allergy and Infectious Disease at the time, but there were no indications that he'd been involved with any action against Mikovits.[7] And yet, in *Plandemic*, she spun the collapse of her career as the result of his malevolent acts.

Fauci was, of course, newly prominent at the time. And Mikovits had a new book to sell.

Willis had deftly refashioned Mikovits's professional failures and longstanding grudges into a trope-laden tale of good versus evil: the Government Cover-Up, the Evil Scientist, the Noble Whistleblower, the Toxic Vaccines. He drew his followers into the effort well in advance of the film's release, even polling them on what its title should be. (The runners-up to *Plandemic* were *The Invisible Enemy* and *The Oath*.) And then, once the story and the participatory distribution plan were set, *Plandemic* launched. "We made the video to go viral," Willis boasted to a reporter interviewing the man behind the moment. "We knew the branding was conspiratorial and shocking. Unfortunately, in this age, you kind of have to be that to get people's attention. But that it would go viral to this degree, I don't think anyone could project."[8]

The Infodemic

Plandemic was just one viral moment in the COVID-19 *infodemic*—the proliferation of information (some reliable, some not) that accompanies an outbreak of a serious disease.[9] Contagions have always been accompanied by confusion, but in 2020 the sheer volume of shifting theories felt overwhelming, destabilizing. On every conceivable topic related to the disease—origins, cures, treatments, policies—the propaganda machine and rumor mill alike repeatedly set online factions ablaze...not only with the conflicting facts expected in an emerging pandemic but with allegations of conspiracies, cover-ups, collusion, and incompetence. You might receive a text from a friend about the National Guard imminently shutting down your city; watch a livestream press conference from a politician outright denying this; and then read a news story suggesting some sort of middle ground—all within thirty minutes.

Some stories were demonstrably false. Some would turn out to be true. In the moment, it was very difficult to tell one from the other. Often it seemed that the facts were simply irrelevant. This was, in large part, because some of the most prominent influencers in the conversation managed to frame every conceivable aspect of a global pandemic not as a fight of humanity against a viral invader but as culture war battles about identity and values. And institutions, unfortunately, were ill-equipped to participate.

Though this chapter focuses on the United States, viral narratives routinely spread far beyond the borders of their country of origin—as did *Plandemic*, in fact, which began to go viral elsewhere even as American fact-checkers were releasing English-language rebuttals. The infodemic, like the pandemic itself, was global. Governments, activists, influencers, and crowds leveraged the crisis to spread narratives in service to their own interest—some for profit, others for power, and many for clout.[10]

The infodemic had begun prior to COVID-19's arrival in the United States; in the early days, it was dominated by Chinese Communist Party (CCP) efforts to obfuscate the virus's origin while attempting to control the narrative about the severity of the outbreak within China. Only a tiny fringe of the American public appeared to believe the Wolf Warrior propaganda about COVID being manufactured in Maryland's Fort

Detrick as a bioweapon. Instead, the origins debate would come to focus on whether the virus had emerged via a Wuhan wet market or had broken free of the Wuhan Institute of Virology in a lab leak. Public health and government institutions were divided and often uncommunicative: the World Health Organization (WHO), the Centers for Disease Control and Prevention (CDC), and various US intelligence agencies all had differing and shifting opinions on the origin question. Public opinion shifted as well: in 2020, a plurality of Americans (43 percent) thought the new coronavirus had most likely come about naturally, though nearly three in ten (29 percent) said it most likely had been created in a lab.[11] By mid-2023, two-thirds of the American public believed the lab-leak hypothesis.[12] Some of this shift in opinion happened as new information trickled out, but it also coincided with declining trust in scientists and institutions. People became progressively less sure that those best positioned to understand the facts were telling them the truth.

Many people across the political spectrum wondered how the pandemic had started; it affected all of us, and the idea of labs researching ways to make diseases more destructive felt horrifying. But within some communities, the origins debate moved beyond topic of interest to fodder for factional warfare. In the summer of 2020, as racial-reckoning protests rocked the United States, a spate of left-leaning media outlets and influencers argued that connecting COVID-19 to China might exacerbate anti-Asian racism.[13] Facebook included the statement that COVID-19 was man-made among the list of topics it was beginning to moderate.[14] While most of the platform's new COVID-related moderation policies focused on stopping the spread of claims about fake cures or other content harmful to individual or public health, the origins debate policy was an outlier—and it sparked much discussion around how to properly define *harm*.

The argument that speculating about the origins of COVID-19 had racist implications quickly became fodder for vocal right-wing factions, who used it to argue that public health had gone "woke." This bolstered the belief among those opposed to pandemic mitigation measures, like lockdowns, that left-wing identity politics was driving health policy.[15]

The decision to moderate the topic galvanized things even further. Now not only were there arguments to be made about wokeness run amok, media incompetence, and purported government cover-ups, but there was also seemingly heavy-handed tech platform moderation. This combination was catnip.

Quite quickly, it became clear that the pandemic would have a profound impact not only on public health and the economy but on *trust*. Coverage by traditional media that largely minimized COVID at first—arguing that it was little more than a flu or making "what about" comparisons to other social ills—cost it considerable credibility.[16] Some prominent figures who were alarmed very early on, in January 2020, were initially mocked. The no-handshake sign posted by influential venture capital firm Andreessen Horowitz became the subject of derision.[17] A handful of technology influencers with large social media followings who criticized what they saw as government inaction,[18] such as Balaji Srinivasan, received flak for being hysterics.

When it became abundantly clear the disease was far more than a flu, some of the articles that had downplayed the novel coronavirus were rightly updated, and tweets promoting them were deleted.[19] Not all outlets prominently called attention to such corrections, though, and the tech influencers who had been maligned then used their own massive platforms to assail feckless media—both for getting it wrong and for not apologizing.[20] Some made collages of mainstream pandemic news headlines that had aged badly, which went viral. People were very angry.

The outrage was not unfounded. Sweeping statements that turned out to be wrong, as new facts emerged, didn't lead to sweeping corrections. The underacknowledged mistakes were a gift to those who benefitted from undermining confidence in "legacy media." A crop of COVID-19 influencers began to gain prominence—some offered rigorous analysis, while others were simply Reflexive Contrarians. It was sometimes difficult to tell which was which, particularly if they peppered their commentary with complex medical terminology.

This divide between those who trusted institutions versus those who looked to "information insurgents" would lead to divergent realities and have profound lasting effects.[21] It became clear early on that many institutions did not appear to understand how best to engage with the factionalized public as the rumor mill and propaganda machine spun story after story. There were the early fights about masks: public health institutions at first lagged behind prominent influencers who argued that the public should be masking. The institutional experts, more accustomed to a slower news pace and higher trust, were sifting through facts before making recommendations. Initially, the CDC advised against masks, only to reverse its stance as more facts emerged. This is expected: rational actors change their views with new information. However, many respected social media figures had been advocating masking for weeks, and the CDC appeared to be leading from behind.[22] People began to question why they'd gotten it wrong; some speculated that public health leaders like Anthony Fauci had misled the public to prevent a mask shortage.[23] It was a noble lie, perhaps, but one that eroded his credibility.

Yet as the government began to push for mask usage, critiques shifted. Contrarians reframed mask advisories as attempts to control the public. Initially presented as incompetent, the public health institutions were now decried as tyrannical.

Prominent hyperpartisan influencers on the right began to equate pandemic mitigation or intervention measures with tyranny. Anti-mask wannabe-influencers emerged: clout-chasers livestreaming themselves in supermarkets, proudly picking fights with exhausted employees of the small businesses that had added masks to their "No Shoes, No Shirt, No Service" requirements. These videos were processed within some realities as "obnoxious trolls haranguing essential workers trying to earn a living," but within others as "warriors sticking it to the man." The worst norms of social media—a willingness to scream at people for the dopamine hit of indignation and attention—increasingly manifested in the real world.

Once masks became a symbol of factional allegiance and political identity, we could no longer have a normal conversation about their efficacy or trade-offs. In fact, it became increasingly difficult for the average person to determine whether or not masks actually worked. New studies were processed and spun by factional media and influencers into whatever narrative fit their niches' preexisting beliefs. Mainstream media, too, often failed to convey the nuance or limitations of a particular study. And so, depending on what media universe you followed, very different headlines hit your field of view about the same finding. Most people do not have access to medical journals online. Even those who do have access to "do their own research" often still lack the time or topical familiarity required to understand the finding. Some tried—and grew followings as Explainers—but the combination of inadequate headlines and personalized algorithmic curation made following the facts an uphill battle.

Even *cures*—cures!—became identity markers. Influential Gurus promoted hydroxychloroquine and vitamin C...and here, too, it felt like a battle to understand the evidence. If a study found that their pet treatment was ineffective, the Gurus—often profiting from sales of the product—simply claimed that the negative studies were *funded by Pharma*. True believers scrutinized the backgrounds of scientists who conducted the studies for evidence that they were "bought"; some were harassed. Government agencies—their heads appointed by Donald Trump—maintained websites covering the best available evidence, but their efforts could be dismissed as institutional lies, incompetence, or a plot to silence the "truth tellers."

My memory of that time in early 2020 is of feeling disoriented. There had never been more people shouting theories into the information space, many with "MD" after their name, and yet somehow it felt impossible to know what was true.

Entirely distinct constellations of COVID-19 experts began to emerge: some focused on lockdowns, some on school closures, some on treatments. Each was boosted by networks of the like-minded and trusted within distinct bespoke realities. Consensus around what was happening varied enormously between them. The Infodemic was at fever pitch—and the vaccines hadn't even been introduced yet.

Meanwhile, half a million people in the United States had died.[24]

Influence, Expertise, and Trust

Filings cabinets full of trafficked children, Central Intelligence Agency supercomputers changing votes, a plandemic: in each of these demonstrably false stories, influencers, algorithms, and committed crowds propelled rumors to mass awareness. Efforts to debunk the claims, meanwhile, were dismissed by the communities who claimed to believe them. By this point, you may be wondering why; you might be shaking your head and thinking, "These are very gullible people" or "Social media companies need to crack down on viral nonsense."

If so, you're part of the community that still trusts institutions and perhaps the mainstream media as well. A sizable community of people, however, no longer do. They don't find experts convincing. And that extends to the expert fact-checks or attempts to debunk even the most seemingly obvious false claims; the rebuttals are coming from someone they don't like, don't trust, and often actively resent. After *Plandemic* went viral, my team and I read many of the comments on Facebook shares of articles that attempted to debunk it. Many people simply did not know what to think. In one representative example, someone had shared an explainer by *Science* into the group Collective Action Against Bill Gates, which had previously discussed the *Plandemic* video. The person expressed confusion: "I seen the Plandemic video and was convinced she was telling the truth. I admire her courage for speaking out against the establishment...NOW I AM CONFUSED." The responses almost uniformly reinforced Mikovits's claims. "It's a scam to make you confused!" one commenter wrote.[25]

People are simply overwhelmed. The world feels unimaginably complex, and millions believe that they are being manipulated—they're just not sure by whom and to what end. Within the QAnon or anti-vaccine true believer communities, members have gone down the proverbial rabbit hole into bespoke realities that most of us would not recognize. There is absolutely no doubt that a vast cabal controls the world, that mainstream media, government, Big Tech, Big Pharma, and the Democratic Party are actively manipulating the public at all times. Attempts by outsiders to shift or add nuance to their views are often met with hostility;

the person trying to inject facts into the conversation is either complicit or a deluded sheep. The comments on *Plandemic* shares in highly conspiratorial communities didn't include much questioning. They were simply exalting, because commenters' beliefs had been confirmed: look here, *they* are being exposed, and the world is going to wake up to what we already know.

But even outside the most extreme spaces, the remarkable thing about COVID-19 was the extent to which bespoke realities seemed to prevail over actual reality, despite extraordinary personal stakes. The constantly mutating coronavirus was a completely indifferent pathogen that could kill people whether they believed in it or not—and in early 2020, many were dying. Yet some prominent influencers—and even world leaders—within highly conspiratorial bespoke realities insisted it was not dangerous, even as media covered refrigerated morgue trucks.[26] They and their followers chose to disregard the risks of exposure or touted pseudoscience to manage it, and many got sick or died.[27] And yet the fantasies persisted.

We're not going to be able to fact-check our way out of the excesses of the rumor mill or the propaganda machine. This problem transcends mere access to facts; at its core, it's a profound crisis of trust.

In *The Death of Expertise*, national security scholar and former Naval War College professor Tom Nichols defines experts in relation to the rest of the public: "Experts are the people who know considerably more on a subject than the rest of us, and are those to whom we turn when we need advice, education, or solutions in a particular area of human knowledge... [E]xperts in any given subject are, by their nature, a minority whose views are more likely to be 'authoritative'—that is, correct or accurate—than anyone else's."[28]

Yet influence and expertise are being decoupled, and trust is shifting. Today, certain audiences may perceive even an influencer with no relevant expertise or credentials as a more trustworthy source than an institutional expert they've never heard of. This is especially true for highly charged, politically tinged topics, where the actual facts may be less important than commitment to an ideological identity. There are so many potential sources of information; many of them conflict. There is a crisis of trust both in the institutions that the experts work for and in the media who usually present their findings. So who really does know best?

Deciding to trust someone, social scientists say, involves answering yes to at least one of two questions. First, does the person have our best interests at heart? This is determined by considering whether we think someone is aligned with us and is making an effort to give us information that is useful to us (and not only to them).[29] Influencers often seem to check these boxes, particularly those who present as Besties or Gurus. Second, does the person know better than we do? For decades, most people answered yes to this question when it came to experts, but now an increasing number aren't so sure.

People are increasingly uncertain about whether experts really do have our best interests at heart; they like *their* doctor, with whom they have a personal connection, but aren't as sure about the medical profession or public health institutions overall. Since the pandemic began in 2020, scientists have managed to retain a high degree of trust overall; nearly all other groups, from religious leaders to public school principals to police officers, were viewed less favorably. However, a February 2022 Pew Research study reported that Americans' trust in scientists to act in the best interests of the public had declined from 43 percent in April 2020 to just 29 percent.[30] The rate for a fair amount of trust remained high, but the shift was significantly partisan; the decline was more pronounced among Republicans.[31] The same goes for prominent health institutions: over the three years of the pandemic, trust in the CDC and the Food and Drug Administration, and in Anthony Fauci personally, all declined significantly among Republicans, but minimally among Democrats.[32]

When we examine trends in trust toward the government or media, a similar pattern emerges. While individuals may trust *their* elected officials or have favorable views of local newspapers, this personal connection doesn't extend to the larger, faceless entities of government, media, or most institutions.

Every year since 2001 the marketing firm Edelman has released an international survey called the Edelman Trust Barometer. The subtitle of each report provides a glimpse into the public zeitgeist in trust that year. In 2006: "A 'Person like Me' Emerges as Credible Spokesperson." In 2018: "The Battle for Truth." In 2022: "The Cycle of Distrust." The 2022 report highlights some concerns that may feel familiar to many readers: "fake news concerns at all time high"; "government and media seen as divisive"; "trust declines for government and media, business still only trusted institution." One in two poll respondents worldwide felt that media and government were divisive forces in society or deliberately lied to the public.

Troublingly, the decline appeared sharper within democratic countries specifically; in several Western countries, institutions were trusted by less than half of respondents in 2022. People surveyed viewed them not as forces for growth and unity but as lacking competence;[33] far higher trust was reported in more authoritarian countries. Media was distrusted, but social media was distrusted even more; everyone is skeptical of the information seen by *those other people*. Indeed, many people are distrustful *of* those "other people": 64 percent of respondents said that people today "lack the ability to have constructive and civil debate about issues they disagree on."[34] The 2023 Edelman Trust Barometer subsequently delved more into why: high polarization, derived in part from economic inequality that has people living in different realities, combined with a fractured media environment in which people live in "echo chambers,"[35] means that there is an ongoing battle over truth.

Compounding this, the internet reduced the seeming value of expertise—who needs an expert if you have Google right there, putting all of the knowledge of the world at your fingertips? Social media accelerated this belief further: Why should a so-called expert's opinion carry greater weight than any other person's? "Do your own research!" became a common refrain within online communities convinced that the experts and the government were lying to them. It was a phrase I saw often in new parenting groups in 2013, applied to every conceivable topic from cosleeping to formula to ear infections. On the surface, it's hard to argue against it: it's an exhortation to be informed, to study up on an important topic. We should all be informed! But it came to carry a particular connotation: it was not an invitation to consult the sorts of peer-reviewed research that offered the best representation of scientific consensus in quainter times; rather it was meant to steer the reader toward alternative sources, because "expert" consensus was compromised. If you did your own research but came to the same conclusions as institutional experts (or, god forbid, Big Pharma), you were doing it wrong.

During the pandemic, people struggled with information glut even as partisan identity shaped their thinking on whether or not to trust scientists. It's hard to know what to believe. I spent the majority of 2021 looking at vaccine rumors. Some, to me, were demonstrably and clearly false. But many were not. People don't actually have the time and energy to "do their own research"—they are going to pick one particular collection of experts to trust and go with it. And it's likely to be the collection of experts that their media, influencers, and friends all trust too—which algorithms will ensure they continue to see.

Distrust has become the default. Polarization increases distrust, which increases polarization. Studies show many citizens of democracies reporting a lack of shared identity. The things that once made democracies strong—like functional institutions—are struggling as society fractures. Psychologist Jonathan Haidt uses the metaphor of the Tower of Babel to describe the situation: "Something went terribly wrong, very suddenly. We are disoriented, unable to speak the same language or recognize the same truth. We are cut off from one another and from the past."[36] Yet even as people express this sense of pervasive distrust, they also report significant fear of problems that can only be solved through collective response—like the pandemic.

Experts face an uphill battle, a result of both actual institutional mistakes and failures, as well as the incentivized exacerbation of distrust.

Institutions made mistakes during COVID-19, both in determining what was happening and in how they engaged with the public. But these mistakes intersected with another dynamic: hyperpartisan media-of-one outlets and Perpetually Aggrieved influencers were actively incentivized to take any error, no matter how minor, by the media or an authority figure and use it to their own advantage. Actively eroding trust in experts and institutions, that strategy of so many invisible rulers, has proven to be a lucrative strategy for attracting and retaining attention. Partisan media outlets have long used phrases like "The media lies to you" and "The experts know nothing." Today, these canards are everywhere. The dynamics of the pandemic—in which consensus was constantly evolving alongside the discovery of new information—offered a continuous stream of opportunities for incentivized influencers to portray media as biased and experts as incompetent and to frame any attempt by tech platforms to mitigate the flood of viral rumors as egregious overreach.

Unfortunately, those attempting to push back found that in the age of social media, the playing field was far from level. The incentives of experts and influencers had diverged years prior; the influencers were products of the new communication ecosystem, while the experts scrambled to catch up.

The Crossroads of Clout and Competence

Long before the pandemic, influencers built up trust within niches, on particular topics, or around particular identities—yoga, perhaps, or healthy cooking. Once COVID-19 began to spread, that preexisting relationship was present even as influencer content switched to commentary about the virus. While tens of thousands of people may have followed that young Instagram mom for her laundry routine or that wellness influencer because they were curious about vegan cooking, they were also going to see their opinions on the COVID vaccine or the next election. The influencer may know absolutely nothing about immunology, but she *does* know what kind of content and language resonates with her audience (who may well have even less knowledge about the topic).

Firebrand Candace Owens, for example, had amassed a following on the political right years prior to COVID as a political commentator on various culture war skirmishes. Profiles describing her appeal emphasize how deftly she blends the political with cultural and lifestyle content (she gardens!), offering daily-living advice alongside searing takedowns of left-wing shenanigans.[37] But she is, unequivocally, a medical novice. So why did her audience of 3.2 million Twitter followers perceive her as a more reputable voice than scientist Anthony Fauci when she told them

COVID vaccines were dangerous? Because her audience trusted her and did not trust Fauci. That distrust is not entirely accidental—in fact, it is deliberately exacerbated. She may not be changing her followers' minds so much as reinforcing their preexisting beliefs or solidifying their understanding of how a new issue intersects with their political identity; it's often difficult to gauge. But even in a matter of life or death, having your beliefs validated by an opinion leader you trust is a powerful force.

We use what cognitive scientist Hugo Mercier calls "coarse cues" to gauge whether someone is trustworthy, like a person's title or prestigious degree.[38] Some influencers look like experts on the surface; a chiropractor might feature "Dr." in his handle as he yells on Instagram about the evils of chemotherapy. It might take some digging to discover that he isn't an oncologist. Another coarse cue is whether the person seems to be validating our preexisting point of view. The chiropractor's followers might not bother to dig into his credentials if he's saying something they agree with in the first place—confirmation bias is potent. If he's positioning his antichemo arguments as defending the people against Big Pharma, well, he's exposing the lies and fighting for the little guy!

Just like the *Plandemic* video.

In a revealing interview with the *LA Times*, Mikki Willis described how *Plandemic* came to be. He'd met Mikovits a year prior through mutual friends and was impressed. Willis told the *LA Times* that as the pandemic unfolded, "there were just so many things that didn't add up," and so he contacted Mikovits to get her opinion. He was motivated by apprehension about vaccine safety (though no COVID-19 vaccines existed at the time) and distrust of the pharmaceutical industry, "concerns he traces back," the *Times* wrote, "to the deaths of his brother from AIDS and his mother from cancer when he was in his 20s, which he believes were hastened by harmful medical treatments."[39] Most of Mikovits's writing and speaking in the near decade following her paper's retraction, and prior to their chat, had focused on spreading the theory that vaccines caused autism. Willis, however, personally trusted her and believed what she told him—and *Plandemic* was the product of that trust.

Yet it was Willis's talent for storytelling, editing, and marketing—and a network of influencer friends and supporters—that made the video a juggernaut. He and his subject came across as good communicators with the best interests of the public at heart.[40]

Social media culture rewards authenticity. Influencers speak like normal people, not like shifty pundits or elite academics. They convey their messages in memes—five words on top of an Instagram picture, not five thousand in an essay. They say what their audience is thinking, even if it's not politically correct. They're not trying to speak for all of America—or all of the world.

Consider one of the most successful influencers in the world: podcaster Joe Rogan, with an audience of eleven million listeners on Spotify, fifteen million subscribers on YouTube, and eighteen million followers on Instagram. Like most influencers, Rogan simply says what's on his mind. His throngs of passionate fans appreciate that candor. He brings on people he finds interesting; I was a guest, in March 2019, and we talked about the Internet Research Agency and Russia's efforts to divide American society.[41] Half of his audience hated me, but he was very friendly and engaging, and I saw it as an opportunity to reach people who might not have trusted mainstream media coverage of the topic but would listen to our conversation with an open mind because of their respect for him.

Rogan has been at the center of multiple controversies over the years in his thousands of hours of podcasting. Tactless things he's said resurface; sometimes he apologizes; other times he explains. Despite these occasional blowups—which often lead to media coverage discussing the power of an influencer with his audience size—Rogan sees himself as an entertainer. As he has put it on numerous occasions, he is just "a moron" with an opinion.[42] In that role, he freely speculates about whatever crosses his mind during his three-hour chats with his guests: Is ivermectin, an antiparasitic dewormer, a cure for COVID? In an April 2021 episode, Rogan mentions a doctor who said it was "99 percent effective," then offers up a common trope: "but you don't hear about it because you can't fund vaccines when it's an effective treatment." However, what comes next is a qualification: "I don't know if this guy is right or wrong. I'm just asking questions"[43] (a rhetorical sibling of "big if true"). Fact-checking organizations responded with articles attempting to clarify that ivermectin was not, in fact, an effective treatment based on the best available evidence. Scientists on social media were frustrated yet again; an influential person with a massive following had boosted a dubious remedy. This pattern repeated as Rogan grew more doubtful of mainstream scientific consensus about COVID-19, often featuring Gurus and Reflexive Contrarians while inviting far fewer conventional medical experts as guests.

But Rogan's freewheeling conversation style is how people talk in real life and on social media. People gossip and speculate. People share rumors. People get things wrong all the time. When you have an audience of over eleven million people, you do have, I would argue, an ethical obligation to try to get potentially impactful things right. But the audience isn't listening to Rogan to hear a litany of disclaimers; they want the casual conversation between him and his guest. He invites influencers, politicians, entertainers, and others to participate in unscripted, unpolished conversations, giving the audience an appealing feeling of being in the room. Many well-meaning influencers have yet to figure out how to have that freewheeling style while also remaining accurate.

Experts, on the other hand, rarely communicate with that kind of compelling ease.

As Nichols notes in *The Death of Expertise*, experts generally have self-awareness about the extent of their knowledge: they know when a question is beyond their capacity and will usually decline to weigh in if they aren't sure of something. This is an admirable trait. Yet, in the age of the influencer, we're surrounded by content created by anyone inclined to put themselves out there. Experts may wait to be sure of something, while influencers take the "big if true" approach. And if it turns out to be false? Oh. Well, they were just sharing their opinion.

The difference in conversational style, the use of casual language and thinking-out-loud commentary, and the willingness to get controversial or pointed at times all make influencers sound honest, often convincing. They sound like people you'd talk to at church or in a bar, while experts sound formal and stilted. The easygoing cool kids versus the nerds. Social media is made for memes and selfie videos—that's what goes viral, gets shared, and gets seen.

Experts generally try to convey nuance: *Well, it may be true in some circumstances that...* But in a world of 280-character tweets and thirty-second Reels, it's hard to do that and still be engaging. Long explanations may come across as making excuses or lacking the confidence of a simple declarative sentence. Academic and institutional experts typically publish research in journals or reports, often accompanied by press releases. Media translate their findings. However, media coverage can be problematic: the need for eye-catching headlines and clicks can lead to sensationalism, distorting complex studies. The public, which often just reads the headline, then sees things like "A harrowing study of 46,000 women shows hair dyes heavily associated with cancer" and misses all the caveats.[44] Even minor findings or flawed studies gain attention if they're sensational enough, inadvertently spreading misinformation.

Because they share knowledge through this process of papers mediated through media, the overwhelming majority of experts don't have the reach or resonance of an influencer. Most people who have truly informed, authoritative opinions about ivermectin haven't spent years building up their Twitter and YouTube followings; they've been doing research in a lab somewhere or treating patients. During the early days of COVID-19, scientists were focused on learning about the disease. They didn't yet know where it had come from or how it spread. They released in-progress findings via preprints or in medical journals that supported rapid peer review. The vast majority weren't doing multiple stream-of-consciousness posts per hour on Twitter or making speculative YouTube livestreams.

But on social media, frequent posting is key to building up an audience. Getting your content curated into a feed takes work—as we discussed, algorithms reward particular posting styles. There are top-notch Explainers with sizable followings—science communicators and physicians who produce excellent and informative YouTube videos for the public—but they began doing so long before COVID-19. Dr. Mikhail

Varshavski—"Dr. Mike"—has been making entertaining health-related videos since 2016 and boasts eleven million subscribers to his YouTube channel, along with another two million followers on TikTok. He answers hard questions and is both authoritative and empathetic. He also has a production team helping him at this point. Dr. Mike was able to use his platform to communicate about COVID-19 to his existing trusted audience—even doing a dedicated debunking of *Plandemic*. Many others, however, who began trying to convey their knowledge, had very small followings. They'd simply not prioritized communicating in that way before.

Over the last few years, many academics have begun investing in a social media presence. But gaining public visibility, growing a Twitter or YouTube audience, is not the primary incentive for experts—they won't get grants or publications by arguing on social media. Their institutions, in fact, might prefer that they don't. As we will discuss, becoming a public figure has some very real trade-offs.

Even as experts were cautious about weighing in on masks, potential remedies, and the disease's spread, influencers were openly speculating about every facet of COVID. Many who had no expertise whatsoever in epidemiology or virology (or China, for that matter) offered up theories—and if they had a lot of engaged followers, those theories were seen. Curation algorithms key off of popularity, not truth. Influencers got tens of thousands of retweets and engagements on pure speculation because their followers and *many* social media users were incessantly searching for information about COVID-19 as they doomscrolled during lockdown. As Naomi Klein wrote in *Doppelganger*, "Nothing had ever been nearly so hot, so potentially clout-rich as COVID-19. It was global. It was synchronous. We were digitally connected, talking about the same thing for weeks, months, years, and on the same global platforms... This squared virality meant that if you put out the right kind of pandemic-themed content—flagged with the right mix and match of keywords ("Great Reset," "WEF," "Bill Gates," "Fascism," "Fauci," "Pfizer") and headlined with tabloid-style teasers ("The Leaders Colluding to Make Us Powerless," "What They Don't Want You to Know About," "Bill Gates Said

WHAT?!?")—you could catch a digital magic carpet ride that would make all previous experiences of virality seem leaden in comparison.[45] Even nonconspiratorial influencers were participating, because moments when massive numbers of people are all paying attention to something searchable are unmissable opportunities. This is why the person you initially followed for makeup tips weighs in on the Russia-Ukraine war, COVID vaccines, and now US inflation and the Israel-Gaza conflict with equal confidence. (They will be talking about something else by the time you read this book.) They're just sharing their opinion. The algorithms, of course, will return the content they have available to them.

Managing a crowd of followers also takes a particular kind of skill. There are many Guru influencers, like supplement salesman and multi-millionaire osteopath Dr. Joseph Mercola, who trade on their credentials as they make far-fetched health claims—such as that spring mattresses amplify harmful radiation—and then sell products to "treat" the problem. Mercola himself has hundreds of thousands of Substack subscribers to his "Censored Library," more than four hundred thousand Twitter followers, an audience of close to three million on Facebook, and distribution on websites like Infowars. He, like Judy Mikovits, says the right words about dark forces conspiring against ordinary folks, and the coarse cues sway many. The people who trust him may not be aware of his profit motive, or they may simply not care. Although a detailed *New York Times* article labeled him "the most influential spreader of coronavirus misinformation online," factions who distrust the *New York Times* would consider that title a point of pride, proof that the "establishment" or the "elites" were out to get him because he was telling the truth.[46]

As the pandemic went on, many of the voices featured on Rogan's massive platform were guests who'd made COVID contrarianism their job, attracting fact-checks from media and often moderation by social platforms. Being written about critically by mainstream media or being moderated or kicked off of a social media platform was a massive *boon* for the influencer—just as it had been for *Plandemic*. The Gurus and the Contrarians could market themselves as the Censored, as Mikovits and Willis had done, even if the extent of the supposed censorship was a fact-check label being appended to one of their claims. In reality, they often had very large followings, far larger than the average scientist, and those followings only grew with the exposure to Rogan's massive audience.

But the critical takeaway here is that influencers have reach and resonance. At a time when people were deeply concerned about a deadly disease, someone with scientific credentials gave a plainspoken interview to a charismatic filmmaker. It wasn't a long PDF. It wasn't a set of statistics. It was material created for social media first, and its essence—as its creator admitted—was a ploy to grab attention and create virality. Content like this wasn't coming out of the expert establishment—they weren't even playing the same game.

Infodemics go hand in hand with epidemics because people are deeply concerned about the potential impact on those they love. Sharing salient rumors is a way that they can help inform their communities and make sense of the world with other impacted people. As with the election rumors we discussed in the last chapter, highly similar tropes and narratives recur, time and time again, because they *resonate*.

In one study of narratives surrounding the 2003 SARS outbreak, aptly titled *An Epidemic of Rumors*, author Jon D. Lee compared rumors about SARS to rumors about AIDS. He found that the narratives were "so analogous as to make it seem the differences lie only in the name of the disease."[47] SARS and AIDS ravaged communities long before social media made it effortless for stories to "go viral." And yet, even in that slower media landscape, the time gap between when people want information about a dangerous disease and when scientific or medical authorities have answers creates opportunities for rumors to set in. Experts write for journals even as media—and now influencers—are writing for the public, and they are often having completely separate conversations.

Beginning in February 2021, a year after the pandemic had started and after half a million Americans had died, the vaccine rollout began, the battles for reality picked up with a vengeance, and the difference between influencer and expert capacity for shaping public opinion was brought into even starker relief.

Network Neglect

Well before scientists had determined whether a COVID-19 vaccine was even possible, the long-standing, committed anti-vaccine faction had begun laying the groundwork for a fear campaign.

Even as the disease had just begun to creep beyond China's borders in early 2020, the very same California anti-vaccine influencers I'd dealt with in 2015 began making videos expressing unbridled excitement at what a pandemic would enable them to accomplish: whatever "rushed" vaccine might be developed would be a gift for their mission to undermine both confidence in *all* vaccines and support for the school requirements they so despised.[48] They would have opportunities to rile up the public about the imminent threat of "forced vaccination"—a phrase they used even for routine school requirements in normal times. Any effort to mitigate the pandemic, they reasoned, could be parlayed into converting people to oppose public health interventions writ large.[49] The propaganda strategy to undermine confidence in COVID-19 shots, and then all shots more broadly, was openly discussed and planned on social media over a year before a vaccine was available.

To put it plainly: the anti-vaccine movement's mobilization around COVID-19 was not in response to safety studies or efficacy findings about COVID-19 vaccines; it *predated* them.

Anti-vaccine activists had self-organized into state-level political advocacy groups on Facebook around the time of the California vaccine law fight in 2015. But the anti-vaccination movement had begun building its sharing networks years prior to the Disneyland measles outbreak. A very official-sounding group called the National Vaccine Information Center (NVIC) created its Facebook page in 2009. NVIC emerged during the broadcast-media-era anti-vaccine movement, which attracted celebrity spokespeople like Jenny McCarthy and got significant media attention on morning shows that aired concerns about vaccines and autism; vaccination rates dipped in response. As claims linking autism and vaccines were repeatedly disproven, however, media stopped giving the movement oxygen. So, the true believers moved to social media and established disciplined activist networks there to circumvent the "media blackout."

Some Gurus and credentialled contrarians (such as Andrew Wakefield, whose paper linking MMR vaccines and autism had been retracted) assembled a large following, alongside profiteers who sold "vaccine detoxes" and at times dangerous autism "cures."[50] Their followers, many of whom were mothers whose lives had been significantly impacted by the challenges of raising children on the autism spectrum, became zealous participants in spreading what they saw as the truth: that vaccines were the problem. These parents were looking for answers, and they had lost confidence in conventional health authorities. They found anti-vaccine movement leaders like Robert F. Kennedy Jr. and figures like Judy Mikovits persuasive; many believed that the truth about links between vaccines and autism were being kept from them by Big Pharma and the government. But they also persuaded each other, sharing personal stories and working to welcome people they met in other parent groups into the community.[51] The Facebook groups they formed ranged in size from the low thousands to over a hundred thousand—not a massive force in terms of percentage of the public overall but with a significant asymmetry of passion.

Most people simply vaccinated their children and moved on with their lives. They didn't post about it on social media. This meant that searching social media for vaccine-related content overwhelmingly returned negative posts and experiences and anti-vaccine activist propaganda—creating a majority illusion in which a relatively small minority looked far larger than it was. The anti-vaccine position began to look like the prevailing public opinion, even as over 80 percent of the public was still vaccinating their kids.

For a long time, algorithms helped the movement expand: anti-vaccine groups and pages and influencer accounts were promoted by the recommendation engines. Groups like Stop Mandatory Vaccination (discussed in Chapter 2) grew their audiences via advertising. Facebook's ad-targeting tool offered "anti-vaccine" as an interest option back in 2015, as we learned when we started Vaccinate California; there was no pro-vaccine ad keyword.[52]

This was the state of affairs until 2019, when a measles outbreak in Samoa killed eighty-three children, with 87 percent under the age of five.[53] Robert F. Kennedy Jr. had played a role there too: in July 2018, a tragic accident led to the deaths of two children immediately follow-ing their MMR vaccines. The government halted the vaccine program for nearly a year during an investigation, which ultimately found that a nurse had made an error in administering the shots.[54] During that time, RFK Jr.'s anti-vaccine group, Children's Health Defense, posted repeat-edly about the tragedy to its Facebook page, highlighting the deaths and questioning the safety of the vaccine program (it did not expend similar energy informing its audiences of the nursing error). Then in September 2019 the measles outbreak struck. As the Samoan government worked to implement an emergency vaccination mandate, RFK Jr. fought against the idea in a letter to local leaders, arguing that perhaps the outbreak itself had been caused by a "mutant strain" from a "defective vaccine." Amer-ican anti-vaccine activists on Facebook began deluging the Samoan gov-ernment's Facebook posts about the outbreak and the emergency vaccine mandate, leaving negative reviews and crazy comments. They held a vita-min drive and boosted local "healers," who were trying to sneak vitamin C into hospitals to encourage parents with sick kids to use that instead.[55]

Facebook, meanwhile, had begun to crack down on vaccine misin-formation in March 2019—following a different measles outbreak and public health emergency in Brooklyn, New York.[56] It created a set of policies, which included removing anti-vaccine groups from recommen-dations and no longer accepting their ads.[57] It enforced these policies during the crisis in Samoa and expanded them to attempt to surface more authoritative information in response to vaccine-related searches. There was some complaining about "censorship" from anti-vaccine ac-tivists but little among the broader public; the deaths of infants and the multiple outbreaks had outraged people. Online lies and anti-vaccine influencers were causing harm.[58]

Despite the platform policy changes, the anti-vaccine influencers and crowds were already well networked, and paid boosts and recommenda-tions were secondary to their more organic strategies. It was this well-established network that drove *Plandemic*'s early spread. And it would go on to be a major player in the online rumor mill speculating about all aspects of COVID-19.

When Mikki Willis posted the *Plandemic* video to his Facebook profile with a call for his audience to share it, Judy Mikovits was already a well-established figure in the anti-vaccine cinematic universe. Her theories about how vaccines caused autism had won her a loyal following of vocal true believers, and though she was not particularly charismatic, they saw her as an authoritative expert. A David standing up to Goliaths. Many COVID contrarians would cast themselves in the same light: top scientists, bravely bucking the elite establishment consensus, *#SilencedForTruth*. Veritable Galileos, all. Their followers—the factions that shared their content—saw themselves as participants in an existential fight.

My team and I watched the spread of *Plandemic* as it happened. We'd become curious about Mikovits's sudden popularity a few weeks prior as she began to promote her book. A new Twitter account she'd made (despite having had one for years) was gaining followers with remarkable speed, including from many newly created handles.[59] It was very obvious to us that *Plandemic* was going to be a viral hit as soon as it was posted. And it was. We watched it break out of the anti-vaccine echo chamber, where a lot of similar content normally stayed, and get pickup within more "mainstream" communities, as commenters debated whether or not to take its claims seriously. They were genuinely curious, trying to figure out whom to trust and what was real. Was it better to err on the side of masks, or not, they wondered?

Meanwhile, it would be nearly forty-eight hours before the fact-checks began to appear. When they did, they would not achieve nearly the same reach.

The lack of networked distribution among public health and science communicators has been a long-standing issue. Local public health officials speak to the communities they care for, but there has been little connectivity between them from a public communication standpoint. There is simply nothing like the distribution of the anti-vaccine movement network on the public health side.[60] Even after battle to pass California's Senate Bill 277—and other laws strengthening routine-vaccine requirements for public schools—institutional experts had not prioritized building up networked social media groups that could amplify accurate information. Some physicians and science communicators did in an ad hoc way, and their efforts should be praised, but there was no coordinated movement to reach the fence-sitters or the confused who saw things like *Plandemic* land in their Facebook feeds. As COVID-19 vaccine development commenced, experts were largely unprepared for the war they were about to find themselves in.

As I watched the COVID infodemic begin to unfold, I often found myself thinking of the CDC official who in 2015 had said to me, "These are just some people on the internet." Public health institutions had believed that the public would continue to trust them and take guidance from their statements. But all of a sudden, an immense number of people simply did not.

The Virality Project

Given the anti-vaccine activists' plainspoken intent to create hesitancy, and having just finished studying the 2020 election delegitimization effort, our team at Stanford Internet Observatory decided to study the narratives surrounding the imminent vaccine rollout. The Virality Project,[61] as we called it, added teams from New York University's Tandon School of Engineering and Center for Social Media and Politics and the nonprofit National Conference on Citizenship to the institutions that worked on the Election Integrity Partnership. We would write weekly briefings summarizing which viral narratives had achieved the most reach or appeared to hop beyond the communities in which they had originated (à la *Plandemic*). These briefings, we hoped, would provide people capable of responding to the viral claims—such as civil society, tech platforms, physicians, and public health officials like the CDC and the Surgeon General's Office—with awareness of what needed a response. They could tailor their messages to address the real concerns of specific communities.

The physicians in particular were passionate about speaking up: they wanted to address misleading narratives by leveraging their own expertise on their own social media accounts. One group of physicians in

California had come up with a hashtag—*#ThisIsOurShot*—and wanted to focus on making relatable, sharable content—posting photos of themselves getting their vaccines or creating funny memes—putting out *good* information as well as pushing back on bad information. Our briefings could help them identify what most urgently needed a response.[62] The social media companies also received our reports, as well as occasional tags on content that seemed to violate their policies. They treated our work as an additional signal to supplement their own understanding of emerging narratives. And, as with the Election Integrity Partnership, the platforms set their own policies and made their own decisions about transparency and what to moderate.

We scoped the Virality Project to look at emerging viral narratives that fell within specific categories: safety; efficacy and necessity; development and distribution; and conspiracy. The categories came from prior research into the anti-vaccine movement that laid out recurring tactics and tropes, some of which dated back well over a century.[63] As scientists in the late 1800s began to conclusively demonstrate that people could be inoculated against smallpox, reducing the prevalence of the deadly disease, some state and local governments began to require inoculation—particularly during outbreaks. Anti-vaccination leagues (as they called themselves) emerged in response, holding protests and making written complaints about affronts to liberty, while also liberally mixing in pseudoscience: inoculation, some argued, would turn people into human-animal hybrids, because cowpox was used in the process.[64] In 1867, one member of a family dated his "syphilitic symptoms" to the time of vaccination, and a prominent leader of an anti-vaccination league argued that this was evidence of unsafe vaccines.[65] By 1897, physicians were writing letters to medical journals bemoaning the extent to which anti-vaccine canards were becoming challenging to refute.[66] Rumors about safety and side effects triggered people's fears and spread widely. Because they were salient, the themes that the rumors and narratives touched on—safety, efficacy, purity, toxicity, and liberty—have persisted over time and are often mixed into conspiracy theorizing.[67] Just as Jon Lee described the

SARS and AIDS rumors as being virtually indistinguishable aside from the names of the diseases, so it is with rumors about vaccines.

As expected, once the rollout began, vaccines were quickly and heavily politicized via both the rumor mill and the propaganda machine. And as with the election narratives, chatter ping-ponged back and forth from the top down and bottom up: political propaganda from media elites was processed by the crowd, reinforcing distrust; user-created content reflected that distrust, influencers boosted it, and media parlayed the resulting viral social media rumors into "some people on the internet are saying" segments.

Influencers were once again overwhelmingly present as mediators, serving as both opinion leaders and content creators. Many created, shaped, and amplified stories that not only served their messaging objectives but at times rewarded them financially as well: wellness and lifestyle influencers had oils to sell, contrarian medical influencers made millions on virtual visits, and conspiracy theory influencers who'd previously been experts in lizard people now peddled theories that vaccines were made from snake venom and offered detox.[68] And, unfortunately, right-wing political influencers played a significant role in turning resisting vaccination into a political identity. Their motivations included clout and power.

Despite the fact that the vaccines were developed via Operation Warp Speed during the presidency of Donald Trump, right-wing political influencers spent extensive amounts of time eroding confidence in their safety. Just as masks, lockdowns, cures, and every other aspect of the pandemic had been politicized into a culture war identity battle, so too were the vaccines. The anti-vaccine movement had become increasingly associated with right-wing politics since California's Senate Bill 277 fight, and the trend continued with the COVID-19 vaccines.[69] Commentary from prominent figures on the political left occasionally veered into the distrustful—Vice President–elect Kamala Harris made remarks about not trusting a "Trump vaccine"—but few political influencers on that side of the aisle made creating hesitancy or delegitimizing COVID-19 vaccines a core theme of their content.

Narratives shifted along with the political winds. Early in the roll-out, when administration of the Johnson & Johnson vaccine was briefly paused because of observed side effects, the "just asking questions" set framed the temporary halt as a conspiracy. Fox News host Tucker Carlson, a man well versed in the art of using innuendo and insinuation to darkly present no facts at all, ominously intoned,

> Now [Anthony] Fauci has declared that because the Johnson & Johnson vaccine has injured six people—and if that's true, by the way, would make that vaccine much safer not just than birth-control pills, but safer than many other vaccines we've distributed in the past—because this one vaccine has hurt six people out of 7 million, we need to stop using it immediately. Does that make sense to you? No, it really doesn't. It seems possible there may be more going on here.

There was no explanation of what was going on there, that night or in any future segment. But insinuations open the door for audience members to fill in the blanks however *they* prefer, while shielding the speaker from a defamation lawsuit. On Facebook, Carlson's speculation session was the most popular post about the Johnson & Johnson pause, even though Fox News journalists had reported on the pause with accuracy and nuance.[70]

The irony was thick: the Johnson & Johnson vaccine was halted after six incidents, generating a segment complaining and expressing suspicion about the halt. Yet the rhetoric from many of the same right-wing influencers a few short months later would allege that the vaccines had been killing and injuring millions. The same public health officials that convened an investigation about six adverse events, we are supposed to believe, then covered up vaccine-induced mass murder.

Although some of the highest-engaged stories overall originated with prominent political and old-media elites, the analysts of the Virality Project were largely seeing rumors moving through very well-established factional rumor mills. While anti-vaccine influencers had reach and disciplined dissemination capabilities through their long-established networks, the popular wellness and political influencers who began to participate had orders of magnitude more. Many rumors stayed within particular communities; the nuttiest conspiracy theories, for example, did not hop across as broad a collection of groups as *Plandemic* had managed to, though conspiracy content about Bill Gates, microchips, and magnetic vaccines spilled out occasionally. Yet, while certain types of content didn't travel far, they went deep, becoming conventional wisdom within bespoke realities. QAnon adherents, for example, came to the conclusion that Anthony Fauci was part of a cabal secretly working to undermine President Trump. This all got significant amounts of engagement *within* the conspiracy communities.

As during the election, if massively popular prominent influencers or celebrities picked up a rumor, it could reach tens of thousands of people nearly instantly. On September 13, 2021, Nicki Minaj tweeted, "My cousin in Trinidad won't get the vaccine cuz his friend got it & became impotent. His testicles became swollen. His friend was weeks away from getting married, now the girl called off the wedding. So just pray on it & make sure you're comfortable with ur decision, not bullied."[71]

This extraordinary piece of content received 252,000 interactions. Some people in the comments tried to convey that this was more commonly a symptom of an STD, not generally a vaccine injury. The Nicki Minaj's Cousin's Friend's Balls discourse dominated the internet that afternoon and, of course, was picked up by the media.[72]

But as funny as the memes were that day, there is actually a more important takeaway: many people are genuinely concerned as they spread "friend-of-a-friend" rumors. Unlike stories about ballots in dumpsters, these stories and first-person posts sharing bad experiences were not the sort that social media companies could dispel with a quick fact-check label and help from an investigative journalist. These stories did need some contextualization—not to disparage them but to compassionately explain things like prevalence or the likelihood that a certain symptom postvaccination was in fact vaccine related. In a past era, these concerns were the sorts of things that a doctor would have responded to one on one in a visit with a concerned patient. But today rumors spread at high velocity and on a global scale. The question of how to respond was immensely complex. Yes, groups of physicians were working to take the signal from the rumors and push back; individual doctors began spending time popping into Clubhouse audio chats and making TikToks to counter viral conspiracy theories (after working their day jobs). But the efforts were all ad hoc. Networks to *share* the physicians' content were ad hoc.

Rumors have "publics," as Jean-Noël Kapferer, the scholar of rumors we encountered in Chapter 1, put it; some groups are going to be more receptive to some stories than others. The Black community, which is very concerned with medical racism and its negative impact on Black women's maternal health outcomes, and which has deep memories of historical atrocities such as the Tuskegee experiments, shared very different types of rumors than the Chinese-language expatriate community, which has a different communal history. And, of course, neither of these groups are themselves monolithic. Since the rumors were moving through niches, effective counterspeech—and effective counterspeakers—might look very different for each rumor.

But building truly networked responses is challenging. Individual civil society organizations or physicians could only respond to so much. The Virality Project had limited resources and could only connect with so many groups. Biden administration officials and other authority figures spoke up, including via the Office of the Surgeon General. However, when trust in authority figures is low, rumors may become *more* compelling. The idea of an "official story" or "official source" reflects a power dynamic: some official has authority to speak, to declare what is true, and the public is expected to believe it. The alternative explanations and theories—the rumors—challenge that authority, highlighting that *official* and *credible* do not always go hand in hand. Today we have both a system that makes rumor spreading effortless *and* the social circumstances that make rumors compelling.

And, of course, even as the rumor mill and domestic propaganda machines were spinning, the state actor propaganda machines were taking advantage of the distrust and unrest too: Russia leveraged its overt state media to express horror about the unfreedom of American vaccine requirements, even as Russian regional governments and businesses imposed nearly identical requirements for certain types of workers and for access to restaurants.[73] It talked up the Sputnik vaccine while fearmongering about the supposed dangers of the Pfizer and AstraZeneca vaccines.[74] One trope used to mock AstraZeneca's vaccine was a throwback to the smallpox-cowpox fears of the 1880s: the Russian talking heads called it "the monkey vaccine," because it was made using a chimpanzee adenovirus, and put memes of chimps on TV. The Sputnik vaccine, of course, contained no monkey parts! (Ironically, the chimpanzee tie would later be used to argue that a monkeypox outbreak, relevant only because of the name, was caused by the AstraZeneca vaccine.)[75] Gray propaganda outlets and bloggers picked up the propaganda touted on state TV, laundering the messages to their own audiences.[76] In another case, a Russia-linked marketing firm registered to a UK address that did not seem to house any business began offering to pay YouTube influencers to talk up the Sputnik vaccine and smear Pfizer as unsafe and dangerous. The effort was exposed by several horrified influencers; a few others, though, did make the paid posts.[77] Facebook subsequently took down a network of pages related to this manipulation campaign.[78]

Moderation and the Mirror World

As with the 2020 election, rapidly evolving circumstances during the pandemic led to new tech company policies that tried to balance free expression and harm prevention. The platforms communicated regularly with public health officials as well to try to surface the best available information. Once again, their efforts to moderate—including basic content labeling—were slammed as "censorship."

Grasping the subtleties of COVID-19 content moderation is crucial for guiding future institutional and platform responses. The real-world consequences of online COVID-19 rumors were stark. Early on, prominent figures like Robert F. Kennedy Jr. and various influencers peddled baseless theories linking 5G wireless towers to the coronavirus. Videos posted to YouTube about the theory accrued hundreds of thousands of views, and—like *Plandemic*—the content spread globally. Some of the social media groups dedicated to 5G theories added nearly half a million followers over a two-week period.[79] A few people were convinced enough to try to burn down towers.[80] Rumors about cures and treatments, meanwhile, led to injuries and deaths.

It's critical to note that audiences were receptive to these theories because of the disorienting state of the world and because of just how hard the pandemic was for many people. Yes, there was a glut of information, and it was incredibly hard to figure out what was true and who was being honest. But people were getting sick, including those without health care. Many families were impacted economically by lockdowns and the loss of childcare; many became frustrated, and some became distrustful of the motivation and competency of institutions that argued for them. The influencers who railed against technology or government or health care weren't entirely wrong: there *are* devastating collective failures, mistakes, and instances of incompetence, and that grain of truth is ripe for exploitation. Rhetoric about the impending threat of tyranny, long present on the political fringe, took on a new tenor and attracted many new adherents. People who had previously vaccinated their kids reported joining anti-lockdown protests or school-reopening activist communities and then losing confidence in the science of vaccination as they spent more time with newfound anti-vaccine allies who became friends.

Social media companies had struggled with how to handle the anti-vaccine movement for years. The 2019 Brooklyn and Samoa measles outbreaks, discussed earlier, showed once again that online rumors and misinformation could lead to very bad situations in the real world. As these epidemics unfolded, major social media companies decided to begin boosting authoritative sources in response to vaccine-related searches. So, as COVID-19 emerged, Meta CEO Mark Zuckerberg mandated that his integrity teams begin working on policies specific to COVID-19 misinformation. He reached out to Anthony Fauci with a proposal to create a "COVID-19 Information Center" to help people find information about the disease.[81]

Following past outbreaks, tech companies had decided that while the anti-vaccine movement could remain on their platforms, its content would not receive algorithmic amplification. Freedom of speech, not freedom of reach. However, when the anti-vaccine movement was primarily spreading fear about proven-safe childhood vaccines, its influence was mostly confined to pregnant women and parents. With the global roll-out of COVID-19 vaccines for all age groups, the movement's potential audience expanded dramatically. Anti-vaccine activists on social media capitalized on this, witnessing a surge in followers. These new adherents eagerly circulated vaccine rumors, misinformation, and conspiracy theories, topics that had become relevant to almost everyone.

This created three challenges for the platforms. First, while some of the claims that captured attention were demonstrably wrong (misinformation), much of what was spreading were rumors rooted in personal stories or opinion commentary. These are not addressable with a fact-check label. Second, the ref-working narrative that "moderation equals censorship," popularized by Trump and his supporters while promoting the Big Lie, was now common knowledge among right-wing factions—and as coalitions formed during COVID-19, it spread to more. Even when the platforms moderated content that could directly affect public health, like the spread of fake cure stories worldwide, their actions were swiftly recast as violations of free speech and liberty, an attempt to suppress debate; the strategy that Willis had deliberately chosen for *Plandemic* worked time and time again. Finally, while the platforms had committed to boosting authoritative sources, institutional communicators struggled with speed and resonance. The organizations that Facebook had announced that it would boost—the WHO and the CDC—rarely produced compelling, shareable content and often were slow to react to communication cycles. Also, many noninstitutional experts had valuable perspectives worth hearing, and platforms like Twitter scrambled to give them "blue check" credentials.

Some of the most challenging posts for platforms were the stories that were superficially true: a nurse named Tiffany Dover, for example, fainted while getting a shot on television. She was fine, but despite the best efforts of fact-checkers, a rumor spread globally that she was dead.[82] Her hospital put her on camera to show that she was fine, but because she was wearing a mask and didn't speak, conspiracy theorists alleged she'd been replaced by a body double. Her life was upended as thousands of people began to harass her friends, neighbors, and employer on Facebook, Instagram, and Twitter.[83] That she had fainted *was* true—everything that came after was not. Should the story have been removed or reduced, or was an information label sufficient? If so, what should the label say? Platforms and fact-checkers often labeled such content as "misleading," and it stayed up, though sometimes with reduced distribution (the posts were no longer curated into people's newsfeeds or could not be retweeted). Groups and accounts that consistently shared misleading content were penalized after some number of strikes. Prominent influencers who had begun to identify as "free-speech absolutists" argued that this was all free expression and that any platform effort to address it was "stifling debate."

In another case, Facebook ads run by unknown actors began to pop up encouraging Americans to self-report vaccine side effects to the national Vaccine Adverse Events Reporting System (VAERS), which the CDC had run for decades to track adverse events. Some prominent influencers who were skeptical of COVID-19 shots began to call for the same. Did you get a headache? Report it! A few months later, anti-vaccine activists used statistics derived from the self-reported data, such as the total number of reports, to allege that the COVID-19 vaccines were phenomenally dangerous.[84] Actual safety studies belie these claims. Nonetheless, there were entries in a database, so people could calculate statistics. Therefore, claims like "There are thousands of reports from people saying they were injured by this vaccine!" didn't necessarily qualify as "misinformation"—after all, it is superficially true. There *were* thousands of reports, but their existence alone was being used to create a very misleading perception.

If a label or context applied by a tech platform to explain how VAERS worked was "censorship," as aggrieved ref-workers opposed to fact-checking argued, then what *was* the appropriate response? Who was supposed to debate this in the marketplace of ideas, and how, so that audiences saw it?

The misleading presentation of VAERS stats, in fact, was an extension of a fudging strategy that anti-vaccine activists had long found highly effective during fights over school shots: VAERS reports for those immunizations, too, included some highly dubious claims. A very small percentage of reports turned into actual Vaccine Injury Compensation Program "vaccine court" cases.[85] Those that did were investigated thoroughly, and some plaintiffs received settlements for demonstrable vaccine injuries—injuries do happen, though they are very rare. Anti-vaccine activists, however, had long touted the number of reports in the database or the total dollar value of the settlements as evidence of the dangers of childhood immunizations—leaving off the fact that the number of injuries relative to the number of shots administered actually showed that a person was more likely to be struck by lightning than injured by a vaccine.

My explanation of how this rhetorical sleight-of-hand works took a full paragraph. Writing "$3 billion was paid out to the vaccine injured!" creates real concern in a lot less time.

Some of the propaganda claims were comically flimsy if you scratched the surface, but they resonated with the target audience. In December 2021, Dr. Peter McCullough, a prominent promoter of hydroxychloroquine and ivermectin, attracted significant attention as a guest on Joe Rogan.[86] During his appearance he implied that the pandemic had been planned, alleged that huge numbers of people had been killed by the vaccine, and argued that the government was suppressing the true facts about, and access to, alternative therapies in an effort to drive people to get vaccinated.[87] Hydroxychloroquine factories were allegedly mysteriously burning down. It was all very evocative of *Plandemic*. McCullough's social media follower count jumped after the appearance.

Soon after, he began to boost the theory that healthy athletes were simply dropping dead after getting COVID vaccines. The claim had been popularized via the release of a documentary called *Died Suddenly*, which alleged that there was an epidemic of sudden deaths linked to blood clots and cardiac arrest. For weeks, any time a prominent person happened to die, the now sizable anti-vaccine Twitter faction would co-opt the tragedy, speculating about whether they were vaccinated and creating huge numbers of posts about the deceased tagged with the hashtag *#DiedSuddenly*.

McCullough—an MD-PhD—had written a letter to the editor of a medical journal alleging that 1,598 athletes had suffered cardiac arrest over about a one-year period; this was presented as quite an ominous outlier, attributable to the vaccines. As 1,598 is a highly specific number, I googled it. It turned out that it came from...a blog. An anonymous blogger at goodsciencing.com had made a list of the deaths of athletes since the vaccine rollout had begun (January 2021), and McCullough cited it in his letter to the journal editor as if it were a solid source.[88] I was enthralled by the shamelessness and began to look through the list. A few more minutes of googling revealed the inconvenient fact that many of the people on the list not only hardly qualified as athletes—some were simply described as sports hobbyists in coverage of their death—but had died by drowning, car accident, or causes unknown. Their vaccine statuses also weren't stated.

An MD-PhD had laundered content from a blog that a middle schooler would've been ashamed to cite into a medical journal by way of a letter. And now his supporters were calling it a "paper."

Meanwhile, as *#DiedSuddenly* captivated the large, highly active, and often vicious anti-vaccine faction on Twitter, the families of people who had died tragically (including by suicide) were subjected to online mobs insisting that their loved ones had really died because of the COVID-19 vaccine.[89] Sometimes the deaths were explained within a day or two, but that gap between when a rumor goes viral and when the truth can be known meant that the rumor generated significant attention (and clout) for those who pushed the stories, while the subsequently revealed facts received little to no attention at all.

This theory of an epidemic of cardiac events rose to national prominence after football player Damar Hamlin collapsed on the field during a game, and Tucker Carlson covered the frightening incident on his nightly Fox News program.[90] He hosted McCullough and discussed his letter as if it had been a study, an explanation for what had happened to Hamlin[91] (who fortunately survived but then found himself the subject of the same Body Double trope that had driven Tiffany Dover into hiding).[92]

Absolute nonsense had been laundered into The Discourse; millions of Tucker Carlson viewers saw the broadcast implying that there was a serious epidemic of sudden athlete deaths. Right-wing and anti-vaccine factions hailed McCullough as a hero for exposing the conspiracy by media, government, and pharma to "suppress" athlete deaths. The fact that he'd previously been suspended ("censored") by Twitter for spreading other COVID-19 misinformation[93] and had his certifications threatened by the American Board of Internal Medicine didn't matter—it might even have given him more cred with the antiestablishment audience he was cultivating.[94] With more than nine hundred thousand Twitter followers and ninety-nine thousand subscribers to his "Courageous Discourse" Substack newsletter, McCullough has far more reach than the overwhelming majority of scientists.

What is the appropriate response to scenarios such as this? Should scientists or the families of victims counter recurring viral hashtags with facts, even if it invites abuse and harassment, amplifies the trend further, and will likely not change the minds of the irate faction anyway? Should Twitter prevent hashtags like *#DiedSuddenly* from trending, or should Facebook downrank or block shares of content from its domain?

These are thorny questions, even as some highly vocal online factions argue that they're simple. "Take more misinformation down because it kills people," some say. "Moderation is censorship," argue others. But the loudest complainers about the status quo rarely offer any specifics for where platforms should draw lines or positive vision for reckoning with a curated, ranked information feed. Vaccines, of course, are highly polarizing, but many, many other health topics do, or will, fall under these policies, and similar questions apply. Should cancer quackery be pushed to newly diagnosed oncology patients because some influencers manage to capture attention? Should teenage girls be barraged with posts about weight loss supplements?

There has been an asymmetry of passion in health misinformation for close to a decade: normal people get vaccinated, and *nothing happens*. This was true of COVID-19 and the billions of vaccines administered worldwide with no massive epidemic of attributable injuries or deaths. Most people who have a completely ordinary experience do not post about it—though the doctors of *#ThisIsOurShot* tried. Meanwhile, platforms curate what is available to them, which means that whatever the rumor mill and propaganda machine churn will surface, unless the platforms have policies that impact the propagation.

Many people, including myself, still hold out hope for a "marketplace of ideas," in which discussion enables the most accurate or best arguments rise to the top. But the structure of our current information environment is not designed to facilitate it. Its incentives encourage sensationalism, and enable grifters to profit from it. People in one bespoke reality are long past listening to those in the others. In *Broken Code*, Wall Street Journal reporter Jeff Horwitz describes leaked internal Facebook memos written by employees of the type of integrity teams that Mark Zuckerberg had instructed to prepare for COVID-19. They describe a mess: Facebook groups served as a staging area for platform-wide assaults on mainstream medical information; doctors posting on the platform were being shouted down; groups were growing because a relatively small number of people were inviting hundreds or thousands of users per day; groups were not arising organically, but had undisclosed ties to political activists. "The company should think about whether it was merely reflecting a widespread skepticism of COVID, or creating one," Horwitz writes while describing a conversation between data scientists. "This is severely impacting public health attitudes," another responds, "I have some upcoming survey data that suggests some baaaad results."[95]

Many moderation calls are debatable by reasonable people: Should something be throttled or just labeled? The battle over the origin of COVID-19—the infamous lab-leak hypothesis—was one example of something that should simply have been left up for debate, because it's unclear that it actually had any real potential for harm. Content that is taken down or banned becomes forbidden knowledge; influencers who are deplatformed now simply move to one of many other different platforms. In her study of writer turned conspiracy theorist Naomi Wolf, who was temporarily deplatformed from Twitter, Naomi Klein writes, "These people don't disappear just because we can no longer see them. They go somewhere else. And many of them go to the Mirror World: a world uncannily like our own, but quite obviously warped."[96] I am generally opposed to the overwhelming majority of takedowns and strongly in favor of reducing reach or labeling, precisely because of the "forbidden knowledge" factor. Other content moderation researchers disagree, arguing that evidence shows that deplatforming people who repeatedly spread lies works, because it reduces their reach. Platforms are private actors under no obligation to offer free speech or free reach, they accurately point out. And yet a quick look at the influencers deplatformed during COVID-19 suggests a significant backfire effect. There were other platforms for them to go to; after being forced from Twitter, YouTube, and Facebook, they regrew their audiences on Telegram, Rumble, and Substack. And many become even more radical.

On Substack in particular, COVID-19 contrarians became a force: Dr. Joseph Mercola, who built a massive business selling quack health products to anti-vaccine activists over many years; tech entrepreneur Steve Kirsch, who had no background in vaccines or epidemiology at all but redefined himself as a COVID contrarian and now fearmongers about childhood vaccines; and "the Pandemic's wrongest man,"[97] Alex Berenson. All are now prominent on the Substack leaderboards with tens of thousands of paid subscribers each at around $5 a month.[98] Some of those suspended by Twitter's old moderation team (including Berenson and McCullough) were welcomed back after Elon Musk acquired the company. They have seen massive follower growth in the time since.

Institutions in the Crosshairs

The Virality Project cataloged the narratives surrounding COVID-19 vaccines for the better part of 2021. Physicians and scientists did attempt to counterspeak, though they often did not have much in the way of individual reach or established networks for amplification. They did come away with an understanding of what they need to do ahead of the next public health crisis. But their ability to adapt—and to build those networks—is now under attack.[99]

The pandemic highlighted many areas in which institutions and authority figures struggled: communication flubs, supply chain shortages, poor contact tracing, dubious border policies, politicized rhetoric, bad coordination, and healthcare access challenges, among other things.[100] There are many trenchant critiques of things that could have been done differently; I wrote several articles about communication failures in 2020 and 2021. Assessments of what specifically went wrong often split according to political perspective: assessments coming from the left have pointed to inadequate consideration of poverty and racism, while libertarian and right-leaning thinking has focused on the economic impact of lockdowns and the validity of mandates.[101] Debates about who got what wrong will no doubt fill many other books; suffice it to say that many people feel that institutions failed, and their confidence in those institutions has diminished.

However, the real struggles of institutions were cynically exaggerated by some, as part of a very deliberate effort to undermine confidence in institutions writ large—to frame them as inherently deceitful and manipulative, staffed by elites out to suppress the people. In late 2022, for example, a narrative took hold among vaccine-distrustful factions that *they* had lied to us about whether or not the vaccines prevented transmission. Evidence was assembled: video snippets, mostly repurposed from early 2021, in which pharmaceutical company executives or government officials made claims suggesting that vaccines would prevent the spread of the virus; video clips with hundreds of thousands of views purporting to expose a pharmaceutical executive "admitting" that they didn't test the vaccine to see if it reduced transmission.[102] The same collages pop up every few months and generate outrage anew, often when an influencer or media-of-one outlet shares them with a rallying cry: *Never forget what they did to you!*

Most people don't recall the circumstances of early 2021: the vaccine manufacturers were not required to test whether the vaccines reduced transmission prior to rollout. To get emergency approval, the companies were supposed to show that the vaccines were safe and prevented vaccinated people from getting sick. They did, for the version of the disease that was circulating at the time. They also, in fact, reduced transmission at that time. But as new variants emerged, they became less effective.[103]

The internet enables the instantaneous resurfacing of any pronouncement of an expert or government official. "The internet is forever," as the saying goes, and this can be a very good thing. However, it also allows for old tweets, writings, and videos to be taken out of context, misrepresenting outdated facts or views as if current circumstances haven't changed. This leads to overreactions, such as labeling those who made these past statements incompetent or dishonest. While some experts do make mistakes or lie, some invisible rulers are incentivized to exploit these gotchas unfairly to undermine the credibility of experts in general.

A Great Retcon is thriving in the communities that were most actively opposed to lockdowns, masks, and vaccines. Some of the most prominent influencers who denigrated vaccines and touted ivermectin and hydroxychloroquine—particularly those who had content labeled or posts removed—now argue that they *deserve an apology*. They feel they were vindicated because, as the vaccines became less effective with each passing variant, their pronouncements that the vaccine would not work *at the very beginning* were borne out. The world changed, and the "cures" they themselves pushed proved useless, but those details can be brushed aside.[104] These influencers rely on people not remembering what happened and internalizing the alternate facts of the bespoke reality.

The fervor and the need to continue to foment distrust are core to their livelihood. The pandemic's end necessitates that they find new topics of monetizable outrage. Some, like Substacker Steve Kirsch, have pivoted to rewarming old vaccine-autism conspiracy theories.[105] The specifics of those discredited theories are new to many, and "investigating" them anew will no doubt appeal to those for whom vaccine distrust and "freethinking" has become a political identity. Others are leaning into elaborate "censorship" conspiracy theories involving corrupt governments and intelligence agencies.

In certain factions where "owning" your enemies is a team sport, members revel in hearing that a vaccine is less effective or that a media outlet got something wrong—the stupidity of the enemy, they think, reflects better on their side. *Of course those sheep got their boosters.* This is not limited to the COVID contrarians; those who most closely hewed to guidance, too, felt considerable schadenfreude when those on the "other side" got sick. This is a game that influencers constantly reinforce but members of the crowd are happy to play.

In this environment, it's not surprising that many institutions (and government bureaucracies) see social media as more of a liability than anything else. Every post carries a nonnegligible chance that an angry online mob might descend on the institution to demand action for an offense given by some expert in its employ.

And sometimes, the research itself—the effort to explain how this trinity works and what the motivations of the new elites are—is precisely what whips the mob up to attack.

This became all too clear to me after Substacker Matt Taibbi was awarded access to Twitter's internal emails by billionaire Elon Musk in December 2022 in an exposé effort that came to be called the "Twitter Files."[106] Having bought the social media platform for $44 billion—a deal he'd tried to back out of but was legally compelled to follow through on—Musk was motivated by the opportunity to embarrass the prior executive team responsible for the moderation rules that he and his fans so despised. He'd fired several executives, including those who made the calls responsible for banning Donald Trump and blocking access to the Hunter Biden laptop stories. Taibbi was one of a handful of journalists offered the opportunity to read Twitter's internal deliberations chronicling those controversial moderation calls.

This could have been an interesting investigative journalism exercise into unaccountable private power. Instead, Taibbi churned out innuendo- and at times error-laden theories in lengthy Twitter threads. Within his (and Musk's) niche, however, the theories were a hit: Taibbi obtained nearly a million new Twitter followers within two weeks of his first thread, as he framed cherry-picked emails as evidence of a biased censorship regime at Twitter. *The government had secretly demanded content takedowns of conservatives!* His Substack subscriber count soared, and he began to earn significantly more money from a new audience eager to read sordid stories of censorship and intrigue.

In March 2023, Taibbi turned his attention to the work we had done at the Virality Project. He wrote a Twitter Files thread (the nineteenth in the series) framing our work not as what it actually was—a research project to understand and chronicle viral narratives and to enable rapid response to get the best available facts out—but as a vast censorship project to take down and suppress those narratives. His "evidence," his purported smoking gun, was an email from a Stanford student researcher to members of Twitter's integrity team:

> Hi Twitter Team. I've attached the biweekly platform escalation summary, which gives insight into the main types of tickets we have been escalating to different platforms. As we continue our work, we would appreciate understanding what kind of content you would find most helpful to be tagged in on Jira. I have noted below which types of content I am currently tagging your platform on. Can you please indicate which of the following types of content you would like to be tagged on going forward?

The rest of the email listed categories we'd been using internally to organize our analyses of the most viral narratives of the week: vaccine misinformation, foreign influence, repeat offenders (the frequent exaggerated or misleading claims by long-standing anti-vaccine activists), and what we called "true content which might promote vaccine hesitancy." The last was a catch-all bucket for stories like that of Tiffany Dover, the fainting nurse, which, while true, were often decontextualized, exaggerated, and spun. The list included some examples of common viral stories that had a grain of truth: "conversation around recent celebrity deaths after a vaccine" and "stories of true vaccine side effects." These were, in fact, the kind of hard-to-verify rumors that were often most in need of contextualizing and counterspeech from physicians and public health officials, who could help people understand prevalence and real risk.

Taibbi cut the email in half.

He called it a "devastating email" as he posted a screenshot of the categories alone, claiming that this was a list of things that *we recommended Big Tech censor*.[107] The entire top half of the inquiry was cropped out, and Taibbi's manufactured context, alleging that we were trying to suppress true stories, completely reframed the outreach. Twitter had, in fact, replied to the email with a list of the kind of content it cared most about—it didn't include the exaggerated true content category. That reply, however, did not make it into the Twitter Files.

The Virality Project was an effort to surface what rumors were going viral in order to help the people trying to address them. Physicians, in particular, were trying to respond to the viral side effect claims by explaining them—not "censoring" them. These were often very scary stories, and putting them in context or helping the public understand what might have happened was critical. A platform throwing up a label or posting a fact-check had the same intent. Furthermore, we weren't the government, we weren't working on behalf of the government, our project wasn't funded by the government, and we had no power over the platform integrity team's decisions.

But the facts don't matter to the incentivized propagandist.

Taibbi's incendiary claim that we had been demanding platforms censor true stories received forty-five million impressions on Twitter. The propaganda machine picked it up instantly, and it became the topic of dozens of right-wing news stories. It generated massive outrage—and if we had, in fact, sent demand lists of entire categories to censor, that outrage would have been justified.

But we hadn't. Taibbi sold a lie to his followers and profited from it.

Meanwhile, our team—especially the students whose names and emails were exposed in his discrediting effort—experienced massive costs. Lies like these don't stop after a moment of outrage. They lead to death threats, harassment, and extended fixation from media-of-one outlets and other influencers, who in turn take their shot at the money and clout machine by being even more extreme than Taibbi.

The most malicious propagandists are very effective at smear campaigns that convince their audience that up is down and that things that never happened were kept from them. In the next chapter we'll discuss this final facet of influence: how invisible rulers leverage the brigading power of an online mob and how the state has begun to leverage it too.

Truth is very rarely cut-and-dried. It never has been. The propagandist has always known that and exploited the kernel of truth, the gray area of uncertainty. Can anyone in a position of authority, for example, say with a straight face and with absolute certainty that no one will get hurt when taking a vaccine? Of course not. The health misinformation influencer leverages that reality, pointing to a prior mistake or overconfident comment: *They are lying to you. They've always been liars. Just look at this PSA from a few years ago where they were saying that fat is bad for you.*

Influencers don't try to suggest that their information is better than the established authorities'. They don't have to. They urge their audiences to rely on a more primitive tool: *What does your gut tell you about who is telling you the truth? Is it me or them?* They make the question not *Whose facts can you trust?* but *Whom can you trust?* And for a variety of reasons, online and off, we are seeing a reallocation of trust from the credentialed experts and authorities of old to people who feel authentic, not elite, "just like me." The ability to influence en masse has expanded from being primarily the purview of people who know *what they are talking about* (think Anthony Fauci), who have been elevated to positions of authority by institutions and the media, to people who know *how to talk persuasively*, how to leverage the tools of social media, built for marketers, to build very strong bonds of trust between themselves and their listeners (think Candace Owens).

And so it was with *Plandemic*. While Judy Mikovits largely faded from public view after her documentary turn, Mikki Willis's star continued to rise. He turned *Plandemic* into a multipart series. He is now a regular on the Guru conference circuit. He has a clothing line, "Rebel Lion." And, of course, he sells supplements.[108]

Of Facts and Factions

The COVID-19 pandemic underscored the indispensable role of institutions and expertise in society. Throughout the crisis, it was scientists, researchers, and healthcare professionals—acting collectively—who developed treatments, introduced vaccines, and combated the spread of the deadly disease. Yet there was also institutional failure: poor communication, botched coordination, and little ownership of bad decisions.

Social media influencers rightfully highlighted, but also at times capitalized on, these failures. "Some people online," to paraphrase the CDC official I spoke with in 2015, have the power to shape perception and make rumors go viral, with an assist from the niche crowds who trust and often agree with them. The pandemic serves as a stark testament to the rising power of the global rumor mill and the chaotic landscape where grains of truth power compelling stories. Truth has always been, in large part, social; now, however, social media have provided us new means for assessing it.[109] The trust in the old top-down system of institutions, experts, authority figures, and mass media isn't simply declining. Within a significant portion of the public it has been *reallocated* to the bottom-up system of influencers, algorithms, and crowds.

This shift matters, because institutions are necessary for society to function, and discoveries borne of expertise are what propel us collectively forward. This has been true for centuries. Institutions serve as stores of collective knowledge. They provide structures in which groups of people can work collectively, and we must be able to work collectively in order to solve real problems (not the pseudo-problems ginned up daily by the outrage machine). "Without the places where professionals like experts and editors and peer reviewers organize conversations and compare propositions and assess competence and provide accountability— everywhere from scientific journals to Wikipedia pages—there is no marketplace of ideas," writes Jonathan Rauch in *The Constitution of Knowledge*.[110] We need experts who understand the specific details and nuances of the challenges we face. We need to be able to trust them, of course; no effort to "combat misinformation" is going to be able to bridge bespoke realities without rectifying this crisis of trust. But while institutions are imperfect, they remain indispensable in orchestrating complex societal functions, embodying collective human wisdom and experience, and fostering stability and continuity in the face of global challenges and uncertainties.

There is a lot of continuing anger. Indeed, well into late 2023—as this book was going to press—allegations of cover-ups, incompetent scientists, and secret research programs related to the origins of COVID-19 continued to spread.[111] The US House of Representatives convened a Republican Freedom Caucus–led "COVID origins cover-up" committee that unfortunately became less a fact-finding mission and more a propaganda producer for the base. Did COVID-19 escape from a lab? Perhaps! But as factional fights persist, it is nearly impossible to find out where the facts lie. Even selecting citations for this chapter felt fraught.

Experts and institutions must adapt, increasing their transparency and their frequency and style of communication. They must prioritize rebuilding trust. Determining a disease's origin or creating an effective vaccine to prevent it is useless if no one trusts the messenger. Millions will simply refuse to get the vaccine.

But the blame for communication struggles during the pandemic does not lie solely with the experts. Many prominent influencers saw an opportunity to increase their clout and grow their following at the expense of institutions...and, sometimes, at the expense of their own audiences; members of right-wing communities died at higher rates.[112]

The public must understand the incentives in play: many of the individuals, particularly the political influencers, who co-opt the language of populism to rail against the "experts" or the "elites" are not looking for *no* elites; they're looking for *new* elites, ones who share their beliefs. If an influencer argues that institutions should be dismantled, defunded, or done away with, the response should be, "Then what will replace them, and how will that happen?"

On the issue of vaccination specifically: there will be challenging times ahead. What Naomi Klein described as the strange-bedfellow coalitions, which manifested in "large protests first against lockdowns and then against any sensible health measure that would have helped make the lockdowns unnecessary,"[113] are now diligently working to overturn the school vaccine laws that have prevented so many other epidemics from even occurring. As anti-vaccine stances are now part and parcel of certain political identities, pushback against resurgent efforts to roll back routine childhood vaccine requirements for school will fall to local parent groups.[114] Staying silent is not an option.

Philosopher Benjamin Bratton used a phrase to describe the pandemic that I thought summed it up better than anything else: "the revenge of the real." COVID-19 was, he wrote, a stark reminder of "the complex biological reality of the planet with which we are entangled, and that underlying reality is apathetic to the plotlines and mythic lessons we may try to project upon it."[115] Actual reality—tornado reality—confronted us, and yet many continued to operate in, or profit from, bespoke realities. And an untold number paid for it with their lives.

8

The Fantasy Industrial Complex

Perhaps the highest form of recognition a propaganda researcher can receive is becoming a target of the very same propaganda machine they've worked to expose. Clearly, your work is having an impact. It's also an intense learning experience. You can study propaganda and conspiracy theories for years, but to really understand their impact, there's no substitute for becoming the subject of a conspiracy theory yourself.

This distinction, however, comes with a steep price. It is jarring, disorienting, to be turned into a character—an avatar—by a person or outlet that intends to use you to further their own agenda. Inane claims cascade through a web of media and media-of-one outlets, getting boosted and remixed by aligned influencers; it feels like the lies are everywhere. The ire of the faction, which now believes you are working against them, brings relentless threats and harassment. It feels like there is no way to push back against the sheer volume of ludicrous claims and misleading commentary. Although you have been accused of things you did not do, quoted as saying words you never said, trying to correct the record feels useless. There's no converting the true believers—they won't trust what you say, and you might just inadvertently call more attention to the lies. For many who are targeted, the easiest decision is simply to go silent. Make peace with the fact that there is now an alternate-universe version of you that many people hate.

A single retaliatory article can generate a maelstrom by itself. But when a propagandist turns you into a recurring Main Character, a villain in a cinematic universe of use to a political machine—well, it turns out, things can go far beyond just inane stories and online harassment. The wild theories spun in the online fever swamps can serve as pretext for something even more sinister: politicians, who wield real power, citing the propaganda as justification for sham investigations and other forms of retaliation.

For me it began on March 2, 2023, when a man claiming to have run cybersecurity at the State Department[1] connected with writer Matt Taibbi in a Twitter Spaces audio chat room hosted by an anonymous guy with a raccoon avatar.

Eight days later, Republican congressman Jim Jordan sent Stanford University a letter demanding that we turn over all email and other communications between Stanford Internet Observatory (SIO) staff and the executive branch or any technology companies dating back to 2015.

Jordan, one of the congressmen who voted not to certify the 2020 election, had recently been given the gavel of the brand-new US House Judiciary Select Subcommittee on the Weaponization of the Federal Government. But the lead-up to his letter had been set in motion months before, in August of the prior year, when attorney-turned-speechwriter Michael Benz set his sights on convincing American conservatives that a vast collusion operation had deprived Donald Trump of his rightful victory in 2020.

Despite his social media boasting, Benz hadn't actually "run cyber" at State. He'd been the deputy assistant secretary for international communications and information policy in the Bureau of Economic and Business Affairs for approximately three months,[2] following a year as a speechwriter for Secretary of Housing and Urban Development Ben Carson. But no matter—after leaving government, Benz simply created an email address, reserved a domain name, and embarked upon a new career as a former cybersecurity expert.

The man whose prior attributable online presence had been scrubbed down to little more than a Pepe-the-frog-throw-pillow Pinterest pinboard was now the head of what he called the Foundation for Freedom Online (FFO)—and also, seemingly, its sole employee. He reinvented himself as "mikebenzcyber" on social media and set about proclaiming that he was going to expose the crime of the century.

The goal of the FFO, Benz wrote in a convoluted blog post, was to expose a vast collusion operation that he claimed had transpired between the government, academia, media, and tech companies. There had been a plot, he alleged, to create a "social media censorship bureau" that "targeted" the speech of *millions* of Americans—particularly those on the populist right.[3]

At the center of this plot—the keeper of an "AI censorship death star superweapon"—was the Election Integrity Partnership (EIP). And the Darth Vader figure in his Death Star analogy? That was me.

In Benz's bespoke reality, the EIP, in cahoots with the Department of Homeland Security, his old employer the State Department, the Federal Bureau of Investigation (FBI), and Big Tech, had colluded to censor *tens of millions of tweets*—twenty-two million to be precise—during our 2020 election work. In his more bombastic media appearances, the number ballooned to *hundreds* of millions, or even *billions*, of posts that we'd supposedly gotten nuked from the internet via some sort of shadowy special access to "internal systems" of government and tech. Government actors had supposedly told us, via these secret systems, what needed be suppressed, and we had supposedly passed their demands on to Big Tech companies. This effort, Benz claimed, had prevented people from seeing *entire narratives* during the 2020 election. We had "pre-censored discussion that predicted the possibility of election fraud."

If this sounds like word salad served up by someone in a tinfoil hat, that's because it is. Benz's theories were remarkable primarily for how utterly wrong they were. When we saw his early posts targeting EIP's work in August 2022, we laughed. His "source" for this list of crazy allegations was something we'd written ourselves: a 292-page final report describing our work, released publicly in March 2021, widely covered by the media and posted publicly to our website for a year and a half before he "discovered" it.[4]

But accuracy wasn't Benz's objective; storytelling was. He was picking out random phrases and numbers from within our report's pages and reassembling them into a sordid spy thriller. Driving this drama was a compelling trope: the Man (or Woman) Behind the Curtain, secretly steering world events unbeknownst to the powerless targets. Benz's long "exposés" were the alternate history of a fantasy world. They included a specific set of villains: real people, reduced to avatars whose lives could be mined for further plot points to generate maximum outrage, engagement, and revenue. His followers and subscribers could enjoy the equivalent of a multiseason drama. But unlike with *Star Wars* or *Game of Thrones*, the audience could actually inhabit the universe, helping harass the villain online and off.

Benz confidently presented his fantasy as fact and himself as the hero, drawing heavily on the Whistleblower trope to sell it. In some right-wing media interviews, Benz postured as an ex-government insider who'd seen terrible abuses in his (very short) tenure at State; in others, he was a concerned citizen who had been "investigating" the rise of a vast censorship apparatus for *nearly a decade*; in still others he was a diplomat offended on behalf of supposedly silenced global populist leaders (like India's president Modi)[5] or a chess champion who had seen the board several positions out and deduced that an "AI censorship death star superweapon" was about to destroy the First Amendment in America.[6]

Those of us who had worked on EIP noticed his sustained effort to get attention, but the attempt to retcon our very public work into some secret conspiracy screamed "crank," and we thought that no reasonable person would take it seriously.

We were wrong.

One challenge of refuting conspiracy theory propaganda is that its authors often present their claims in what's known as a *Gish gallop*: a litany of allegations so numerous that the target is temporarily paralyzed, unable to decide what to respond to first. It takes an extraordinary amount of time to address them point by point, since some are based on twisted or decontextualized grains of truth. And so it was with Benz.

The Election Integrity Partnership work that Benz refashioned into a plot had taken place in 2020, when the government bureaucracies were run by Trump appointees. In Benz's alternate universe, the government had been in the tank for Joe Biden. There was no "secret access" to "internal systems" or data portals. The 2020 EIP effort and 2021 Virality

Project had no government funding, although Stanford Internet Observatory and the University of Washington did subsequently receive a National Science Foundation grant to study rapid responses to rumors in late 2021—a grain of truth that Benz twisted to label us "government-funded censors" and imply that we had been rewarded for helping Biden win.[7] The soon-to-be-infamous "22 million tweets" statistic he bandied about had nothing to do with anything getting "censored"—it was a figure from a table in our report, calculated well after Election Day, that tallied the number of tweets discussing the prominent election rumors we'd studied. This simple act of addition was refashioned into evidence of a plot in his alternate reality.

Online cranks are a dime a dozen. But it quickly became clear that the Foundation for Freedom Online was linked to a broader network of right-wing advocacy organizations with ties to a small group of congressional partisans. The FFO's website footer, later removed, described it as "a project of Empower Oversight,"[8] an effort started by a long-time Republican combatant who'd previously wondered if Senator Joe McCarthy—he of the 1950s Red Scare hysteria—had gotten a bad rap.[9] Empower Oversight primarily worked to procure "whistle-blowers" for congressional hearings,[10] and FFO came to serve as the primary source for the now growing chorus of right-wing media and legislative rumblings about censorship. Benz had a limited understanding of the "cyber" topics he presented himself as an expert in, but with the backing of a partisan machine, he was able to step into the role of spokesperson for the grievance and was rewarded with glowing profiles that bolstered his credibility.[11]

And so, an absurd alternate history, overwhelmingly sourced to one man, proliferated. Far Right outlets, influencers, and media-of-one figures were thrilled to give Benz's claims airtime: *Some people on the internet are saying that Stanford censored tens of millions of YOUR tweets! Some people are saying Stanford rebooted a CIA mind control project!*[12] Steve Bannon, Sebastian Gorka, and John Solomon eagerly had Benz on as a guest. Narrative laundering began—a very old propaganda strategy in which claims attributed to a seemingly authoritative source appear in one small outlet, then propagate across a daisy chain of ideologically aligned outlets, each citing the last. It goes something like this: Outlet B repeats a baseless claim, but attributes it to A—"Outlet A is reporting that the Election Integrity Partnership..." Outlet B is just reporting on the reporting, after all. Outlet C can then cite Outlet B, and so on. Very few readers will take the time to look at the original source material if they trust the outlet restating the claim. The repetition, meanwhile, gives the impression that the story is important and ensures it remains on the audience's mind.

But today narrative laundering across propaganda rags is only half the ballgame. There's also the social media rumor mill. Indeed, several of the "repeat spreader" influencers described in EIP's report—the pivotal figures who'd repeatedly helped election rumors *go wildly viral*—shared the coverage of Benz's claims. They reframed our work summarizing their demonstrated massive reach as preemptively targeting them, *suppressing them*, and alleged that we were motivated by anticonservative bias.[13] These allegations, of course, went viral.

As the lies spread, they ignited harassment from the influencers' fans. People who were turned into villains in this alternate history were battered with outrage, abuse, and sometimes threats. Meanwhile, growing interest from partisan politicians was setting the stage for harassment from another entity: the political machine. This was not accidental; Benz's avowed goal, very plainly stated on his blog, was to have a congressional committee "armed with subpoena power" investigate the villains he described in his reports.[14]

There's a term for the kind of material the FFO produced and the network boosted: *bullshit*. Bullshit is speech intended to persuade without regard for the truth.[15] It is simply a means to an end; veracity is not worth worrying about. As absurd as it was, Benz's cosplay as a cybersecurity whistle-blower would have real-world consequences for me and my colleagues. That's because even the people in the world best-equipped to understand the mechanics of these Kafkaesque claims have a difficult time refuting them. It takes an order of magnitude more effort to debunk bullshit than it does to produce it.[16]

Institutions, as we've discussed, are ill equipped to respond to bad-faith attacks. Their inclination is to say nothing and hope that the news cycle passes—a strategy that is a relic of a different media era—or to put out a fact-check. Today the "news cycle" rarely dies; instead, within the niche the rumors recur, the machine churns along, and the faction continuously builds upon the alternate history—and stable of villains—underpinning its bespoke reality. After right-wing media had picked up Benz's bullshit for several weeks in a row, we put up a detailed post on the Election Integrity Partnership's blog, on October 5, 2022, patiently explaining what he'd gotten wrong.[17] But the outlets that covered the crank theory were undeterred.

Propagandists driving smear campaigns are not dissuaded by a fact-check. If one exists, they will write around it, undermine its neutrality, or double down on whatever claim in the Gish gallop the target failed to address. The modern propagandist's goal is to activate the niche, to advance an ideological agenda, and, often, to profit from the process.

The incentives of the hyperpartisan media-of-one figures and influencers present one challenge for shared reality: there are few consequences for pumping out bullshit and significant upsides in terms of money and clout. But the other challenge we faced was the issue of trust: in the age of bespoke realities, audiences who believed claims that election lies had somehow been "precensored" were unlikely to trust our rebuttals of even the most ridiculous theories. We were saying one thing, but on the other side was a man elevated into an authority figure by media who spoke to and for the faction—and he was one of them. He was weaving a story of woke academics who'd colluded with the Deep State to censor them—familiar tropes that informed so many adjacent grievances. And so, within this bespoke reality, the Election Integrity Partnership came to be seen not as a research project studying claims about the election but as part of a government-backed plot to suppress conservative speech and deprive Donald Trump—their candidate!—of his rightful victory. The implication of this alternate history was that we were therefore also responsible for denying *them* their rightful president. And that, you will not be surprised to hear, translated into waves of harassment.

The Power of Harassment

Throughout this book we've analyzed rumors, propaganda, and disinformation and how they're leveraged by the powerful, who want to accrue more power, and by profit-motivated people, who want to earn more money.

Shaping public opinion is one way to go about doing this, as invisible rulers have long known. But today's social media ecosystem affords the influencer-algorithm-crowd trinity another method for shaping public opinion: harassment.

Harassment campaigns have also evolved as a result of the collision between the propaganda machine and the rumor mill; as we have discussed, mobs may target a random Main Character of the day or may focus instead on a reoccurring bogeyman. Online harassment—the intentional use of platforms to maliciously target a person or group with the intent of causing them distress, harm, or significant disruption to everyday life—has become an acceptable and rewarding blood sport, a way to solidify factional camaraderie and influencer-crowd ties by targeting some common enemy. The inclination most people have in the physical world to refrain from behaving aggressively toward others seems to disappear when they are online.[18] This has made once-taboo behavior—threats, bullying, intimidation, stalking—fairly commonplace. Even when the harassment happens online, it often carries hints of "real-world" danger: posting a target's address, for example, or photos of their children or place of employment. Intimidation is often the point; online mobs can feel very threatening, particularly if they also begin to call, email, or write letters to their targets. Those targeted envision worst-case situations, such as what happened with Pizzagate: an armed person with a tenuous grasp on reality showing up to investigate.

Online harassment goes hand in hand with smear campaigns. Smears are a form of propaganda that aims to discredit an individual or institution, often using innuendo and insinuation to attack their reputation. Smearing a target isn't a new strategy, but it has changed in the age of social media. There are fewer editorial controls; influencers and media-of-one figures with massive reach can smear their opponents relatively effortlessly. Smear campaigns have long been a cost of doing business when researching any online influence effort, foreign or domestic. Russian and Chinese state media, Indian troll brigades, and even an Azerbaijani network have written retaliatory articles or sent nasty messages targeting my team and me when we've exposed how some of their online networks have operated. A wall in my office displays some of the most egregious and amusing examples. They retaliate, however, because real power is at stake, and discrediting the people exposing them is the best way to cast doubt on the findings. Domestically, too, the Gurus, Propagandists, and Perpetually Aggrieved influencers don't want their power games or grift interrupted. Pesky journalists or academics highlighting how this system of incentives works or how a specific influence effort took shape threatens them—it lifts the curtain and reveals that Oz the Great and Powerful is just a cynical troll with a megaphone and a bank account. And since they can't refute that truth, they instead try to discredit their critics.

The smears, of course, then incite more harassment. Influential figures—even those within the US government—make claims about their perceived political enemies, and online mobs stand ready to attack. The target can be anyone, but in the present moment in American politics, there is extensive focus on scientists, researchers, teachers, and even poll workers—politically expedient targets who have become avatars in culture war battles.

The Age of Rage

Politicians need to capture attention to win. In the United States, this is particularly true in crowded primaries, which are often the elections that matter most. Many are taking a page from the rhetorical style and tactics of influencers—such as posting primarily to influence the algorithm. Some seek the support of popular influencers so they can piggyback on an existing faction to build their own online armies. Making themselves political figureheads for a niche is a shrewd strategy. Unfortunately, many choose to become online brawlers to do it.

The issue isn't about having different policy opinions—disagreement is healthy in a democracy. The problem lies in how these disagreements are expressed. Between 2009 and 2019, tweets from members of Congress, for example, became noticeably more uncivil and hostile.[19] Candidates who rely on meme policies and "owning" their enemies are molding themselves to the moment as they reinforce its worst dynamics. Social media is increasingly the barometer people use for understanding social norms, and vitriolic attacks and outrage directed at the right enemies are signals to others of good partisanship.[20] Extreme or nasty behavior displayed by the most vocal and visible members not only shapes how outsiders view the group but also influences the sense of what's okay within the group.

The popularity of figures like Marjorie Taylor Greene, a former QAnon blogger[21] who once followed a teen survivor of a mass shooting around the US Capitol grounds,[22] can be attributed, at least in part, to the incentives of this environment. She has had remarkably few legislative successes but excels in her role as a one-woman pseudo-event machine. Most of her media coverage is for doing outrageous things that she does for coverage. She behaves the way she does because it increases her clout, inspires adulation among her online faction, and generates an angry response from enemy factions—all of which social media algorithms process as engagement worthy of more attention. In 2023 she displayed nude images of Hunter Biden blown up on posters on the floor of the US House of Representatives in a hearing. Many across the political spectrum felt this was a new low, but some of the most vocal influencers of the extremely online Right saw as her owning their enemies; partisan schadenfreude is a driving force in American politics.[23] Hunter Biden, arguably, is at least a public figure. But Greene also baselessly accused a former Twitter executive of endorsing child sexualization, helping to trigger harassment campaigns and death threats that led the executive to flee his home.[24] What had the executive done to earn her ire? He'd been one of several participants who'd contributed to making the content moderation call to block links to the *New York Post* coverage of Hunter Biden's laptop and was involved in the decision to block one of her accounts.[25]

Rage, conspiracism, and mob pursuit of retribution are poisoning politics. Rather than leading, some aspiring politicians choose to cater to the alternate histories of niche factions because becoming popular with a highly activist and vocal faction will increase attention paid to them. This extends, ironically, to delegitimizing the same processes that brought them to the offices they hold; rather than speaking truth to conspiracists, dozens within Congress wholeheartedly embraced conspiracism themselves in order to signal their membership in a shared identity and factional affiliation.[26] A few of the political influencers who rose to prominence in 2020 for denying the results of the presidential election leveraged their newfound popularity to run for office themselves, trying to parlay their online clout into victory at the ballot box in 2022.[27] Some ran for local offices responsible for managing elections, pledging to investigate "the steal." Results were mixed—many lost, particularly in battleground states, though the number of election deniers in the House of Representatives increased.[28] Five joined the Senate, including the former attorney general of Missouri, Eric Schmitt.[29] A cadre of these politicians would become participants, as we will soon discuss, in investigations into the Election Integrity Partnership and other academic and civil society organizations, using the writings of partisan cranks as a pretext for targeting those who had pushed back against the Big Lie.

Elections are not the only targets in the battle for reality. Political influencers don't quiet down between presidential elections or hang up their Twitter handles when an issue is resolved. Instead, they pivot their content to topics with high potential to keep fueling the crowds and the algorithms. Many political influencers who promoted the Big Lie and amassed significant followings as election truthers realized they needed novelty to continue growing their audiences and earning money.

In September 2022, as the US midterm elections approached, data journalist Jeremy Merrill and investigative journalist Elizabeth Dwoskin of the *Washington Post* published an analysis of what prominent election rumormongers had been doing since November 2020.[30] They examined a group of seventy-seven influencers, some of whom had grown their initial audience with election denials, and found that they'd pivoted to other arenas, where they now had cachet, too.

"The 'big lie' wasn't just a plan to overturn the election. It was a massive clout-building exercise that spawned a generation of influencers,"

Dwoskin wrote in the *Washington Post*.[31] To maintain their energy between elections, most pivoted their focus to something equally political but evergreen: the culture wars.

Culture war content and online kerfuffles were tangentially related to actual, important social issues: racism, for example, or pandemic lockdown protocols. However, arguing about big issues is hard, and so the fights devolved into ridiculous manufactured controversies, primarily driven by factions performing their identities and alleviating their ennui, but dressed up as being *really about* something else. There were pitched battles about whether some author was entitled to write Young Adult literature (was she of the "correct" ethnicity or ability status to be able to "authentically" write a character)[32] or about the anthropomorphized green M&M's shoes (was the shift from heels to sneakers a result of feminist "wokism"?).[33] Apocryphal rumors become sources of rage: *Did you hear that kids are identifying as cats and demanding schools provide litter boxes in the bathrooms? Gender ideology, it's out of control. Oh, there were no litter boxes? Well, it's still out of control.* This may all seem very stupid—and truly, it *is* very stupid!—but books were pulled, M&M's abandoned its spokescandies, and multiple politicians ominously intoned about the dangers of litter boxes for children.[34]

The culture war is a propaganda battle. It has been for decades. As Noam Chomsky pointed out in *Manufacturing Consent*, the media in the 1980s had the power to define worthy and unworthy victims; fear of some *other* was one of its five filters, an incentive that shaped its coverage. At the time of Chomsky's writing, in the 1980s, the worthy and unworthy victims were largely divided along the lines of "America and its allies" and "people at war with America or its allies." But as the propaganda machine devolved into niches, the political influencers and media-of-one figures who obtain profit and power from capturing audience attention have made you or your neighbor into that worthy or unworthy victim. Any community that can be held up as an unworthy enemy faction that *hates you* is a fair target for the rage of a mob steered by an influencer.

This tactic has become common enough to earn its own slang: *nutpicking*. Nutpicking occurs when one person online (often an influencer like the Perpetually Aggrieved) singles out another, often ordinary person. The first will share a post by the second, usually a controversial or inelegant take on some culture war issue that captures a lot of attention or riles up a faction. That unfortunate poster is then positioned as an avatar (an effigy, really) of the faction's common enemies. There is rarely a direct call to harass the target, but there doesn't need to be. The person riling up the mob simply casts the target as a reprehensible person or Haver of Bad Opinions and wrings their hands about the state of affairs. This is a long-established art form: "Will no one rid me of this meddlesome priest?" asked King Henry II in 1170, referring to the archbishop of Canterbury. Four knights read between the lines; the resulting violence solved the king's problem.

Likewise, factions today know what to do: the incitement post is retweeted by the crowd and perhaps pushed out as a trend by the algorithm. The target becomes the Main Character of the moment on social media. Amateur sleuths dig in, posting personal information (doxxing) or dredging up some tenuous connection to another bad person that the faction already hates (the Transitive Property of Bad People). Any tenuous connection produces significant glee and a wave of posts about how the target has been "exposed!"

Sometimes the faction will pull the target's employer into the barrage of harassment, demanding that the person be punished or fired. The faction may pull in friends, family, or associates of the target and harass them as proxies—a different sort of punishment, as the target, feeling terrible that their near and dear have been sucked into the terrible drama, may now self-isolate to avoid calling attention to anyone else.

If the target tries to correct the record, their explanation will often be ignored (if they have few followers, it may not even be seen) unless another faction chooses to fight back on their behalf. If they set their account to private or delete it in the face of the mob, they look guilty. The rumor must be true; otherwise why are they hiding?

"Some people on the internet are saying" media coverage and Substack posts may begin to appear over the next few days, and the manufactured controversy may become the target's top Google search result for some time. Eventually the mob will tire, and the instigators will move on to something (or someone) else. But for the target, the impact of the experience will remain.

The right calls this *cancel culture*; the left debates whether cancel culture exists. It does. And all factions do it, justifying it as "calling someone out," perhaps, or "exposing an enemy of the people." For the mob, in the heat of the moment, the end justifies the means.

The goal is to chill participation and speech, and it works. Fear of an experience like this leads some to self-censor or to avoid criticizing powerful influencers. There's an old adage, apocryphally attributed to Mark Twain: never pick a fight with a man who buys ink by the barrel.[35] We can update it in the age of social media: never pick a fight with a man who wields an online mob.

Essayist and cultural critic Venkatesh Rao gave this state of affairs a name: the Internet of Beefs.[36] (*Beef* is slang for a long-standing grudge or conflict between people.)

As it became clear that influencers could capture attention and profit from performative aggrievement—and that both algorithms and crowds would derive satisfaction from participation—online beefing became the norm. Virtual public spaces were increasingly dominated by "beef-only thinkers," Rao wrote in early 2020, and infinite opportunities for culture warring yielded a background state of continuous conflict. None of the highly visible, often viral battles reflected actual individualized conflicts, he pointed out. Rather, they were purely factional, fought by "charismatic celebrity knights loosely affiliated with various citadel-like strongholds peopled by opt-in armies of mooks."

But why? What motivates the participants?

The influencers get engagement and its spoils: more clout, more money. The troops get the camaraderie of a fight and a sense of mission—maybe even the recognition of a coveted retweet from an influencer-hero. Sometimes the crowd is composed of true believers, who sincerely believe that "beefing" advances a cause; if you make it trend, you make it true. But another big motivator is simply the lulz—being a troll can be *fun*.

Winning—actually advancing a cause—is not the point. The point is the fight. Winning might, in fact, negatively impact the influencer because resolution would reduce the potential for future monetizable content.

Why is this happening? One intriguing explanation from social science research argues that the design of social media platforms not only creates opportunities for constant baiting of and fighting with other factions but also inadvertently increases the breadth of topics that people consider to *be* bait.[37] In your local neighborhood, you might agree with your neighbor on abortion but disagree with her on student debt relief. In the real world, that would be something you'd come to terms with. She's your neighbor, and your community has basic civility norms. Also, hot-button issues for Democrats three states away may simply not be particularly polarizing in your town.

Online, however, algorithmic sorting means that political factions are global rather than local. If a topic is polarizing for some part of the faction, it becomes part of the list of potential topics to be fought over by *all* of the faction. A thing that would not matter in your neighborhood becomes incorporated into part of core Democratic identity (for example) in the online arena. The moderating effects of things like local geography and knowing the real people behind the opinions fade away. The inadvertent result is that an increasing number of identities, beliefs, opinions, and cultural preferences become fronts of stark social division—and therefore fodder for the Internet of Beefs. As one social scientist who studies these dynamics put it, the effect is similar to *Lord of the Flies*.[38]

Meanwhile, another dynamic compounds the problem. Studies have found that political animosity—affective polarization—happens when people with one political identity overestimate the prevalence of extreme-outlier views that are actually only held by a small minority of the "other side."[39] Think of the majority-illusion example from our small English village in Chapter 1, but blown up to a global scale. People who live within highly partisan bespoke realities have a warped perception of what's happening outside. They see caricatures, presented by incentivized media and influencers, which constantly reinforce the idea that people outside their bubble are raving racists or woke snowflakes.

However, because of this extreme dislike of what they believe their ideological enemies to be, they don't engage, and the perception persists. Yes, there are people who make TikToks spouting off about obscure gender ideas or who make unabashedly white supremacist Facebook posts about crime in the inner city—but these are not the average person. Were we to encounter the colorful characters chosen by the nutpickers in our local neighborhoods, we'd recognize them as outliers.

So people are hypersensitive about more issues than ever before, while also markedly misinterpreting the other side's stance on those issues. The upshot of all this? Shifting norms, as beefing and harassment become acceptable. And individual transformations—just ask families with a relative who has been sucked into a brigade of keyboard warriors and rendered almost unrecognizable. Amid all this, the people who do *not* want to participate have to expend effort to leave—to block, mute, and ultimately extricate themselves from the pervasive hostility and harassment, even as the beefers shriek that they are cowards incapable of defending their views.

But as stupid as the culture war pseudo-events powering all this may feel, they have an impact. And make no mistake, the Internet of Beefs cascades offline, also, in two key ways. First, it is changing incentives for politicians, who recognize that they can harness this energy to get themselves elected; this reinforces toxic partisanship. Second, it is increasing harassment of completely ordinary people—including the local and largely unknown public servants charged with keeping the machinery of our democracy running.[40]

From Platform to Plaza

In quainter media environments, the culture war was fought largely with faceless archetypes—the welfare queen, the promiscuous teenager. Smears were largely reserved for the famous or the powerful and remained mostly confined to the media; politicians or executives might occasionally experience a real-world protest, but rarely did crowds show up to scream outside the home of an ordinary person.

But today, ordinary people become fodder for the knights driving the Internet of Beefs, and what happens online sometimes spills into the real world in frightening ways. This dynamic of online-to-offline action is increasingly impacting public servants, many of whom are accustomed to criticism and acknowledge that their roles give them power. They do not believe that they are beyond oversight or criticism. But threats and intimidation aren't criticism and oversight. Most people would find being recorded or photographed by a stranger as they walked down the street disconcerting and threatening; having the moment livestreamed for a mob makes it worse.

During both the 2020 and 2022 elections, election truthers who believed the Big Lie congregated in Telegram channels to share the names and photographs of poll workers and election officials who they thought were "up to something." People in vote-counting facilities were targeted. Media-of-one outlet Gateway Pundit accused two election workers, by name and with a photo included, of "pulling out suitcases of ballots"; President Trump and his inner circle began to talk about them as well, and they had to flee their homes after a barrage of threats.[41] In 2022, things ratcheted up once again: ordinary people were influenced by lurid propaganda films like *2000 Mules*, a documentary by right-wing activist Dinesh D'Souza that played on the baseless allegation of widespread ballot mules to allege that a mass theft had happened in 2020 and was similarly underway in the 2022 election. The innuendo-laden film inspired a litany of fact-checks, though largely from outside the media ecosystem trusted by the community. Meanwhile, groups popped up on Truth Social to coordinate ballot-box observation; those who found the film persuasive took to sitting in front of drop boxes, armed, recording their neighbors dropping off their ballots.[42]

In addition to elections, school board and city council meetings have also become hotbeds of harassment. These gatherings have always attracted a handful of deeply committed eccentrics and gadflies, but COVID-19 policies created real resentment and increased vitriol. People occasionally followed doctors or teachers to their cars after school board and city council meetings. Mask policies, which might have been civilly debated within communities with input from public health data, instead turned into a war with people protesting (and livestreaming) outside the homes, rather than the offices, of public health officials.[43] The videos are processed differently depending on what faction you align with; some see the protestors as brave warriors: others, as annoying neighbors; still others, as domestic terrorists. Many public servants decided the potential costs were simply too high and quit their jobs.[44]

Disputes that originate online also hop offline. On June 17, 2023, at 7:05 a.m. Central Time, professor of pediatrics and molecular virology Dr. Peter Hotez shared a *Vice* magazine article criticizing popular podcaster Joe Rogan for hosting Robert F. Kennedy Jr., then a newly announced presidential candidate for the Democratic Party, on his podcast.[45] The *Vice* piece that Hotez tweeted chronicled Kennedy's usual schtick—pushing baseless theories about 5G and Wi-Fi making people sick, fearmongering about vaccines (COVID and childhood), and talking up discredited cures—but then also noted that Spotify, the platform that carries Rogan's show, had stopped trying to stem vaccine misinformation on the podcast.

Dr. Hotez had previously gone on Rogan's podcast as a guest before the pandemic to dispel vaccine-autism conspiracy theories and again at the start of the pandemic to discuss COVID-19.[46] But since those appearances, Rogan had become increasingly skeptical of mainstream scientific consensus on COVID vaccines and treatments. He also took to Twitter to respond to Hotez's criticism: "Peter, if you claim what RFKjr is saying is 'misinformation' I am offering you $100,000.00 to the charity of your choice if you're willing to debate him on my show with no time limit."[47] RFK Jr., who in a past life was primarily known as an attorney, quickly said he'd do it. Elon Musk amplified the exchange, saying Hotez was "afraid of a public debate" because he knew he was wrong.[48] Hotez declined the debate invitation but offered to go on the podcast to correct the record one-on-one (plus eleven million listeners) with Joe Rogan.

However, the kindling was lit: at the time of the argument, Rogan had 11 million Twitter followers, Musk had 144 million, and RFK Jr. had 1.5 million.[49] Each has a highly active army on the Internet of Beefs.

The ensuing tiff was ostensibly about debating:[50] Should experts debate cranks? Was Rogan capable of moderating a debate? Was it cowardly *not* to debate? Why don't experts want to debate people if they're such experts?[51] The brouhaha was similar to the debates-about-debate that periodically pop up when creationists challenge evolutionary biologists.

The interaction trended, leading to a deluge of comments and replies. Many were extremely nasty. Other prominent COVID vaccine opponents got in the game, offering their own money to enrich the pot and drawing their factions into the conversation. Hotez, who has 460,100 followers, generally maintains a positive tone in his posts; he is not a culture warrior, though he does have a long-standing collection of anti-vaccine reply guys whose commentary he occasionally highlights to his own audience. Hotez is influential and not exempt from critique—his expertise informs public health policies, and he has developed several vaccines in use globally. He is also clearly a public figure: he is regularly on television and podcasts, has written books, and testified in front of Congress. He is capable of holding his own in response to public criticism and he good-naturedly did so during the barrage. Mainstream media outlets sympathetically covered his effort.

But many of the online brawlers were not interested in actual debate. Much of the mob's barrage consisted primarily of personal attacks and smears. And on June 18 at 10:50 a.m., Hotez tweeted that two people had showed up at his door, filming him as he stood outside.[52] They posted the video online. It had taken just over twenty-four hours from the first interaction on Twitter to a pair of individuals showing up on his front stoop. Apparently Rogan, Musk, and RFK Jr. had nothing to say about that.

These two citizen journalists of the Fifth Estate were there to clout-chase: to film Hotez, hoping to provoke him into doing something they could use to gin up further harassment on the internet. If he got angry, if he slammed the door, if he threatened them or called the police—well, that would be fodder for the online mob. Hotez stayed calm, and the people at his door were fortunately not inclined to violence, but the effect was horrifying for observers who work in public health and science communication. This was intimidation, not debate.

The *Journal of the American Medical Association* recently published a study surveying physicians' and scientists' experiences with harassment. Unsurprisingly, two-thirds of respondents reported being harassed online (sexual images sent to them, review bombing, doxxing, and violent threats); prior to the pandemic, only 23 percent had reported such things. Some, however, also reported being harassed offline (stalking and assaults). Many respondents said that online threats of offline harm had significantly impacted their willingness to engage.[53]

The normalization of this behavior matters for far more than the individual target. In the introduction, I discussed my experience as a mom who decided to speak up in favor of a bill to eliminate a loophole to vaccine requirements for California public schools in the aftermath of the Disneyland measles outbreak. I wasn't a public figure at all at the time, and used social media primarily to talk to family, friends, and colleagues. But I wanted to advocate for a belief that had become important to me: that the overwhelmingly safe vaccines that prevent communicable diseases should be a requirement for public school, because no one has the right to put other people's kids at risk of deadly diseases out of misguided beliefs in disproven theories. This was not a particularly controversial opinion in the offline world at the time; over 80 percent of kids in California were vaccinated, so it was arguably fairly mainstream, even if the asymmetry of passion created a different perception online. Yet the extent of the doxxing, targeting, and harassment Vaccinate California advocates received made me feel like it was some sort of risky fringe belief. We were followed and recorded, clips of us were posted to YouTube, and anti-vaccine activists made public social media posts discussing what would happen if they protested on sidewalks outside of our homes or sent us Christmas cards. It was jarring—I'd never wanted a visible online presence as any kind of activist, and at the time I was very nervous about having even a limited one suddenly thrust upon me. I worried that it would impact my future career, for example, if employers googled me and found weird anti-vax hate videos. I ultimately chose to be vocal anyway, but even in 2015 the harassment made it feel more like a war than a policy fight.[54] I was reluctant to encourage others to speak up as well.

A few years later, in 2021—by then, rather accustomed to attracting online controversy—I spoke up in favor of reopening my district's schools as evidence increasingly suggested that the pandemic and vaccination effort had reached a point at which kids could safely return to the classroom. A moderate parent group had formed to request that the San Francisco district formulate a reopening plan; I joined and became a "reopener mom." Shortly after, I got involved in another parent-led campaign, this time to reform the California math curriculum: a few years prior low pass rates for some student groups led the San Francisco school district to make the decision to no longer offer algebra in eighth grade. I thought this was an inequitable solution that didn't help either struggling or advanced kids, so I spoke up about both reversing the policy and warning other districts in California not to adopt such a disastrous approach.[55] In each of these situations, I purposefully chose to take a visible advocacy role on social media—the causes were important to me, and I wanted to raise awareness and shape local public opinion. Many people saw my posts and reached out in direct messages asking how they could get involved—but a significant number noted that they were very wary of saying anything publicly. They were afraid of trolling or putting their families or jobs at risk by advocating for anything remotely controversial. One single mom had a small business and was afraid of people who disagreed with her political beliefs leaving bad reviews and tanking her livelihood.

You may not share my beliefs on these issues—you may even hate them—but in a healthy democracy these are the sorts of things we have to be able to discuss. Yet each of these three local issues turned into a social media brouhaha. The local fight was blue versus bluer—local Democrats versus local Democratic Socialists. But California also takes up a lot of space in the heads of people who don't live there—trolls from other cities often weigh in on San Francisco's "woke governance" issues in particular—and these policy fights devolved into vitriol, smears, and doxxing. Some people see the attacks and back away: they're understandably afraid of becoming the focus of the mob. Causing people to refrain from participation, known as the *chilling effect*, is one of the main goals of this kind of behavior. Seeing a person become the Main Character—seeing them face ridicule, smears, professional consequences, threats, and harassment and recognizing how random it all is—is frightening. In the back of their minds, bystanders watching it happen to an unfortunate target know that next time it could be them. There but for the grace of God go I.

Others, by contrast, see the attacks and are motivated to participate because the "debate" gives them cover to troll and be nasty.

One consistent finding in polarization research is that members within a community often don't feel comfortable criticizing or pushing back against the excesses of their own political faction. This relates to our earlier discussion of political identities becoming more global than local, as people are sorted on social media. Many participants fear that by speaking up against something they think is a bridge too far, they will be attacked by their own "team" for disloyalty or tarred as "bad progressives" or "bad conservatives" if they don't align fully with the faction. They don't want their own faction to come for them! And so they self-silence.[56]

They may also not want to be seen as undermining their side; after all, the other guys are worse. A progressive may have privately believed that their school district should have reopened earlier, but then again, *Tucker Carlson supports school reopening.* A conservative may have privately been disgusted by Trump's lies about stolen elections but avoided saying so given vicious attacks from members of their own party. Indeed, fellow Republicans who opposed Jim Jordan's bid for the House speakership in October 2023 reported receiving credible death threats from his supporters.[57]

The people who are not self-silencing, meanwhile, are the most extreme voices—particularly the knights with armies of mooks who are willing to deploy harassment and smears for the sake of their clout. Their visibility further cements the perception that the most extreme people reflect the majority consensus... which in turn offers up more fodder for nutpicking and creates more of an appetite for fighting those "extremists."

People are exhausted by this. Attempting to have an earnest, good-faith conversation on social media carries the risk of having an inartful comment rendered into bait for a mob—and nuance is difficult to express within the constraints of a social media post. It takes courage to defend the target of a nutpicking brigade—even just to stand up for common human decency, regardless of the specific opinion expressed—because no one wants to have the mob turn on them. Harassment is not just "mean speech"—it has real cascading consequences for social dynamics and norms.

The effect of the harassment, smears, and threats is that over time people become wary of expressing their opinion. This kind of toxicity— which some influencers try to normalize as "calling out" an opponent or engaging in "free speech"—contributes to an environment that stifles speech. It stifles online assembly. It makes others pull out of the debate because the cost of speaking up feels too high. Deciding it's not worth the risk to their reputations, careers, or families, they shut up and stop participating. And that is, in fact, the entire goal.

The Cinematic Universe Expands

I experienced another online mob just ahead of the 2022 midterms. Elon Musk favorably retweeted Yoel Roth,[58] then head of Twitter's Trust and Safety Department, who had posted about work the Stanford Internet Observatory had done jointly with Twitter, examining Iranian and Chinese networks masquerading as Americans in election conversations on the platform.[59] The Iranians pretended to be left-wing Americans and encouraged support for pro-Palestinian, progressive-left candidates, while the Chinese primarily focused on attacking politicians and candidates they saw as anti-China, such as Senator Marco Rubio.

Sharing the work was beneficial for Musk, who could show that his new company was protecting the midterm elections from foreign interference.

Roth's tweet—and by extension Musk's retweet—quoted me. For two days after the retweet by Musk, I gained followers by the thousands, but I was also deluged with harassment from his most vocal admirers— including Pizzagater Jack Posobiec. Posobiec was not happy that Musk had favorably boosted the work of someone who'd done research into Russian interference in the 2016 election (the "Russiagate hoax," in Posobiec's reality) and who had studied the Big Lie in the 2020 election ("censored conservatives"). To push back against the positive attention, Posobiec baselessly announced to his then 1.8 million followers, and later his podcast audience, that EIP colleague and professor Kate Starbird and I were "behind censoring the Hunter Biden laptop."[60] It was pure fabrication, an utter lie, intended to discredit us and rile up the mob. While I might *seem* like a good guy for exposing Chinese and Iranian operations targeting Americans, Posobiec was telling his fans, I was in fact a very bad person—a villain.

In reality, my only comment on Twitter's moderation of the Hunter Biden laptop story was that it had been overly heavy-handed. I thought it was a bad call. But social media makes decontextualization effortless: facts take work to find, and Posobiec knew that his followers wouldn't bother to check. They would simply trust him—and attack me. Sure enough, immediately after he posted the lie, his flying monkeys swarmed. Some sent me emails—commentary along the lines of "blood refreshes the tree of liberty" and "traitors who violate the Constitution are hung for sedition." Others just screamed at me on Twitter; I wound up blocking around six thousand people that day.

Posobiec knew that he would never be held accountable in any way. His following had increased by orders of magnitude since the online lies about Pizzagate had inspired a gunman to show up to a small restaurant in the real world. Rather than reckoning with what he'd inspired there, he simply alleged that the gunman was part of a plot to silence him: "False Flag. Planted Comet Pizza Gunman will be used to push for censorship of independent news sources that are not corporate owned."[61] The primary form of accountability for precipitating a mob has been platform moderation, and the biggest influencers are rarely punished because they're not the ones who actually go and harass or threaten the targets. The faction handles this for them, taking care of the proverbial meddlesome priest on the influencer's behalf.

It's hard to differentiate between the pursuits of power, money, and clout. I have often wondered to what extent the conspiracy theorist political influencers actually believe what they're pushing. There were no search results for me and that laptop story, and a two-second glance at LinkedIn makes clear I've never worked at Twitter. Posobiec, in all likelihood, simply fired off some bullshit; it didn't *matter* to him if it was true. He needed only to invoke the shibboleth "Hunter Biden's Laptop," and his followers would instantly know what to do. They were convinced that a vast cabal had colluded to disenfranchise them, to snatch away Trump's win by censoring the laptop story, and if I was mentioned in this way, then I must have been a part of it. Familiarity, a dash of novelty, and a slew of repetition. It did not matter to Jack Posobiec (or to Mike Benz) what the cost of their lies was for the people they targeted and smeared. What mattered was keeping fans engaged, aggrieved, and subscribed. And so, later that evening, Posobiec repeated his claims on his podcast—making money from the advertisers who paid to reach his listeners—and a new wave of harassment hit my inbox.

Posobiec was adept at generating online harassment, but his theories remained largely confined to a right-wing echo chamber. A few months later, allegations linking us to everything from Hunter Biden's laptop to the censorship of "tens of millions of tweets" would go far more mainstream . . . ushered in by the scribes of what had come to be known as The Twitter Files.

On February 28, 2023, I received an email from writer Matt Taibbi, who at the time was still going through Twitter's internal emails and crafting "Twitter Files" stories about purported malfeasance. "Hello from Matt Taibbi," it began. "Obviously you're familiar with my work, as you've written critically of it." The inquiry asked me to comment on two things: the fact that I'd worked at the CIA and the fact that an executive at Twitter had written an email about me in 2017, saying that he felt I "lacked expertise."

I did know Taibbi's work. He'd got his start as a lefty darling, lambasting Wall Street and calling Goldman Sachs a "vampire squid" in the pages of *Rolling Stone*. But then, at the height of the *#MeToo* movement in 2017, his career took a hit after his early writings, some of which detailed abusive and degrading behavior toward women during his time in Russia, came to light.[62] He issued a public apology and dismissed those writings as "satire," but the damage was done. After the uproar caused his publisher to drop him, Taibbi became deeply resentful of cancel culture on the left and gradually progressed from taking on billionaires to caping for one. Unlike Posobiec, however, Taibbi was still broadly perceived as a legitimate journalist, making it easier for people to buy into his alternate universe—and for congressmen to cite it.

As I read his email, I was struck by the lack of any actual questions. The "facts" I was being asked to comment on were useful to Taibbi solely as tools to smear me personally. *CIA! Spooky... and did you hear someone once said she was dumb?*

In fact, I'd interned for the CIA while an undergraduate—two decades earlier, and years prior to the founding of Twitter. This wasn't a secret; although in my forties I rarely bring up my college internships, it had been referenced by journalists and the subject of jokes in public speech and panel introductions. Taibbi's other point—that an executive from a company I'd once pushed for Congress to investigate had called me unqualified at the time—mostly struck me as funny. The executive and I had gone on to collaborate in subsequent years. OK, he said something dismissive five years prior. So? What was I supposed to say about that now? Where were the questions about my actual work with Twitter?

I didn't reply. I didn't trust Taibbi to treat me fairly.

I'd seen his recent backchannel conversations with a colleague of mine, in which it seemed obvious that the "reporter" was working backward: from his own pet theories to the emails in front of him, not the other way around.

His comment that I'd written critically of his work, however, was entirely correct. I'd initially been optimistic about the potential of the Twitter Files but was soon disappointed. Taibbi spun sensational viral tales out of the emails he cherry-picked, but they didn't stand up to scrutiny. His very first expose, posted as a Twitter thread, made an incendiary allegation that the Biden campaign had demanded Twitter take down content...but the requested content turned out to be non-consensual nudes of Hunter Biden. Free speech doesn't include the right to spread stolen nude images, and the platform had rightly taken them down. Ignoring the substance of a request while framing its mere existence as evidence of pressure to "censor" was dishonest.

Taibbi's anecdotes certainly created heat, but they generated little light. As someone who'd studied platform content moderation for years, I thought the whole thing was a missed opportunity to ask far more important questions and really get into Twitter's internal data.[63]

Tech journalists who knew something about how platform trust and safety teams operated were, by turns, amused by and embarrassed for the Twitter Files writers. They'd been chosen by Musk because of a shared distaste for mainstream journalism and content moderation—not because they knew anything about the topic.[64] As a result, there was an abundance of what Michael Crichton once called "wet-streets-cause-rain" mistakes—basic misinterpretations, confusion of cause and effect.[65] But more importantly, it quickly became clear that the writers were requesting internal Twitter documents, then trying to shoehorn what they got into the story they already planned to tell.

Although I distrusted Taibbi from the start, I made the mistake of trusting one of the other Twitter Files authors: Michael Shellenberger. He wasn't a journalist by training but a PR flack, a man after Edward Bernays's own heart, with quite the impressive roster of clients; Hugo Chavez had hired him when the Venezuelan strongman needed to improve his image in the United States.[66] Today, he runs a Substack newsletter purporting to expose all manner of nefarious evils and does media hits, presenting himself as an expert on topics ranging from climate, to homelessness, to drug abuse, to city governance, to crime, to epidemiology, to gender, to race, to AI, to UFOs, to whales. In December 2022, he added content moderation and free speech to the list.

Shellenberger, too, revealed a knack for misunderstanding material in ways that corroborated his preexisting beliefs. One of his early Twitter Files threads, a fifty-post opus, alleged the discovery of "evidence pointing to an organized effort by representatives of the intelligence community" to discredit the story of Hunter Biden's laptop. Again, the moderation of the laptop story was indeed a heavy-handed debacle, as Twitter's then CEO had quickly acknowledged. However, Shellenberger elevated a bad call into a vast government conspiracy: one of Twitter's internal emails revealed *that the FBI had sent payments to Twitter.*

When the FBI sends legal requests, it is obligated to pay the recipient of the request for time spent fulfilling it. Shellenberger, however, implied that the payments, which dated back to 2019, were part of a plot—that a supposed FBI "influence campaign" to suppress the laptop was greased because the bureau was paying Twitter.[67] Twitter's general counsel, fired by Musk a few weeks prior, had previously been general counsel at the FBI. There was no evidence presented of any connection between people, payments, and moderation and no indication of further journalistic digging into the requests—the innuendo was enough. Elon Musk boosted the thread, spinning Shellenberger's take into an even broader incendiary clam: "Government paid Twitter millions of dollars to censor info from the public."[68]

Congressman Jim Jordan piled on, demanding Twitter's "censorship" records.[69] Fact-checkers did eventually explain how the legal request reimbursement process worked, but by then the theory was canon within the cinematic universe, bolstered by Jordan's involvement and willingness to play along with the fiction.[70]

Shellenberger reached out to me in a private message on December 29, 2022, ten days after posting his FBI thread. He wanted to learn more about content moderation. Granted, this glimmer of self-awareness had happened *after* his misleading allegation had gone viral, but I decided to help. As long as the Twitter Files project was happening, I figured, it'd be good to have informed reporters looking at the emails, whatever their ideology. Over the next three months we had friendly conversations about content moderation, both privately and publicly.[71] We didn't always agree, but I felt good about the interactions; if I could help him convey the nuanced reality of content moderation decisions to his audience, perhaps the topic might become less fraught.

I was wrong.

Public Square or Gladiatorial Arena?

A lot of people use the "public square" metaphor to describe social media, particularly those concerned that moderation policies are a form of censorship. It's an appealing metaphor for American politicians and activists, who leverage it to argue that platforms should have to adhere to the rules of free speech as enumerated in the US Constitution. It's also a completely misleading metaphor: these "public squares" are in reality private companies serving global audiences. The exceptions would be those that the First Amendment specifies: defamation, fraud, obscenity, child abuse material, content that constitutes direct incitement to violence, and the "imminent lawless action" of the 1969 Supreme Court case *Brandenburg v. Ohio.*

In a physical public square, people also behave quite differently. Civility is still mostly a norm. The harassment mobs—from simple bullies to unhinged truthers—would not be tolerated. You do not get to follow your neighbors around offline, screaming obscenities at them. You do not get to chase after them with pitchforks or get your hundred closest friends to follow them down the street, shrieking at them. You don't get to post doctored naked photos of them on their office doors or stand outside telling everyone who approaches their places of work that they're really a criminal. There are time, place, and manner restrictions on speech, public nuisance laws, noise ordinances, and other ways of keeping the peace.

Sometimes the private companies that own the "square" decide that influencers using mobs to target random people on the internet is, in fact, bad for business. But when they make calls that lead to takedowns or strikes against instigators, the factions attempt to work the refs. They use platitudes about censorship, even when their goal is to push *other* people out of the conversation—ironically, violating a different sort of virtualized First Amendment value: the right to free assembly.

In 2013 former Twitter CEO Dick Costolo talked about the platform's role as reminiscent of the Greek agora, where people came to talk about what was going on, to hear politicians and preachers and people from the next town over, to have unfiltered conversations and debate. But the incessant, roiling culture war skirmishes have made these spaces more like Roman gladiatorial arenas, venues more for a fight to the death than a deliberative dialogue.

In these gladiatorial brawls, taking down an account is one of the most drastic moderation actions that a social media company can undertake. In our studies of platform moderation actions, as noted earlier, we see that the smaller accounts often receive this kind of enforcement, while the accounts of larger influencers, media figures, celebrities, or politicians who say the same things are often left untouched. Sometimes they might receive a strike or be asked to delete a specific tweet. But they are rarely taken down because the platforms know that such an action will create outrage and blowback.

Indeed, one of the useful glimpses into moderation that came from the Twitter Files, via a thread from former *New York Times* journalist Bari Weiss, who founded center-right media outlet The Free Press, was that Twitter had put certain accounts onto a list that required upper-management approval for action—essentially giving these high-profile accounts an extra layer of protection *against* moderation (the opposite of censorship, one might argue).[72] One of them was Libs of TikTok,[73] a popular nutpicker who often highlighted her ideological enemies on LGBT issues; her targets regularly received harassment and threats. But because of her popularity, Twitter was concerned about the blowback of taking action on the account. When it had done so on a few occasions, factional outrage over the decision led to media coverage from Tucker Carlson and right-wing media outlets, as well as commentary from sitting Republican politicians.

The challenge of content moderation is that the policies are enforced by people. As such, it is easy for those who are moderated to allege that the people who made the call were biased against their identity or politics. When millions of moderation decisions are made each month on Twitter, Facebook, YouTube, and TikTok, there will be bad calls. Since the decisions are rarely transparently laid out, arguments about systematic bias against a particular group are often very persuasive to angry crowds. Investigations into partisan bias and anticonservative censorship in particular have consistently found the opposite—that conservatives tend to dominate mainstream social media platforms—but the anecdotes remain persuasive.[74]

As social media platforms tried to address some of the worst elements of the rumor-and-misinformation dynamics—for example, by trying to minimize rumors that delegitimized elections, led people to drink fishtank cleaner, or incited harassment mobs—their efforts were recontextualized as anticonservative bias and censorship. When platforms sought to strike a balance between free expression and hate speech or dehumanization, that too was recontextualized as censorship. Actual bad calls, overreach, and inconsistently applied policies meant that there was always fodder to leverage toward delegitimizing the entire enterprise of content moderation. New platforms sprang up that explicitly declared themselves free speech zones: early on, deplatformed Far Right anti-Semites and avowed racists went to Gab. However, since most people do not actually want to participate in avowedly racist communities, it got little mainstream traction. Other platforms, such as Parler, Gettr, and Truth Social (begun by former president Donald Trump), emerged to cater primarily to MAGA audiences and attracted some top influencer and commentator talent. However, they didn't gain a lot of traction for a very simple reason: there were no libs to own.

Free speech is a cherished and foundational human right, one that people who believe in democratic societies should support in spirit even if the letter of the constitutional amendment applies specifically to the US government. However, the term—like its opposite, *censorship*—has undergone an extended reframing effort by factions who want wholly unencumbered attention and elimination of any kind of intervention by the private actors who host their speech. Downranking ragebait is censorship; actioning the accounts of individuals who started harassment mobs is censorship; labeling disputed or false claims is censorship, these very loud voices argue. In reality, platforms have their own freedom of speech and association rights as they decide what they will carry and what they will amplify. Even *Infowars*, a website run by Alex Jones, which caters to conspiracy theorists and has produced the sort of mobs that harass victims of mass shootings, has a terms of service: "remember: you are a guest here. it is not censorship if you violate the rules and your post is deleted. all civilizations have rules and if you violate them you can expect to be ostracized from the tribe."[75] Social media platforms and most online comments sections belong to private businesses, not the government, and their business depends on keeping the greatest possible number of users happy. But the ref-working ragemongers of the Internet of Beefs don't want (their audiences) to see it that way.

The fight over "free speech" is about preferential dissemination. It is a fight about algorithmic amplification, share of voice, and the ability to reach vast audiences at no cost—recast as if they were rights. It's a fight for power, for dominance of communication infrastructure and the capacity to shape public opinion.

A Different Form of Harassment

By 2023, having studied disinformation and propaganda campaigns for years, I was accustomed to facing harassment from the occasional online mob or being smeared by the occasional hyperpartisan or state-controlled media outlet.

But then, on March 2, 2023, Matt Taibbi entered that Twitter Spaces voice chat room—run by the anonymous man with a raccoon-face profile picture—to talk about his latest Twitter Files findings with fans.[76] And in that chat room was Mike Benz.

Benz, who'd been trying to make Taibbi notice him for weeks, seized the opportunity, effusively praising Taibbi's work for a long, embarrassing moment before letting the audience know that it was actually he, Benz, who had "all of the missing pieces of the puzzle" detailing the evil cabal purportedly censoring right-wing speech.

"I can tell you literally everything," Benz told Taibbi, promising him that he would have "superpowers" at the end of the conversation. In a rambling monologue, Benz breathlessly recounted the alternate history he'd so painstakingly crafted. He fixated on me: I was the puppet master of this vast cabal, with "special privileged access" to "DHS' 24/7 cyber mission control" and "DHS FBI powers." My supposed powers came with a secret deputization authorizing me to censor "22 million tweets," he burbled, dropping the twisted statistic he'd harped on for months on his blog. Then he ran through the laundry list of conspiracy theories he'd been feeding right-wing media. Basking in the audience attention, he enthusiastically upped the number of posts we'd somehow censored to *hundreds* of millions. "Wow," Taibbi solemnly replied, as if he were Bob Woodward speaking to Deep Throat in an underground DC parking lot.

"This is a scale of censorship the world has never experienced before!" Benz exclaimed.

A few days later, on March 9, 2023, Matt Taibbi and Michael Shellenberger testified in a public hearing before Jim Jordan and his Select Subcommittee on the Weaponization of the Federal Government. Under oath, and in chaotic written testimony, the two witnesses regurgitated Benz's claims—the nonsense about "millions of tweets" and targeting of conservatives, my supposed "undisclosed CIA ties," and all the rest of the bullshit, now entered into the congressional record as if they'd uncovered it while sleuthing through Twitter's files.

The appearance made Benz's dream of congressional hearings before a committee with subpoena power—the stated goal in his first blog post—come true. He sat behind them in the hearing room as Shellenberger called on Congress to limit the ability of social media platforms to remove harmful content and to cut all public funding for our work.

Shellenberger, with whom I'd been regularly speaking until just a few days prior, submitted an error-riddled, sixty-eight-page Gish Gallop of a testimony to Jordan's committee; he mentioned me by name over fifty times, assigning me opinions I don't hold and mixing up work I'd done with work done by others.[77] The words *censor* and *censorship* appeared more than two hundred times, stuffed into every conceivable sentence—a PR man's effort to create reality through relentless repetition. Shellenberger could have reached out to confirm his claims about "undisclosed ties" or "22 million tweets" in advance, but he chose not to. He did, however, reach out after the fact, to an SIO colleague, asking if he'd gotten anything wrong in his testimony. And if he had, he asked, should he be censored?

Normally, this would have been funny. Propagandists have been mad at us on the internet before. It was amusing to see vaunted muckraker Matt Taibbi fall for the claims of a fawning bullshitter he met in a Twitter Space and to hear Michael Shellenberger call Benz the "head of cyber at the State Department" in a post-testimony victory lap on Joe Rogan's podcast. But, unfortunately, irate trolls on the internet came out in force, and there were threats to deal with.

This time, however, the most impactful consequence of the smear wasn't the resulting online harassment.

Rather, it was a different form of harassment, one that is far more significant. It turned out that Shellenberger and Taibbi's faux-journalism blockbuster provided the pretext needed for Jim Jordan and his Select Subcommittee on the Weaponization of the Federal Government to announce an investigation into the role that the Stanford Internet Observatory, the Election Integrity Partnership, and the Virality Project had played in a "censorship regime" by "advising on so-called misinformation."[78]

By the end of that week, the EIP member institutions—Stanford University, the University of Washington, Graphika, and the Digital Forensic Research Lab—had received letters from Jordan demanding that we turn over all of our emails with government and tech companies dating back to 2015. Shortly afterward, SIO's letter turned into a subpoena. Hundreds of letters would go out from the Jordan committee over the next nine months as he aggressively, and ironically, used his congressional subpoena power to seek evidence of the "weaponization of the federal government."[79]

An ideological ally making an accusatory insinuation was all it took to justify a letter. Matt Taibbi said something in a Twitter thread, and Jim Jordan got to read my emails.

The time since the subpoena arrived has been a surreal journey into a mirror world.

Not to be outdone by his colleague, Republican representative Dan Bishop, another congressman who voted against certifying the 2020 election and praised Mike Benz as "indispensable in bringing to light the largest government censorship scheme in US history,"[80] began to demand we turn over documents for his House Homeland Security committee.

Shellenberger, meanwhile, made me the recurring Main Character of his newly launched Substack. He took over as the lead screenwriter extending Benz's cinematic universe, spinning more episodes about the

"CIA Fellow" he'd supposedly "exposed," the evil mastermind of the "Censorship Industrial Complex" who was also, in turn, a malignant narcissist, a snob, and quite possibly a bad mom. She was "linked to" every stupid thing anyone in disinformation research had ever done, leading a conspiracy in every email she was cc'd on, and secretly behind every bad idea the Biden administration had ever had. In one remarkable post, she had even deluded *President Obama* into "supporting censorship." Most importantly, though, this fictional character who shared my name and face was the nemesis in *his* hero epic: Michael Shellenberger, self-styled champion of American liberty, was on a crusade to dismantle, defund, and disempower Renée DiResta, someone who'd risen to "the highest levels" of the intelligence community, one of "the most dangerous people in America right now."[81] Readers captivated by his valiant stand, he frequently reminded them, could show their support by subscribing to his Substack for $9.99/month.

Shortly after, in June 2023, came the lawfare: legal proceedings, such as vexatious lawsuits that bog down the target, tying up their time, energy, and money. Stephen Miller—the Trump advisor best known for his family-separating immigration policy, now leading the "America First Legal" lawsuit mill—sued me and my colleagues on behalf of the Gateway Pundit's founder (he of the ballots-in-dumpsters stories) and a random "health freedom" activist we'd never heard of. Their legal complaint regurgitated the now familiar lie: our supposed collusion with tech platforms and the government, it claimed, had deprived entire classes of people of their First Amendment rights in "probably the largest mass-surveillance and mass-censorship program in American history."[82] Naturally, the lawsuit cited the Twitter Files—and the Foundation for Freedom Online.

The lawsuit was filed in a federal courthouse in Louisiana with only one active judge, a Trump appointee. That judge was also presiding over *Missouri v. Biden*, a case in which the attorneys general of Missouri and Louisiana (who'd previously filed an amicus brief supporting efforts to overturn the 2020 election) alleged that the Biden administration had engaged in a vast jawboning operation to censor speech. (*Jawboning* is jargon for the government coercing companies to behave in a particular way, under credible threat of regulation or other retaliation.) The Gateway Pundit's founder was also a plaintiff in *that* lawsuit. On July 4, 2023, the judge issued a sweeping injunction in *Missouri v. Biden*, banning the government from, among other things, collaborating or partnering with the Stanford Internet Observatory. As I sat in the yard barbequing with my family on that Independence Day, I was shocked to read that the judge had mentioned me, personally, in the injunction. According to the judge, I'd declared that the Election Integrity Partnership was designed to "get around unclear legal authorities" and circumvent the First Amendment.[83]

It was a manufactured quotation. And it wasn't true.

The experience was maddening. It was against my interests in the lawsuit to immediately, publicly point out that the quote attributed to me was simply made up[84]—but that meant watching as the rumor mill and the propaganda machine batted the lie back and forth between them, over and over again, in dozens of articles and innumerable viral tweets.

Meanwhile, back in Congress, Jordan and Bishop requested that members of EIP, including recently graduated students who'd participated, attend "voluntary interviews"—behind closed doors—to discuss our work. In such interviews, the committee staff questions the witness, on videotape, for many hours; colleagues who went through them spent between five and seven hours answering questions. The witness gets neither a copy of the tape nor a transcript. Jordan and Bishop, in other words, could selectively leak out-of-context dribs and drabs to partisan media or favored influencers who could produce retaliatory smears. Meanwhile, those they interviewed had no immediate access to material with which to correct the record. The endeavor was profoundly skewed against those targeted. As Cardinal Richelieu once said, "If you give me six lines written by the hand of the most honest of men, I will find something in them which will hang him." Imagine what's possible with not only six hours of video but thousands of emails and a collection of Jira tickets tracking election and vaccine rumors...all of which we produced in response to the subpoena. A normal Congress would use its interview and subpoena powers in good faith, in pursuit of a true legislative or oversight purpose. But that is not what we have today. In an unprecedented abrogation of congressional norms, Jordan took excerpts from the closed-door testimony of one of my colleagues and documents produced via the subpoena and turned them over to Stephen Miller and America First Legal, which used them to write an amicus brief on behalf of Jordan, supporting the plaintiffs in *Missouri v. Biden*. Our congressional testimonies were being handed off to the lawfare side of the political machine—to the very team suing us! Other material was spun into committee reports that misrepresented the statements of those who'd attempted to honestly engage.[85]

I declined the "voluntary" interrogation, informing one congressman that if there was compelling public interest in hearing from me, then I'd happily discuss our public work in a public hearing, where the American public and any media who were interested could hear what I had to say directly. Yet despite the "Weaponization" committee sending out hundreds of letters targeting academics and institutions, it seems that no one accused has testified publicly. Instead, in November 2023, Shellenberger and Taibbi were invited back to talk about our work yet again in a commemorative hearing celebrating the one-year anniversary of the Twitter Files.

This entire enterprise—from the useful idiots of Elon Musk's Twitter Files laundering the inane theories of Benz's "foundation" into the congressional record, to the pipeline between the congressional hearings and the lawfare—fulfilled the aims of a political machine.[86] And every accusation was a confession: Shellenberger's testimony depicted me as someone engaged in collusion with the government, as part of a vast conspiracy to silence opinions; yet here was a federal judge misquoting me to justify telling the executive branch it could not speak to us. So-called free speech activists were working with a hyperpartisan congressional subcommittee to halt our First Amendment–protected work. And even as Jordan worked hand-in-hand with the attorneys general and Stephen Miller, *we* were accused of "intertwinement" with the government.

The problem with the 2020 election, in the mirror world of the hyperpartisan smear machine, had been not *Trump's attempt to steal it* but rather the effort of academics, tech platforms, and Trump's own Department of Homeland Security *to chronicle and respond to it*. We were not the government, our projects hadn't been funded by the government, the government wasn't telling us what to do, and we had our own First Amendment rights to do our research and to speak to tech companies—even to flag the occasional viral post that we thought violated their policies. Sixty-five percent of the time, the companies did nothing in response.

But when the facts refuted the conspiracy theory, the smear artists doubled down to mere innuendo.

The Serengeti Strategy

Creating alternate universes and making individual people the face of conspiracy theories and the target of mobs is going to continue because it works. As the *New York Times* reported, "Republican lawmakers and activists are mounting a sweeping legal campaign against universities, think tanks and private companies that study the spread of disinformation, accusing them of colluding with the government to suppress conservative speech online."[87]

And yet, institutions, uncertain how to respond, continue to treat this playbook as just some normal quasi-partisan shenanigans.

Perhaps what has been most frustrating about living through this experience is that this has happened before. In 2010 historians Naomi Oreskes and Erik M. Conway published *Merchants of Doubt*, a book exploring the history and tactics used by powerful individuals and interest groups to sow doubt and spread misinformation on various scientific issues. They connected the dots between playbooks used to undermine the scientific findings that cigarettes were causing cancer and those that were being used at the time to try to discredit the scientists who were raising the alarm about human-influenced climate change.

Certain industries and ideologically motivated groups have employed similar tactics to cast doubt on well-established scientific findings for many decades now—things that might be harmful to their profits or ideological beliefs. If they could cast doubt on the findings, the science, and the scientists, then they could continue to amass power and profit. "Doubt is our product," one tobacco industry executive wrote in 1969, "since it is the best means of competing with the 'body of fact' that exists in the minds of the general public."[88] Credentialed contrarians who could create a measure of doubt were bolstered by industry PR machines. Partisan-front think tanks were spun up to oppose the findings. Scientists were smeared personally. Some were sued. Some were hauled in front of Congress for hearings led by congressmen wishing to make an example of them—and to protect the congressmen's own interests. Documents obtained through the Freedom of Information Act and a cache of hacked emails (which came to be called "Climategate") were spun to create the impression of corruption, incompetence, or dishonesty.

One of the prominent targeted climate scientists, Dr. Michael Mann, wrote a book about being in the maelstrom himself. When I read it, I felt like I was reading a recounting of my own story: "The attacks are typically carried out by organizations and groups with names like 'Citizens for a Sound Economy' that masquerade as grassroots entities but in reality represent powerful industries and have hence been termed 'Astroturf' organizations. These groups employ ideologically aligned media outlets and a network of lawyers, lobbyists, and politicians to advance their message."[89] Fake foundations, propaganda outlets, and a network of lawyers and politicians created an alternate reality then, too. It is easier, Mann astutely notes, to target an individual and to make that person an avatar for an idea—just as longtime PR flack Shellenberger did, giving his mob someone specific to hate. Mann termed this the "Serengeti strategy": just as predators pick off a vulnerable animal from the herd, the people going after climate scientists at the time would pick off one prominent researcher, making them not only a target but an avatar for everything wrong with the industry, isolating them, and setting them up as an example of what might happen should others poke their heads up. And when these targeted attacks happened, members of the field often tried to keep their heads down to avoid being next.

The goal, in the context of tobacco and climate, was to create confusion and delay policy actions, ultimately hindering efforts to address pressing environmental and public health issues. Today's merchants of doubt are the political influencers who sowed confusion about—and reaped profits from—"stolen election" propaganda. They are leading the charge to harass and sue the researchers who studied their handi-work and that of their ideological allies in 2020, in anticipation of the 2024 election. And to update Mann: as the merchants have no leg to stand on, their weapons of choice are manufactured claims of incompe-tence and malfeasance, laden with innuendo and vilification; intimida-tion campaigns of ridicule and harassment; and the threat of an online mob.[90]

Amid all this, unfortunately, many universities on the receiving end of the harassment—both government and mob—chose the wrong com-munications strategy: stay silent and hope the media cycle passes.

The people who *did* continue to speak were Mike Benz, Matt Taibbi, Michael Shellenberger, and the other propagandists, screenwriters of cin-ematic universes, and scribes of bespoke realities, who filled their paid subscribers' inboxes and newsfeeds with the "truths" they wanted to hear. Benz and his blog continued to be a primary source for Far Right alche-mists; he opined, and they spun his conspiratorial ramblings into "facts" for the Far Right bespoke reality. Taibbi was humiliated on television by journalist Medhi Hasan, who looked into the claim that the Election Integrity Partnership had flagged "22 million tweets" and pointed out that Taibbi had been off by approximately 21,997,000.[91] Immediately afterward, Taibbi had a falling out with Elon Musk and lost access to his treasure trove of Twitter's internal documents; he now makes plaintive YouTube videos complaining that Musk has suppressed his reach and is impacting his Substack subscriber numbers.

Some readers may wonder why those who get targeted by smear artists don't file defamation lawsuits. The simple answer is that it is extremely expensive and takes a lot of time; years go by before cases are heard. But it's worth noting, perhaps, that British libel laws are far more favorable to those defamed than laws in the United States. And in June 2023, when Michael Shellenberger went to England to appear onstage with Russell Brand and Matt Taibbi to "expose" the so-called censorship-industrial complex, he suddenly declined to use my name. This wasn't about "nam-ing names," he said, piously, across the pond. It was about freedom.

Four months after that panel in England, Benz was the subject of a damning exposé by NBC News. He had, as I mentioned earlier, erased nearly all of his social media profiles before starting his "foundation"— a move that suggested he perhaps had something to hide. Indeed, an October 2023 news story revealed that Benz had "a secret history as an alt-right persona" known as "Frame Game."[92] Frame Game had run an anonymous YouTube channel called "Frame Game Radio" where he ranted about "white genocide" in the United States, a purported Jewish cabal, his desire to set up a "White Mother Fertility Fund," and the IQs of racial minorities. He posted similar content to Twitter and Gab. When caught by NBC, he declared that his secret past persona had been an effort to *deradicalize anti-Semites* (an excuse that his past social media contacts, including prominent neo-Nazi Richard Spencer, publicly mocked).[93] However, Frame Game/Mike Benz's past posts still lingered in some corners of the web, where his own words spoke for him: "If I, a Jew, a member of the Tribe, Hebrew Schooled, can read Mein Kampf & think 'holy shit, Hitler actually had some decent points.' Then NO ONE is safe from hating you once they find out who is behind the White genocide happening all over the world."[94]

And, across his oeuvre, he was angry that social media platforms were censoring him.

This was the man who retconned his brief stint as a relative nobody in the State Department into a sexy cyber-whistleblower origin story and was treated as a trustworthy source by Michael Shellenberger and Matt Taibbi. But as incredible as it all is, it is also very serious: the lies and half-truths begat harassment, threats, two congressional investigations, and two lawsuits.[96] And that is just for us.

The lawsuits are utter nonsense; they should have been swiftly dismissed. But that isn't the point. Stanford has already been forced to rack up legal fees in the seven figures to fend off frivolous lawsuits and manage the document production and testimony preparation for the subpoenas. Each week, I spend time talking to lawyers and reviewing the documentation that is needed to fight back. Meanwhile Miller and his cronies are fund-raising off their efforts, portraying themselves as champions of free speech even as they try to stifle ours.

The government agencies, nonprofits, and state and local officials that had worked to defend American elections in 2020 and 2022 have stepped back in the face of these attacks, concerned about their safety and uncertain about what they were legally allowed to do now. Tech companies have backed away as well; some continue to investigate state actor influence operations independently, but have noted that they are no longer receiving any government tips about foreign meddling.[96]

Self-censorship has begun, at the individual and government levels; the National Institutes of Health paused—some say killed—a grant program to study health communications out of concern that it would trigger investigations.[97] Academics at state universities have been deluged by FOIAs, slowing their work to a crawl. [98] And there is a lingering fear, among all of those targeted, that whipped-up true believers might resort to real-world violence or intimidation, as they did with Pizzagate and Peter Hotez.

In *A Lot of People Are Saying*, a 2019 book about the rise of conspiracy theories in American political life, authors Russell Muirhead and Nancy Rosenblum sum up this state of affairs eloquently: "The attack on shared modes of understanding is fatiguing. The consequences of incessant charges of secret plots and nefarious plotters are political, but at the same time they affect us personally and individually."[99]

The harassment works precisely as intended. The cinematic universes keep expanding. And the truth gets obliterated. Where can we go from here?

9

The Path Forward

Father Coughlin

Until now, we have focused on the ways in which, over the last decade, invisible rulers have transformed, propaganda and rumor have become pervasive, and millions of people have become entrenched in bespoke realities. The challenges facing us feel unique to the twenty-first century. But we have faced similar challenges before, as we will see in the dramatic story of Father Coughlin, who became a propagandist for Nazism in the 1930s. The dilemma then, as now, was what the response should be.

Charles Coughlin, a Detroit-based Catholic priest, began his radio broadcasting career in 1926 with the intent to grow his church flock. Coughlin was uniquely charismatic, blessed with a mesmerizing rich, mellow voice and a talent for persuasive yet accessible rhetoric, honed by decades of delivering sermons. Radio was growing in popularity, and Coughlin was tailor-made for the new medium, a man in the right place at the right time.[1]

Coughlin's early radio sermons focused on religious content, but by 1930 they were almost exclusively about politics. As the Great Depression ravaged America, ruining millions of lives, Coughlin's words resonated with poor and middle-class families alike. He affirmed for his audience the sense that their values and institutions were threatened, validated their struggles, and offered them not only an explanation but a set of villains and scapegoats.[2] Even prior to his pivot into politics, he had an audience that trusted him and believed him. He was a priest, and for Catholics in particular, his words channeled the Lord. He was in a unique position to moralize about who was good and who was bad.

And for those who were not Catholic or religious, he could speak as one patriot to another.

Coughlin's political content focused on "capitalism, currency, and communism." He was a proponent of social justice, using his radio broadcasts to criticize manipulative capitalist businessmen, indifferent politicians, and Communists alike. While he'd been a staunch supporter of Franklin D. Roosevelt during the 1932 presidential race, he became disillusioned. By 1934, President Roosevelt—in Coughlin's telling, a liar, a betrayer, a double-crosser, and "anti-God"—had become a frequent target of his wrath. He started his own political organization, the National Union for Social Justice. As he grew angrier at the state of the world, he became increasingly sympathetic to rising fascism in Europe.

All of this was within the realm of constitutionally protected free speech and political activism. Yet the rising ferocity of the rhetoric alarmed a portion of his early supporters. By 1935, some American leaders within the Catholic Church were describing Coughlin as a "hysterical demagogue." A profile in *The Atlantic* opened with a vignette of his youth movement to fight Communists: schoolchildren pledging to surrender their lives rather than obey the dictates of Karl Marx.[3] Coughlin's fiery calls to actions could generate letter-writing campaigns, rallies, and in-the-streets action. By 1936, he had taken a stance: "This is our last election. It is fascism or communism. We are at the crossroads. I take the road to fascism."[4] Democracy, he claimed, was doomed.

Father Coughlin was one of the most influential people of his time. While measurements vary, at the peak of his popularity an audience of up to 30 million listeners tuned in to his Sunday sermons—at a time when the population of the United States was 120 million people. They were not all supporters; some Gallup surveys estimated that one-third of his listeners actually disagreed with what he said.[5] Hate listeners, perhaps, were there for the controversy and entertainment. But Coughlin shaped public opinion. His audience acted in response to his provocations.[6] And he generated such massive engagement that a new post office was built in his town to process the tens of thousands of letters received each week from fans.[7]

There were moments in the early 1930s when radio syndicates had indicated discomfort with his anti-Semitism and suggested he moderate his "vigor";[8] Coughlin told his audience that he'd been gagged, and they flooded the broadcasting offices with complaints. By 1938, his vigorous speech had extended from criticism of Jewish bankers to vocal support for the Nazis. His print newsletter *Social Justice* republished excerpts from "The Protocols of the Elders of Zion," a notorious piece of anti-Semitic propaganda.[9] Media figures and religious leaders criticized him, and some of his audience did drop off. Academics and journalists in a group called the Institute for Propaganda Analysis undertook an effort to educate the public about the rhetorical tactics and effects of Coughlin's propaganda.

Then, in November 1938, Coughlin crossed a line. On November 9, mobs of Nazis burned hundreds of synagogues, destroyed thousands of Jewish-owned businesses, and arrested tens of thousands of Jewish people in a night of violence that came to be known as Kristallnacht. On November 20, Coughlin took to the airwaves to explain what had happened in Germany to his American audience—and he blamed the Jews. His radio address about Kristallnacht leveraged the fascist propaganda technique of reversing victim and offender: It was not the Jews who were persecuted, Coughlin argued.[10] No, Kristallnacht was a justified response to Jewish persecution of *Christians*.[11] The Nazis had been lenient, their real target was Communists, and only a few synagogues were burned, he lied.[12]

The response from radio broadcasters was swift. An announcer from WMCA, a New York station that carried Coughlin's program, responded immediately afterward, "Unfortunately, Father Coughlin has made some mistakes of fact."[13] The station wrote a letter declaring that the broadcast "was calculated to incite religious and racial strife in America," noting that it had pointed this out to Coughlin in advance and that he'd agreed to remove the lies intended to have that effect but had not done so.[14] WMCA informed Coughlin that it would no longer broadcast his program at all unless he submitted scripts in advance for approval, and it did not air his next homily when Coughlin didn't send a script (giving the time slot to alternative Catholic programming instead).[15] Radio stations that carried his show in other cities canceled his broadcasts.

Coughlin argued he'd been misunderstood, that the (Jewish-owned) media coverage of his Nazi-sympathetic address was unfair. Nazi media in Germany weighed in, arguing that stifling Coughlin's reach showed American hypocrisy. Americans were not allowed to hear the truth, Nazi media crowed: "a typical case of Jewish terrorism of American public opinion."[16] Coughlin became a hero in Nazi Germany.

Private media companies responded to the use of their platforms for the incitement of hate and the excusing of religious persecution.[17] As broadcasting licensers began to cancel programs and impose requirements, however, a few thousand of Coughlin's fans picketed;[18] for more than six consecutive months, his supporters protested weekly outside one radio station that cut his feed.[19] They argued that stations should be compelled to carry Coughlin, that he had a right to broadcast and that depriving them of their right to hear him was a civil rights issue. Opponents argued that the civil rights issue went the other way: Coughlin was praising and advocating for violence and calling for the persecution of groups of people.[20]

Even as the Kristallnacht broadcast controversy roiled, Coughlin published a speech, under his own byline in his newsletter, plagiarizing Nazi propaganda minister Paul Joseph Goebbels.[21] Shortly after, some of the more extreme among his supporters, including members of a small paramilitary activist group known as the Christian Front—started not *by* Coughlin but in response to his call for a crusade against anti-Christian forces—began to commit acts of violence in the streets.[22] The group was eventually raided by the Federal Bureau of Investigation (FBI) for planning a bombing campaign and talking of overthrowing the government, though historians disagree on how serious the effort was.[23] Upon their arrest, Coughlin reiterated that he stood with the broader idea, and movement, of a Christian front.

Although Roosevelt didn't want to act, prominent journalists wrote letters encouraging the suspensions and suggested that the Federal Communications Commission itself should take Coughlin off the air.[24] As

Coughlin began to advocate for authoritarianism and fascist dictator-ship, the Roosevelt administration decided that the radio spectrum was "a limited national resource," and so broadcasting was not entitled to full protection under the First Amendment.[25] In July 1939, the National Association of Broadcasters changed its code to put limitations on the sale of air time to "spokesmen of controversial public issues" and made explicit that radio could not be used to "convey attacks upon another's race or religion."[26] The association debated the question of what could be covered in radio addresses and how (or to what extent) religious content on the radio should promote consensus and spiritual harmony versus denigrating other religions to bolster one's own.[27] Questions about how best to treat these issues helped shape the regulatory effort known as the Fairness Doctrine,[28] which required that broadcast media afford equal time to presenting opposing sides on controversial topics.

On September 23, 1940, Coughlin wrote in his newsletter that he had been "forced from the air." In 1942, the US Post Office revoked the second-class mailing privilege of his *Social Justice* newsletter, and the attorney general initiated an investigation into it as a source of pro-Axis propaganda.

The deplatforming of Coughlin significantly reduced his influence; he became increasingly irrelevant after the United States entered World War II and ultimately returned to a quiet life as a preacher. But his pop-ularity in his heyday is an interesting case study of the power of char-ismatic individuals with an innate understanding of both the structure and the substance of influence to shape public opinion.

Very few people would argue that Father Coughlin was on the right side of history or a force for good by the late 1930s. Coughlin's contem-porary, the philosopher Karl Popper, speculated about the "the paradox of tolerance"—how a liberal society tolerant of authoritarian viewpoints in the interests of free expression might undermine its own survival. In-deed, Coughlin's example is directly relevant to the present moment be-cause of the multifaceted and ethically complex response from private enterprise, government, media, and civil society to the rise of a dema-gogue. There were government regulatory responses. There were public-education efforts. And there were private entities that made a choice to deny him a platform—with vocal crowds in both support of and opposition to that choice.

These same questions face us today, albeit on a different type of technological infrastructure. The stakes are also similar.

Responding to the Rumor Mill and Propaganda Machine

The modern parallels to the Coughlin story are numerous. A powerful new technology, radio, transformed how people received information and learned about the world. It became a source of entertainment; radio broadcasters became cultural influencers, stars. Moments like Orson Welles's 1938 radio adaptation of H. G. Wells's *War of the Worlds*, a novel about a Martian invasion of America, revealed how uniquely potent it could be for conveying both reality and unreality. The president of the United States, Franklin D. Roosevelt, used radio for his "fireside chats," evening broadcasts about issues ranging from the Depression to fighting fascism in Europe. And as with every prior technological medium, radio became a tool for propaganda, used by state actors as well as demagogues like Coughlin.

A little over ten years ago, the most recent major communication technology shift—social media—gave rise to the trinity of influencers, algorithms, and crowds. Private-platform design decisions began to influence whom we knew and what we saw, leading to a proliferation of new relationships and new voices. These decisions also increased the supply of unfiltered information—and facilitated the rise of bespoke realities. People who share not only Coughlin's talents—charisma, a knack for storytelling, a deep connection with their audience—but also his demagoguery and authoritarian streak are extraordinarily well served by this new medium.

So how do we answer this? How do we think about free expression in an algorithmically mediated communication ecosystem? Can the way we create and share information be redesigned so that we not only have an increasing proliferation of voices but also an increased capacity to hear them? How do we position ourselves to achieve consensus or tackle "tornado reality" without resurfacing the problems stemming from what Noam Chomsky called manufacturing consent?

We're in a period of adaptation. Each revolution in communication technology has delivered a period of disruption: access to information increases, traditional hierarchies are toppled, new voices are amplified, culture changes, and the potential for mobilization and activism evolves. This often results in social upheaval: the printing press, as we saw, played a significant role in the Reformation and the Thirty Years' War. Guardrails eventually appear, as regulation attempts to mitigate the worst negative externalities; for instance, in the nineteenth century, as newspapers became more prominent, countries introduced laws that penalized libel and minimized monopoly control. Society gradually adapts: most people have internalized that supermarket tabloids often don't tell the truth. There are structural responses and media literacy efforts—as well as a rise of counterspeakers who address the substance of newly popular arguments.

Now, after the social media revolution, which guardrails might temper the negative effects of the collision of the propaganda machine and the rumor mill?

American leaders in the late 1930s addressed the unique challenge presented by the radio priest influencer through policy, both regulatory and self-regulatory. They created relevant forms of education—and there's a lot we can learn from their response. Today's communication infrastructure is more full featured and participatory than radio, so design offers a powerful third lever.

But technology is only part of the story. Users have agency, and ordinary people can take steps to eschew murmurations, resist the ragebait of persecution profiteers and toxic Gurus, and create healthier norms.

Policy

The response to Father Coughlin is an interesting case study in content moderation from a bygone era. There was "labeling," as the station announcer immediately alerted listeners that Coughlin had misled them. There was content review. There was a temporary ban and then a permanent one. There was also industry-level policy change to try to prevent a repeat scenario.

And when the broadcasters did act, Coughlin's supporters protested.

The parallels are obvious. Today, social media companies are the powerful governors of online speech, setting the rules about whom and what they'll carry.[29]

Rethinking Content Moderation

Society has a complicated relationship with content moderation. Many people would argue that while a modern-day Father Coughlin doesn't have a right to be featured on television or quoted in the newspapers, social media is different. Many view these platforms as the new public square. And yet, poll after poll, year after year, reinforces that a large majority of people also support content moderation.[30] They don't want the public square to be a cesspool.

Policies shape propagation; the rules lay out what may be hosted, monetized, and made to go viral. But there are differences in opinion about what should be permitted, and enforcement is rarely uniform. This tension, together with the lack of a clear bright line around what should be allowed, is often exploited by precisely the people who benefit most from no moderation, like the Propagandists and the Perpetually Aggrieved. Just as Coughlin once did, current demagogues leverage moderation actions taken against them both to harden factional divides and to delegitimize the authority of the platforms to decide what they host, curate, and amplify. *The policies are unfair; their very existence is censorship!* goes the simplistic argument. Who are the platforms to decide what is hate speech or to take down posts promoting fake cures for contagious diseases? The point of this rhetoric is to normalize the idea that the platforms shouldn't be allowed to set the rules of engagement . . . because in the short term, it's only the platforms that can.

Other influencers, crowds, and factions, meanwhile, lament that certain types of content are not taken down *fast enough*; some argue that words are violence and call on platforms to stem the tide of "lawful but awful" content that, while it does not run afoul of speech laws, was once confined to far less visible realms.[31] They frame moderation calls that leave offensive content *up* as platforms' endangering vulnerable groups or abdicating their responsibility to users.

Meanwhile, academic leaders and technologists debate whether faster fact-checking might solve the problem, or attempt to engage in good-faith debate about bias in moderation. There's a fundamental disconnect here, driven by underestimation and misinterpretation. The factional combatants view this as a tactical arms race in a Hobbesian information war of all against all, where "working the refs" is a means to a strategic advantage. The others see it as a peacetime civil governance problem.[32]

But if we boot off the bad actors, filter nasty speech, or kill off the algorithms that help wild conspiracy theories trend, will we return to a less polarized, more harmonious way of relating to each other?

No.

That's because the content itself reflects real opinions. Real demand. Coughlin resonated because he spoke to communities that struggled deeply during the Great Depression, acknowledging their frustration and rage.

It's also because the internet has a place for everyone. Getting kicked off a large platform may reduce mainstream attention, but there are alt-platforms developed specifically for niche political identities. Telegram largely does not moderate and hosts many channels started by big influencers who were kicked off Twitter, YouTube, and Facebook. There are closed spaces, such as Discord servers and WhatsApp groups. There are email newsletters. The internet is a largely borderless ecosystem; social platforms, web content, media, and social media all blend together, and users are the bridge between the spaces. Banning a community on one platform will not prevent its ideas from spreading if they're compelling or novel enough.[33]

The censorship-resistant structure of the internet makes it hard to silence dissidents or stifle social movements—and that is a good thing. Yet, as Karl Popper noted, tolerance has its limits; a complete free-for-all results in unusable, unpleasant platforms. Mainstream social platforms—which are, ultimately, businesses—are not obligated to give megaphones to demagogues, to accept their ad dollars, or to recommend them to new users. Fortunately, a whole spectrum of available moderation options can create guardrails, balancing the trade-offs between moderation and free expression.

Tech companies have significant discretion in setting policies. They have to adhere to local laws, like blocking pro-Nazi content in Germany, where it's illegal. But in countries without such laws, platforms can decide whether to host Nazi sympathizers or to ban them. In the United States, the First Amendment (which does permit hate speech) does not restrict private companies; a social media company operating in the United States that wanted to ban any post with the word *cat* could go ahead and do it—though it might be bad for business. There is a trade-off here: some people feel that platforms should not be allowed to carry certain kinds of speech; others feel that they should be made to carry all speech that isn't explicitly illegal. Yet, if private companies are setting the policies for their online spaces—as opposed to a government setting the standards for all platforms within a country—people can vote with their feet (or fingers) and spend their time on platforms with more palatable (or cat-friendly) policies.[34]

Indeed, business is a significant driver in setting policy. While platforms generally hew to the value of maximizing free expression, they also recognize that roving factions of jerks screaming epithets are bad for the bottom line: they can chase away users and advertisers alike. Thus some platforms, including Twitter, have long made certain content ineligible for trends, or for monetization, or for serving alongside ads.

Here, too, battles ensue, because what is often framed as a fight over *speech* is actually a fight over *reach*.

On June 1, 2023, the *Daily Wire* announced that *What Is a Woman?*—contributor Matt Walsh's gender-ideology related documentary—would stream for free on Twitter. The date marked the one-year anniversary of its release and coincided with Pride Month.

However, later that day, Walsh and others at the *Daily Wire* announced that Twitter was reneging. "Twitter canceled a deal with @realdailywire to premiere What is a Woman? for free on the platform because of two instances of 'misgendering.' I'm not kidding," wrote *Daily Wire* CEO Jeremy Boering.[35] He detailed the events in a thread: Twitter had offered the *Daily Wire* a package to stream and promote the documentary to every user of the site but wanted to review the film first. Upon its review, Twitter's team noticed the instances within the film and labeled it under its hateful content policy.[36] Their decision would lead to a reduction in the film's visibility, as users could not easily share it.

A fracas unfolded: Boering said Twitter was picking a side in the "trans debate." Twitter's trust and safety team said they were simply following their long-standing policy. Musk, sympathetic to the *Daily Wire*, admonished his team and removed the hateful conduct labels—but also said Twitter wouldn't actively *recommend* "sensitive content."[37] This did not go over well with several of the online factions. On June 2, he relented, saying the film could be shared with no restrictions but would not run next to advertising. He also personally promoted it. The head of trust and safety and two members of the brand integrity team resigned.[38]

The film was never unavailable. I watched it; it was the sort of reductive culture war documentary content that exists all over Amazon and other streaming services, created to be provocative and polarizing but not clearly outside the bounds of what a platform should host. However, mere hosting was not the concern—the ease of going viral was the point of contention. Even once the film was shareable, supporters remained outraged about the ads restriction, since it would impact reach. Positioning the film as "censored by Twitter," meanwhile, likely garnered it far more attention than it would have otherwise received.

Robert Cialdini, a psychologist who studies influence, noted years ago that censorship appears to increase not only attention to a viewpoint but sympathy with it: "This raises the worrisome possibility that especially clever individuals holding a weak or unpopular position on an interest can get us to agree with that position by arranging to have their message restricted. The irony is that for such people—members of fringe political groups, for example—the most effective strategy may not be to publicize their unpopular views but to get those views officially censored and then to publicize the censorship."[39] Today the strategy is so effective that some influencers proclaim their silencing purely speculatively. Even *after* Musk acquired the company, gave "amnesty" to the previously suspended, and loosened the moderation policies that right-wing factional activists hated, influencers with very large followings continued to allege that they were being silenced by some nefarious force. *My engagement is down! Something strange is going on. Twitter is still shadowbanning me! Some of Elon's employees must still be loyal to the old regime!*

The speech-reach designation is important. Moderation is fraught but necessary. A total free-for-all will produce real harms—like the riots and radicalization discussed in earlier chapters, which have manifested far beyond the borders of the United States. And yet, free expression is also a critical democratic value.

Platforms can do three things here. First, they can create moderation frameworks guided by international human rights law. These companies serve a global community, and there are existing principles and standards to draw on that balance freedom of expression with preventing harm. TikTok, which has a parent company founded by Chinese entrepreneurs, notes its commitment to this approach: "Our principles are centered on balancing expression with harm prevention, embracing human dignity, and ensuring our actions are fair."[40] The commitment to dignity involves fostering civility, respecting local context, championing inclusion, and protecting individual privacy. Facebook's Oversight Board, which serves as a judicial body that reviews contested moderation decisions, also uses an international human rights framework to guide its decisions.[41]

Second, platforms can ensure that policies are informed by empirical research into harms. Harms on social media can include cyberbullying, hate speech, certain types of misinformation (regarding health, for example), and the spread of extremist ideologies. However, conceptualizations of harm differ greatly from community to community. Some communities argue that words are violence. Others find this ridiculous. As societies grapple with the impact of social media on individuals and communities, research is crucial to differentiate between harms and moral panic. This might involve studies of what topics should be handled more carefully: Google has had a policy called "Your Money or Your Life" since 2013, which requires that search results related to health and financial queries be held to a higher standard of care. Positioning scammers trying to sell juice fasts at the top of results for queries about treating cancer would be harmful. However, the policy is narrowly tailored to demonstrably significant categories.

The trade-off between speech and harm might also be determined by the potential to drive real-world action. Certain powerful users—such as world leaders or major influencers—have far greater potential to incite real-world violence, for example, because they have followers who they can mobilize to actually riot. By contrast, low-follower accounts that use incitement or violence-tinged language would have a far harder time whipping up a real mob. Yet powerful people are often handled with kid gloves because platforms are afraid they will rile up their fans or aligned politicians *against the platform*.[42] Social media companies need to create policies that they are comfortable defending and then actually defend them, even in the face of ref-working.

Third, platforms can prioritize transparent enforcement with an appeals process. Platforms make mistakes. With millions of posts flagged for action, automated or human moderators will inevitably make the wrong call at times. My team at the Stanford Internet Observatory has studied social media content moderation issues related to terrorism, state actor manipulation, harassment, election delegitimization, health misinformation, and child safety. Our findings suggest that policies are often reactive, and moderation *is* often demonstrably ad hoc or unevenly applied. And that's because the hardest decisions are ultimately made by *people*, operating with incomplete information and sometimes under significant pressure.

Initial moderation efforts are often automated. The "AI mods" are trained on content that violates platform policies and then try to pattern-match against new content that they encounter. They are used because the scale of moderation is enormous on large platforms—millions of accounts and posts are actioned each quarter—and also to protect the mental health of human moderators, who otherwise have to look at truly terrible things.[43]

And yet, a sense that one group gets moderated more or one individual gets flagged for saying something while other accounts don't can cause feelings of resentment and distrust in the process. Over time, outrage merchants gain ground with moderation delegitimization efforts because there are actual bad calls they can point to. The challenge is similar to that faced by institutions: one error anywhere is cited as evidence of incompetence or bias everywhere.

This is why platforms must commit to detailed transparency around enforcement. If an account is downranked ("shadowbanned," colloquially) or put on an unsafe-for-advertising list, let them know (and potentially appeal). If an account or post is taken down, indicate why on the suspension page so that bystanders can understand the decision as well. Was it a state actor account? Was it for hate speech? What policy was violated? These statistics are sometimes released in aggregate, but granularity can help increase legitimacy.

Rethinking and refining content moderation policies is one approach for improving online discourse, but it is presently at the discretion of the companies themselves. Policies can whipsaw around depending on who owns the company. There is another, broader approach, however, which comes from outside the platforms: public policy.

Rethinking Regulation

Government regulation works to rein in unaccountable private power across most industries and ensures that companies, in their pursuit of profit, don't negatively impact the public. Social media companies reaped extraordinary profit with almost no oversight for many years, even as unintended consequences led to significant harm for some communities; the propaganda-fueled genocide in Myanmar is one glaring example. Therefore, governments worldwide have begun to involve themselves in the conversation about online harms. The focus of government regulatory efforts, however, should be on creating a system of oversight and accountability, not on the day-to-day adjudication of content moderation decisions.

Some countries have created laws giving them leverage over particular types of content. India and Singapore, for example, require social media companies to take down posts at the government's request.[44] But even as unaccountable private power has created significant challenges, government power, with the risk of punishment it carries, is equally troubling. India's social media law has been used by the Bharatiya Janata Party government to prevent international dissidents' content from reaching Indian audiences.[45]

In the United States, meanwhile, congressional legislators from both parties have drafted bills that threaten to revoke or reform Section 230 of the Communications Decency Act (which immunizes platforms from liability for content that users post). On the left, the bills often try to require that platforms moderate things like election interference. On the right, bills often threaten to revoke Section 230 protections if platforms take content *down* and argue that platforms should be required to host all First Amendment–protected speech—including hate speech. Donald Trump tried to take this approach by passing an executive order a few days after Twitter labeled some of his tweets alleging election fraud;[46] it was overturned by Joe Biden in May 2021.[47]

One area where regulators should concentrate, however, is commercial speech and paid political speech that goes undisclosed by influencers. Consumers have a right to be informed about the financial incentives of the people who promote products and politicians. Here, existing agencies like the Federal Trade Commission and the Federal Election Commission have both the authority and the experience to act and to enforce existing disclosure rules.

More generally, however, rather than focusing on the specifics of moderation, government regulators can focus on increasing transparency surrounding the practice. Transparency is vital for an informed public, and government can prioritize it in three areas: in disclosing state actor influence operations to the public, in declaring their own takedown requests, and in ensuring that outside researchers have the tools necessary to study the powerful private actors of Big Tech.

Deterrence

Government responses to foreign propaganda long predate social media companies. The Active Measures Working Group (AMWG), convened in 1981 by Ronald Reagan, confronted Soviet disinformation with a simple methodology: "Report-Analyze-Publicize."[48] The Central Intelligence Agency (CIA), Department of Defense, State Department, FBI, and others

324 | INVISIBLE RULERS

collected and analyzed Soviet forgeries and manipulation campaigns. Materials and reports were put out transparently to the public. The AMWG exposed myriad influence operations, including KGB-forged racist hate mail purportedly from the Ku Klux Klan that threatened Asian and African athletes planning to compete in the 1984 Los Angeles Olympic Games.[49] The story caused a stir; indeed, it is the type of story one could easily envision going viral on social media in 2024.

In exposing these campaigns to the public, AMWG revealed how the Soviet Union manipulated its targets, to reinforce the threat both for domestic audiences and foreign observers. It avoided giving credence to the Soviet disinformation by attempting to counter it. By keeping a narrow scope—the AMWG only addressed the mechanics of disinformation campaigns, not the broad-spectrum propaganda of Soviet media writ large—it didn't get caught up in ideological arguments. By focusing on producing airtight reports and communicating transparently, it maintained a state of high regard and trust with the American public. The effort also enjoyed broad bipartisan support at all levels of the executive branch and Congress. Former Republican Speaker of the House Newt Gingrich in particular was a vocal supporter (these days, it's unclear where Gingrich would stand on such an effort).

This kind of collaborative effort could be reimplemented today to address contemporary influence operations and disinformation campaigns by state actors. Americans pride ourselves on our commitment to free speech, and an open internet is part of that core value. However, as Herbert Romerstein, former director of the US Information Agency's Office to Counter Soviet Disinformation, put it, "Democracy need not let its institutions serve as delivery systems for enemy propaganda."[50]

The challenge is that disinformation campaigns today move through a different media ecosystem, and engaging with social media companies is necessary. But interagency collaboration and public-private partnerships alike are now being reframed as "collusion" by factions, influencers, and incentivized politicians. The press on the Far Right fringe has spent years convincing their audience that Russian interference in 2016 was a "hoax." Politicians like Jim Jordan and Dan Bishop have wholeheartedly embraced conspiracy theorists who pretend that state actors on social media are all just a construct of Deep Staters and woke academics in the tank for Joe Biden. This is not only a lie but a gift: it aids Chinese, Iranian, and Russian interference efforts by reducing America's capacity for response. Indeed, other Republicans who believe these lies have called for the defunding of the very agencies tasked with countering foreign propaganda and protecting American elections.

Despite the misleading theories, government must engage with social media companies around these issues, which brings us to our second area requiring transparency: responsible disclosure of government engagement itself.

Transparency

One issue the Twitter Files did surface was how this engagement is often sloppy: occasionally, lists of suspected foreign accounts that the government sent to tech platforms to look into included accounts of people who weren't foreign trolls at all. Attribution is difficult, but the glimpse into government efforts did not inspire confidence. Ultimately, action was not taken on the mistaken accounts due to platforms' due diligence—they checked the tips and didn't remove those that were not, in fact, state-linked trolls. But the issue highlights why multiple stakeholders must examine influence operations and that transparency is needed when accounts do come down.

A major civil liberties concern when the United States government engages with a social media company is *jawboning* (a government actor using informal pressure to coerce business to behave in a particular way).[51] The lawsuit *Missouri v. Biden* is about just this. And, as you'll recall, in that case the judge issued a preliminary injunction that barred the government from speaking with tech platforms—and my team.[52]

The judge's injunction was stayed and later significantly reduced by the extremely conservative Fifth Circuit Court of Appeals. The Fifth Circuit panel of judges found that certain parts of the Biden administration had likely engaged in impermissible coercion but that the lower court judge's injunction was overbroad. It vacated nine of its ten provisions, among them the injunction against the Stanford Internet Observatory—rightfully pointing out that the judge's order impacted *our* freedom of speech.[53] The case was heard by the Supreme Court on March 18, 2024.[54] The Court's decision is expected after the publication of this book—however, most legal experts agreed that the hearing did not go well for the alleged victims of censorship. The Justices—including several conservative appointees—questioned the characterization of the government's interaction with Big Tech as "coercion," and critiqued the integrity of the claims themselves. "I have such a problem with your brief, counselor," Justice Sonia Sotomayor said to the Solicitor General of Louisiana, who argued the case. "You omit information that changes the context of some of your claims; you attribute things to people who it didn't happen to."

Multiple things are true in this situation: the original ruling was plainly incorrect, the case was based on fabricated quotes and misleading claims,[55] jawboning is a bad thing, *and* the government has a right and indeed an obligation to speak to private companies at times. In fact, even the original overbroad injunction had acknowledged multiple types of harm and national security concerns necessitating government and platform cooperation, among them "foreign attempts to influence elections," "criminal efforts to suppress voting," "exercising permissible public government speech promoting government policies or views on matters of public concern," and "informing social-media companies of postings intending to mislead voters about voting requirements and procedures."[56]

There is an incoherence to the current discourse around platform engagements with governments and academia. If platforms, for example, set public health policies independently, they are attacked for being "arbiters of truth" or overstepping their area of expertise. If they reach out to government public health officials or academic experts, they are slammed as "colluding" to silence incorrect opinions. *Reason*, a libertarian magazine, took material obtained in *Missouri v. Biden* and released it as "The Facebook Files," reframing Meta's outreach to the Centers for Disease Control and Prevention (CDC), inquiring about viral rumors in an effort to curate accurate content as something nefarious.[57] But what should Facebook have done? Are we to live in a world in which experts and companies or companies and governments can't discuss critical issues?

The same people were also aggrieved when the government reached out to platforms. So, again...what should happen?

We can avoid the actual risk of jawboning fairly simply: create regulatory or self-regulatory guardrails that introduce more transparency into exchanges like these. If the government is requesting a takedown of a post or account, or if a platform takes down a network of accounts following a tip from the government, this could be put into a public database, enabling watchdogs to examine overreach. The Lumen database does this with copyright-related and other external requests for platforms to take down content, though participation is voluntary. Twitter, for example, ceased filing Lumen reports after reporters found that it was taking down instances of a documentary at the request of the Indian government.[58] Google, by contrast, currently discloses content takedown requests on its own site; all other social media companies should follow suit.

The final role for government in ensuring transparency is to empower independent researchers. This feels like a niche and boring topic. It isn't. If we want to understand the structure of our information system, the substance that flows across it, and the speakers who drive it, then researchers and journalists who study social media platforms need access to data. Are right-wing voices being censored? Did Social Media Company X create policies that treated some category of speech unfairly? Let's have a look.

In the United States, platform share data with researchers voluntarily. These partnerships have been critical for understanding influence operations, manipulation, election misinformation, and more. But after Elon Musk purchased Twitter, the company shut down its Twitter Moderation Research Consortium effort. And in June 2023, it began to charge $42,000 a month for the type of researcher API access that had previously been free. There is now nearly no outside visibility into issues ranging from child exploitation to foreign influence operations on one of the world's most powerful public-opinion-shaping tools. There is legislation in the United States that aims to fix this—the Platform Accountability and Transparency Act—but it has struggled to gain momentum. What's more promising (and also stark evidence of the United States' failed leadership here) is the EU's Digital Services Act. The legislation went into effect in 2023 and provides data access for European researchers.

While transparency in moderation and government requests is a crucial foundation for both regulatory and self-regulatory efforts, addressing content at the end stage is still fundamentally *reactive*. It's like fixing a leaky faucet—necessary, but it doesn't improve the whole plumbing system. But what if we were to look at the design of the system instead? Unlike the largely passive listeners of Coughlin's radio audience, today's social media users are active participants; the design of social media affordances shapes their experience. When it comes to *proactive* measures for navigating the rumor mill and propaganda machine, design can have a profound impact.

Design

In 1971, Herbert Simon, a Nobel laureate and professor of computer science and organizational psychology, turned a now famous phrase: "A wealth of information creates a poverty of attention." That quip resonates with audiences today as much as it did in the early 1970s. People bombarded with messages must decide how to allocate their attention, because there is simply not enough time to take in everything—and most of us feel overwhelmed. The full quote, however, reveals the important part: "In an information-rich world, the wealth of information means a dearth of something else: a scarcity of whatever it is that information consumes. What information consumes is rather obvious: it consumes the attention of its recipients. Hence, a wealth of information creates a poverty of attention and a need to allocate that attention efficiently among the overabundance of information sources that might consume it."[59]

In the golden age of broadcast television, Simon saw that while attention is a finite resource, there was an ever-growing abundance of information. Most of the cost of information is the cost incurred by the recipient, Simon argued; the cost of the *New York Times* was not only the price of the paper but the time spent to read it. The incentives of the media outlet and the reader were not always aligned.

The abundance of information is now a deluge. The internet and our devices deliver information twenty-four hours a day, seven days a week. Newly democratized AI technology has reduced the cost of creating content—even video—to virtually nothing. As the attention economy has grown, so has the attention deficit.

Simon foresaw the direction in which things were headed and began to strongly advocate for better computer systems to help people process the abundance of information that was soon to confront them. Information-processor systems, he theorized, could reduce the drag on an organization or individual's attention if they prioritized effective curation. We are still waiting for them.

Simon's colleagues were skeptical about computerized curation: what mattered might be what the machines *withheld*. Karl Deutsch, a professor of government at Harvard, was concerned that filtering might result in people seeing only things they would feel favorably about, leading to bad policy creation or suboptimal organizational behavior. What if the filtering process withheld criticism or a challenge to the prevailing consensus? Martin Shubik, an economics professor at Yale, wondered about the evolving technology of computing and its potential impact on democracy: "Within a few years it may be possible to have a virtually instant referendum on many political issues," he said. "This could represent a technical triumph—and a social disaster if instability resulted from instantaneous public reaction to incompletely understood affairs magnified by quick feedback."

Simon, Deutsch, and Shubik were discussing one of social media's biggest challenges decades before online platforms existed: content curation, the art of deciding what information reaches whom. The algorithmic curation of today is key to influence and to shaping consensus, and yet it is overshadowed by content moderation, which attempts to sift the "good" from the "bad."[60]

The design principle that "attention is scarce and must be preserved" is very different from "the more information the better." Designers and design ethicists argue that curation systems should help us focus on things of importance or, at a minimum, things that we intentionally choose to engage with (even if that is supermarket tabloid content). There's a common saying among those in tech product design: "the devil is in the defaults." There is no neutral feed; posts have to be weighted and ordered somehow. But how? Should early popularity be the most important factor? If so, then influencers and other creators are incentivized to use a combination of sensational language alongside fake accounts or coordinated engagement to try to make something popular. Should algorithms simply default to a reverse-chronological feed, which places the most recent post from among those followed at the top? If so, then that would incentivize frequent posting and quantity over quality.

Right now, notifications about sensational ragebait, Main Character harassment mobs, or feeds that reward spamming are the default. But three broad design shifts could mitigate these destructive dynamics and minimize the risk of technical triumphs becoming social disasters. The first applies Simon's guidance to the curation systems that steer our attention. The second puts more control directly in the hands of the user. And the third creates friction: slowing virality down so facts can catch up with rumors (which, ironically, journalism aimed to do as pamphlets evolved into newspapers).

Bursting the Bubbles

Earlier, we examined how recommendation algorithms built new social networks by connecting people to each other in closed and open crowds. There was very little consideration of what was recommended or who was suggested in those early days of community establishment, and the result included conspiratorial cults like QAnon. Platforms are more aware of the unintended consequences of what they suggest now, but the question of how to address the shattering of consensus reality offers no easy answers. Recent research on YouTube suggests that consumption of extreme content is now far more a function of active *demand*, not an algorithm funneling naive and unwitting users toward a dark future.[61]

There are challenges beyond outright extremism too—like polarization. A collaborative research project between social scientists and Meta researchers with access to the platform's internal data found evidence that recommendations and curation do contribute to echo chambers and ideological segregation.[62] Yet, when social scientists ran experiments on Facebook during the 2020 election, they discovered that tweaking curation was not a magic bullet for depolarization: interventions to change what users saw, such as by switching their feeds away from algorithmically curated to reverse-chronological order or reducing the amount of content they saw from "like-minded" sources, achieved little.[63] Additionally, reducing the prevalence of political content in the feeds of partisans reduced their time on Facebook but didn't depolarize them.

After years of algorithmic and social reinforcement, some people may simply be too entrenched in bespoke realities: their networks are set; their beliefs are settled; they enjoy the time spent with fellow members of their faction. The studies' interventions were explored during a fairly limited window; the findings contain a lot of nuance, and the authors cautioned against an overbroad reading and sweeping generalizations. Research into the impact of algorithmic curation should certainly continue; however, fixing feeds alone will not be a panacea for deeper issues of polarization and ideological segregation.[64]

But there are still avenues to explore. Many social media researchers still believe that recommender systems can be designed to depolarize or to bridge divides between groups.[65] Engagement signals might be weighed less heavily when choosing what to surface—or at least coupled with other indicators.[66] Civility might become more heavily weighted, particularly around political topics, rather than the moral language and sensationalism that often gets boosted today.[67] News-related content might default to high authoritativeness or trustworthiness.[68] It's become controversial to say that some sources are more reliable than others, but it's a fact; users themselves could provide signals for which sources are trustworthy, crowdsourcing the ratings.[69]

Rethinking curation extends beyond content suggestions. Nicholas Christakis, a sociology professor and physician at Yale, has long argued that whom we are connected to is profoundly important and that it is possible to make prosocial behaviors (such as healthy eating or not smoking) contagious in a community.[70] Platforms already have internal metrics for characterizing whether communities are pro- or antisocial (recall Facebook's concerns about some of the groups that popped up after election 2020; they were flagged not because of their politics but because of a rising prevalence of posts advocating violence). Recommendation and feed-ranking algorithms could draw on this signal. It might be worth experimenting with being transparent here too: surfacing group rankings might increase certain types of positive behavior. Designing to reinforce positive social norms is a growing area of research.[71]

Since feed ranking is central to how much attention—and potentially revenue—an influencer receives, many of the Generals and the Perpetually Aggrieved cast the feed ranking algorithm as somehow sacrosanct and any change as censorship. For example, Facebook's "Break the Glass" measures, which reduced political content after the January 6 riot, led to outrage from prominent political influencers who temporarily fell off the Top 10 Most Popular Posts list (after enjoying a significant presence for months immediately following the election).[72] In reality, the current system is simply an attention- and revenue-maximization engine built by a for-profit company; you'll recall that Facebook also changed the Watch feed recommendations in a way that penalized Rick Lax's wholly apolitical cheating-spouse videos.

People who want to see negativity, profanity, deeply polarizing figures, or fringe media still can, even if the algorithm changes; those accounts will still exist. But as a guiding principle, "freedom of speech not freedom of reach" is the way to go. Hosting content and promoting content are two different things.[73] Even in the days of newsstands, certain magazines focused around more adult topics were strategically shelved. Platforms can decide to enable freedom of expression by hosting controversial or even offensive content. If users follow the content proactively, platforms can certainly surface it in their feeds. But they don't have to promote it on all surfaces, or recommend it to potential new followers, or run ads against it. In fact, noted free speech champion Elon Musk made this principle the cornerstone of Twitter's content moderation framework in 2023[74] and enshrined it in the code of his company's recommender system, which he transparently published on Github.[75]

Put More Control in the Hands of Users

There is another option: giving users the ability to explicitly define their feed, moderation, and recommendation preferences themselves. The idea of increasing user autonomy has percolated for years, often in the context of popping filter bubbles. In 2017, Ethan Zuckerman, then director of the Center for Civic Media at the Massachusetts Institute of Technology, created a tool called Gobo that enabled users to see their social media feeds with their own curation rules.[76] Do you want to see more posts by women? By family? Within a particular category? This allows users to build a feed that aligns with their interests and values, not those of the platforms.

"Middleware"—curation by third parties[77]—expands on this idea. Anyone can create a feed, such as in the form of a list to which they add contributors, and share it publicly, perhaps splitting revenue with platforms in exchange for delivering a sustained audience. Users, in turn, can subscribe to feeds curated by editors with verified topical expertise or even a particular partisan identity.

Upstart social media company Bluesky already offers this. I use it, and in addition to participating in the typical following experience, I subscribe to feeds with names like "Gardening," "What Is Science?," "Urbanism," "Shitposters," and "UkrainianView" (posts from people in Ukraine). I can click between them depending on my mood, and I see posts related to those topics from people I don't even follow. The possibilities are endless; more adventurous users can follow "OnlyPosts" (OnlyFans-type adult content), AI art feeds, and a whole array of identity-based communities. People who use these tools are directly conveying their interests and intentionally choosing what (or whom) they want to see; recommendation engines are not intuiting or nudging.

The outstanding question, of course, is what impact self-selection at scale would have on warring factions. Would most people opt in to something extreme that simply reinforces their preexisting bespoke realities? I would like to think the answer is no, but we don't know enough yet to have an answer. Regardless, while this shift may reinforce bespoke realities for some, a combination of the two approaches—changing the defaults and giving more power to the user—could reduce some of the bait and bullshit that gets unintentionally pushed toward the susceptible.

Putting humans back in the loop in certain capacities, such as through middleware, is potentially transformative. So is scaling back the algorithms. It's probably time to get rid of wholly automated trends features. Gaming them is a key element in creating majority illusions, projecting false consensus, and driving abuse toward Main Characters. They are a boon to the most destructive elements of the rumor mill and the propaganda machine alike. Presently, they are a net negative.

However, the idea of trends remains valuable. Crises like the Maui wildfires of 2023 reinforced the need for government or local media to be able to rapidly communicate with the public on social media as well as through emergency broadcasts. And sports fans enjoy sharing game highlights in team trends on Sundays—it's a temporary virtual gathering place. Middleware or human-curated approaches could be hugely beneficial here as well. In order to support breaking news while minimizing the downsides, a curated-newsroom model—which both Twitter and Facebook employed in the past—could be reimplemented.

Giving users more control of what they see at the individual or community level has many benefits: increased agency, a feeling of inclusion, an increased sense of legitimacy. This applies to content moderation as well. Rather than a "customer service" model of content moderation, in which centralized authority regulates the space, this would be a return to community governance.[78] Users might opt into particular moderation approaches that align with their values. They could also subscribe to shared block lists.

Posts that are beginning to go viral could be thrown into a queue for a crowd-sourced fact-check, akin to the Community Notes feature on Twitter. Indeed, crowd-sourced fact-checks show great promise in certain cases; diverse crowds of differing perspectives often display extremely high accuracy or are very familiar with the context of specific events. Unfortunately, Community Notes itself quickly became politicized (with factions gaming it by selecting the tweets of their enemies for correction; blatantly false tweets by Elon Musk himself were often ignored). However, a combination of the methodical pace of a professional fact-check and the faster response of crowd clarification might confer more legitimacy on the process in a time of significant distrust.

Friction: Not Always a Bad Thing

The seamless structure of social media lends itself to viral rumors and reactive behaviors. Many designers argue that a bit of strategic friction can put people in a less impulsive, more reflective mind-set, making media literacy maxims like "Think before you share" a little bit easier to follow.[79]

You may have encountered some friction-inducing nudges already: if you draft a profanity-laden comment, some platforms will alert you that most users don't talk like that with a pop-up asking if you still want to post. It's a way to subtly articulate that you're about to violate a social norm—which you can still do, if you so choose. Sometimes interstitials appear over a social media post (they gray it out or blur it) to inform you that the content underneath is disputed or might be disturbing; they create momentary friction so that you can decide if you still want to click through to see it. Certain platforms, like Twitter, have experimented with asking users who go to reshare an article if they want to read it first.[80] It's a gentle reminder that headlines can be misleading or clickbait and that it's always a good idea to see what's inside the article before amplifying it.

There has always been a tension between speed and accuracy. Professional journalism introduced friction into the process of knowledge sharing. Reporters went off to corroborate facts, then communicated their findings to the public. Sure, the (geographically constrained) rumor mill might have been humming simultaneously, but journalists made an effort to connect with sources to try to get as accurate a story as possible.

Since the rumor mill is now a global free-for-all, it's worth considering strategic friction beyond the individual level also. There's an intervention on Wall Street exchanges known as the "circuit breaker": if a stock price begins to go haywire because a rumor or some news has come out, the circuit breakers give the market time to digest the new information without the stock being whipsawed around, which might create unwarranted bad feedback loops.[81]

We need not have circuit breakers for all types of viral content, but improving the capabilities of algorithms to quickly detect rapid virality in specific categories—perhaps the sudden rapid sharing of the same photo of an explosion—can create a marketplace of ideas hardened against manipulation. Rather than seeing early virality as a signal to boost, for example, a photo claiming to be an explosion at the Pentagon to yet more people—helping the trend become the truth—it might instead be an indication to do the opposite, to temporarily reduce distribution. The photo can then be evaluated—by fact-checkers, journalists, or a Community Notes–like body—to determine whether it's real or an AI-generated hoax.[82] Social media companies are currently exploring machine-readable watermarking and other detection mechanisms for generative-AI image and video content for just this reason.

Some will howl about the rumor mill being vox populi and declare any friction impeding it to be "censorship" or some sort of slippery slope toward it. But we recognize the negative impact that rumors and panics have in other circumstances, and it's worth experimenting with slower social media as well.

America's free speech tradition is predicated on the idea that fact and falsehood will meet in the marketplace of ideas, that both will be heard, and that good ideas will overcome the bad. However, our current communication ecosystem actively stymies that process. We have not a public square but a gladiatorial arena. Debates in the public square don't often involve people gathering to follow one hapless individual down the street, screaming obscenities at them for hours; time, place, and manner restrictions on speech contribute to keeping local discourse civil. We can experiment with what they might look like online.[83] By incorporating measures that introduce more friction, even if only momentarily, platforms can manage the novel challenges of a virtual public square while upholding the principles of free speech.[84]

The Future Is Decentralized

Design mitigations can improve the social media ecosystem as it presently exists. But social media is likely not going to be a handful of behemoths forever.

In 2018—as ref-working and theories of deliberate suppression began to delegitimize content moderation within some bespoke realities—I began to wonder what federalism looked like in the digital age. Was it possible to create a consensus framework in an interconnected yet divergent online society? Is it possible to create moderation rules that are palatable to a large majority of people? Polls consistently show that people want moderation on the internet—most favor restricting false information and violent content.[85] But polls rarely ask people to offer up the details of what exactly their ideal system looks like.

Reddit has an interesting federalist approach to moderation: beyond top-level, platform-wide rules that govern serious abuse, power largely resides in the hands of the subreddit mods (topical forum moderators), volunteers who create and enforce specific rules and appeals processes for their communities.[86] If you want, for instance, to forbid people from posting pictures of dogs in your cat subreddit, you can do that. The rules are laid out clearly; if a new member joins and decides to post dogs, well, they saw the rules and chose to violate them, and mods will take action. The dog poster can cry censorship, but the community will be unsympathetic. Members came together to share a space about their love for cats, opting into and then helping shape community norms. They do not want their cat picture space overrun with dog-posting trolls. And so the person will be booted. Community-led moderation is often viewed as having higher legitimacy than top-down, centralized moderation; Reddit's decentralized model enables context-specific decisions by mods who are members of the group and well versed in its norms.[87] The community is also empowered to downvote bad comments and uninteresting posts, serving as both informal moderators and curators.

But the designs of Facebook, Twitter, and YouTube do not lend themselves to Reddit's approach. Instead, as the moderation wars raged, alt-platforms emerged that were built to serve the moderation proclivities of particular communities: Gab, Parler, Gettr, Truth Social, and other enterprising companies saw an opportunity to create pleasant fiefdoms for right-wing users. One, Truth Social, was backed by President Donald Trump, who'd been banned from mainstream social media for his role in inciting the events of January 6. Another, Gettr, had heavy involvement from Chinese billionaire dissident Miles Guo, a close associate of Steve Bannon, resulting in a unique audience mix of anti–Chinese Communist

Party and MAGA users.[88] But something interesting happened: with the exception of Gab,[89] which catered to an extremely Far Right and often white-nationalist audience, most MAGA-oriented spaces did not gain traction. A critical engagement dynamic was missing: there were no libs to own. It wasn't an arena; it was a space largely dominated by a single faction. Prominent political influencers and politicians such as Senator Ted Cruz proclaimed that they would become regulars on Parler; they did not.

There was no opportunity to spin up an aggrievement fest over being wrongfully moderated. A few years after their founding, most of the alt-platforms catering to the Right had largely flopped. Gettr attempted a pivot; Miles Guo announced that it would become a marketplace for unvaccinated sperm.[90]

After Elon Musk bought Twitter in late 2022, a second, and perhaps more important, social media diaspora emerged—one that intersected with technological protocols that offer real decentralization.

When Musk bought Twitter, he instituted not only moderation policy changes but major design shifts that were (rather predictably) a boon for spammers, manipulators, and extremists: for example, selling access to verified "blue check" profile icons without the account verification part and then changing the comment-ranking framework to put the new "paid check" accounts at the top. Dissatisfied folks—chiefly liberal and leftist influencers and crowds—moved to an existing technologically federated platform: Mastodon.

Launched in 2016, Mastodon is a decentralized and open-source social media network built on a protocol called ActivityPub. People can run individual "instances" of Mastodon, but they are all connected via the protocol, which means that all instances can see public posts from the broader network. Social media companies like Twitter, Facebook, Parler, Truth Social, and TikTok, by contrast, are centralized and proprietary: you cannot run your own Facebook instance or contribute code to it.

Using Mastodon feels a lot like using Twitter: you can follow people, post, reply, repost, and share media within and across the instances. But the decentralized approach means that moderation frameworks can be specific to each instance. Instance "owners" set the moderation rules—as they do on Reddit, though not with the granularity of limiting, say, posts of dogs. The rules are intended to handle adult content, hate speech, and other "lawful but awful" content. Instances may choose to defederate from other servers with rules that they find lax, so posts from users in that laxer space do not show up on the more restrictive instance.

As I, too, got fed up with Twitter, I found myself increasingly on Mastodon experiencing the "online federalism" that I'd wondered about. It was not an arena: Mastodon had no algorithmic curated feed and no quote-tweet button. It was purely chronological; when I popped I saw what people were discussing at that moment. Overall I found it very friendly. It was left leaning, though not overwhelmingly. There was no quote-tweet dunking, no Main Character, and no owning of factional enemies. It was a nice reminder that social media does not have to be toxic and horrible.

Similar options soon followed. Bluesky, mentioned earlier in the context of its useful feed-subscription feature, is another protocol-based decentralized social network. Meta, Facebook's parent company, launched Twitter competitor Threads and announced plans to make it compatible with ActivityPub as part of the Fediverse. Unlike Mastodon and Bluesky, however, Threads has an opinionated and centralized moderation framework that draws on Instagram's policies. This means that it strongly enforces rules against hate speech and other violations.

The trend toward decentralization is still emerging, but it will significantly shape social media in the future. Centralized, top-down moderation on social media has a legitimacy problem; while the Right's complaining is the most audible, many groups distrust it. It's opaque. It often feels unfair. On a federated social network, by contrast, I can join an instance run by a person who is aligned with my values and has similar sensibilities around moderation. If I don't like her rules, I can leave and find a new instance, and my past posts and profile go with me. Other people who want maximal free speech or adult content in their social media experience have options as well. Some communities, like the early adopters of Bluesky (many of whom were from rose-in-bio, anarchist, and antifascist factions on Twitter; the *New Yorker* described it as having the vibes of a "Portland coffee shop"),[91] wanted strong left-leaning curation and moderation values. Its users quickly developed shared block lists along the same lines. This is also a form of community moderation, and, as with every other facet of platform design, there are trade-offs: shared blocklists can enable communities to kill trolling efforts and create spaces where they feel comfortable. But if they're based on opinions rather than behavior, they can also reinforce bespoke realities.

The growing trend of decentralization and protocols will not be for everyone. Major platforms offer an appealing degree of ease. But many people feel exhausted by the current state of social media. Early chatter on Bluesky repeatedly expressed a basic ask: *I just don't want to deal with Nazis.* Chris Cox, chief product officer at Meta, reflected this sentiment when expressing how Threads would differ from its competitors: "We've been hearing from creators and public figures who are interested in having a platform that is sanely run."[92] Centralized companies, however, will continue to face the challenge of trying to craft universal rules for a complex global audience, even as incentivized ref-workers and grandstanding politicians try to undermine them at every turn.

Protocol-based options are showing us that digital federalism is possible. I'm enjoying my time on Mastodon, Bluesky, and Threads. But there's a degree of resignation in what's happening. We are not finding ways to create healthier networks, or to arrive at shared norms and values, or to have more productive dialogue between people of divergent perspectives. We aren't solving the problem of how to achieve consensus. We're moving back to smaller networks and reinforcing our niches.

"We shape our tools, and thereafter they shape us," argued Dr. John Culkin, a contemporary and friend of media theorist Marshall McLuhan. Theorists like Culkin and McLuhan—working in the 1960s, when television had seemingly upended the social order—operated on the premise that a given technological system engendered norms. The system, the infrastructure itself, shaped society, which shaped behavior, which shaped society. The programming—the substance, the content—was somewhat secondary.[93] And this is why we must ensure that the future study of social media design (and its impact) spans disciplines, in recognition of the fact that these are complex systems that drive collective behavior.[94]

By the time this book comes out, there will likely be new technologies and new platforms and new features. Each will come with a set of trade-offs and unintended consequences. But the key takeaway is that our communication systems should be designed to serve us. Wise men in past eras knew this: "Information does not have to be attended to (now) just because it exists in the environment," Herbert Simon offered. Centuries before, Marcus Aurelius said much the same thing: "You are not compelled to form any opinion about this matter before you, not to disturb your peace of mind at all. Things in themselves have no power to extort a verdict from you."[95]

Policy and design can shift the incentives of the system, perhaps making propaganda less lucrative or rumors less explosive. But policy and design specifics will change as technology evolves and new platforms and capabilities emerge and fade away. Perhaps the most impactful lever for change is not tweaks to the rules and features of social media but an improved awareness of our own behavior as users—our capacity to shape murmurations, our responsibility as one of the "seven birds" our friends and families see. As people who work in content moderation often put it (over drinks), the problem with social media is people.

Explaining how the system works may help reduce its worst facets. Noam Chomsky in *Manufacturing Consent*, Neil Postman in *Amusing Ourselves to Death*, and Daniel Boorstin in *The Image* did so for the eras in which they wrote. Learning now about how algorithms function, how tropes and rhetoric work, and why we might be incentivized to spin up outrage can help us recognize when and how we are being manipulated and make us more informed participants. And so, education is our final, and perhaps most powerful, lever.

Education

In 1937, as Father Coughlin descended into overt fascism, a group of academics and journalists deeply concerned about both domestic and Nazi propaganda decided that they would educate people on how it worked. This group, led by journalist Clyde Miller, formed the Institute for Propaganda Analysis (IPA) and set about creating content that exposed the rhetorical tricks of the invisible rulers. Propaganda was deeply harmful to American democracy, they believed; by oversimplifying complex situations and appealing to emotion, it undermined free thought. Their educational materials took the form of practical and engaging guides for community groups and high school students, with titles such as "Propaganda, How to Recognize It and Deal with It."

There were three ways to deal with it. The first, suppression, was contrary to democratic principles of open debate. The second, counter-propaganda, matched the manipulation and potentially intensified social divides. The Institute for Propaganda Analysis rejected both approaches. The best way to deal with propaganda, its leaders felt, was to give people the tools to recognize it.[96] Revealing rhetorical devices and methods of manipulation could enhance critical thinking and build immunity to propaganda's influence. It could help create the sort of rational, participatory citizens that John Dewey had argued for in debates with Walter Lippmann.

Like Edward Bernays, the IPA took a broad view of "propaganda," describing it as "conscious attempts to influence others irrespective of whether the appeal is made to the intellect or to the emotions; whether the propagandist is sincere or insincere; whether his motives are selfish or altruistic; whether his power as a propagandist depends upon conscious calculation or comes from some unconscious force."[97] The point was not to dissect the intent of any specific invisible ruler but to explain how, specifically, resonance was achieved.

One IPA framework, the "ABCs of Propaganda Analysis,"[98] emphasized self-reflection and the importance of recognizing one's emotional response to media. For example, F, "Find the Facts," reminded people that there was plenty of time to study a topic before coming to a conclusion; there was no need to rush to judgment on the timeline of the propagandist, and the responsible listener should interrogate why the propagandist might want them to. G, "Guard Against Omnibus Words," highlighted the importance of being alert to words and symbols redefined by the propagandist to serve his needs (like *censorship* has been today).

Another IPA guide laid out seven "tricks of the trade"—rhetorical devices by which the invisible ruler attempts to sway the crowd:

1. *Name calling*—giving an idea a bad label—is used to make us reject and condemn the idea without evidence.
2. *Glittering generality*—associating something with a "virtue word"—is used to make us accept and approve the thing without evidence.
3. *Transfer* carries over the authority, sanction, or prestige of something respected and revered in order to make the latter acceptable; or it carries authority, sanction, and disapproval to cause us to reject and disapprove something that the propagandist would have us reject and disapprove.
4. *Testimonial* consists in having some respected or hated person say that a given idea, program, product, or person is good or bad.
5. *Plain folks* is the method by which a speaker attempts to convince his audience that he and his ideas are good because they are "of the people," the "plain folks."
6. *Card stacking* involves the selection and use of facts or falsehoods, illustrations or distractions, and logical or illogical statements in order to give the best or worst possible case for an idea, program, person, or product.
7. *Band wagoning* has as its theme that "everybody—at least all of *us*—is doing it"; with it, the propagandist attempts to convince us all that members of a group to which we belong are accepting his program and that we must therefore follow our crowd and "jump on the band wagon."

When I first tracked down the IPA pamphlets, I was struck by how immediately applicable the long out-of-print, poorly scanned documents still are today. And they used emojis! Little pictographs assigned to the rhetorical techniques appeared in the texts the IPA analyzed.[99] I do this in slide decks for my own talks; I'd thought it was a fun way to make the audience remember things, to break up text with something a little exciting but still familiar. The IPA had gotten there a solid ninety years before me. Why had this type of education disappeared?

The IPA produced multiple analyses specific to Coughlin—not fact-checks but deconstructions. But more importantly, as broadcasters and governments scrambled to determine appropriate regulatory responses to radio demagogues, their approach proactively reduced the likelihood of a future Coughlin.

However, the effort was not a success at scale. The IPA's book, *The Fine Art of Propaganda: A Study of Father Coughlin's Speeches*, sold thirty thousand copies, and an estimated one million children received IPA materials overall. Coughlin had tens of millions of listeners.

The IPA also became politically contentious—precisely because it took on invisible rulers both foreign and domestic: "In a democracy there are many voices, many opinions, and many propagandas," the IPA noted. It argued, fifty years before Chomsky, that media capture through ownership, advertising, and state control were problems to be overcome. When World War II started, its mission clashed with America's own propaganda effort. It lasted five years prior to running out of funding, publishing its last weekly newsletter in 1942. Clyde Miller, meanwhile, was subsequently fired by Columbia University's Teachers College during the Red Scare—a victim of McCarthyism and smear campaigns. And the House Un-American Activities Committee attacked the IPA in 1947, calling it a "Communist front."[100]

The IPA's approach feels resonant decades later because the rhetorical devices of propaganda, like the tropes in stories, stay fairly consistent. They work on an emotional level, and although evolving technology may change the delivery, the target—people—remains the same.

Propaganda literacy efforts like the IPA are not a panacea. However, educating the public to recognize manipulative rhetoric seems worth attempting again, particularly given that approaches like the broadcasters' simply turning Coughlin off are increasingly ineffective today. Podcasts such as *Decoding the Gurus* and *Conspirituality* are attempting this for their audiences, using entertaining case studies and humor to explain how specific online Gurus operate. Lively subreddits discuss the episodes, collaboratively dissecting the podcasts of mid-tier COVID contrarians who are still earning nearly $10,000 a month on Patreon alone. Science communicators, too, have begun to recognize that this approach can be compelling; educators create infographics with characters like "The Faux-Persecuted Truthtellers" and "The Uncertainty Inflaters" to unpack folks whom everyone has encountered on the internet.[101] These skewerings are entertaining; even though it's educational content, people share it. The learning process doesn't have to involve sitting in a room reading a rhetoric textbook. It can be made fun.

And in addition to educating people about propaganda, we can educate them about the algorithms that facilitate its spread. Algorithms reflect the incentives of the tech platforms, and teaching people how the digital invisible rulers actually work can help us understand the powerful roles we as users, as members of crowds, play today.[102] Algorithmic literacy can help people understand why not all of their friends see all of their posts (hint: it's not censorship). Understanding how recommender systems sort people into networks can help us be more cognizant of polarizing factions. Learning about curation and engagement helps people understand why minority opinions feel like the majority.

Rumors: How to Recognize and Deal with Them

But what of rumors? In the 1910s, a rumor may have stayed confined to a village or town. In the 1960s, it might have percolated across television programs, if it could get past powerful gatekeepers. Now, in the 2020s, it moves through a murmuration of millions, trends on Twitter, and is picked up by 24/7 mass media. Rumors are more pervasive and fly farther today than ever before, and political rumors are especially potent.[103] Understanding and knowing how to respond to them is as critical today as understanding propaganda was in the twentieth century. Rumors, of course, are more organic and less deliberate; they're core to how we socialize. But they play a significant role in shaping consensus within the niches we inhabit, even as they impact our ability to reach consensus across them. And they are very, very sticky: rumors recur, and they're hard to refute—particularly when people don't trust those doing the refuting.

Just as Wayfair was accused of selling kids in filing cabinets, in the early 1980s Procter & Gamble (P&G) was accused of ties to satanism. Satanic panics were coming for many unexpected targets around the time; conspiracy-prone churches that railed against rock-and-roll bands also went after P&G. Some of the rumors focused on its logo, in use for over fifty years: the beard on the logo's face had what looked like three upside-down sixes (the mark of the beast). Fifteen thousand people called the company in under two months to inquire about this as the rumor began (a fraction, of course, of the engagement on major viral rumors today). The rumor seemed to die down in 1982 but resurfaced in 1985; a tall tale alleged that *someone* (attribution varied) had seen the company's CEO on *The Phil Donohue Show*, a popular TV talk show at the time, admitting to the nefarious relationship.[104] Procter & Gamble painstakingly attempted to correct the record: the company hired investigators to look into the origin of the rumor, distributed thousands of antirumor media kits, and made efforts to engage religious leaders—including Jerry Fallwell and Billy Graham—to quash the inane theory.[105] After hundreds of thousands of phone calls over a period of a few months, P&G removed the logo from all of its products in April 1985.[106] But this too blew up. *What were they hiding?*

The rumor returned in 1991. Believers distributed fliers to alert their friends and encourage a boycott. Pastors handed them out to their church congregations, which news coverage suggested persuaded some to participate in the boycott. "Our pastor presented it to us. And if a person of trust presents something to you, you believe it," one person told the *Washington Post*, expressing surprise when the reporter informed him that the supposed *Donohue* broadcast had never happened.[107] P&G eventually began aggressively suing people spreading the rumor—including distributors for its competitor, Amway, who were leaving voicemails in hopes of gaining boycotting P&G customers.

Jean-Noël Kapferer, the rumor scholar we first encountered in Chapter 1, studied the response of P&G and other companies faced with similar challenges. He found that refuting the false claims was very difficult for targeted companies and individuals alike: simply denying the rumor often reinforced it in people's minds or inadvertently communicated the misleading claims to still more people. Denials were challenging: they weren't really "news" because they were expected, and they were something of a killjoy. They "plunge[d] us back into the banality of reality" and offered little novelty.[108] If the correction carried a frisson of drama— perhaps a countersmear—it might get more attention, but companies and institutions were often loath to play that game.

And yet, not bothering to put out a refutation was also a bad strategy, because the lie went unchallenged.

Two questions mattered: whether to respond and how. To the question of whether, Kapferer argued that four groups were in play: enemies who will always believe the rumor, the uninvolved (who won't pay attention), allies who will support the targeted person or company, and then the hesitant, who don't know what to think. The last group mattered the most; if they weren't engaging, silence was possibly the best response. If they seemed to be paying attention and sharing the rumor—remember *Plandemic*, which hopped out of the anti-vaccine niche and into the corgi clubs and the church groups—then a response was necessary.

The ability to quickly examine spread—not simply in terms of engagement numbers but in terms of the communities that were engaging—was an attempted focus of the Virality Project. It's hard to assess community spread quickly, but it's key for enabling rapid response counterspeech. It ensures that the response is relevant, comes from the right messenger, and reaches the right audience.

But there is still the question of how to respond, once it's deemed necessary.

P&G responded with statements and community engagement and media comments, but lawsuits against the competitors who defamed them played perhaps the most significant role in ending the rumors. Similarly, Dominion—which was scapegoated in Election 2020 rumors— filed a massive defamation lawsuit and won a nine-figure settlement from Fox News. In the Wayfair case, the actions of social media companies primarily reduced the trend; we've discussed the trade-offs of private actors throttling rumors already and the challenge of doing so on decentralized social networks.

Kapferer examined other case studies: a false allegation that McDonalds put worms in its meat and an actress struggling to overcome lies that she was severely ill. He described some strategies that worked. Repositioning rumors and making them embarrassing to share was one approach. This might be a more uphill battle today, as norms have fractured along with reality. However, people do respond to learning that they've spread something demonstrably false: one of the early sharers of the Wayfair rumor—now enrolled in a PhD program to study algorithmic bias—acknowledged that when people eventually told her the Wayfair rumors were debunked, she felt uncomfortable and deleted her posts. She clarified for her followers that some of the children they'd been making collages about weren't actually missing at all. But she also knew that she couldn't take it back; some would continue to believe.[109]

There was another approach that Kapferer highlighted as effective, something very similar to the IPA's take on exposing propagandist rhetoric: explaining why people believe the rumor. In 2021, as the Election Integrity Partnership reviewed viral election rumors in the months after January 6, a handful of recurring themes stuck out.[110] "Bussed-in voters" rumors popped up in multiple places in 2020 but had also made the rounds in 2016 and 2012;[111] indeed, the trope dates back decades. Similarly, rumors about dead voters and rigged machines popped up year after year. Mail-in ballot concerns were newer, and COVID-19 certainly made them more salient, but they popped up on a weekly basis despite repeated efforts to reiterate the facts.

In Chapter 3 we discussed the concept of tropes: familiar building blocks for stories that writers (and influencers) commonly rely on. When the movie opens with a large fin slicing through the water as a woman jumps into the ocean, you know where it's headed. And who among us hasn't seen a political thriller in which a cabal hacks something to steal an election.

Tropes are comforting for their familiarity; the audience feels up-to-speed instantly. And the same held with election rumors. There was a finite set of elements: Found Ballots. Dead Voters. Nefarious Pens. Hacked Machines. The plotlines were so familiar—evocative of popular Netflix thrillers at times[112]—that audiences would often reply to influencers' tweets or Facebook posts with something like "Oh, they're at it again," or "Of course!" or "They keep doing this, the cheaters." Yet they didn't appear to lose interest.

That's in part because influencers would add a dash of novelty. Each of the "hacked machines" conspiracy theories had a distinctive element: they had been compromised by evil Democratic operatives, by CIA supercomputers, by Russians, or, in one memorable instance, by Italian satellites.[113] The "new" story was then worth sharing, and the faction could feel that it was participating in the fight for their candidate by doing so.

Tropes also make conspiracy-theory narratives transferable across topics. The QAnon omniconspiracy theory incorporated elements of others that were rooted in the idea that a Nefarious Government Cabal existed. The Man Behind the Curtain is a common trope in many conspiracy theories, from vaccines to chemtrails to UFO cover-ups.[114]

But the fact that these manipulative tropes are so common could also be their undoing. Years ago, I stumbled across an amazing website called TV Tropes. It's like Wikipedia but written by people whose passion in life is documenting every narrative device that's ever appeared on a screen, large or small. It's illuminating. The "Expository Hairstyle Change" entry explains (and in doing so, skewers) the common visual device, used in films ranging from *The Matrix* to *Frozen*, that conveys a character's personal growth. When you see a technician alone in a lab in a white coat "Playing With Syringes," you know that dinosaurs or a virus will escape imminently.

What does this have to do with rumors? The current system for countering rumors is largely reactive: fact-checkers play Whac-A-Mole with the latest specific inflection. They debunk ballot claims in Sonoma and voting machine theories in North Carolina after they've spread. The truth is, it's not yet clear how effective the resulting fact-check labels are: some studies suggest they have an impact; others say it's limited.[115] Content that is taken down in one place or labeled in another continues to spread elsewhere in the ecosystem.[116] But there's promising research into what's known as inoculation theory, or *prebunking*—the temporal opposite of debunking.[117] The strategy is similar to that of the Institute for Propaganda Analysis's "tricks of the trade" guide. Instead of fact-checking specific claims reactively, what if we discussed their underpinnings preemptively, explaining how and why they work?[118] By illustrating how certain types of rhetoric or tropes function, what rumors recur, and how invisible rulers use them, people "could be inoculated against persuasive attacks in much the same way that one's immune system can be inoculated against viral attacks."[119] No one likes to be manipulated, and prebunking taps into that inherently human desire to maintain autonomy.

Another argument for prebunking is that tropes are nonpartisan. Teaching audiences how to spot building blocks can be empowering and need not criticize anyone's favorite influencer or political party. It might even lead to what TV Tropes calls the "Everybody Helps Out" denouement, when the story ends with all the characters coming together to make the world a better place.[120]

Reset Norms

There was one response to Father Coughlin that we haven't yet discussed: the church's reaction.

The church approved of Coughlin's early radio broadcasts, as he combined Catholic teachings with broader economic and political commentary. However, as his broadcasts became more political and controversial, and as his views increasingly delved into conspiracy theories, anti-Semitism, and fascism, the church distanced itself. Prominent Catholic leaders like Cardinal George Mundelein of Chicago openly disapproved of Coughlin's divisive and inflammatory statements. Eventually, in 1942, his superiors in the church intervened, ordering Coughlin to cease his political activities and concentrate on his priestly duties. The church took a stand against divisive rhetoric and actions inconsistent with its teachings.

Cyberbullying and online harassment are serious problems; people across the political spectrum are rightly very concerned when either happens to young people. Yet it's often adults who troll each other, screaming epithets at, disparaging, or haranguing some perceived enemy or unfortunate Main Character over the most mundane things. The provocation can be anything. Recall the woman mentioned in Chapter 2 who in 2022 posted about enjoying coffee in the garden with her husband each morning only to receive thousands of replies. Strangers attacked her for not "acknowledging her privilege" and thinking of how her words might impact those in worse circumstances or without husbands, gardens, or coffee.[121] That situation was absurd but not surprising. Platform affordances, coupled with mobs' moral righteousness and satisfaction, make it routine. The targets lock down or delete their accounts and often think twice before posting again. Gamergate wasn't an isolated event—it was a norm shift. *New York Times* columnist Ezra Klein put it concisely in a 2022 essay: "Twitter rewards decent people for acting indecently."[122]

If we want virtual public squares, we have to act like the people on them are our neighbors. If we want to come together and have open debates about important issues, the norms of participating and reacting have to change. Because at the moment, people are finding the Great Decentralization preferable to trying to get along on the same social media platforms.

Media-of-one and political influencers who smear people, tacitly incite whack jobs, and then disclaim responsibility should be seen for what they are, no matter the faction: assholes. And it's people *within* their faction who should call them on it, as the church did with Coughlin. Criticism from the outside is more easily dismissed.

Influencers can play a major role in creating healthier communities by modeling better behavior themselves—and platforms can incentivize this in recommendations and content curation. Increasing the visibility of less sensational, less popular, or less nasty accounts in feeds could be transformative.

Chris Bail of the Duke Polarization Lab argues that it's important to increase awareness of how algorithms intersect with online crowds. Teaching people to "see the prism"—to recognize, for example, the majority illusion that happens when small groups of extremely strident people dominate The Discourse—can be very useful. Raising awareness of the misperceptions people have about their political opponents—making them aware of the opinions of the majority of the group rather than those of the loud fringe—can have a strong depolarizing effect.[123] By realizing that extreme opinions often get more attention, while quieter, moderate views stay hidden, people might start reacting differently to posts that are designed to provoke strong reactions.

We all need to speak up, debate, and engage—and visibly support those who are targeted by harassment mobs for doing so. Otherwise, the most extreme voices—those most willing to resort to threats, cancellations, and mob dynamics—control the conversation.

Updating the Playbook: Notes for the Targeted

As Bernays pointed out a century ago, invisible rulers are incentivized to tear down the current system of authority. If you or your institution works on an issue that one of the Perpetually Aggrieved influencers or some incentivized propagandist can use as fodder for the culture war, you or members of your team will eventually be targeted. You must have a strategy in advance so that you are not scrambling when it happens.

Don't think that it won't come for you or your field, industry, or brand. It will. In 2023, some online factions began harassing *librarians*.

For academic institutions in particular, it is paramount to recognize bad-faith attacks and not hang people out to dry. Bad-faith mobs demanding firings are targeting the principle of academic freedom and working to silence the speech of the researchers they attack. Hyperpartisan legislators now also regularly act in bad faith, demanding documents using the flimsy pretext of a half-baked smear campaign—they are abusing their power. They are not acting for a legitimate legislative purpose. Their intent is to chill good work and silence good people in pursuit of political aims. The people who stood up to McCarthyism are the ones history remembers.

Your communication strategy is as important as your legal strategy. Playing ostrich does not stop the rumors or end the story; it simply lets someone else control the narrative. If you are sufficiently interesting or useful as a villain in a conspiracy theory, the propaganda machine and the rumor mill can keep recycling claims and allegations endlessly. If you wait for a "news cycle" to pass to begin doing your work or speaking publicly again, you will be waiting forever—the people writing the smears are not "news" outlets. Once your institution or a team member, manager, or CEO is part of some conspiracy theorist's monetized cinematic universe, he will always find a way to work that entity or person back into the story. Niche media are fully aware that you will not sue them because of the cost and time commitment involved in a defamation complaint; there is no cost or consequence for continuing to lie.

The universities targeted by Jim Jordan in 2023 learned all this the hard way. When the weaponized congressional committee demanded information, many quickly complied. Most of the institutions confronted with these subpoenas treated them as if they were dealing with a legitimate investigative oversight effort rather than the second coming of the House Un-American Activities Committee. If they played nice, the thinking went, maybe Congress would read the documents they turned over, see there was nothing to any of this, and go away. Receiving a subpoena comes with legal obligations, of course—subpoenas are hard to fight, and institutions often have many lines of work and relationships with other parts of Congress that they need to maintain. But many institutions also ran a doomed communication strategy, trying to keep their heads down and hoping the news cycle would just move on. Correcting the record or denying the lies would only attract more attention, they thought. After all, even if people *were* talking about it on Joe Rogan and it was attracting tens of millions of views on Twitter, it wasn't in the *Washington Post*.

This was terribly naive. The point of the exercise was punishment, not oversight. It was glaringly obvious to those of us who study propaganda and disinformation what was going to happen: documents and excerpts of interviews would be leaked to ideologically aligned propaganda outlets, and those mentioned in the resulting coverage would be targeted by online mobs. And yet, since institutions did not fully comprehend what game they were playing, many communications teams struggled to formulate a plan. They gambled on the tiny chance that the leaks and bad-faith targeting wouldn't happen—and lost. The strategy was decided by the institution, but the consequences were borne by the individuals.

Targets of these campaigns need not respond to each and every attack or smear; you don't want to inadvertently amplify something that has gotten little pickup and seems likely to quickly fizzle out. However, if something begins to spread outside an echo chamber, rapid transparent responses are key. There is no need to fight in the mud with pigs, but getting your own story out is important. When people search for information about the rumor, the search engine may well return the smear content—unless you make the facts available. Write your own post detailing the facts in plain language and share it through your network. Make sure any Wikipedia articles about you or your work reflect the truth—because today's AI-enhanced search engines increasingly incorporate Wikipedia content into generated summaries. Wikipedia attacks can be managed with help from the site's volunteer editors. If you are FOIA'd, consider posting the documents preemptively yourself on an official website to prebunk the claims and reduce the impact of the "secret documents exposed!!!!" stories. Consider sharing them with a good-faith media outlet. If you receive bad-faith media inquiries from recurringly dishonest outlets, consider posting the full email, along with your response, publicly on your site or sharing it to social media.

If you are an individual who is targeted, reach out to someone who's been through a smear campaign before for advice on how to respond and how to protect yourself (from legal, security, and reputational standpoints). Your interests—particularly if you are the zebra in the Serengeti strategy—may not be aligned with your institution's, and you should be clear-eyed about what that means. The climate scientists learned this quickly, which is why they formed field-protection efforts such as the Climate Science Legal Defense Fund.[124] Members of the field can also mutually support each other, particularly when the targeted person can't speak up. Physicians, too, have developed community-assistance groups that help targeted individuals push back against harassment and smear campaigns. More fields need to form these efforts in advance of when they're needed.

Above all else, make sure that the person at your institution leading the response understands modern smear campaigns and also the internet.

In addition to internalizing that the political game has changed, institutions of all types must adapt to the modern communication environment more generally—the CDC's failures during COVID offer a vivid explanation of why. There are two areas for immediate focus: first, communicating transparently and frequently; second, building networks of compelling speakers and amplifiers.

Years ago, shortly after Senate Bill 277—the bill to remove the personal-belief loophole from school vaccine requirements—became law in California, I was asked to join Dr. Richard Pan, the state senator who led the bill, and Leah Russin, the founder of Vaccinate California, to speak to a class of public health master's degree students at the University of California, Berkeley. Dr. Pan talked about the bill, and Leah spoke about the importance of parent advocacy. I talked about the data analysis I'd done of the evolving anti-vaccine Twitter conversation—including the observation that the public health officials were largely outside it. Several communities had been frequent participants in the hashtag: long-standing anti-vaccine activists, a new "medical freedom" cluster, and Tea Party conservatives in particular. There were influencers local to these communities who drove the conversation—they got retweeted, and their memes were picked up by other members. There wasn't really anything like that on the public health side. One student asked me if they should be doing more. Should they all join Twitter? I'd experienced a significant amount of harassment on Twitter during that campaign, and Twitter hadn't seemed interested in moderating even doxxing and stalking, so I hedged a bit—why would I encourage other people to go sign up for that? These were students who had *actual public health work* to be doing, I thought.

My answer is different now. Engaging on social media is part of the job. Period. It is not optional. Individuals can do more or less of it, of course, but the field must train communicators, and it must train them for *this* communication era, not the old one where they might occasionally go on TV or NPR. And that is because today if you are not communicating, well, others still are. And their content is what is available for curation, for amplification, and for shaping the online conversation.

The tendency among experts is often to wait until they know all the facts. But this is no longer the right approach; silence simply gives others the opportunity to shape the narrative via the rumor mill.[125] It's fine to say, "We don't know yet" or "Information is still coming in; please be patient"—even these comments reinforce that the institution is aware of the concern, paying attention, and trying to figure out the facts. But simply waiting it out and not participating in the conversation because consensus hasn't solidified leaves a void for others to fill.

As Naomi Oreskes and Erik Conway put it in *Merchants of Doubt*, "Scientists have long believed that their job is to figure out what the truth is. Someone else can best popularize it. Someone else can better communicate it. And if there's garbage being promoted somewhere, someone else can deal with it." Scientists may want to avoid jumping into the fray on science-related rumors or misinformation at all, lest they be accused of "politicizing the science."[126] Yet if their voices are absent, the world will be worse off. It was often not scientific consensus (or even debate) that trended during COVID but what we might call the "consensus of the most likes"; if enough people engaged with a post, more saw it. The algorithms are not equipped to judge accuracy or authoritativeness—and in emerging situations, it's not always clear what *is* accurate.

Building up an audience through regular public communication is key. Brands have begun to do it. Some public service accounts, like the National Parks Service, numerous state agencies ranging from sewer management to wildlife conservation, and even the US Consumer Product Safety Commission, now aim to be engaging and funny.[127] Their content gets shared because it feels relevant and it's something of a novelty—but the important messages are getting out there. Influencers on social media are, above all else, storytellers, and good storytellers are authentic, honest, knowledgeable, and entertaining.[128] The people communicating on behalf of institutions need to be equally good storytellers, responding simply, directly, and quickly.

But taking part in online discussions and sharing engaging material is just the first step. In today's world, where rumors and propaganda spread through networks, institutions need networks to spread their messages. This was one of my main takeaways following our work on the Election Integrity Partnership and the Virality Project. Networked institutions matter. We could show local election officials or doctors what misleading information was picking up steam, and they could respond by posting their own messages, creating their own counterspeech. Doctors were very good at making their messages resonant, because they'd talked to vaccine-hesitant patients face-to-face for a long time. However, they often didn't have large audiences online, so the messages only traveled so far. Meanwhile, the "repeat spreaders" had not only individual large audiences but *networked distribution*. They moved information from person to person, crowd to crowd. The influencer-algorithm-crowd trinity is a networked distribution system. When we tried to create a network of institutions to help get the most accurate information out to the public, those who wanted to manipulate the discourse unopposed tried to reframe it as a cabal.

Form partnerships, build networks. They are key.

For a time of niches and polarization, the communication strategy of "right audience, right message, right time" requires *right messenger* as the fourth critical element. Connecting *with* influencers is one option. In the summer of 2021, for example, the Biden White House worked to bring influencers with existing large followings into the COVID-19 vaccine conversation. The White House connected with more than fifty Twitch streamers, YouTubers, TikTokers, and other celebrities with large online audiences. Many were excited about an opportunity to push back against other influencers who'd spread misinformation. In another outreach effort, one vaccine-hesitant influencer, a Mexican actor with nearly seventeen million Instagram followers at the time, livestreamed an open discussion with Anthony Fauci, where he expressed his concerns and Dr. Fauci responded. This was a one-on-one conversation, but it leveraged technology to reach millions. State and local governments also reached out to those with existing large followings, sometimes paying local micro-influencers to help spread pro-vaccine messages.[129] It is paramount that these public service announcement campaigns be transparent, unlike the political influencer campaigns that earn sponsorship and affiliate revenue and don't disclose their incentives to their audience.

Networked counterspeech serves another important purpose: When just a few people speak up, they can be easily overwhelmed by a harassment brigade. But a groundswell of outspoken participants can stand up against this harassment and ensure that the viewpoints on social media platforms are more fully representative.

Mediating Consensus, Sharing Reality

Coughlin was the man for the medium, and invisible rulers of today are the men and women who understand the medium. But Coughlin also spoke to a deep and real resentment—he started out not as a fascist but rather as a man who spoke for, and to, some part of the public. The political influencers we've discussed are also giving voice to real concerns. Many are important spokespeople for communities and movements.

The collision of the rumor mill and the propaganda machine can't be undone. There will be no return to a handful of media translating respectable institutional thinking for the masses. Nor should we pine for that: it is not immediately obvious that centralized lies pushed by the old power structure are preferable to the thousands of small lies pushed by the new. Chomsky's critique of manufacturing consent was trenchant—and true.

But the pervasive, acrimonious dissensus we find ourselves in is simply untenable for democratic society. There is, of course, a deep irony that platforms built to connect the world have severed our ability to find common ground. We now have an actively disinformed citizenry, spread across bespoke realities. The factions fight the institutions, and they fight each other. The nihilistic, loud voices among them, like the Perpetually Aggrieved, speak for the rage but offer no vision for the future. The alienation of bystanders makes their words appealing, and fear of standing up to the mobs makes pushback less likely. Yet the delegitimization of everything that surrounds them does not make them any more capable of building a lasting movement with a vision. They cannot form consensus sufficient to build new institutions; the old institutions, meanwhile, struggle to form consensus sufficient to govern.

Many of us stand on the sidelines, afraid to engage and unsure who to trust. Meanwhile, generative technologies are adding *unreality* to the equation: AI-created accounts, videos, audio, and text.

All of this occurs at a time when we desperately need consensus—when we face profound collective challenges. Addressing issues like climate change, pandemics, and technology transforming the workforce is impossible if we remain locked in factional warfare.

Something has to change.

It won't be human nature. Factions have always been part of American society; in 1787, James Madison argued they're part of our very essence: "The latent causes of faction are thus sown in the nature of man," he wrote in the Federalist Papers, noting that we are "more disposed to vex and oppress each other than to co-operate for [the] common good."

The desire to shape public opinion won't change either. Reaching consensus will always be a messy, grueling process. There will always be invisible rulers operating behind the scenes—the next Father Coughlin, a new Amazing Polly, a novel algorithm. And the medium will always evolve, just as the printing press and radio gave way to successors.

But we can focus—as Madison did—on mitigating their harmful effects. Platforms can design with incentives beyond engagement in mind. Governments can prioritize transparency and the restoration of trust. Counterspeakers—*all of us*—can leverage the very same networked tools that propagandists do.

The path forward requires systems to mediate, not manufacture, consent. We need systems that are resistant to top-down control and corruption but also to bottom-up, breakneck rumors. This requires a heightened awareness from, again, *all of us*: a recognition of our own biases and preferences, a commitment to balancing skepticism and trust, and a genuine desire to share the same reality.

Acknowledgments

THIS BOOK would not have been written but for the crowds of extraordinary people I've met on the Internet. The bold parents of Vaccinate California and the science communicators and physicians I've been honored to work alongside. The Bay Area Refactorings community, curated and corralled by Venkatesh Rao, who helped me refine many of these ideas; early versions of several concepts appear as essays on *Ribbonfarm*. Justin Hendrix, Roger McNamee, and the other good folks in civil society and academia who came together to call for tech hearings and accountability in 2017, establishing lasting interdisciplinary connections and a shared commitment to working toward a prosocial internet. The tech friends with whom I discussed ways to create a healthier communication ecosystem, including Tristan Harris, Guillaume Chaslot, Sandy Parakilas, Tobias Rose-Stockwell, and Aza Raskin (who also deserves credit for the Chapter 6 subtitle "From Russia with Likes"). The San Francisco parent activists from across the political spectrum who used social media to help others find their voices and galvanized real change while remaining positive and constructive. The tech policy, OSINT, and disinformation research communities, from whom I've learned so much. The dear friends, allies, and co-conspirators* in myriad Slacks, Signal groups, and WhatsApp chats—iykyk. You keep me sane. And, of course, the trolls and malcontents who harangued me along the way...thank you for the inspiration.

I owe a deep debt of gratitude to my wonderful colleagues at the Stanford Internet Observatory (SIO) who work tirelessly to understand the mechanics of online manipulation in all of its various forms—Alex

---

* This is a joke.

Stamos, David Thiel, Elena Cryst, John Perrino, Shelby Grossman, and Jeff Hancock—as well as our extraordinary student research assistants, postdocs, and alums. Several invaluable collaborators from SIO worked with me on projects that informed this book: Isabella Garcia-Camargo, Matt DeButts, Chase Small, Dan Bateyko, Josh Goldstein, Samantha Bradshaw, Ronald Robertson, and Carly Miller, thank you. I have felt truly welcomed by a broad community of colleagues and collaborators, both within the Stanford Cyber Policy Center and in the field more broadly, who have shown me the ropes and mentored me over the last few years as I moved into academia. Special thanks to Kate Starbird, Mike Caulfield, Joe Bak-Coleman, Laura Edelson, Rebekah Tromble, Cameron Hickey, Kate Klonick, Yoel Roth, and danah boyd for all of the discussions, feedback, idea refinement, and support, both on this project and writ large.

I also want to thank the extraordinary community of colleagues—now friends—on both sides of the aisle who do pro-democracy and election integrity work and who always put country above party. You are doing selfless, patriotic work, and I am inspired by your efforts and proud to be part of the same team. During some very challenging times, your steadfast support, wisdom, and check-in messages have been a source of strength and means of recalibration. Along these same lines, special thanks to my fellow members of the 2017 class of Presidential Leadership Scholars, who have transformed into a second family.

I have been incredibly fortunate to have received support from very generous people who helped make my work possible and extended its reach, including the Mozilla Foundation, Emerson Collective, and Craig Newmark, as well as the editors who have helped me turn thoughts into words—particularly at *Wired*, *The Atlantic*, and *Noema*. Scholars at the Knight First Amendment Institute have also been invaluably helpful.

This book's realization owes everything to support I received from the fellowship team at Emerson Collective. They saw value in the story I wanted to tell and provided thoughtful guidance throughout the process; I am immensely grateful for their belief in me and this project. Similarly, I want to thank my agent, Susan Rabiner, whose unvarnished feedback helped me execute, as well as the editorial, marketing, and design teams at PublicAffairs, particularly John Mahaney, for their dedication to turning this project into a tangible, bound book. I am also indebted to Kevin Zawacki, Gary Zhexi Zhang, Claire Cronin, James Hider, and Eden Beck, who helped me get through the writing, editing, and fact-checking process—making the thing coherent, in other words—as well as to Avik Roy, Romina Boccia, Ann Florini, Jed Bailey, Peter Mellgard, Nils Gilman, and Jon Askonas, who read early drafts of various bits. The title of Chapter 8 was inspired by the work of Kurt Andersen. Thank you all so much. A special thanks is also due to my lawyers, who helped me make good decisions.

Finally, I want to thank my family. My parents, who have no social media accounts and still don't understand what I do but are coming around to thinking it's a real job. My sister. My three beautiful children, who inspire and challenge and make me truly happy every day—an embodied reminder of the future and the role I play in shaping it. And, most importantly, my husband, partner, and best friend, who patiently reads all my writing, helps me refine my thoughts, and scans my mentions when the internet gets mad at me. Justin, you mean the world to me, and I am so very, very grateful for your presence and love in my life.

Notes

INTRODUCTION

1 "Thundering herd," *The Economist*, September 26, 2015, https://www.economist.com/united-states/2015/09/26/thundering-herd.

2 Olga Khazan, "Wealthy L.A. Schools' Vaccination Rates Are as Low as South Sudan's," *The Atlantic*, September 16, 2014, https://www.theatlantic.com/health/archive/2014/09/wealthy-la-schools-vaccination-rates-are-as-low-as-south-sudans/380252.

3 Gil Kaufman, "Vaccine Skeptic Eric Clapton Claims 'Subliminal' Messages Are Convincing People to Fall in Line," *Billboard*, January 24, 2022, https://www.billboard.com/music/rock/eric-clapton-subliminal-messages-covid-interview-1235022031/.

CHAPTER 1: THE MILL AND THE MACHINE

1 NBA.com Staff, "Kyrie Irving on Flat-Earth Comments: 'I'm Sorry,'" NBA, October 2, 2018, https://www.nba.com/news/kyrie-irving-regrets-flat-earth-comments.

2 Rob Picheta, "The Flat-Earth Conspiracy Is Spreading Around the Globe. Does It Hide a Darker Core?," *CNN*, November 18, 2019, https://edition.cnn.com/2019/11/16/us/flat-earth-conference-conspiracy-theories-scli-intl/index.html.

3 Dustin Gardiner and Kyle Cheney, "Prosecutors Grapple with Alternative Reality Defense in Paul Pelosi Trial," *Politico*, November 15, 2023, https://www.politico.com/news/2023/11/15/paul-pelosi-jan-6-riot-00127267.

4 *Consensus reality* is the shared understanding and agreement within a group about what is real and true. It encompasses the commonly accepted beliefs, perceptions, and interpretations that shape our collective understanding of the world and is shaped by media, institutions (educational, governmental, scientific), and the public (including civil society, social movements, and collective memory). For more on consensus reality in the current cultural moment, see J. M. Berger, "Our Consensus Reality Has Shattered," *The Atlantic*, October 9, 2020, https://www.theatlantic.com/ideas/archive/2020/10/year-living-uncertainly/616648.

5 Jean-Noël Kapferer, *Rumors: Uses, Interpretations and Images* (New Brunswick, NJ: Transaction Publishers, 2013), 3.

6 People participate in spreading rumors to compare their thinking to a group with which they identify; to arrive at consensus; for clout (being the one to reveal the rumor shows that they're in the know); to participate in group dynamics and culture; or to persuade or convince others about something. For some people, transmitting rumors is akin to starting a crusade, and the rumor is a kind of revealed truth. Ibid., chap. 3.

7 Kristina Lerman, Xiaoran Yan, and Xin-Zeng Wu, "The 'Majority Illusion' in Social Networks," *PLoS One* 11, no. 2 (2016), https://doi.org/10.1371/journal.pone.0147617.

8 There are many definitions of *propaganda*; this one is adapted from Garth S. Jowett and Victoria O'Donnell, *Propaganda and Persuasion: Fifth Edition* (Los Angeles: SAGE Publications, Inc., 2012), 7, which states in full, "Propaganda is the deliberate, systematic attempt to shape perceptions, manipulate cognitions, and direct behavior to achieve a response that furthers the desired intent of the propagandist."

9 Nicholas Difonzo and Prashant Bordia, "Rumors Influence: Toward a Dynamic Social Impact Theory of Rumor," in *The Science of Social Influence: Advances and Future Progress*, ed. Anthony R. Pratkanis (New York: Psychology Group, 2007), 271–295.

10 Edward Bernays, *Propaganda* (Brooklyn, NY: Ig Publishing, 2005), 61.

11 Ibid., 77.

12 Ibid., 109.

13 The details of this have been debated by scholars. The oft-repeated version of this story, where Luther nails the theses to the church door himself, was spread by Luther's contemporary and biographer, Philipp Melanchton. However, Melanchton was not in Wittenberg at the time, and no other evidence has been found that shows that Luther performed this dramatic action. An alternative explanation, put forth by several historians, including Peter Marshall, is that Luther simply mailed the theses to an archbishop.

14 As historian Niall Ferguson writes in his examination of social networks and hierarchies, *The Square and the Tower*, "Printing was crucial to the Reformation's success. Cities with at least one printing press in 1500 were significantly more likely to adopt Protestantism than cities without printing, but it was cities with multiple competing printers that were most likely to turn Protestant." Niall Ferguson, *The Square and the Tower: Networks and Power, from the Freemasons to Facebook* (New York: Penguin Press, 2018), 83.

15 Matthew Baker, "Flying Writings," in *Wild Boar in the Vineyard: Martin Luther at the Birth of the Modern World* (online version of a 2017 exhibit showcasing early printed works by Martin Luther, primarily from the holdings of the Burke Library at Union Theological Seminary, Columbia University), Columbia University Libraries, Digital Collections & Online Exhibitions, https://exhibitions.library.columbia.edu/exhibits/show/martin-luther/flug.

16 Ronald James Deibert, *Parchment, Printing, and Hypermedia: Communication in World Order Transformation* (New York: Columbia University Press, 1997), 72.

17 Benedict Anderson, *Imagined Communities: Reflections on the Origin and Spread of Nationalism*, rev. ed. (London: Verso, 2006), 40.

18 The "Pamphlet wars" began after the adoption of the printing press, when inexpensive, short booklets were used to spread ideas in polemical or propagandist ways. Pamphlets fostered debate about religious beliefs, government policies, political philosophy, and controversial civic issues across England, France, Germany, and North America. The Protestant Reformation, the French Revolution, and the American Revolution were all periods of heavy pamphleteering. For a collected list of examples spanning regions throughout the period, see "List of Pamphlet Wars," Wikipedia, last modified March 21, 2022, https://en.wikipedia.org/wiki/List_of_pamphlet_wars.

19 Peter H. Wilson, "The Causes of the Thirty Years War 1618–48," *English Historical Review* 123, no. 502 (2008): 554, https://doi.org/10.1093/ehr/cen160.

20 Pope Gregory chose a rarer Latin verb form, the gerundive, which contained in its very construction an emphasis that something must or ought to be done. This stylistic choice, which also appears in the famous imperialist rhetoric of Cato the Elder—*Carthago delenda est!* (Carthage must be destroyed)—and the writings of Cicero, likely emphasized the sense of a religious crusade. See Maria Teresa Prendergast and Thomas A. Prendergast, "The Invention of Propaganda: A Critical Commentary on and Translation of *Inscrutabili Divinae Providentiae Arcano*," in *The Oxford Handbook of Propaganda Studies*, ed. Jonathan Auerbach and Russ Castronovo (Oxford: Oxford University Press, 2013), 19–27. Thanks also to Dr. Katie Clark for raising the parallel in an online conversation.

21 Baker, "Flying Writings," Flugschriften 1.

22 Barbara Basbanes Richter, "Benjamin Franklin and the Pamphlet Wars," National Endowment for the Humanities, March 17, 2020, https://www.neh.gov/article/benjamin-franklin-and-pamphlet-wars.

23 While historians debate the extent to which the papers were influential in their time, they were written and published in large part to urge New Yorkers specifically to support ratification. See "Full Text of the Federalist Papers," Research Guides, Library of Congress, September 5, 2023, https://guides.loc.gov/federalist-papers/full-text.

24 Leonard Downie Jr. and Michael Schudson, "The Reconstruction of American Journalism," *Columbia Journalism Review*, November/December 2009, https://archives.cjr.org/reconstruction /the_reconstruction_of_american.php.

25 There are various types of state media. According to the State Media Matrix created by Marius Dragomir and Astrid Söderström, on one side of the spectrum, "state-controlled media" is fully

state funded, and the government controls editorial decisions and the organizational structure of the media company. On the other end of the spectrum, independent public media are created for the public interest with government backing but are editorially independent and do not rely on government funding. Between these poles, the State Media Matrix names five other hybrid models, which are either independent (operating without government interference in editorial decisions) or captured (where messaging is controlled by the government). Based on their levels of government funding and control, these are given different names: captured public or state-managed media, captured private media, independent state-funded and state-managed media, independent state-funded media, and independent state-managed media. See Marius Dragomir and Astrid Söderström, *The State of State Media: A Global Analysis of the Editorial Independence of State Media and an Introduction of a New State Media Typology*, CEU Democracy Institute: Center for Media, Data and Society, 2021, https://cmds.ceu.edu/sites/cmcs.ceu.hu/files/attachment /article/2091/thestateofstatemedia.pdf.

26 George Creel, *Rebel at Large: Recollections of Fifty Crowded Years* (New York: G. P. Putnam's Sons, 1947), 158.

27 Bernays, *Propaganda*, 37.

28 See George Creel, *How We Advertised America: The First Telling of the Amazing Story of the Committee on Public Information That Carried the Gospel of Americanism to Every Corner of the Globe* (New York: Harper and Brother's Publishers, 1920).

29 Walter Lippmann, *Public Opinion* (New York: Harcourt, Brace and Company, 1922), 20.

30 Since the late 1960s, American confidence in the government has been declining. According to researchers, this is due to a number of factors, including the belief that government leaders are incompetent or unethical. Additionally, as economic inequality and political polarization have increased over the decades, this has led to a sense of unfairness and distrust of members of the opposing party or social group.

    A PEW study finds that since the late 1960s, Americans' trust in the government has been plummeting from 77 percent of people trusting the federal government "to do the right thing nearly always or most of the time" to around 25 percent in 1979. After brief rebounds in trust at certain moments in the 1980s and 1990s and after 9/11, trust began to fall again and has been at around 20 percent through the 2010s and early 2020s. See "Public Trust in Government: 1958–2022," Pew Research Center, June 6, 2022, https://www.pewresearch.org/politics/2022 /06/06/public-trust-in-government-1958-2022.

    Trust in media has also declined as news sources have proliferated. Since the advent of talk radio and the twenty-four-hour cable news cycle, opinion has blended into objective news coverage in ways that are sometimes different for audiences to disentangle, leading to perceptions of bias. Scholars also point to the decline of local news and the rise of politicized critiques of the media, particularly from the right, as fueling a distrust of journalists.

31 Zines had originated within science fiction fandoms in the 1930s but proliferated in the 1950s and 1960s as members of counterculture communities, including those horrified by the Vietnam War, sought a way to network and communicate with each other. Laura Van Leuven, "A Brief History of Zines," *Chapel Hill Rare Book Blog*, October 25, 2017, https://blogs.lib.unc.edu /rbc/2017/10/25/a-brief-history-of-zines.

32 Mark Hampton, "The Fourth Estate Ideal in Journalism History," in *The Routledge Companion to News and Journalism*, ed. Stuart Allan, 1st ed. (London and New York: Routledge, 2010), 3.

33 Notably, the Bush administration claimed that war with Iraq was justified because the country possessed weapons of mass destruction and were seeking to buy large quantities of yellowcake uranium to produce more nuclear warheads. Less than a year after the March 2003 invasion of Iraq, however, it was announced that no weapons of mass destruction had been found. The only yellowcake uranium discovered in Iraq had been there since before 1991. See Wright Bryan and Douglas Hopper, "Iraq WMD Timeline: How the Mystery Unraveled," *NPR*, November 15, 2005, https://www.npr.org/2005/11/15/4996218/iraq-wmd-timeline-how-the -mystery-unraveled. Also see Julian Borger, "There Were No Weapons of Mass Destruction in Iraq," *The Guardian*, October 7, 2004, https://www.theguardian.com/world/2004/oct/07/usa .iraq1.

34 Lasswell's original formulation is "Who, Says What, in Which Channel, to Whom, with What Effect?" See Harold Lasswell, "The Structure and Function of Communication in Society," in *The Communication of Ideas: A Series of Addresses* (New York: Institute for Religious and Social Studies, 1948), 37.

35 Elihu Katz and Paul F. Lazarsfeld, *Personal Influence: The Part Played by People in the Flow of Mass Communications* (New York: Free Press, 1955), 16.

36 Paul F. Lazarsfeld, Bernard Berelson, and Hazel Gaudet, *The People's Choice: How the Voter Makes Up His Mind in a Presidential Campaign*, 3rd ed. (New York: Columbia University Press, 1968).

37 Katz and Lazarsfeld, *Personal Influence*, 32.

38 Ibid., 1.

39 Ibid., 32.

40 This term, used somewhat interchangeably with *Magic Bullet model* in communication theory, has been apocryphally attributed to Harold Lasswell's writings on propaganda per "Hypodermic Needle Model," Wikipedia, last modified March 29, 2023, https://en.wikipedia.org/wiki/Hypodermic_needle_model.

41 Katz and Lazarsfeld, *Personal Influence*, 33.

42 Jon Askonas, "Life in an Alternate Reality Game," *New Atlantis*, no. 68 (Spring 2022): 6–28, published online as "Reality Is Just a Game Now," *New Atlantis*, https://www.thenewatlantis.com/publications/reality-is-just-a-game-now.

43 See Lippmann, *Public Opinion*; Walter Lippmann, *The Phantom Public* (New York: MacMillan, 1925). Discussion of his debate with Dewey is examined at length in Zac Gershberg and Sean Illing, *The Paradox of Democracy: Free Speech, Open Media, and Perilous Persuasion* (Chicago: University of Chicago Press, 2022).

CHAPTER 2: IF YOU MAKE IT TREND, YOU MAKE IT TRUE

1 Geoff Herbert, "Wayfair Responds to Sex Trafficking Conspiracy Theory over Cabinets with Human Names," Syracuse.com, July 13, 2020, https://www.syracuse.com/business/2020/07/wayfair-responds-to-sex-trafficking-conspiracy-theory-over-cabinets-with-human-names.html.

2 Jessica Contrera, "A QAnon Con: How the Viral Wayfair Sex Trafficking Lie Hurt Real Kids," *Washington Post*, December 16, 2021, https://www.washingtonpost.com/dc-md-va/interactive/2021/wayfair-qanon-sex-trafficking-conspiracy.

3 Marc-André Argentino (@_MAArgentino), "13/ Spike B came at 5:36 am. This tweet was retweeted 71K & liked 139K times...." Twitter, July 11, 2020, 5:27 p.m., https://twitter.com/_MAArgentino/status/1282063878571032579.

4 Contrera, "A QAnon Con."

5 Amanda Seitz, "QAnon's 'Save the Children' Morphs into Popular Slogan," *Associated Press*, October 28, 2020, https://apnews.com/article/election-2020-donald-trump-child-trafficking-illinois-morris-aab978bb7e9b89cd2cea151ca13421a0; E. J. Dickson, "What Is #SaveTheChildren and Why Did Facebook Block It?," *Rolling Stone*, August 12, 2020, https://www.rollingstone.com/culture/culture-features/savethechildren-qanon-pizzagate-facebook-block-hashtag-1041812; "Save the Children Statement on Use of Its Name in Unaffiliated Campaigns," Save the Children, August 7, 2020, https://www.savethechildren.org/us/about-us/media-and-news/2020-press-releases/save-the-children-statement-on-use-of-its-name-in-unaffiliated-c.

6 US Attorney's Office, District of Columbia, "North Carolina Man Sentenced to Four-Year Prison Term for Armed Assault at Northwest Washington Pizza Restaurant," US Department of Justice, June 22, 2017, https://www.justice.gov/usao-dc/pr/north-carolina-man-sentenced-four-year-prison-term-armed-assault-northwest-washington.

7 Adam Goldman, "The Comet Ping Pong Gunman Answers Our Reporter's Questions," *New York Times*, December 7, 2016, https://www.nytimes.com/2016/12/07/us/edgar-welch-comet-pizza-fake-news.html.

8 German Lopez, "Pizzagate, the Fake News Conspiracy Theory That Led a Gunman to DC's Comet Ping Pong, Explained," *Vox*, December 8, 2016, https://www.vox.com/policy-and-politics/2016/12/5/13842258/pizzagate-comet-ping-pong-fake-news.

9 Paul Farhi, "'False Flag' Planted at a Pizza Place? It's Just One More Conspiracy to Digest," *Washington Post*, December 5, 2016, https://www.washingtonpost.com/lifestyle/style/false-flag-planted-at-a-pizza-place-its-just-one-more-conspiracy-to-digest/2016/12/05/fc154b1e-bb09-11e6-94ac-3d324840106c_story.html. This was an ironic accusation, because in November 2016 Posobiec had himself been involved in an effort in which a hooded protestor held up an offensive sign—"Rape Melania"—at a Trump rally in an attempt to malign anti-Trump protestors. The phrase trended on Twitter, with Trump and Clinton supporters alike expressing outrage, and garnered widespread press coverage across the political spectrum until leaked texts covered in the media exposed Posobiec's involvement in January 2017. Joseph Bernstein, "Inside The Alt-Right's Campaign to Smear Trump Protesters as Anarchists," *BuzzFeed News*, January 11, 2017, https://www.buzzfeednews.com/article/josephbernstein/inside-the-alt-rights-campaign-to-smear-trump-protesters-as#.bmwXWKz23.

10 The anonymous "Q" of QAnon began communicating in October 2017, and the influence of the group spread from there. Edward Tian, "The QAnon Timeline: Four Years, 5,000 Drops and Countless Failed Prophecies," *Bellingcat*, January 29, 2012, https://www.bellingcat.com/news/americas/2021/01/29/the-qanon-timeline.

11 Contrera, "A QAnon Con."

12 Ben Collins (@oneunderscore__), "Pizzagate/QAnon people have Wayfair trending today. They falsely claim price glitches on storage boxes prove that the company is trafficking children . . . ," Twitter, July 10, 2020, Internet Archive, https://web.archive.org/web/20200711192428/https://twitter.com/oneunderscore__/status/1281616606012092419.

13 Chris Armenta, "Case 5:20-Cv-07502," Digital Commons, October 26, 2020, https://digitalcommons.law.scu.edu/cgi/viewcontent.cgi?article=3345&context=historical; Polly, "@99freemind Twitter Account," Internet Archive, January 2017, https://web.archive.org/web/20201125235053/twitter.com/99freemind.

14 According to Nick Hayes in *Influencer Marketing: Who Really Influences Your Customers?*, agencies began working on word-of-mouth marketing projects for large corporations in the mid-2000s as an alternative to relying on more traditional, expensive advertising and PR campaigns. Around this time, marketers like Hayes began to rank and target influencers and strategize about how best to use them. Nick Hayes, *Influencer Marketing: Who Really Influences Your Customers?* 1st ed. (Abingdon, UK: Routledge, 2015).

15 According to the *OED*, the term *influencer* can be traced back centuries under its definition of "one who or that which influences," The earliest example of *influencer* as a marketing term comes in 1968 and is defined as "a person who has the ability to influence other people's decisions about the purchase of particular goods or services," The Internet-era influencer, "a well-known or prominent person who uses the Internet or social media to promote or generate interest in products, often for payments," first appears in 2007. "Influencer, n.," Oxford English Dictionary, last modified September 2022, https://www.oed.com/view/Entry/95522; "influencer, n.," Oxford English Dictionary, April 2023, https://doi.org/10.1093/OED/2106254973.

16 Dan Gillmor, *We the Media: Grassroots Journalism by the People, for the People* (Sebastopol, CA: O'Reilly Media Inc., 2004).

17 Edward L. Bernays, *Propaganda* (New York: Ig, 2005), 61.

18 Clive Thompson, "Is the Tipping Point Toast?," *Fast Company*, February 1, 2008, https://www.fastcompany.com/641124/tipping-point-toast.

19 Thanks to Jeff Jarvis for conversations that helped to define this difference.

20 In his 1962 book *The Image*, Boorstin's definition reads, "The celebrity is a person who is known for his well-knownness" (Daniel Boorstin, *The Image: A Guide to Pseudo-Events in America* [New York: Random House, 1992], 78). One of Kim Kardashian's gifts—indeed, a gift shared by many successful influencers—was that she had the power to create a media spectacle that would be covered by media simply because it was a spectacle, and she was famous. One example involved breathless coverage of Kim "breaking the internet" because she showed skin on a magazine cover. A lot of people talked about it, and media talked about the people talking about it.

21 Alice E. Marwick and danah boyd, "I Tweet Honestly, I Tweet Passionately: Twitter Users, Context Collapse, and the Imagined Audience," *New Media & Society*, July 7, 2010, http://nms.sagepub.com/content/early/2010/06/22/1461444810365313.

22 Brian Solis, "The Rise of Digital Influence, by Brian Solis," *SlideShare*, March 20, 2012, https:// www.slideshare.net/Altimeter/the-rise-of-digital-influence; Brian Solis, "Report: The Rise of Digital Influence and How to Measure It," Brian Solis, March 21, 2012, https://www.briansolis .com/2012/03/report-the-rise-of-digital-influence.

23 Lauren Edmonds, "Jeffree Star Said Slaughtering His Yaks Is the 'Wyoming Way' and Showed a Group of Animals Scheduled to Be Killed the Next Day," *Insider*, June 7, 2022, https://www .insider.com/jeffree-star-defends-killing-yaks-at-ranch-wyoming-way-2022-6.

24 Sapna Maheshwari, "Are You Ready for the NanoInfluencers?" *New York Times*, November 11, 2018, https://www.nytimes.com/2018/11/11/business/media/nanoinfluencers-instagram-influencers.html.

25 For an interview-rich examination of how influencers themselves describe their skills, goals, monetization strategies, and relationship to their audience, see Emily Hund, *The Influencer Industry: The Quest for Authenticity on Social Media* (Princeton: Princeton University Press, 2023).

26 For an extended examination of ways in which bias manifests in search engines, see Safiya Noble, *Algorithms of Oppression: How Search Engines Reinforce Racism* (New York: NYU Press, 2018).

27 For more on the relationship between search queries, rare keywords or phrases, and online rabbit holes, see Michael Golebiewski and danah boyd, "Data Voids," *Data & Society*, October 29, 2019, https://datasociety.net/library/data-voids; Francesca Tripodi, "Searching for Alternative Facts," *Data & Society*, May 16, 2018, https://datasociety.net/library/searching-for-alternative-facts; Ronald E. Robertson et al., "Identifying Search Directives on Social Media," *Journal of Online Trust & Safety*, September 21, 2023, https://tsjournal.org/index.php/jots/article/view/133.

28 Cassidy George, "How Charli D'Amelio Became the Face of TikTok," *New Yorker*, September 5, 2020, https://www.newyorker.com/culture/cultural-comment/how-charli-damelio-became-the -face-of-tiktok.

29 When Charli D'Amelio reached one hundred million followers, TikTok wrote a blog post congratulating her. "Congratulations Charli for 100M Followers, Paving the Way for Creators Everywhere," TikTok, November 22, 2020, https://newsroom.tiktok.com/en-us/congratulations -charli-damelio-for-100-million-followers-paving-the-way-for-creators-everywhere. Her remarkable success has been analyzed in great detail, as people attempt to understand how her content and TikTok's For You algorithm intersect. One such video, by "Richard the YouTube Strategist," breaks down the early posts by D'Amelio and charts which helped her take off. "How Charli d'Amelio Became Famous," video posted to YouTube by Richard the Youtube strategist, May 7, 2020, https://www.youtube.com/watch?v=Ks8kpjhVxVE.

30 Steven Levy, "The Untold History of Facebook's Most Controversial Growth Tool," *Medium*, February 25, 2020, https://marker.medium.com/the-untold-history-of-facebooks-most -controversial-growth-tool-2ea3bfeaaa66.

31 Kashmir Hill, "How Facebook Figures Out Everyone You've Ever Met," *Gizmodo*, November 7, 2017, https://gizmodo.com/how-facebook-figures-out-everyone-youve-ever-met-1819822691.

32 Kashmir Hill, "Facebook Recommended That This Psychiatrist's Patients Friend Each Other," *Splinter*, August 29, 2016, https://splinternews.com/facebook-recommended-that-this-psychiatrists -patients-f-1793861472.

33 Anil Dash, "Nobody Has a Million Twitter Followers," Anil Dash, January 5, 2010, https:// www.anildash.com/2010/01/05/nobody_has_a_million_twitter_followers.

34 Julia Zappei, "Twitter Scrapping Its Suggested User List," *NBC News*, November 16, 2009, https://www.nbcnews.com/id/wbna33964694.

35 Gerrick De Vynck, "High-Profile Republicans Gain Followers in First Weeks of Musk's Reign," *Washington Post*, November 27, 2022, https://www.washingtonpost.com/technology/2022/11/27 /musk-followers-bernie-cruz.

36 J. M. Berger and Jonathon Morgan, "The ISIS Twitter Census: Defining and Describing the Population of ISIS Supporters on Twitter," Brookings, March 2015, https://www.brookings.edu /wp-content/uploads/2016/06/isis_twitter_census_berger_morgan.pdf.

37 Renée DiResta, "Social Network Algorithms Are Distorting Reality by Boosting Conspiracy Theories," *Fast Company*, May 11, 2016, https://www.fastcompany.com/3059742/social -network-algorithms-are-distorting-reality-by-boosting-conspiracy-theories.

38 Anna Merlan, "The Conspiracy Singularity Has Arrived," *Vice*, July 17, 2020, https://www.vice.com/en/article/v7gz53/the-conspiracy-singularity-has-arrived.

39 Jeff Horwitz and Katherine Blunt, "Instagram Connects Vast Pedophile Network," *Wall Street Journal*, June 7, 2023, https://www.wsj.com/articles/instagram-vast-pedophile-network-4ab7189.

40 Renée DiResta, "Online Conspiracy Groups Are a Lot Like Cults," *Wired*, November 13, 2018, https://www.wired.com/story/online-conspiracy-groups-qanon-cults.

41 With 272,000 members as of December 11, 2023. "QAnonCasualties Subreddit," Reddit, accessed December 11, 2023, https://www.reddit.com/r/QAnonCasualties.

42 Brandy Zadrozny, "On Facebook, Anti-vaxxers Urged a Mom Not to Give Her Son Tamiflu. He Later Died," *NBC News*, February 7, 2020, https://www.nbcnews.com/tech/social-media/facebook-anti-vaxxers-pushed-mom-not-give-her-son-tamiflu-n1131936.

43 Renée DiResta, "The Complexity of Simply Searching for Medical Advice," *Wired*, July 3, 2018, https://www.wired.com/story/the-complexity-of-simply-searching-for-medical-advice.

44 Jeff Horwitz and Deepa Seetharaman, "Facebook Executives Shut Down Efforts to Make the Site Less Divisive," *Wall Street Journal*, May 26, 2020, https://www.wsj.com/articles/facebook-knows-it-encourages-division-top-executives-nixed-solutions-11590507499.

45 Brandy Zadrozny, "'Carol's Journey': What Facebook Knew About How It Radicalized Users," *NBC News*, October 22, 2021, https://www.nbcnews.com/tech/tech-news/facebook-knew-radicalized-users-rcna3581.

46 Taylor Hatmaker, "Facebook Hits Pause on Algorithmic Recommendations for Political and Social Issue Groups," *TechCrunch*, October 30, 2020, https://techcrunch.com/2020/10/30/facebook-group-recommendations-election.

47 Ben Collins and Brandy Zadrozny, "Facebook Bans QAnon Across Its Platforms," *NBC News*, October 6, 2020, https://www.nbcnews.com/tech/tech-news/facebook-bans-qanon-across-its-platforms-n1242339.

48 L. M. Sacasas, "From Common Sense to Bespoke Realities," *Convivial Society*, July 12, 2022, https://theconvivialsociety.substack.com/p/from-common-sense-to-bespoke-realities.

49 In Chapter 3 of his book *The Hype Machine: How Social Media Disrupts Our Elections, Our Economy, and Our Health—and How We Must Adapt* (New York: Currency, 2020), computational social scientist Sinan Aral of MIT describes connections between users (networks) as the "substrate"—the foundation upon which everything else happens. On social media, whom we know and follow is connected to what we see. Just as in our village example from Chapter 1, our networks shape what we see, hear, and are potentially influenced by. That's because the people you choose to follow or friend and the groups you choose to join, whether proactively or via a recommender system, largely determine what you're going to see in your subsequent social media experience. Influencers, of course, with their large followings, have disproportionate reach and impact relative to "ordinary" users. But each node in the network—the followers, too, in other words—plays a role in shaping what the others see and do and, by extension, how they feel, act, and think about the world around them.

50 Chris Meserole, "How Do Recommender Systems Work on Digital Platforms?," Brookings, September 21, 2022, https://www.brookings.edu/techstream/how-do-recommender-systems-work-on-digital-platforms-social-media-recommendation-algorithms.

51 Smriti Bhagat et al., "When Do Recommender Systems Amplify User Preferences? A Theoretical Framework and Mitigation Strategies," Meta, August 6, 2021, https://research.facebook.com/blog/2021/8/when-do-recommender-systems-amplify-user-preferences-a-theoretical-framework-and-mitigation-strategies.

52 Akos Lada, Meihong Wang, and Tak Yan, "How Does News Feed Predict What You Want to See?," Meta, January 26, 2021, https://tech.facebook.com/engineering/2021/1/news-feed-ranking.

53 Casey Newton, "How YouTube Perfected the Feed," *The Verge*, August 30, 2017, https://www.theverge.com/2017/8/30/16222850/youtube-google-brain-algorithm-video-recommendation-personalized-feed.

54 Emma Lurie, Dan Bateyko, and Frances Schroeder, "TikTok Just Announced the Data It's Willing to Share. What's Missing?," Stanford Internet Observatory Cyber Policy Center, February 24, 2023, https://cyber.fsi.stanford.edu/io/news/tiktok-just-announced-data-its-willing-share-whats-missing.

55 Emily Baker-White, "TikTok's Secret 'Heating' Button Can Make Anyone Go Viral," *Forbes*, January 20, 2023, https://www.forbes.com/sites/emilybaker-white/2023/01/20/tiktoks-secret -heating-button-can-make-anyone-go-viral.

56 The acknowledgment that a combination of an opaque algorithm and incentivized employees was shaping content consumption on the platform was met with considerable concern, in part because TikTok's parent company was founded in China and remains partially Chinese-owned; some prominent congressmen and tech policy voices harbor concern about that power being abused by an authoritarian government. For more discussion of this, see Kari Paul and Johana Bhuiyan, "Key Takeaways from TikTok Hearing in Congress—and the Uncertain Road Ahead," *The Guardian*, March 23, 2023, https://www.theguardian.com/technology/2023 /mar/23/key-takeaways-tiktok-hearing-congress-shou-zi-chew. Full committee hearing: Scott Duke Kominers and Liang Wu, "Threads Foreshadows a Big—and Surprising—Shift in Social Media," *Harvard Business Review*, July 13, 2023, https://hbr.org/2023/07/threads-foreshadows -a-big-and-surprising-shift-in-social-media.

57 Kelley Cotter, "Playing the Visibility Game: How Digital Influencers and Algorithms Negotiate Influence on Instagram," *New Media & Society* 21, no. 4 (December 14, 2018), https://journals .sagepub.com/doi/10.1177/1461444818815684.

58 Brendan Koerner, "Watch This Guy Work, and You'll Finally Understand the TikTok Era," *Wired*, October 19, 2023, https://www.wired.com/story/tiktok-talent-factory-ursus-magana -creator-economy.

59 Drew Harwell, "How TikTok Ate the Internet," *Washington Post*, October 14, 2023, https:// www.washingtonpost.com/technology/interactive/2022/tiktok-popularity.

60 Ryan Broderick, "Your Least Favorite Gross Viral Food Videos Are All Connected to This Guy," *Eater*, May 11, 2021, https://www.eater.com/2021/5/11/22430383/why-are-gross-viral-food-videos -popular-rick-lax-facebook-watch.

61 Ashley Mears, "Hocus Focus: How Magicians Made a Fortune on Facebook," *The Economist*, July 28, 2022, https://www.economist.com/1843/2022/07/28/hocus-focus-how-magicians-made -a-fortune-on-facebook.

62 Horwitz and Seetharaman, "Facebook Executives Shut Down Efforts to Make the Site Less Divisive."

63 This is the title of one of my favorite books: Charles Mackay, *Extraordinary Popular Delusions and the Madness of Crowds* (1841; reis. New York: Noonday Press, 1932).

64 Renée DiResta, "Crowds and Technology," *Ribbonfarm*, September 15, 2016, https://www .ribbonfarm.com/2016/09/15/crowds-and-technology.

65 Ryan Schocket, "This Woman Tweeted About Having Coffee Every Day with Her Husband—the Internet Tore Her Apart," *BuzzFeed*, October 24, 2022, https://www.buzzfeed.com /ryanschocket2/woman-backlash-for-coffee-husband-tweet.

66 Joon Ian Wong, Dave Gershgorn, and Mike Murphy, "Facebook Is Trying to Get Rid of Bias in Trending News by Getting Rid of Humans," *Quartz*, August 26, 2016, https://qz.com/768122 /facebook-fires-human-editors-moves-to-algorithm-for-trending-topics.

67 Hannah Ritchie, "Read All About It: The Biggest Fake News Stories of 2016," *CNBC*, December 30, 2016, https://www.cnbc.com/2016/12/30/read-all-about-it-the-biggest-fake-news-stories -of-2016.html.

68 Olivia Solon, "In Firing Human Editors, Facebook Has Lost the Fight Against Fake News," *The Guardian*, August 29, 2016, https://www.theguardian.com/technology/2016/aug/29/facebook -trending-news-editors-fake-news-stories.

69 Boorstin, *The Image*.

70 Edward Bernays, *Crystallizing Public Opinion* (New York: Boni and Liveright, 1923), 171.

71 Boorstin, *The Image*, 10.

72 Brian Welk and Rosemary Rossi, "Bean Dad Makes His 9-Year-Old Struggle to Open Can of Beans for 6 Hours, Infuriates Twitter: 'Self-Absorbed A–Hat,'" *The Wrap*, January 3, 2021, https://www.thewrap.com/bean-dad-9-year-old-open-can-6-hours-infuriates-twitter.

73 Israel ישראל (@Israel), "Things that shouldn't be trending on @Twitter: 'The Jews' @TwitterSafety do your job," Twitter, May 16, 2023, 5:02 a.m., https://twitter.com/Israel/status /1658397528398737408.

74 Sarah Mervosh and Emily S. Rueb, "Fuller Picture Emerges of Viral Video of Native American Man and Catholic Students," *New York Times*, January 20, 2021, https://www.nytimes.com /2019/01/20/us/nathan-phillips-covington.html.

75 Joshua Rothman, "How to Escape Pseudo-events in America: The Lessons of Covington," *New Yorker*, 2019, https://www.newyorker.com/culture/cultural-comment/what-the-covington-saga -reveals-about-our-media-landscape.

CHAPTER 3: GURUS, BESTIES, AND PROPAGANDISTS

1 Jason Horowitz and Taylor Lorenz, "Khaby Lame, the Everyman of the Internet," *New York Times*, June 2, 2021, https://www.nytimes.com/2021/06/02/style/khaby-lame-tiktok.html.

2 *Thirst traps* are provocative images or videos in which the creator is trying to appear attractive or enticing.

3 Clare Malone, "The Gospel of Candace Owens," *New Yorker*, April 22, 2023, https://www .newyorker.com/news/annals-of-communications/the-gospel-of-candace-owens.

4 While there are many journalistic profiles of MrBeast, his frequently updated Wikipedia page provides the most up-to-date summary of his content and philanthropic efforts. "MrBeast," Wikipedia, last modified September 8, 2023, https://en.wikipedia.org/wiki/MrBeast.

5 "I Helped 2000 Amputees Walk Again," video posted to YouTube by Beast Philanthropy, May 7, 2023, https://www.youtube.com/watch?v=l5PvwYZQtT8.

6 Keffals became known in part for successfully trolling her ideological opponents, posting things like "I've always wanted to ratio…" and then pointing followers to a quote-tweeted post or other mention of a prominent media figure, politician, or corporate target whom she felt had done something stupid or malicious. Her followers would then go and comment on the post or reply to the poster. The term *ratio* refers to the number of comments relative to likes on a social media post; a post with many more comments than likes often indicates to observers that the person got a lot of flak and little support for what they expressed. Taylor Lorenz, "The Trans Twitch Star Delivering News to a Legion of LGBTQ Teens," *Washington Post*, June 26, 2022, https://www .washingtonpost.com/technology/2022/06/26/keffals-trans-twitch-streaming-news.

7 Sinan Aral, Lev Muchnik, and Arun Sundararajan, "Distinguishing Influence-Based Contagion from Homophily-Driven Diffusion in Dynamic Networks," *Proceedings of the National Academy of Sciences of the United States of America* 106, no. 51 (2009): 21544–21549, https://doi.org /10.1073/pnas.0908800106.

8 Talcott Parsons, "On the Concept of Influence," *Public Opinion Quarterly* 27, no. 1 (1963): 37–62, https://doi.org/10.1086/267148.

9 Cartwright's formula in its academic construction specified an agent, O, who was exerting influence; a method of exerting influence; and the agent subjected to the influence, which he labeled P. Agent O → does something → to Agent P. I use the term *target* here for clarity. Cartwright uses *agent* to describe both the person being influenced and the person doing the influencing. While Cartwright's formula for how influence works is simple, he acknowledges that the reality is often more complex: "Breaking down the process of influence in this way does violence to its essential nature, for above all influence is a social relationship. Influence cannot be properly understood by treating the properties of O or of P in isolation." Dorwin Cartwright, "Influence, Leadership, Control," in *Handbook of Organizations (RLE: Organizations)*, ed. James G. March (Routledge, 2013), 1–47.

10 Chloe Sorvino, "Could MrBeast Be the First YouTuber Billionaire?," *Forbes*, November 30, 2022, https://www.forbes.com/sites/chloesorvino/2022/11/30/could-mrbeast-be-the-first-youtuber -billionaire.

11 Alan Neves et al., "Quantifying Complementarity Among Strategies for Influencers' Detection on Twitter," *Procedia Computer Science* 51 (2015): 2435–2444, https://doi.org/10.1016/j.procs .2015.05.428.

12 Jon Ronson, "How One Stupid Tweet Blew Up Justine Sacco's Life," *New York Times*, February 12, 2015, https://www.nytimes.com/2015/02/15/magazine/how-one-stupid-tweet-ruined-justine -saccos-life.html.

13 Cartwright, "Influence, Leadership, Control," 1–47.

14 Jesse Singal, "The Strange Tale of Social Autopsy, the Anti-harassment Start-up That Descended into Gamergate Trutherism," *Intelligencer*, April 18, 2016, https://nymag.com/intelligencer/2016/04/how-social-autopsy-fell-for-gamergate-trutherism.html. Owens, who herself had been the target of real-world bullying, achieved some visibility as a side story during Gamergate. She was the founder of an effort called Social Autopsy, which launched a Kickstarter to catalog the abuses of trolls and bullies by deanonymizing them and making their words easily discoverable. This effort caused its own online blowup, as both Gamergate and anti-Gamergate participants, as well as anti-harassment advocates (including two of the women who had been a sustained focus of Gamergate attacks), pointed out the ways it would be abused, leading Owens to accuse them of targeting her.

15 Jakob Nielsen, "The 90-9-1 Rule for Participation Inequality in Social Media and Online Communities," Nielsen Norman Group, October 8, 2006, https://www.nngroup.com/articles/participation-inequality.

16 Shannon C. McGregor, "Social Media as Public Opinion: How Journalists Use Social Media to Represent Public Opinion," *Journalism: Theory, Practice & Criticism* 20, no. 8 (May 9, 2019): 1070–1086, https://doi.org/10.1177/1464884919845458. McGregor points this out and additionally highlights the fact that social media participants are not reflective of the public, despite the fact that media considers social media majorities as a sort of unofficial poll and uses commentary from participants as vox populi opinions.

17 Renée DiResta, "Election-Fraud Rumors Are Always the Same," *The Atlantic*, December 15, 2022, https://www.theatlantic.com/ideas/archive/2022/11/arizona-election-voting-machines-fraud-conspiracy-tv-tropes/672100.

18 Aumyo Hassan and Sarah J. Barber, "The Effects of Repetition Frequency on the Illusory Truth Effect," *Cognitive Research: Principles and Implications* 6, no. 1 (May 13, 2021), https://doi.org/10.1186/s41235-021-00301-5.

19 Eytan Bakshy et al., "Everyone's an Influencer: Quantifying Influence on Twitter," Proceedings of the Fourth ACM International Conference on Web Search and Data Mining, Hong Kong, February 9, 2011, https://doi.org/10.1145/1935826.1935845.

20 Jeff Guo, "The Bonkers Seth Rich Conspiracy Theory, Explained," *Vox*, May 24, 2017, https://www.vox.com/policy-and-politics/2017/5/24/15685560/seth-rich-conspiracy-theory-explained-fox-news-hannity.

21 Damon Centola, "Influencers, Backfire Effects, and the Power of the Periphery," *Personal Networks: Classic Readings and New Directions in Egocentric Analysis* 51 (2021): 73–86. The concept of complex contagion, and the roles that influencers and networks play in helping ideas go viral, is explored by Centola in depth throughout his book *Change: How to Make Big Things Happen* (New York: Little, Brown Spark, 2021).

22 Ibid.

23 Megan Hoins, "What 'The Discourse' Has to Do with Internet Discomfort," *Medium*, April 26, 2018, https://medium.com/@meganhoins/what-the-discourse-has-to-do-with-internet-discomfort-6a554408966b; Sakshi, "Discourse (Slang)," Know Your Meme, August 30, 2023, https://knowyourmeme.com/memes/discourse-slang. "The Discourse" has an academic definition, which internet culture appropriated largely mockingly; rather than referring to important and serious issues, it is most often applied to rather esoteric nonsense that breaks out of its main community and is viewed with some bemusement by those outside the argument. "The Discourse" in its meme sense was popularized on tumblr in 2015 and was originally deployed when a fight broke out between a few people on the internet, often over an obscure niche issue, and an observer noted the argument and its somewhat ridiculous valence.

24 Allison P. Davis, "A Vibe Shift Is Coming," *The Cut*, February 16, 2022, https://www.thecut.com/2022/02/a-vibe-shift-is-coming.html.

25 Ryan Holiday, "Trading Up the Chain: Mainstream Media Takes Cues from Blogosphere," *Observer*, April 4, 2014, https://observer.com/2014/04/mainstream-media-takes-cues-from-blogosphere.

26 Seth Rich was murdered in July 2016. Nearly a year later, in April 2017, Jack Posobiec began tweeting conspiracy theories about Seth Rich as the party responsible for the Democratic National Convention leak (arguing that this absolved Russia). In May 2017, Posobiec temporarily gained White House press credentials from his job at Rebel Media. He used one of the press

conferences to ask Trump about Seth Rich, but the question was ignored (James LaPorta, "Jack Posobiec, Pizzagate and Seth Rich Conspiracy Theorist, Has Top Secret Security Clearance," *Daily Beast*, updated August 17, 2017, https://www.thedailybeast.com/jack-posobiec-pizzagate -and-seth-rich-conspiracy-theorist-has-top-secret-security-clearance). On May 16, 2017, Fox News published a story about investigating Rich's murder and connecting it (without evidence) to Wikileaks. After this, Hannity pushed the story (THR Staff, "Sean Hannity Backs Off Seth Rich Story 'For Now' Out of Respect for His Family," *Hollywood Reporter*, May 23, 2017, https://www.hollywoodreporter.com/news/general-news/sean-hannity-backs-seth-rich-story -respect-family-999155). A week later, Fox News retracted the story ("The Origins of the Seth Rich Conspiracy Theory," *NPR*, July 11, 2019, https://www.npr.org/2019/07/11/740608323 /the-origins-of-the-seth-rich-conspiracy-theory). An in-depth case study of the Seth Rich story and Fox's coverage can also be found in Brian Stelter's book *Hoax: Donald Trump, Fox News, and the Dangerous Distortion of Truth* (New York: One Signal Publishers), 2020.

27 Most of the work in academic literature and the field of brand marketing alike primarily differentiates influencers by tiers according to their reach. Guides written by agencies that help companies develop an influencer marketing strategy additionally differentiate by the influencer's topical niche. This gap is interesting because brand marketing strategists precisely and extensively define brand personalities (for example, in terms of one of the twelve personality archetypes of Carl Jung: "The Everyman," "The Sage," "The Jester," "The Rebel"). Similar assessments of influencers (many of whom are brands) do not appear to exist at the moment, though one study attempted a taxonomy based on keywords within LinkedIn profiles: visionary, strategist, mentor, tutor, teacher, and so forth. "Brand Archetypes," OVO, n.d., https://brandsbyovo.com /expertise/brand-archetypes; James Barry and John T. Gironda, "Operationalizing Thought Leadership for Online B2B Marketing," *Industrial Marketing Management* 81 (August 1, 2019): 138–159, https://doi.org/10.1016/j.indmarman.2017.11.005.

28 "Special Episode: Calibrating the Gurometer," Decoding the Gurus, January 9, 2021, https:// decoding-the-gurus.captivate.fm/episode/calibrating-the-gurometer. Scholars Christopher Kavanagh (a cognitive anthropologist and social psychologist) and Matthew Browne (a psychology professor) host a podcast called *Decoding the Gurus*, which broached the idea of a "Gurometer" that defined ten key characteristics of modern secular gurus, among them antiestablishment inclinations.

29 Helen Lewis's podcast *The New Gurus* goes deeply into the motivations and value propositions that gurus offer their audiences in several different topical categories. Simplification and an easy guide for how to live is common among them. *The New Gurus* Apple Podcasts, April 17, 2023, https://podcasts.apple.com/us/podcast/the-new-gurus/id1659385785.

30 "The Virus, the Vaccine, and the Dark Side of Wellness," *Harper's Bazaar*, March 16, 2021, https://www.harpersbazaar.com/culture/features/a35823360/covid-19-vaccine-qanon-wellness -influencers; E. J. Dickson, "Wellness Influencers Are Calling Out QAnon Conspiracy Theorists for Spreading Lies," *Rolling Stone*, September 15, 2020, https://www.rollingstone.com/culture /culture-news/qanon-wellness-influencers-seane-corn-yoga-1059856.

31 Kaitlyn Tiffany, "The Women Making Conspiracy Theories Beautiful," *The Atlantic*, August 18, 2020, https://www.theatlantic.com/technology/archive/2020/08/how-instagram-aesthetics -repackage-qanon/615364.

32 Derek Beres, Julian Walker, and Matthew Remski, *Conspirituality: How New Age Conspiracy Theories Became a Health Threat* (New York: Public Affairs, 2023), chap. 1.

33 Charlotte Ward and David Voas, "The Emergence of Conspirituality," *Journal of Contemporary Religion* 26, no. 1 (January 1, 2011): 103–121, https://doi.org/10.1080/13537903.2011.539846.

34 Martin Riedl, Josephine Lukito, and Samuel Woolley, "Political Influencers on Social Media: An Introduction," *Social Media and Society* 9, no. 2 (June 7, 2023): 205630512311779, https://doi .org/10.1177/20563051231177938.

35 For an interesting profile of Chris Rufo that examines his avowed leveraging of propaganda tactics (such as deliberately setting out to redefine the term *critical race theory*) in service to accomplishing his goals, see Benjamin Wallace-Wells, "How a Conservative Activist Invented the Conflict over Critical Race Theory," *New Yorker*, June 18, 2021, https://www.newyorker.com/news /annals-of-inquiry/how-a-conservative-activist-invented-the-conflict-over-critical-race-theory.

36 Philipp Margolin, "Distort, Discredit, Dismiss: The Manipulation Playbook of Anti-science Actors, Part 2," *The Protagonist Future?*, May 15, 2023, https://protagonistfuture.substack.com/p/distort-discredit-dismiss.

37 Robert Tracinski, "The Populist Right Isn't Interested in Elite Accountability," *The UnPopulist*, November 18, 2022, https://www.theunpopulist.net/p/the-populist-right-isnt-interested.

38 Adam, "Twitter's Main Character," Know Your Meme, July 13, 2023, https://knowyourmeme.com/memes/twitters-main-character; Maple Cocaine (@maplecocaine), "Each day on twitter there is one main character. The goal is to never be it," Twitter, January 2, 2019, https://twitter.com/maplecocaine/status/1080665226410889217.

39 Reeves Wiedeman, "PissPigGranddad, the Punk-Rock Florist Who Fought ISIS in Syria, Is Coming Home," *Intelligencer*, April 3, 2017, https://nymag.com/intelligencer/2017/04/brace-belden-pisspiggranddad-syria-isis.html.

40 Sam Jaffe Goldstein, "Jeffrey Epstein Is a Feature of Our System: A Conversation with Liz Franczak and Brace Belden, Hosts of 'Trueanon,'" *Los Angeles Review of Books*, January 30, 2020, https://lareviewofbooks.org/article/jeffrey-epstein-is-a-feature-of-our-system-a-conversation-with-liz-franczak-and-brace-belden-hosts-of-trueanon.

41 These two topics, in quick succession, dominated The Discourse in one week of June 2023.

42 Helen Lewis, "Extremophiles, the Internet's Favorite Personality Type," *The Atlantic*, January 31, 2023, https://www.theatlantic.com/ideas/archive/2023/01/internet-youtube-podcast-guru-influencers-andrew-tate/672867.

43 David A. Graham, "The Unlabelling of an 'Anti-Muslim Extremist,'" *The Atlantic*, June 18, 2018, https://www.theatlantic.com/politics/archive/2018/06/maajid-nawaz-v-splc/562646.

44 Vanessa Thorpe, "LBC's Maajid Nawaz's Fascination with Conspiracies Raises Alarm," *The Guardian*, January 31, 2021, https://www.theguardian.com/tv-and-radio/2021/jan/31/lbcs-maajid-nawazs-fascination-with-conspiracies-raises-alarm.

45 Gurwinder Bhogal, "The Perils of Audience Capture: How Influencers Become Brainwashed by Their Audience," *The Prism* (blog), Substack, June 30, 2022. https://gurwinder.substack.com/p/the-perils-of-audience-capture.

46 Maajid Nawaz (@MaajidNawaz), "Titan sub search & oxygen countdown= scam...," Twitter, June 24, 2023, https://twitter.com/MaajidNawaz/status/1672698980558307333.

47 Naomi Klein, *Doppelganger: A Trip into the Mirror World* (New York: Farrar, Straus and Giroux, 2023), 106–107.

48 Gurwinder Bhogal defines *audience capture*, in a very thorough explainer post, as a feedback loop that "involves the gradual and unwitting replacement of a person's identity with one custom-made for the audience." Bhogal, "The Perils of Audience Capture."

49 Klein, *Doppelganger*, 131.

50 Ibid., 106–107.

51 Charli, https://www.charlidamelio.com.

52 X (@x), "Surprise! Today we launched our Creator Ads Revenue Sharing program...," Twitter, July 14, 2023, https://twitter.com/X/status/1679572360695824384.

53 Taylor Lorenz, "Far-Right Twitter Influencers First on Elon Musk's Monetization Scheme," *Washington Post*, updated July 14, 2023, https://www.washingtonpost.com/technology/2023/07/13/twitter-creators-payments-right-wing.

54 Zeynep Alkan and Sevilay Ulaş, "Trust in Social Media Influencers and Purchase Intention: An Empirical Analysis," *Online Journal of Communication and Media Technologies* 13, no. 1 (January 1, 2023): e202301, https://doi.org/10.30935/ojcmt/12783. While there is not much literature on the implications of trust in influencers on political attitude shifts or belief formation, influencers expressing opinions increased the trust toward them, and there is a positive correlation between trust in the influencer and purchasing intent.

55 "For Shopping, Americans Turn to Mobile Phones While Influencers Become a Factor," Pew Research Center, November 21, 2022, https://www.pewresearch.org/fact-tank/2022/11/21/for-shopping-phones-are-common-and-influencers-have-become-a-factor-especially-for-young-adults.

56 *Supplement to the 2022 Edelman Trust Barometer: The New Cascade of Influence: Brands in a Feed-First World*, Edelman Trust Institute, August 2022, https://www.edelman.com/sites/g/files

/aatuss191/files/2022-08/2022%20Edelman%20Trust%20Barometer%20SUPPLEMENT%20to%20The%20New%20Cascade%20of%20Influence%20FINAL.pdf, 16–17.

57 Paris Martineau, "Inside the Pricey War to Influence Your Instagram Feed," *Wired*, November 18, 2018, https://www.wired.com/story/pricey-war-influence-your-instagram-feed.

58 Alexandra Sternlicht, "The World's Most Followed Tiktoker Gets Paid as Much as $750K per Post, but to Reach His Greatest Business Goal Khaby Lame Is Binge-Watching American Cartoons," *Fortune*, September 14, 2022, https://fortune.com/2022/09/14/how-khaby-lame-plans-expand-business-that-gets-750k-dollars-for-tiktok-post.

59 Alexandra Sternlicht, "Top Creators 2022," *Forbes*, September 6, 2022, https://www.forbes.com/sites/alexandrasternlicht/2022/09/06/top-creators-2022.

60 Carly Porterfield, "Right-Wing Pundits Ben Shapiro and Steven Crowder Clash Over $50 Million Media Deal," *Forbes*, January 20, 2023, https://www.forbes.com/sites/carlieporterfield/2023/01/20/right-wing-pundits-ben-shapiro-and-steven-crowder-clash-over-50-million-media-deal.

61 Laurence Scott, "A History of the Influencer, from Shakespeare to Instagram," *New Yorker*, April 21, 2019. https://www.newyorker.com/culture/annals-of-inquiry/a-history-of-the-influencer-from-shakespeare-to-instagram.

62 A case study by Shannon McGregor details how the Trump campaign used influencers to drive online conversations during the 2016 campaign: "The campaign then identified the top 10 percent of users with the highest influence in terms of follower counts and their ability to drive social media conversations. These users were invited to join the campaign's rapid response team, 'The Big-League Trump Team.' As [Gary] Coby, [a digital strategist with the Trump campaign], said, 'Basically, during the debate we were sending a text out to this small group every three to five minutes. Those pieces of content we sent out, were getting up to 500 percent additional increase in reach [on social media] relative to everything else. Trump had a big footprint, but then we were behind the scenes kind of putting gasoline on all of that.'" More broadly, McGregor's paper provides a list of ways in which political campaigns in 2016 (notably Sanders, Trump, some quotes from Cruz's campaign team) were using social media listening to try to find emergent chatter—to pull things up from the crowd. She writes, "Reading social media messages from supporters informed campaign messaging, as well as strategy more broadly." Shannon C. McGregor, "'Taking the Temperature of the Room': How Political Campaigns Use Social Media to Understand and Represent Public Opinion," *Public Opinion Quarterly* 84, no. S1 (July 15, 2020): 236–256.

63 Kate Knibbs, "Mike Bloomberg's Meme Campaign Is Just the Beginning," *Wired*, February 13, 2020, https://www.wired.com/story/election-2020-influncers.

64 Benjamin Wofford, "Meet the Lobbyist Next Door," *Wired*, July 14, 2022, https://www.wired.com/story/meet-the-lobbyist-next-door.

65 Johnatan Reiss and Michelle R. Smith, "Inside One Network Cashing in on Vaccine Disinformation," *AP News*, August 14, 2023, https://apnews.com/article/anti-vaccine-bollinger-coronavirus-disinformation-a7b8e1f33990670563b4c469b462c9bf.

66 Anastasia Goodwin and Samuel Woolley, "Political Groups Are Paying Influencers to Spread Partisan Messaging," *Teen Vogue*, October 7, 2021, https://www.teenvogue.com/story/tiktok-influencers-political-campaigns.

67 "These Are 'Not' Political Ads," Mozilla Foundation, n.d., https://foundation.mozilla.org/en/campaigns/tiktok-political-ads.

68 Robert Downen, "Gen Z Influencers Are Being Quietly Recruited to Defend Ken Paxton," *Texas Tribune*, August 20, 2023, https://www.texastribune.org/2023/08/14/influenceable-texas-politics-ken-paxton.

69 Despite apocryphal stories of gladiators endorsing olive oil in ancient Rome, the earliest documented example comes from Josiah Wedgwood in the 1760s. He aligned his tea sets with British royalty by calling himself "Potter to her Majesty" and from there built his brand. In the late nineteenth century, endorsements from both prominent and everyday people appeared alongside ads for patent medicines, or what we would today call "snake oil." Many of these testimonials had been paid for, while others were wholly faked. The disrepute of patent medicines cast endorsements in a negative light until they reemerged in the years following World War I, amid a massive rise in media consumption and the advertising industry. For more work on this topic, see Kerry

Segrave, *Endorsements in Advertising: A Social History* (Jefferson, NC: McFarland & Co., 2005), or Peter Suciu, "History of Influencer Marketing Predates Social Media by Centuries—but Is There Enough Transparency in the 21st Century?," *Forbes*, December 7, 2020.

70 "Guides Concerning the Use of Endorsements and Testimonials in Advertising Federal Acquisition Regulation; Final Rule," Federal Trade Commission, October 15, 2009, https://www.ftc .gov/sites/default/files/documents/federal_register_notices/guides-concerning-use-endorsements -and-testimonials-advertising-16-cfr-part-255/091015guidesconcerningtestimonials.pdf.

71 Jessica Camille Aguirre, "When Does Mom's Blog Become an Ad?," *NPR*, August 17, 2012, https://www.npr.org/sections/health-shots/2012/08/16/158938607/when-does-moms-blog -become-an-ad. To be clear, the FTC did mandate that celebrities had to disclose engagements if they were "outside the context of traditional ads, such as on talk shows or in social media." "FTC Publishes Final Guides Governing Endorsements, Testimonials," Federal Trade Commission, June 22, 2017, https://www.ftc.gov/news-events/news/press-releases/2009/10/ftc-publishes -final-guides-governing-endorsements-testimonials.

72 Marisa Taylor, "FTC Not Sure How to Enforce Blogger Disclosure Rules," *Wall Street Journal*, January 15, 2010, https://www.wsj.com/articles/BL-DGB-10282.

73 Louise Matsakis, "YouTube and Pinterest Influencers Almost Never Disclose Marketing Relationships," *Wired*, March 27, 2018, https://www.wired.com/story/youtube-pinterest-influencers -never-disclose-affiliate-links.

74 "FTC Releases Advertising Disclosures Guidance for Online Influencers," Federal Trade Commission, November 5, 2019, https://www.ftc.gov/news-events/news/press-releases/2019/11/ftc-releases -advertising-disclosures-guidance-online-influencers.

75 The FTC has filed and won a handful of high-profile lawsuits in recent years, such as *FTC vs. Teami, LLC*, a "detoxifying" tea and skincare company that made deceptive health claims and promoted its products with undisclosed celebrity endorsements on social media. In general, however, the FTC has trouble enforcing its guidelines because they are nonbonding instructions rather than formal rules and therefore are more open to interpretation. For recent work on this topic, see Keith Coop, "Influencers: Not So Fluent in Disclosure Compliance," *Loyola of Los Angeles Entertainment Law Review* 41, no. 1 (2021).

76 Giovanni De Gregorio and Catalina Goanta, "The Influencer Republic: Monetizing Political Speech on Social Media," *German Law Journal* 23, no. 2 (March 23, 2022): 204–225, https:// doi.org/10.1017/glj.2022.15.

77 Renée DiResta, "How the Creator Economy Is Incentivizing Propaganda," *NOEMA*, June 7, 2023, https://www.noemamag.com/the-new-media-goliaths.

78 Edward L. Bernays, *Crystallizing Public Opinion* (1923; reis., New York: Ig Publishing, 2011), 92.

79 Jemima Kelly, "Substack's Success Shows Readers Have Had Enough of Polarised Media," *Financial Times*, March 31, 2021, https://www.ft.com/content/3e565df2-0cb2-4126-a879-eb2710 eef03a.

80 Glenn Greenwald, "Glenn Greenwald," Rumble, n.d., https://rumble.com/GGreenwald. Audience count as of December 3, 2023.

81 Clio Chang, "The Substackerati," *Columbia Journalism Review*, November 16, 2020, https:// www.cjr.org/special_report/substackerati.php.

CHAPTER 4: THE CROWD

1 George F. Young et al., "Starling Flock Networks Manage Uncertainty in Consensus at Low Cost," *PLoS Computational Biology* 9, no. 1 (2013), https://doi.org/10.1371/journal.pcbi.1002894.

2 Renée DiResta, "How Online Mobs Act like Flocks of Birds," *NOEMA*, November 3, 2022, https://www.noemamag.com/how-online-mobs-act-like-flocks-of-birds.

3 As with birds, that behavior does not necessarily have to be rational. In 2016, the games company "Cards against Humanity" launched a crowdfunding site that invited people to donate their hard-earned cash to pay for a backhoe that was digging a hole in a field—for absolutely no reason at all. They livestreamed the digger excavating the pointless hole somewhere in America, explaining that "as long as money keeps coming in, we'll keep digging," In the end, they raised more than $100,000. See Laura Wagner, "People Knowingly Donated $100,000 to Dig a Big,

Pointless Hole in the Ground," *The Guardian*, November 27, 2016, https://www.theguardian.com/technology/2016/nov/28/cards-against-humanity-hole.

4   Sara Brin Rosenthal et al., "Revealing the Hidden Networks of Interaction in Mobile Animal Groups Allows Prediction of Complex Behavioral Contagion," *Proceedings of the National Academy of Sciences* 112, no. 15 (2015): 4690–4695, https://doi.org/10.1073/pnas.1420068112.

5   Naomi Forman-Katz and Katerina Eva Matsa, "News Platform Fact Sheet," Pew Research Center, September 20, 2022, https://www.pewresearch.org/journalism/fact-sheet/news-platform-fact-sheet.

6   David Shor, "One Needle to Predict Them All: Does the *New York Times* Needle Really Need to Exist?" (interview by Mike Pesca, *The Gist* [podcast], January 5, 2021), https://slate.com/podcasts/the-gist/2021/01/new-york-times-polling-and-georgia.

7   David Shor (@davidshor), "Post-MLK-assasination race riots reduced Democratic vote share…," Twitter, May 28, 2020, https://twitter.com/davidshor/status/1265998625836019712.

8   Benjamin Dixon (@BenjaminPDixon), "So we're really concern trolling for the purposes of increasing democratic turnout. Tell you what, go to Minneapolis…," Twitter, May 28, 2020, https://twitter.com/BenjaminPDixon/status/1266119727665029120.

9   Ari Trujillo Wesler (@TheReFTW), "Post-MLK-assasination race riots reduced Democratic vote share…," Twitter, https://twitter.com/TheReFTW/status/1266146619805728768.

10 Eric Levitz, "David Shor's Unified Theory of American Politics," *Intelligencer*, July 17, 2020, https://nymag.com/intelligencer/2020/07/david-shor-cancel-culture-2020-election-theory-polls.html.

11 Yascha Mounk, "Stop Firing the Innocent," *The Atlantic*, June 27, 2020, https://www.theatlantic.com/ideas/archive/2020/06/stop-firing-innocent/613615.

12 Jonathan Chait, "The Still-Vital Case for Liberalism in a Radical Age," *Intelligencer*, June 11, 2020, https://nymag.com/intelligencer/2020/06/case-for-liberalism-tom-cotton-new-york-times-james-bennet.html.

13 Jonathan Chait, "An Elite Progressive LISTSERV Melts Down over a Bogus Racism Charge," *Intelligencer*, June 23, 2020, https://nymag.com/intelligencer/2020/06/case-for-liberalism-tom-cotton-new-york-times-james-bennet.html.

14 Matthew Yglesias, "The Real Stakes in the David Shor Saga," *Vox*, July 29, 2020, https://www.vox.com/2020/7/29/21340308/david-shor-omar-wasow-speech.

15 Renée DiResta, "Mediating Consent," *The Feed*, Ribbonfarm, December 17, 2019, https://www.ribbonfarm.com/2019/12/17/mediating-consent.

16 For a full examination of the means by which the internet transformed advocacy and organizing, see David Karpf, *The MoveOn Effect: The Unexpected Transformation of American Political Advocacy, Oxford Studies in Digital Politics* (New York: Oxford University Press, 2012).

17 Zeynep Tufekci, *Twitter and Tear Gas: The Power and Fragility of Networked Protest* (New Haven, CT: Yale University Press, 2017), introduction.

18 Stephan Lewandowsky, Ronald E. Robertson, and Renée DiResta, "Challenges in Understanding Human-Algorithm Entanglement During Online Information Consumption," *Perspectives on Psychological Science*, July 10, 2023, https://doi.org/10.1177/17456916231180809.

19 Sinan Aral, *The Hype Machine: How Social Media Disrupts Our Elections, Our Economy, and Our Health—and How We Must Adapt* (New York: Currency, 2020), 194–197.

20 Elias Canetti, *Crowds and Power* (1960; reis., New York: Seabury Press, 1978), 29.

21 Renée DiResta, "Crowds and Technology," *Ribbonfarm*, September 15, 2016, https://www.ribbonfarm.com/2016/09/15/crowds-and-technology.

22 Renée DiResta, "Elon Musk Is Fighting for Attention, Not Free Speech," *The Atlantic*, April 14, 2022, https://www.theatlantic.com/ideas/archive/2022/04/elon-musk-buy-twitter-free-speech/629571.

23 I've chosen to use Wikipedia for some citations on controversial topics, including this one, because of the "negotiated facts" and consensus process that results in the creation of Wikipedia's articles. See "Gamergate (Harassment Campaign)," Wikipedia, last modified August 12, 2023, https://en.wikipedia.org/wiki/Gamergate_(harassment_campaign).

24 *USA Today* quotes Steve Bannon, who took over *Breitbart* News in 2012, describing the rise of the alt-right movement that *Breitbart* helped to galvanize: "You can activate that army. They come in through Gamergate or whatever and then get turned onto politics and Trump." Mike

Snider, "Steve Bannon Learned to Harness Troll Army from 'World of Warcraft,'" *USA To-day*, July 18, 2017, https://www.usatoday.com/story/tech/talkingtech/2017/07/18/steve-bannon-learned-harness-troll-army-world-warcraft/489713001.

25 Emily St. James, "#Gamergate: Here's Why Everybody in the Video Game World Is Fighting," *Vox*, October 13, 2014, https://www.vox.com/2014/9/6/6111065/gamergate-explained-everybody-fighting.

26 Caitlin Dewey, "The Only Guide to Gamergate You Will Ever Need to Read," *Washington Post*, October 14, 2014, https://www.washingtonpost.com/news/the-intersect/wp/2014/10/14/the-only-guide-to-gamergate-you-will-ever-need-to-read.

27 Study methodologies vary but range from 7 to 15 percent for staunchly antivaccine and up to 30 percent for vaccine hesitant. See Timothy B. Gravelle et al., "Estimating the Size of 'Anti-vax' and Vaccine Hesitant Populations in the US, UK, and Canada: Comparative Latent Class Modeling of Vaccine Attitudes," *Human Vaccines & Immunotherapeutics* 18, no. 1 (2022), https://doi.org/10.1080/21645515.2021.2008214; Hannah A. Roberts et al., "To Vax or Not to Vax: Predictors of Anti-vax Attitudes and COVID-19 Vaccine Hesitancy Prior to Widespread Vaccine Availability," *PLoS One* 17, no. 2 (2022), https://doi.org/10.1371/journal.pone.0264019.

28 Sarah Elbeshbishi and Mabinty Quarshie, "Fewer Than 1 in 5 Support 'Defund the Police' Movement, USA TODAY/Ipsos Poll Finds," *USA Today*, March 7, 2021, https://www.usatoday.com/story/news/politics/2021/03/07/usa-today-ipsos-poll-just-18-support-defund-police-movement/4599232001.

29 Political keywords in bios also became more prevalent. A study of keywords in Twitter user bios found that indicators of political identity almost tripled between 2015 and 2018. N. Rogers and J. J. Jones, "Using Twitter Bios to Measure Changes in Self-Identity: Are Americans Defining Themselves More Politically over Time?," *Journal of Social Computing* 2, no. 1 (March 2021): 1–13, https://doi.org/10.23919/JSC.2021.0002.

30 B. J. Bethel, "GamerGate Meme War Shares DNA with Pro–Donald Trump Trolls," *Sydney Morning Herald*, September 14, 2016, https://www.smh.com.au/world/north-america/gamergate-meme-war-shares-dna-with-prodonald-trump-trolls-20160914-grg052.html.

31 Sam Levin, "Millionaire Tells Millennials: If You Want a House, Stop Buying Avocado Toast," *Guardian*, May 15, 2017, https://www.theguardian.com/lifeandstyle/2017/may/15/australian-millionaire-millennials-avocado-toast-house.

32 Renée DiResta, "It's Not Misinformation. It's Amplified Propaganda," *The Atlantic*, October 9, 2021, https://www.theatlantic.com/ideas/archive/2021/10/disinformation-propaganda-amplification-ampliganda/620334.

33 Shahid Buttar (@ShahidForChange), "Why do you think #PelosiMustGo?," Twitter, July 12, 2020, 11:59 a.m., Internet Archive, https://web.archive.org/web/20200712201533/https://twitter.com/ShahidForChange/status/1282389059768213504.

34 Emily Zanotti, "'Pelosi Must Go': Speaker Blasted from the Left over 'Corporate Interests,'" *Daily Wire*, July 14, 2020, https://www.dailywire.com/news/pelosi-must-go-speaker-blasted-from-the-left-over-corporate-interests.

35 Chris Bail, *Breaking the Social Media Prism: How to Make Our Platforms Less Polarizing* (Princeton, NJ: Princeton University Press, 2021), 31–32.

36 Jay Van Bavel and Dominic Packer, *The Power of Us: Harnessing Our Shared Identities for Personal and Collective Success* (New York: Little, Brown Spark, 2021), 29.

37 Robert B. Cialdini, *Influence: Science and Practice*, 5th ed. (1984; reis., Boston: Pearson, 2009), 99.

38 Cass R. Sunstein, "The Law of Group Polarization," *Journal of Political Philosophy* 10, no. 2 (2002): 175–195.

39 Todd Rose, *Collective Illusions: Conformity, Complicity and the Science of Why We Make Bad Decisions* (New York: Hachette, 2022), 39–42.

40 Van Bavel and Packer, *The Power of Us*, 77.

41 Ibid., 170–171.

42 Steve Rathje, Jay J. Van Bavel, and Sander van der Linden, "Out-Group Animosity Drives Engagement on Social Media," *PNAS* 118, no. 26 (2021), https://www.pnas.org/doi/10.1073/pnas.2024292118.

43 Freddie deBoer, "The YIMBYs and Social Capture," *FdB*, Substack, February 27, 2023, https://freddiedeboer.substack.com/p/the-yimby-movement-demonstrates-social.

44 Sandra González-Bailón and Yphtach Lelkes, "Do Social Media Undermine Social Cohesion? A Critical Review," *Social Issues and Policy Review* 17, no. 1 (January 2023): 155–180, https://doi.org/10.1111/sipr.12091.

45 Thanks to Gary Zhexi Zhang for the metaphor.

46 Helen C. Harton, Matthew Gunderson, and Martin J. Bourgeois, "'I'll Be There with You': Social Influence and Cultural Emergence at the Capitol on January 6," *Group Dynamics: Theory, Research, and Practice* 26, no. 3 (2022): 220–238, https://doi.org/10.1037/gdn0000185.

47 Eric Hoffer, *The True Believer: Thoughts on the Nature of Mass Movements* (New York: Perennial Library, 1989), preface.

48 Ibid., 91.

49 Clay Shirky, "A Group Is Its Own Worst Enemy," in *The Best Software Writing I*, ed. Joel Spolsky (Berkeley, CA: Apress, 2005), 183–209, https://doi.org/10.1007/978-1-4302-0038-3_23.

50 J. M. Berger and Jonathon Morgan, "The ISIS Twitter Census: Defining and Describing the Population of ISIS Supporters on Twitter," Brookings, March 5, 2015, https://www.brookings.edu/articles/the-isis-twitter-census-defining-and-describing-the-population-of-isis-supporters-on-twitter.

51 "We consider a particular role to be influential in the spread of information, when a link posted by that role induces an account in another role to post the same link with high probability. We find that for information originating from extremist sources, educators and solicitors are the most influential in triggering other roles to also spread such content. Whereas, motivators influence other roles spreading biased news, flamers are influential in the spread of fake news." See Shruti Phadke and Tanushree Mitra, "Educators, Solicitors, Flamers, Motivators, Sympathizers: Characterizing Roles in Online Extremist Movements," *Proceedings of the ACM on Human-Computer Interaction* 5, no. CSCW2 (2021): 1–35.

52 Hoffer, *The True Believer*, 130–140.

53 Ibid., 114.

54 Jacques Ellul, *Propaganda: The Formation of Men's Attitudes* (New York: Vintage Books, 1973), 29.

55 Tufekci, *Twitter and Tear Gas*, xxiii.

56 Aidan Walker, "What's the Deal with 'Stonks'?," Know Your Meme, 2022, https://knowyourmeme.com/editorials/guides/whats-the-deal-with-stonks.

57 "Elon Musk Charged with Securities Fraud for Misleading Tweets," US Securities and Exchange Commission, September 27, 2018, https://www.sec.gov/news/press-release/2018-219.

58 Allison Morrow, "Elon Musk Tweet Fuels Frenzied GameStop Surge," *CNN Business*, January 28, 2021, https://edition.cnn.com/2021/01/26/investing/gamestop-stock-elon-musk-reddit/index.html.

59 Steve Goldstein, "GameStop Stock Hits as High as $500 in Premarket Action," *MarketWatch*, January 28, 2021, https://www.marketwatch.com/story/gamestop-stock-hits-as-high-as-500-in-premarket-action-2021-01-28.

60 Emily Stewart and Rani Molla, "Robinhood, and Its Role in the GameStop Saga, Explained," *Vox*, January 30, 2021, https://www.vox.com/recode/22254270/robinhood-gamestop-amc-block-wallstreetbets-day-trading.

61 Matt Levine, "The GameStop Game Never Stops," *Bloomberg*, January 25, 2021, https://www.bloomberg.com/opinion/articles/2021-01-25/the-game-never-stops.

62 Robert J. Shiller, *Narrative Economics: How Stories Go Viral and Drive Major Economic Events* (Princeton, NJ: Princeton University Press, 2019), 273–274.

63 DiResta, "It's Not Misinformation."

CHAPTER 5: BUILDING THE BIG LIE

1 Atlantic Council's DFRLab, "#StopTheSteal: Timeline of Social Media and Extremist Activities Leading to 1/6 Insurrection," Just Security, May 18, 2021, https://www.justsecurity.org/74622/stopthesteal-timeline-of-social-media-and-extremist-activities-leading-to-1-6-insurrection.

2 Will Sommer, "How the Ilhan Omar Marriage Smear Went from an Anonymous Post on an Obscure Forum to Being Embraced by Trump," *Daily Beast*, July 19, 2019, https://www.thedaily beast.com/how-the-ilhan-omar-marriage-smear-went-from-an-anonymous-post-on-an-obscure -forum-to-being-embraced-by-trump.

3 Paul Farhi, "John McCain Knew How to Make Journalists Love Him," *Washington Post*, August 27, 2018, https://www.washingtonpost.com/lifestyle/style/john-mccain-knew-how-to-make-journalists -love-him/2018/08/27/9b156f80-a9bc-11e8-8a0c-70b618c98d3c_story.html.

4 Journalism and Media Staff, "McCain vs. Obama on the Web," Pew Research Center's Journal- ism Project, August 18, 2020, https://www.pewresearch.org/journalism/2008/09/15/mccain-vs -obama-on-the-web.

5 Roger Sollenberger, "Right-Wing Trolls Launch Stop the Steal PAC to Cash In on Election Lies," *Salon*, November 18, 2020, https://www.salon.com/2020/11/18/right-wing-trolls-launch-stop -the-steal-pac-to-cash-in-on-election-lies.

6 Rob Kuznia et al., "Stop the Steal's Massive Disinformation Campaign Connected to Roger Stone," *CNN*, November 14, 2020, https://www.cnn.com/2020/11/13/business/stop -the-steal-disinformation-campaign-invs/index.html. Roger Stone is credited with first using the phrase "Stop the Steal" in 2016 in association with the Trump campaign as it anticipated a loss.

7 Zach Sweat, "Field Guide to Political Emojis," Know Your Meme, April 12, 2023, https:// knowyourmeme.com/editorials/guides/field-guide-to-political-emojis.

8 Nick Corasaniti, Sheera Frenkel, and Nicole Perlroth, "App Used to Tabulate Votes Is Said to Have Been Inadequately Tested," *New York Times*, February 4, 2020, https://www.nytimes .com/2020/02/03/us/politics/iowa-caucus-app.html; "Nevada Hopes to Avoid Chaos of Iowa Caucuses as Bloomberg Tries to Recover," *NBC News*, February 21, 2020, https://www.nbcnews .com/politics/2020-election/how-iowa-caucuses-fell-apart-tarnished-vote-n1140346.

9 "Bernie Sanders' Supporters Shouldn't Fall for Republicans' Impeachment Conspiracy," *NBC News*, January 16, 2020, https://www.nbcnews.com/think/opinion/bernie-sanders-supporters -shouldn-t-fall-republicans-impeachment-conspiracy-ncna1116576.

10 Ilhan Omar (@IlhanMN), "This can't be!," Twitter, February 4, 2020, https://twitter.com/IlhanMN /status/1224575334248566784.

11 Renée DiResta, "The Conspiracies Are Coming from Inside the House," *The Atlantic*, March 10, 2020, https://www.theatlantic.com/ideas/archive/2020/03/internet-conspiracies-are-coming -inside-country/607645.

12 "Online Conspiracy Theories Flourish After Iowa Caucus Fiasco," *AP News*, May 1, 2021, https:// apnews.com/article/iowa-elections-lindsey-graham-ia-state-wire-donald-trump-8ae0e5172130f 81265172fbd3e65094a,%20; Ben Nimmo (@ebenimmo), "Looking into Twitter traffic…," Twitter, February 5, 2020, https://twitter.com/benimmo/status/1224832953458614272.

13 Data compiled from the Stanford Internet Observatory, analyzed in DiResta, "The Conspiracies Are Coming from Inside the House"; trend additionally archived at "United States Trends | 04/02/2020," (C) 2022, n.d., https://archive.twitter-trending.com/united-states/04-02-2020.

14 Elizabeth Bruenig (@ebruenig), "Clinton's '16 campaign manager…," Twitter, February 4, 2020, Internet Archive, https://web.archive.org/web/20200205111150/https://twitter.com/ebruenig/status /1224710768546996225.

15 Robby Mook (@RobbyMook), "Sorry, folks…," Twitter, February 4, 2020, Internet Archive, https://web.archive.org/web/20221123092124/https://twitter.com/RobbyMook/status/1224 555538790395904.

16 "Fact-Checking Trump's Claim That Mail-In Ballots Lead to Voter Fraud," *NBC News*, April 10, 2020, https://www.nbcnews.com/politics/donald-trump/trump-pushes-false-claims-about-mail -vote-fraud-here-are-n1180566.

17 "Report: Trump Commission Did Not Find Widespread Voter Fraud," *AP News*, April 20, 2021, https://apnews.com/article/north-america-donald-trump-us-news-ap-top-news-elections -f5f6a73b2af546ee97816bb35e82c18d; Michael Tackett and Michael Wines, "Trump Dis- bands Commission on Voter Fraud," *New York Times*, January 4, 2018, https://www.nytimes .com/2018/01/03/us/politics/trump-voter-fraud-commission.html.

18 "Voters Line Up to Cast Ballot in Wisconsin Primary Despite Coronavirus Risk," *NBC News*, April 10, 2020, https://www.nbcnews.com/politics/2020-election/coronavirus-has-ignited-battle -over-voting-my-mail-here-s-n1178531.

19 Tucker Carlson, "Tom Fitton Explains Why Vote-by-Mail Invites Voter Fraud," *Fox News*, April 10, 2020, https://sports.yahoo.com/tom-fitton-explains-why-vote-010533405.html; Tucker Carlson, "Ex-Nevada AG Describes Ballots 'Piled Up in Apartments and Trash Cans and in Hallways' Due to Mail-In Voting," *Fox News*, May 26, 2020, https://www.foxnews.com /media/nevada-adam-laxalt-mail-in-voting-election-fraud; Newt Gingrich, "Newt Gingrich: Democrats Want to Steal November Election—Here's How," *Fox News*, June 7, 2020, https:// www.foxnews.com/opinion/voter-fraud-newt-gingrich; Paul Steinhauser, "Trump Says Surge in Voting by Mail His 'Biggest Risk,'" *Fox News*, June 19, 2020, https://www.foxnews.com /politics/trump-says-surge-in-voting-by-mail-my-biggest-risk; John Binder, "Court Brief: 23K Dead Registered Voters Could Get Mail-In Ballots in California," *Breitbart*, June 25, 2020, https://www.breitbart.com/politics/2020/06/25/court-brief-23k-dead-registered-voters-could -get-mail-in-ballots-in-california; Julia Musto, "Texas AG Ken Paxton Says There's 'a Lot of Voter Fraud' Involving Mail-In Ballots," *Fox News*, June 27, 2020, https://www.foxnews.com/media /tx-ag-ken-paxton-mail-in-voting-fraud-supreme-court-win; "West Virginia Mail Carrier Ad- mits Attempted Election Fraud, Says It Comes from AP Reporting," *Fox News*, July 12, 2020, https://www.foxnews.com/us/west-virginia-mail-carrier-admits-attempted-election-fraud; Gregg Re, "Mail-In Voting Faces Slew of Issues Nationwide, as Emergency USPS Memo Sounds Alarm," *Fox News*, July 22, 2020, https://www.foxnews.com/politics/mail-in-voting-faces -slew-of-issues-nationwide; John Binder, "*NPR* Analysis: 65,000 Mail-In Votes Thrown Out This Year for Arriving Late," *Breitbart*, July 13, 2020, https://www.breitbart.com/politics/2020/07/13 /npr-analysis-65000-mail-in-votes-thrown-out-this-year-for-arriving-late; John Binder, "Exclusive— Catherine Engelbrecht: Mail-In Voting Is 'Engineered Chaos' to Manipulate 2020 Election," *Breitbart*, July 19, 2020, https://www.breitbart.com/politics/2020/07/19/exclusive-catherine -engelbrecht-mail-voting-engineered-chaos; Charles Creitz, "Tucker Bashes Dems over Claims Trump 'Stealing Mailboxes': They're Making US 'Even More Paranoid and Fearful,'" *Fox News*, August 17, 2020, https://www.foxnews.com/opinion/tucker-bashes-democrats-trump -usps-stealing-mailboxes; John Binder, "Democrat Insider Details Mail-In Voting Fraud Operation: 'This Is a Real Thing,'" *Breitbart*, August 30, 2020, https://www.breitbart.com /politics/2020/08/30/democrat-details-mass-voter-fraud-operation; John Binder, "Fact Check: DNC Falsely Says 'Absolutely Zero Difference Between Voting by Mail and Voting Absentee,'" *Breitbart*, August 20, 2020, https://www.breitbart.com/politics/2020/08/20/fact-check-mail-in -voting-and-absentee-voting-are-not-the-same; "Tucker: Why Silicon Valley Is Doing All It Can to Help the Biden-Harris Ticket," *Fox News*, September 4, 2020, https://www.foxnews.com /transcript/tucker-why-silicon-valley-is-doing-all-it-can-to-help-the-biden-harris-ticket; Talia Kaplan, "Anonymous Democrat Operative's Account of How Election Fraud Is Allegedly Com- mitted Was 'Revealing' and 'Chilling': NY Post Reporter," *Fox News*, September 1, 2020, https:// www.foxnews.com/politics/anonymous-dem-operatives-account-of-how-election-fraud-is -allegedly-committed-was-revealing-and-chilling-ny-post-reporter; John Binder, "Georgia Elec- tion Officials Receive Referrals for Nearly 100 Cases of Voter Fraud," *Breitbart*, September 1, 2020, https://www.breitbart.com/politics/2020/09/13/georgia-election-officials-receive-referrals-100 -cases-voter-fraud; John Binder, "Feds: 19 Non-citizens Charged with Voting in 2016 Election in Swing State," *Breitbart*, September 3, 2020, https://www.breitbart.com/politics/2020/09/03 /feds-19-non-citizens-charged-with-voting-in-2016-election-in-swing-state; Julia Musto, "Mich- igan Gov. Gretchen Whitmer Vetoes 'Fearmongering' Bill Targeting Voter Fraud," *Fox News*, October 17, 2020, https://www.foxnews.com/politics/michigan-governor-gretchen-whitmer -vetoes-bill-targeting-voter-fraud-citing-confusion; Robert Kraychick, "Catherine Engelbrecht: Patriots Must Volunteer Their 'Eyes and Ears' for 'Ballot Security,'" *Breitbart*, October 21, 2020, https://www.breitbart.com/radio/2020/10/21/catherine-engelbrecht-patriots-must-volunteer -their-eyes-and-ears-for-ballot-security; John Binder, "Texas Mayoral Candidate Arrested on 109 Counts of Mail-In Voter Fraud," *Breitbart*, October 8, 2020, https://www.breitbart.com /politics/2020/10/08/texas-mayoral-candidate-arrested-on-109-counts-of-mail-in-voter-fraud.

20 Political scientists have observed a "winner effect" among those on the winning side of an election, in which the positive influence of being on the winning side increases trust, perceptions of fairness, and consent to the outcome of an election. In turn, there appear to be negative effects on attitudes about government among citizens on the losing side, which cause concern about the effects of elections on system legitimacy, though it is not clear that those attitudes endure. Betsy Sinclair, Steven S. Smith, and Patrick D. Tucker, " 'It's Largely a Rigged System': Voter Confidence and the Winner Effect in 2016," *Political Research Quarterly* 71, no. 4 (April 21, 2018): 854–868, https://doi.org/10.1177/1065912918768006.

21 Stephen Collinson, "Why Trump's Talk of a Rigged Vote Is So Dangerous," *CNN Politics*, October 19, 2016, https://edition.cnn.com/2016/10/18/politics/donald-trump-rigged-election/index.html.

22 Jessica Taylor, "Clinton Says She Was 'Right' About 'Vast Russia Conspiracy'; Investigations Ongoing," *NPR*, June 1, 2017, https://www.npr.org/2017/06/01/530941011/clinton-says-she-was-right-about-vast-russia-conspiracy-investigations-ongoing.

23 According to Attorney General William Barr's summary of Robert Mueller's investigation, they "did not find that the Trump campaign or anyone associated with it conspired or coordinated with Russia in its efforts to influence the 2016 U.S. presidential election." Regarding obstruction of justice, the report laid out evidence on both sides without drawing a conclusion, leaving Barr and Deputy Attorney General Rod Rosenstein to conclude, "The evidence developed during the Special Counsel's investigation is not sufficient to establish that the President committed an obstruction-of-justice offense." Trump reacted to this news by declaring on Twitter on March 24, 2019, "No Collusion, No Obstruction, Complete and Total EXONERATION. KEEP AMERICA GREAT!," https://x.com/realDonaldTrump/status/1109918388133023744. Mueller refuted this a few months later in testimony before Congress, saying his investigation did not assess " 'collusion,' which is not a legal term" and that Trump "was not exculpated for the acts that he allegedly committed." Mueller clarified that the investigation "focused on whether the evidence was sufficient to charge any member of the campaign with taking part in a criminal conspiracy. It was not." "Full Transcript: Mueller Testimony Before House Judiciary, Intelligence Committees," *NBC News*, July 25, 2019, https://www.nbcnews.com/politics/congress/full-transcript-robert-mueller-house-committee-testimony-n1033216.

24 "Russian Active Measures Campaigns and Interference in the 2016 U.S. Election: Report," US Senate Select Committee on Intelligence, November 10, 2020, https://www.intelligence.senate.gov/publications/report-select-committee-intelligence-united-states-senate-russian-active-measures.

25 Chris Kahn, "Despite Report Findings, Almost Half of Americans Think Trump Colluded with Russia," *Reuters*, March 27, 2019, https://www.reuters.com/article/us-usa-trump-russia-poll/despite-report-findings-almost-half-of-americans-think-trump-colluded-with-russia-reuters-ipsos-poll-idUSKCN1R72S0.

26 A survey of evolving election integrity policies ahead of the 2020 election can be found in Chapter 6 of the Election Integrity Partnership final report: "The Long Fuse: Misinformation and the 2020 Election," Stanford Digital Repository, March 3, 2021, https://purl.stanford.edu/tr171zs0069.

27 Tessa Lyons, "The Three-Part Recipe for Cleaning up Your News Feed," Meta, May 22, 2018, https://about.fb.com/news/2018/05/inside-feed-reduce-remove-inform.

28 Sheera Frenkel and Mike Isaac, "Inside Facebook's Election 'War Room.'" *New York Times*, September 19, 2018, https://www.nytimes.com/2018/09/19/technology/facebook-election-war-room.html.

29 For example, two right-wing figures, Jacob Wohl and Jack Burkman, were charged in 2020 with telecommunications fraud and intimidating voters after they made tens of thousands of robocalls to minority areas in the Midwest. The calls falsely claimed that if citizens voted by mail, their information would be used for mandatory vaccination programs and given to law enforcement and collection agencies. Christine Hauser, "Two Right-Wing Operatives Plead Guilty in 2020 Robocall Scheme," *New York Times*, October 25, 2022, https://www.nytimes.com/2022/10/25/us/politics/ohio-robocalls-wohl-burkman-guilty.html.

30 For more on "bot armies," see Samuel C. Woolley and Philip N. Howard, eds., *Computational Propaganda: Political Parties, Politicians, and Political Manipulation on Social Media* (Oxford: Oxford University Press, 2018).

31 "Social Media Influencer Douglass Mackey Convicted of Election Interference in 2016 Presidential Race," US Department of Justice, March 31, 2023, https://www.justice.gov/usao-edny/pr/social-media-influencer-douglass-mackey-convicted-election-interference-2016.

32 Colin Moynihan, "Online Troll Named Microchip Tells of Sowing 'Chaos' in 2016 Election," *New York Times*, March 23, 2023, https://www.nytimes.com/2023/03/22/nyregion/douglass-mackey-microchip-hillary-clinton-election.html.

33 Scott Shane and Alan Blinder, "Democrats Faked Online Push to Outlaw Alcohol in Alabama Race," *New York Times*, January 7, 2019, https://www.nytimes.com/2019/01/07/us/politics/alabama-senate-facebook-roy-moore.html.

34 Reporting about the effort also alleged that the company, New Knowledge, had created a ruse involving a network of Russian Twitter accounts that began to follow candidate Roy Moore, generating mainstream media coverage that Russian bots supported him. The CEO disputed the claim. I did not work at the company at the time and learned of these allegations through media coverage. Scott Shane and Alan Blinder, "Secret Experiment in Alabama Senate Race Imitated Russian Tactics," *New York Times*, June 20, 2019, https://www.nytimes.com/2018/12/19/us/alabama-senate-roy-jones-russia.html.

35 Tony Romm and Craig Timberg, "Facebook Suspends Five Accounts, Including That of a Social Media Researcher, for Misleading Tactics in Alabama Election," *Washington Post*, December 22, 2018, https://www.washingtonpost.com/technology/2018/12/22/facebook-suspends-five-accounts-including-social-media-researcher-misleading-tactics-alabama-election.

36 Matt Osborne, "Swinging a US Senate Race in Alabama, Kremlin-Style Isn't Illegal, but It Should Be," *Crooks and Liars*, January 7, 2019, https://crooksandliars.com/2019/01/how-swing-us-senate-race-alabama-kremlin.

37 Isaac Stanley-Becker, "Facebook Bans Marketing Firm Running 'Troll Farm' for Pro-Trump Youth Group," *Washington Post*, October 8, 2020, https://www.washingtonpost.com/technology/2020/10/08/facebook-bans-media-consultancy-running-troll-farm-pro-trump-youth-group.

38 "Analysis of an October 2020 Facebook Takedown Linked to U.S.," Stanford Internet Observatory Cyber Policy Center, October 8, 2020, https://cyber.fsi.stanford.edu/io/news/oct-2020-fb-rally-forge.

39 Priyanjana Bengani, "Hundreds of 'Pink Slime' Local News Outlets Are Distributing Algorithmic Stories and Conservative Talking Points," *Columbia Journalism Review*, December 18, 2019, https://www.cjr.org/tow_center_reports/hundreds-of-pink-slime-local-news-outlets-are-distributing-algorithmic-stories-conservative-talking-points.php.

40 Davey Alba and Jack Nicas, "As Local News Dies, a Pay-for-Play Network Rises in Its Place," *New York Times*, October 20, 2020, https://www.nytimes.com/2020/10/18/technology/timpone-local-news-metric-media.html.

41 Sean Hannity (@seanhannity), "Suspicious! Milwaukee Voting...," Twitter, November 5, 2020, https://twitter.com/seanhannity/status/1324355153185656832.

42 Ethan Duran, "Conservative Backed Website Spread Misleading Claims During Election," *Urban Milwaukee*, November 12, 2020, https://urbanmilwaukee.com/2020/11/12/conservative-backed-website-spread-misleading-claims-during-election.

43 Despite their rhetoric, these sites in fact do moderate.

44 Renée DiResta, "Free Speech Is Not the Same as Free Reach," *Wired*, August 30, 2018, https://www.wired.com/story/free-speech-is-not-the-same-as-free-reach.

45 Jeff Kosseff, "First Amendment Protection for Online Platforms," *Computer Law & Security Review* 35, no. 5 (October 1, 2019): 105340, https://doi.org/10.1016/j.clsr.2019.105340.

46 There have been many assessments by journalists as well as academics discussing the evidence surrounding this persistent theory—for example, Danielle Keats Citron and Mary Ann Franks, "The Internet as a Speech Machine and Other Myths Confounding Section 230 Reform," *University of Chicago Legal Forum* 2020, no. 3 (2020), https://chicagounbound.uchicago.edu/uclf/vol2020/iss1/3; "Despite Cries of Censorship, Conservatives Dominate Social Media," *Politico*,

October 27, 2020, https://www.politico.com/news/2020/10/26/censorship-conservatives-social-media-432643; Siva Vaidhyanathan, "Why Conservatives Allege Big Tech Is Muzzling Them," *The Atlantic*, July 28, 2019, https://www.theatlantic.com/ideas/archive/2019/07/conservatives-pretend-big-tech-biased-against-them/594916; Mathew Ingram, "Republicans Still Convinced Facebook and Twitter Are Biased Against Them," *Columbia Journalism Review*, July 18, 2018, https://www.cjr.org/the_media_today/tech-biased-against-conservatives.php; Nitasha Tiku, "Leaked Audio Reveals Google's Efforts to Woo Conservatives," *Wired*, December 10, 2018, https://www.wired.com/story/leaked-audio-reveals-googles-efforts-woo-conservatives; Nicholas Thompson and Fred Vogelstein, "Inside the Two Years That Shook Facebook—and the World," *Wired*, February 12, 2018, https://www.wired.com/story/inside-facebook-mark-zuckerberg-2-years-of-hell; Paul M. Barrett and J. Grant Sims, "False Accusation: The Unfounded Claim That Social Media Companies Censor Conservatives," New York University, February 2021, https://bhr.stern.nyu.edu/bias-report-release-page. One ongoing challenge with assessing it empirically is that access to data on both moderation and curation algorithms is limited by technology platforms.

47 Ferenc Huszár et al., "Algorithmic Amplification of Politics on Twitter," *PNAS* 119, no. 1 (December 21, 2021): e2025334119, https://doi.org/10.1073/pnas.2025334119.

48 "An Update on Senator Kyl's Review of Potential Anti-conservative Bias," Meta, June 22, 2020, https://about.fb.com/news/2019/08/update-on-potential-anti-conservative-bias; Kerry Flynn, "Facebook Commissioned a Study of Alleged Anti-conservative Bias. Here's What It Found," *CNN Business*, August 20, 2019, https://www.cnn.com/2019/08/20/media/facebook-anti-conservative-bias-report/index.html; Jon Kyl, "Why Conservatives Don't Trust Facebook," *Wall Street Journal*, August 20, 2019, Internet Archive, https://web.archive.org/web/20190820161311/https://www.wsj.com/articles/why-conservatives-dont-trust-facebook-11566309603.

49 Thomas Kaplan and Sarah Almukhtar, "How Trump Is Outspending Every 2020 Democrat on Facebook," *New York Times*, June 11, 2020, https://www.nytimes.com/interactive/2019/05/21/us/politics/trump-2020-facebook-ads.html.

50 Ferenc Huszár et al., "Algorithmic Amplification of Politics on Twitter," *Proceedings of the National Academy of Sciences of the United States of America* 119, no. 1 (December 21, 2021), https://doi.org/10.1073/pnas.2025334119.

51 Reem Nadeem, "Most Americans Think Social Media Sites Censor Political Viewpoints," Pew Research Center: Internet, Science & Tech, August 19, 2020, https://www.pewresearch.org/internet/2020/08/19/most-americans-think-social-media-sites-censor-political-viewpoints.

52 Renée DiResta, "How the Creator Economy Is Incentivizing Propaganda," *NOEMA*, June 7, 2023, https://www.noemamag.com/the-new-media-goliaths.

53 Liam Stack, "Trump Wants Your Tales of Social Media Censorship and Your Contact Info," *New York Times*, May 16, 2019, https://www.nytimes.com/2019/05/15/us/donald-trump-twitter-facebook-youtube.html.

54 Oliver Darcy, "'Circus Show' Summit: Trump Delivers Meandering Speech to His Digital Army of Supporters at the White House," *CNN Business*, July 12, 2019, https://edition.cnn.com/2019/07/11/tech/trump-speech-social-media-summit/index.html.

55 Kirsten Grind and John D. McKinnon, "Facebook, Twitter Turn to Right-Leaning Groups to Help Referee Political Speech," *Wall Street Journal*, January 8, 2019, https://www.wsj.com/articles/facebook-twitter-solicit-outside-groups-often-on-the-right-to-referee-political-speech-11546966779.

56 Craig Silverman and Jane Lytvynenko, "A New Racist Campaign Against Kamala Harris Is Taking Shape," *BuzzFeed*, June 28, 2019, https://www.buzzfeednews.com/article/craigsilverman/kamala-harris-black-citizenship.

57 Ben Schreckinger, "Trump's Culture Warriors Go Home." *Politico*, November/December 2018, https://www.politico.com/magazine/story/2018/10/29/trump-cernovich-milo-yiannopoulos-richard-spencer-alt-right-2018-221916.

58 "Widower Asks Twitter to Delete Trump's Conspiracy Tweets," *NBC News*, May 27, 2020, https://www.nbcnews.com/politics/donald-trump/twitter-fact-checks-trump-s-misleading-tweet-mail-voting-n1215151.

59 Elizabeth Dwoskin, "Twitter Labels Trump's Tweets with a Fact Check for the First Time," *Washington Post*, May 27, 2020, https://www.washingtonpost.com/technology/2020/05/26/trump-twitter-label-fact-check.

60 Donald Trump (@realDonaldTrumpl), "@Twitter is now interfering in the 2020 Presidential Election...," Twitter, May 27, 2020, https://twitter.com/realDonaldTrump/status/1265427538140188676; Donald Trump (@realDonaldTrumpl), "Twitter is completely stifling FREE SPEECH, and I, as President, will not allow it to happen!," Twitter, May 27, 2020, https://twitter.com/realDonaldTrump/status/1265427539008380928.

61 "Executive Order on Preventing Online Censorship," White House, May 28, 2020, https://trumpwhitehouse.archives.gov/presidential-actions/executive-order-preventing-online-censorship.

62 "Remarks by President Trump Announcing an Executive Order on Preventing Online Censorship," White House, May 28, 2020, https://trumpwhitehouse.archives.gov/briefings-statements/remarks-president-trump-announcing-executive-order-preventing-online-censorship.

63 David Shepardson, "Biden Revokes Trump Order That Sought to Limit Social Media Firms' Protections," *Reuters*, May 17, 2021, https://www.reuters.com/technology/biden-revokes-trump-order-that-sought-limit-social-media-firms-protections-2021-05-15.

64 Anne Applebaum, "Democracy Is Surprisingly Easy to Undermine," *Atlantic*, June 17, 2021, https://www.theatlantic.com/ideas/archive/2021/06/trump-fraud-stop-steal-copycats/619226/.

65 Russell Muirhead and Nancy L. Rosenblum, *A Lot of People Are Saying: The New Conpiracism and the Assault on Democracy* (Princeton, NJ: Princeton University Press, 2019), 7–14.

66 Ibid., 34–35, 74.

67 Benkler describes this cycle as an elite-driven mass media disinformation campaign, coming from the top, propagated through Trump's statements, and spread through right-wing supports (communication teams at the White House and for reelection, the Republican National Convention, Republican officials, right-wing media) and through mainstream media coverage. Cable, network, and local TV and news are more important than some people assume—lots of folks get their political info here rather than from online debates. Yet Trump's Twitter handle (@RealDonaldTrump) is "on par with the most influential media sites" and is "the most influential source with a right-wing audience orientation." Trump tweets something, and because he is president, it triggers a wave of coverage across the media ecosystem—including in centrist/mainstream media. The right-wing influencers repeat his claims and develop them; then mainstream media covers this as if it's a fair, partisan debate rather than disinformation. Yochai Benkler et al., "Mail-In Voter Fraud: Anatomy of a Disinformation Campaign," Social Science Research Network, January 1, 2020, https://doi.org/10.2139/ssrn.3703701.

68 "Statement from CISA Director Krebs on Security and Resilience of 2020 Elections," Cybersecurity and Infrastructure Security Agency, October 20, 2020, https://www.cisa.gov/news-events/news/statement-cisa-director-krebs-security-and-resilience-2020-elections.

69 Center for Internet Security, "Reporting Misinformation to the EI-ISAC," US Election Assistance Commission, https://www.eac.gov/sites/default/files/partners/EI_ISAC_Reporting_Misinformation_Sheet102820.pdf.

70 The "Long Fuse" report. See Chapter 1 of the EIP final report, "The Long Fuse," for a full description of outside partnerships and workflows. Online at "The Long Fuse: Misinformation and the 2020 Election," Stanford Digital Repository, March 3, 2021, https://purl.stanford.edu/tr171zs0069.

71 Casey Nelson, "Postal Service Investigating Mail Found in Greenville Ditch," 94.3 Jack FM [Green Bay, WI], September 23, 2020, https://943jackfm.com/2020/09/23/postal-service-investigating-mail-found-in-greenville-ditch.

72 Jim Hoft, "BREAKING: US Mail Found in Ditch in Rural Wisconsin—Included Absentee Ballots," Gateway Pundit, September 23, 2020, Internet Archive, https://web.archive.org/web/20200926103923/https://www.thegatewaypundit.com/2020/09/breaking-us-mail-found-ditch-greenville-wisconsin-included-absentee-ballots.

73 Center for an Informed Public, Digital Forensic Research Lab, Graphika, and Stanford Internet Observatory, "The Long Fuse: Misinformation and the 2020 Election," Stanford Digital Repository: Election Integrity Partnership, March 3, 2021, https://purl.stanford.edu/tr171zs0069.

74 Patrick Marley, "Mail Found in Greenville Ditch Did Not Include Any Wisconsin Ballots," *Milwaukee Journal Sentinel*, October 1, 2020, https://www.jsonline.com/story/news/politics /elections/2020/10/01/mail-found-greenville-ditch-did-not-include-any-wisconsin-ballots /5883960002.

75 E (@ElijahSchaffer), "If you have further evidence that these are legitimate...," Twitter, September 25, 2020, https://twitter.com/ElijahSchaffer/status/1309400335988019201.

76 Jim Hoft, "UPDATED: California Man Finds THOUSANDS of Unopened Ballots in Garbage Dumpster—Workers Quickly Try to Cover Them Up—County Says Returned Ballots from 2018?," *Gateway Pundit*, September 29, 2020, Internet Archive, https://web.archive.org /web/20200925152834/https://www.thegatewaypundit.com/2020/09/exclusive-california-man -finds-thousands-unopened-ballots-garbage-dumpster-workers-quickly-try-cover-photos.

77 Joe Bak-Coleman et al., "Foreign vs Domestic: An Examination of Amplification in a Ballot Misinformation Story," Election Integrity Partnership, June 24, 2022, https://www.eipartnership .net/2020/vast-majority-of-discarded-ballot-amplification-isnt-from-foreign-sources.

78 Angelo Fichera, "Photos of Recycled Election Materials in California Prompt False Claim," Fact Check.org, September 29, 2020, https://www.factcheck.org/2020/09/photos-of-recycled-election -materials-in-california-prompt-false-claim.

79 Hoft, "UPDATED: California Man Finds THOUSANDS."

80 "Two Iranian Nationals Charged for Cyber-enabled Disinformation and Threat Campaign Designed to Influence the 2020 U.S. Presidential Election," US Justice Department, January 25, 2022, https://www.justice.gov/opa/pr/two-iranian-nationals-charged-cyber-enabled-disinformation -and-threat-campaign-designed.

81 Emma S. Spiro and Kate Starbird, "Rumors Have Rules," *Issues in Science and Technology* 39, no. 3 (Spring 2023): 47–49, https://doi.org/10.58875/CXGL5395.

82 Nicholas DiFonzo and Prashant Bordia, "Rumor, Gossip and Urban Legends," *Diogenes* 54, no. 1 (February 1, 2007): 19–35, https://doi.org/10.1177/0392192107073433.

83 "Election Security Rumor vs. Reality," Cybersecurity and Infrastructure Security Agency, n.d., https://www.cisa.gov/rumor-vs-reality#rumor18.

84 One interesting thing about the repetitive pathways we observed in our 2020 analysis of election rumors was that even sensational, blatantly conspiratorial ideas—CIA supercomputers changing votes, MaidenGate, other outlandish-seeming conspiracy theories—appeared to have already gone from something that one might expect to fall under complex contagion (something that might be a reputational concern for the influencer propagating it) and instead moved via simple-contagion pathways, suggesting the presence of an echo chamber. The influencers behaved as if the audience was already receptive even to truly outlandish claims, and indeed there was little sign of pushback to any claim of fraud. In the case of Sharpiegate, for example, the primed audience no longer needed extensive additional confirmation or evidence to believe that deliberate fraud had occurred, and so the narrative did move from the periphery to the influencer, but then was quickly boosted by a series of credentialed, large influencers.

85 Kate Starbird, Renée DiResta, and Matt DeButts, "Influence and Improvisation: Participatory Disinformation During the 2020 US Election," *Social Media and Society* 9, no. 2 (2023): 205630512311779–205630512311779, https://doi.org/10.1177/20563051231177943.

86 Jean-Noel Kapferer, *Rumors: Uses, Interpretation, and Necessity* (London: Routledge, 2013), 69.

87 Brian Slodysko, "How Trump's MAGA Movement Helped a 29-Year-Old Activist Become a Millionaire," *ABC News*, October 10, 2023, https://abcnews.go.com/Politics/wireStory/trumps -maga-movement-helped-29-year-activist-become-103849365.

88 University of Washington research scholar Michael Caulfield has written about this process extensively in a series of case studies on his blog: Michael Caulfield, "Tropes and Networked Digital Activism #1: Trope-Field Fit," *Hapgood*, June 12, 2021, https://hapgood.us/2021/06/12 /participatory-propaganda-tropes-and-trope-field-fit-part-one. For more of Caulfield's work on how tropes and evidence are related, see Charlie Warzel, "'Evidence Maximalism' Is How the Internet Argues Now," *Atlantic*, February 8, 2024, https://www.theatlantic.com/technology/archive /2024/02/evidence-maximalism-conspiracy-theories-taylor-swift/677390/.

89 Natalie Dagenhardt, "Maidengate Scandal Breaks: Democrats Allegedly Registered Women Under Their Previous Names," *Right Journalism*, November 11, 2020, Internet Archive, https://web.archive.org/web/20201111150137/https://www.rightjournalism.com/maidengate-scandal-breaks-democrats-allegedly-registered-women-under-their-previous-names.

90 For an overview of "Sharpiegate" in Maricopa County, see Rachel Leingang and McKenzie Sadeghi, "Fact Check: Arizona Election Departments Confirm Sharpies Can Be Used on Ballots," *USA Today*, November 5, 2020, https://www.usatoday.com/story/news/factcheck/2020/11/04/fact-check-sharpiegate-controversy-arizona-false-claim/6164820002.

91 Ibid.

92 Bill Goodykoontz, "Fox News Correctly Called Arizona for Joe Biden a Year Ago. That Night Changed Everything," *Arizona Republic*, November 3, 2021, https://www.azcentral.com/story/entertainment/media/2021/11/03/fox-news-biden-arizona-call-election-night/8544699002.

93 Meg Warner et al., "Presidential Election Results 2020," *CNN Politics*, November 23, 2020, https://www.cnn.com/politics/live-news/election-results-and-news-11-03-20/index.html.

94 Fox announces that Biden has won Arizona at 11:20 p.m. EST. Trump tweets at 12:45 a.m., "I will be making a statement tonight. A big WIN!" and again around 1:25 a.m., "We are up BIG, but they are trying to STEAL the Election," which Twitter labels shortly after. He spoke just before 2:30 a.m. EST. Christina Wilkie, "Trump Tries to Claim Victory Even as Ballots Are Being Counted in Several States—NBC Has Not Made a Call," *CNBC*, November 6, 2020, https://www.cnbc.com/2020/11/04/trump-tries-to-claim-victory-even-as-ballots-are-being-counted-in-several-states-nbc-has-not-made-a-call.html.

95 David Bauder, Randall Chase, and Geoff Mulvihill, "Fox, Dominion Reach $787.5M Settlement over False Election Claims," *AP News*, April 20, 2023, https://apnews.com/article/fox-news-dominion-lawsuit-trial-trump-2020-0ac71f75acfacc52ea80b3e747fb0afe.

96 Olivia Rubin, "What Fox News Hosts Allegedly Said Privately Versus On-Air About False Election Fraud Claims," *ABC News*, April 24, 2023, https://abcnews.go.com/Politics/fox-news-hosts-allegedly-privately-versus-air-false/story?id=97662551.

97 Center for an Informed Public, Digital Forensic Research Lab, Graphika, and Stanford Internet Observatory, "The Long Fuse: Misinformation and the 2020 Election," Stanford Digital Repository: Election Integrity Partnership, March 3, 2021, https://purl.stanford.edu/tr171zs0069.

98 Joey Garrison and Jessica Guynn, "Facebook Readying 'Break-Glass' Tools to Restrict Content if Violence Erupts After Election," *USA Today*, September 23, 2020, https://www.usatoday.com/story/news/politics/elections/2020/09/22/election-2020-facebook-has-break-glass-measures-if-violence-erupts/5866803002.

99 Jeff Horwitz, *Broken Code: Inside Facebook and the Fight to Expose Its Harmful Secrets* (New York: Knopf Doubleday Publishing Group, 2023), 214.

100 Bauder, Chase, and Mulvihill, "Fox, Dominion Reach $787.5M Settlement."

101 Davey Alba, "No Proof People Stole Maiden Names to Vote," *New York Times*, November 11, 2020, https://www.nytimes.com/2020/11/11/technology/no-proof-maiden-names-vote.html.

102 Lt. Gen. Thomas McInerney, Dennis Montgomery, and Steve Bannon, "What Is THE HAMMER What Is The Scorecard War Room Pandemic Episode 470," November 2, 2020, Internet Archive, https://archive.org/details/what-is-the-hammer-what-is-the-scorecard-war-room-pandemic-episode.

103 Nicole Leaver and Joan Donovan, "Viral Slogan: Hammer and Scorecard," Media Manipulation Casebook, February 10, 2021, https://mediamanipulation.org/case-studies/viral-slogan-hammer-and-scorecard.

104 Emma-Jo Morris and Gabrielle Fonrouge, "Smoking-Gun Email Reveals How Hunter Biden Introduced Ukrainian Businessman to VP Dad," *New York Post*, October 14, 2020, https://nypost.com/2020/10/14/email-reveals-how-hunter-biden-introduced-ukrainian-biz-man-to-dad.

105 Fox News reportedly passed on the story and, interestingly, even the *New York Post* attributed the explosive story to two reporters who may not have been the ones to actually author it. According to two anonymous *Post* employees who spoke with the *New York Times*, the article was written by staff reporter Bruce Golding, who didn't want his byline used because he "had concerns over the article's credibility." Katie Robertson, "*New York Post* Published Hunter Biden

Report amid Newsroom Doubts," *New York Times*, October 18, 2020, https://www.nytimes.com/2020/10/18/business/media/new-york-post-hunter-biden.html.

106 The Hunter Biden laptop story was out of scope for EIP because it didn't relate to voting or election delegitimization—but I found it interesting as an example of two companies taking different moderation approaches to the same incident. I thought Facebook had made the right call by reducing distribution while allowing the story to remain and be shared by users and that Twitter had made the wrong one. The calls were made under the "hacked materials" policy. Blocking the nudes seemed fully reasonable, under the hacked materials policy as well as from an individual privacy standpoint—there is no free speech argument that justifies propagating someone else's leaked private photos—but blocking the sharing of the newspaper URL was the wrong call. Twitter, responding to outcry, reversed the call several hours later.

107 " 'This Will Be Awesome': Musk Leaks Twitter's Hunter Biden Files," *Politico*, December 2, 2022, https://www.politico.com/news/2022/12/02/musk-leak-twitter-hunter-biden-files-00072015.

108 Jessica Bursztynsky, "Twitter CEO Jack Dorsey Says Blocking *New York Post* Story Was 'Wrong,' " *CNBC*, October 16, 2020, https://www.cnbc.com/2020/10/16/twitter-ceo-jack-dorsey-says-blocking-post-story-was-wrong.html.

109 Craig Silverman, Ryan Mac, and Jane Lytvynenko, "How Facebook Failed to Prevent Stop the Steal," *BuzzFeed News*, April 22, 2021, https://www.buzzfeednews.com/article/craigsilverman/facebook-failed-stop-the-steal-insurrection.

110 Jessica Guynn, "Facebook Deploys Emergency Measures to Curb Misinformation as Nation Awaits Election Results," *USA Today*, November 5, 2020, https://www.usatoday.com/story/tech/2020/11/05/facebook-election-misinformation-crackdown-emergency-measures-trump/6182001002; Horwitz, *Broken Code*, 220.

111 Jessica Guynn, "Facebook Shuts Down Pro-Trump 'Stop the Steal' Group over 'Worrying Calls for Violence,' " *Time*, November 5, 2020, https://time.com/5907902/stop-the-steal-facebook-group-trump-election.

112 Ryan Mac, Craig Silverman, and Jane Lytvynenko, "Facebook Stopped Employees from Reading an Internal Report About Its Role in the Insurrection. You Can Read It Here," *BuzzFeed News*, April 26, 2021, https://www.buzzfeednews.com/article/ryanmac/full-facebook-stop-the-steal-internal-report.

113 Mac, Silverman, and Lytvynenko, "Facebook Stopped Employees from Reading an Internal Report."

114 Craig Silverman, Ryan Mac, and Jane Lytvynenko, "Facebook Knows It Was Used to Help Incite the Capitol Insurrection," *BuzzFeed News*, April 21, 2021, https://www.buzzfeednews.com/article/craigsilverman/facebook-failed-stop-the-steal-insurrection.

115 Silverman, Mac, and Lytvynenko, "Facebook Knows It Was Used."

116 Teo Armus, "A 'Stop the Steal' Organizer, Now Banned by Twitter, Said Three GOP Lawmakers Helped Plan His D.C. Rally," *Washington Post*, January 13, 2021, https://www.washingtonpost.com/nation/2021/01/13/ali-alexander-capitol-biggs-gosar/.

117 "How the 'Stop the Steal' Movement Outwitted Facebook Ahead of the Jan. 6 Insurrection," *NPR*, October 22, 2021, https://www.npr.org/2021/10/22/1048543513/facebook-groups-jan-6-insurrection.

118 "View of Repeat Spreaders and Election Delegitimization," *Journal of Quantitative Description: Digital Media* 2 (2022): 1–49, https://journalqd.org/article/view/3137/2635.

119 Top twenty-one spreaders of election misinformation on Twitter: Center for an Informed Public, Digital Forensic Research Lab, Graphika, and Stanford Internet Observatory, "The Long Fuse: Misinformation and the 2020 Election," Stanford Digital Repository: Election Integrity Partnership, March 3, 2021, https://purl.stanford.edu/tr171zs0069.

120 "Project Veritas #BallotHarvesting Amplification," Election Integrity Partnership, September 29, 2020, https://www.eipartnership.net/2020/project-veritas-ballotharvesting.

121 Ian Kennedy et al., "Repeat Spreaders and Election Delegitimization," *Journal of Quantitative Description: Digital Media* 2 (2022), https://doi.org/10.51685/jqd.2022.013.

122 Yochai Benkler, Robert Farris, and Hal Roberts, *Network Propaganda: Manipulation, Disinformation, and Radicalization in American Politics* (Oxford: Oxford University Press, 2018).

123 Renée DiResta, "The Misinformation Campaign Was Distinctly One-Sided," *The Atlantic*, March 15, 2021, https://www.theatlantic.com/ideas/archive/2021/03/right-wing-propagandists -were-doing-something-unique/618267. To understand the dynamics of relative engagement with misinformation news sources across the political spectrum, see Laura Edelson et al., "Understanding Engagement with U.S. (Mis)Information News Sources on Facebook," *ICM '21: Proceedings of the 21st ACM Internet Measurement Conference*, November 2021, 444–463, https:// dl.acm.org/doi/abs/10.1145/3487552.3487859.

124 Benkler et al., "Mail-In Voter Fraud: Anatomy of a Disinformation Campaign," Berkman Klein Center, October 2, 2020, https://cyber.harvard.edu/publication/2020/Mail-in-Voter-Fraud -Disinformation-2020.

125 University of Washington Center for an Informed Public professor Kate Starbird describes the concept of evidence being assembled to fit an existing frame in a February 3, 2021, Usenix Enigma conference talk titled "Online Rumors, Misinformation and Disinformation: The Perfect Storm of Covid-19 and Election2020," https://www.usenix.org/conference/enigma2021 /presentation/starbird.

126 Starbird, DiResta, and DeButts, "Influence and Improvisation."

127 Ryan Quinn, "Conservatives Sue, Investigate Disinformation Researchers," *Inside Higher Ed*, June 23, 2023, https://www.insidehighered.com/news/faculty-issues/research/2023/06/23 /stanford-u-wash-faculty-fought-disinformation-got-sued; Naomi Nix and Joseph Menn, "These Academics Studied Falsehoods Spread by Trump. Now the GOP Wants Answers," *Washington Post*, June 6, 2023, https://www.washingtonpost.com/technology/2023/06/06/disinformation -researchers-congress-jim-jordan.

128 "Addressing False Claims and Misperceptions of the UW Center for an Informed Public's Research," Center for an Informed Public, March 16, 2023, https://www.cip.uw.edu/2023/03/16 /uw-cip-election-integrity-partnership-research-claims.

129 After the election, some Stanford Internet Observatory researchers examined platform moderation of content that we had tracked via the Election Integrity Partnership's Jira ticketing system. See Samantha Bradshaw, Shelby Grossman, and Miles McCain, "An Investigation of Social Media Labeling Decisions Preceding the 2020 U.S. Election," *PloS One* 18, no. 11 (2023): 1–18, https://doi.org/10.1371/journal.pone.0289683.

130 "Summary of Investigative Findings," *Tech Policy Press*, n.d., accessed September 3, 2023, https://techpolicy.press/wp-content/uploads/2023/01/J6-Committee-Draft-Social-Media -Report-TPP.pdf.

131 "Far-Right Influencer Known as 'Baked Alaska' Sentenced over Capitol Attack," *The Guardian*, January 10, 2023, https://www.theguardian.com/us-news/2023/jan/10/baked-alaska-anthime -gionet-sentenced-capitol-attack.

132 Craig Timberg, "Gallows or Guillotines? The Chilling Debate on TheDonald.win Before the Capitol Siege," *Washington Post*, April 15, 2021, https://www.washingtonpost.com/technology /2021/04/15/thedonald-capitol-attack-advance-democracy.

133 Jonathan A. Greenblatt, "No One Is Born an Extremist. Jan. 6 Shows Virtually Anyone Can Be Swept Up by Hate Groups," *USA Today*, January 6, 2022, https://www.usatoday.com/story /opinion/2022/01/06/january-6-hate-groups-adl-research/8995472002.

134 Cass Sunstein, *Going to Extremes: How Like Minds Unite and Divide* (Oxford: Oxford University Press, 2009).

135 Zicheng Cheng, Hugo Marcos-Marne, and Homero Gil de Zúñiga, "Birds of a Feather Get Angrier Together: Social Media News Use and Social Media Political Homophily as Antecedents of Political Anger," *Political Behavior*, March 6, 2023, https://doi.org/10.1007/s11109-023-09864-z.

136 Lyn Van Swol, Sangwon Lee, and Rachel Hutchins, "The Banality of Extremism: The Role of Group Dynamics and Communication of Norms in Polarization on January 6," *Group Dynamics: Theory, Research and Practice* 26, no. 3 (2022): 239–251, https://doi.org/10.1037/gdn0000180.

137 As Van Swol, Lee, and Hutchins put it, "The fact that participants posted themselves on social media participating in the attack, without consideration of the consequences, suggests just how embedded they were in the norms of their network and isolated from dissent" (ibid.).

138 See P. B. Paulus and J. B. Kenworthy, "The Crowd Dynamics and Collective Stupidity of the January 6 Riot: Theoretical Analyses and Prescriptions for a Collectively Wiser Future," *Group Dynamics: Theory, Research, and Practice* 26, no. 3 (2022): 199–219, https://doi.org/10.1037 /gdn0000184: "Even with a limited security force, the crowd did not surge through the police lines until some crowd members (apparently instigated by certain crowd elements such as the Proud Boys and the Oath Keepers) were able to breach the police lines with little consequence. The restriction of movement of crowd members on the Capitol grounds was thus disinhibited due to the lack of serious consequences. Contagion and imitation followed." Paulus and Kenworthy examined the multifaceted psychological dynamics of mobilization in depth: "The crowd members were mobilized for action by both the social media process and the rally speakers to go to the Capitol to protest the election and demand a reassessment of the outcome. At that point, social control factors become the key elements that determine the outcome of the collective movement or action. Respected leaders inside and outside of the collective, the press, and clear messages from security elements or officials about the appropriate and inappropriate collective actions and consequences for violations can help minimize the potential for violent and destructive actions. An important factor in the occurrence of a hostile outburst is leadership. The leadership may be unintentional when the individual behaviors of some group members lead others to follow. In the case of the breaching of the police lines, the simple act of some in the crowd breaking through the lines may have led others to follow."

139 Maria Polletta and Andrew Oxford, "Arizona GOP Asks Followers If They're Willing to Die in Effort to Overturn Election Results," *AZ Central*, December 8, 2020, https://www.azcentral.com /story/news/politics/elections/2020/12/08/arizona-republican-party-asks-if-followers-die -election-president-donald-trump/6488952002/.

140 Zachary Petrizzo, "'Stop the Steal' Leader Threatens 'Something Bad' Might Happen to D.C. Hotel After It Closes Doors to MAGA March," *Daily Dot*, December 29, 2020, https://www .dailydot.com/debug/stop-the-steal-something-bad-hotel-harrington.

141 Daniel Lippman, "Facebook Bans Stop the Steal Organizer Ali Alexander," *Politico*. January 12, 2021, https://www.politico.com/news/2021/01/12/facebook-bans-stop-the-steal-organizer-ali -alexander-458267.

142 Will Sommer, "'Stop the Steal' Organizer in Hiding After Denying Blame for Riot," *Daily Beast*, January 10, 2021, https://www.thedailybeast.com/stop-the-steal-organizer-in-hiding-after-denying -blame-for-riot.

143 Sommer, "'Stop the Steal' Organizer in Hiding."

144 Derek Hawkins, Sarah Ellison, and Blair Guild, "What Tucker Carlson Said About Trump in Private Texts vs. on Fox News," *Washington Post*, March 9, 2023, https://www.washingtonpost .com/media/2023/03/09/tucker-carlson-trump-texts-fox-news.

145 Brian Fung, "Parler Has Now Been Booted by Amazon, Apple and Google," *CNN Business*, January 9, 2021, https://www.cnn.com/2021/01/09/tech/parler-suspended-apple-app-store/index.html.

146 Alexander posted this to his Telegram channel on October 30, 2022, following the election; the post can be found at https://t.me/alialexander/5435.

147 "Post-election Lawsuits Related to the 2020 U.S. Presidential Election," Wikipedia, November 28, 2022, https://en.wikipedia.org/wiki/Post-election_lawsuits_related_to_the_2020_U.S ._presidential_election.

148 Jennifer Agiest and Ariel Edwards-Levy, "CNN Poll: Most Republicans Care More About Picking a 2024 GOP Nominee Who Agrees with Them on Issues Than One Who Can Beat Biden," *CNN Politics*, March 14, 2023, https://edition.cnn.com/2023/03/14/politics/cnn-poll-republicans -2024-nominee/index.html.

149 Ryan Quinn, "Conservatives Sue, Investigate Disinformation Researchers," *Inside Higher Ed*, June 23, 2023, https://www.insidehighered.com/news/faculty-issues/research/2023/06/23 /stanford-u-wash-faculty-fought-disinformation-got-sued; Nix and Menn, "These Academics Studied Falsehoods Spread by Trump."

150 "Addressing False Claims and Misperceptions of the UW Center for an Informed Public's Research," Center for an Informed Public, March 16, 2023, https://www.cip.uw.edu/2023/03/16 /uw-cip-election-integrity-partnership-research-claims.

CHAPTER 6: AGENTS OF INFLUENCE

1 Matt Kodama, "#ColumbianChemicals Hoax: Trolling the Gulf Coast for Deceptive Patterns," *Recorded Future* blog, June 12, 2015, https://www.recordedfuture.com/blog/columbianchemicals-hoax-analysis.

2 Adrian Chen, "The Agency," *New York Times*, June 2, 2015, https://www.nytimes.com/2015/06/07/magazine/the-agency.html.

3 John Borthwick, "Media Hacking," *Medium*, March 7, 2015, https://render.betaworks.com/media-hacking-3b1e350d619c.

4 Kodama, "#ColumbianChemicals Hoax."

5 Borthwick, "Media Hacking."

6 Chen, "The Agency."

7 Haley Ott, Kerry Breen, and Duarte Dias, "What Is the Wagner Group, and Who Is Yevgeny Prigozhin? What to Know About the Russian Private Military Company," *CBS News*, August 24, 2023, https://www.cbsnews.com/news/wagner-group-who-is-yevgeny-prigozhin-russia-mercenary-private-military-company.

8 Associated Press, "A Russian Businessman Linked to Putin Admits to U.S. Election Meddling," *NPR*, November 7, 2022, https://www.npr.org/2022/11/07/1134878028/yevgeny-prigozhin-russia-election-interference-putin.

9 "Amid Infighting Among Putin's Lieutenants, Head of Mercenary Force Appears to Take a Step Too Far," *AP News*, June 23, 2023, https://apnews.com/article/putin-russia-ukraine-war-prigozhin-infighting-0e051f0a43522f57ef1810a8b03f6e62.

10 Patrick Smith, "Prigozhin Dismissed Security Fears Days Before Plane Crash, Video Appears to Show," *NBC News*, August 31, 2023, https://www.nbcnews.com/news/world/prigozhin-dismissed-security-fears-days-plane-crash-video-appears-show-rcna102699.

11 Nicholas J. Cull, "Master of American Propaganda: How George Creel Sold the Great War to America, and America to the World," *PBS*, accessed September 7, 2023, https://www.pbs.org/wgbh/americanexperience/features/the-great-war-master-of-american-propaganda. Bernays worked alongside award-winning storytellers, artists, and advertisers, as well as national celebrities and around seventy-five thousand local citizens, who were prepped with pro-war talking points to deliver in presentations at community centers.

12 Thomas Rid, *Active Measures: The Secret History of Disinformation and Political Warfare* (London: Profile Books Ltd., 2020).

13 Jacques Ellul, *Propaganda: The Formation of Men's Attitudes* (New York: Vintage Books, 1973).

14 Renée DiResta and Joshua Goldstein, "Full-Spectrum Propaganda in the Social Media Era," working paper currently under review. Available at http://reneediresta.com/fullspectrumpropaganda.pdf.

15 Philip N. Howard, "Why Governments Use Broadcast TV and Dissidents Use Twitter," *The Atlantic*, June 14, 2013, https://www.theatlantic.com/international/archive/2013/06/why-governments-use-broadcast-tv-and-dissidents-use-twitter/276896.

16 In their study of the Tahrir Square protests, Zeynep Tufekci and Christopher Wilson found that Facebook and other social media platforms were critical to driving protest participation and spreading information that was not controlled by politicians. Zeynep Tufekci and Christopher Wilson, "Social Media and the Decision to Participate in Political Protest: Observations from Tahrir Square," *Journal of Communication* 62, no. 2 (March 6, 2012): 363–379, https://doi.org/10.1111/j.1460-2466.2012.01629.

17 David Patrikarakos, *War in 140 Characters: How Social Media Is Reshaping Conflict in the Twenty-First Century* (New York: Basic Books, 2017).

18 For more on the concept of computational propaganda, see Samuel C. Woolley and Philip N. Howard, eds., *Computational Propaganda: Political Parties, Politicians, and Political Manipulation on Social Media* (New York: Oxford University Press, 2019).

19 Julian E. Barnes and Sheera Frenkel, "Pentagon Orders Review of Its Overseas Social Media Campaigns," *New York Times*, September 19, 2022, https://www.nytimes.com/2022/09/19/us/politics/pentagon-social-media.html.

20 Niko Vorobyov, "Meduza Editor: 'Russia's State Media Is Terrifyingly Effective,'" *Aljazeera*, April 7, 2022, https://www.aljazeera.com/news/2022/4/7/meduza-editor-kovalyov-there-is-no-media -landscape-in-russia.

21 "About," Facebook, September 2, 2009, https://www.facebook.com/cctvcom/about_profile _transparency.

22 Renée DiResta and John Perrino, "U.S. Influence Operations: The Military's Resurrected Digital Campaign for Hearts and Minds," *Lawfare*, October 11, 2022, https://www.lawfaremedia .org/article/us-influence-operations-militarys-resurrected-digital-campaign-hearts-and-minds.

23 Michael J. Waller, "Putin Propaganda Picks Up Ex-Pentagon Contractors," February 11, 2016, Internet Archive, https://web.archive.org/web/20160317024555/http://aminewswire.com/stories /510662541-putin-propaganda-picks-up-ex-pentagon-contractors.

24 Graphika and Stanford Internet Observatory, "Unheard Voice," *Graphika*, August 24, 2022, https://graphika.com/reports/unheard-voice.

25 Lizzie Dearden, "Isis Using Kittens and Honey Bees in Bid to Soften Image in Dabiq Propaganda Magazine," *The Independent*, August 2, 2016, https://www.independent.co.uk/news /world/middle-east/isis-kittens-honey-bees-dabiq-propaganda-recruits-photo-soften-image-terror -a7168586.html.

26 A term originating with anarchists of the First International to refer to a propaganda strategy in which an atrocity is committed to raise awareness of a group and its mission—specifically, to incite a revolution. Constance Bantman, "Introduction," in *The French Anarchists in London: Exile and Transnationalism in the First Globalisation* (Liverpool, UK: Liverpool University Press, 2013), 1–12.

27 J. M. Berger, "The Evolution of Terrorist Propaganda: The Paris Attack and Social Media," Brookings, January 27, 2015, https://www.brookings.edu/articles/the-evolution-of-terrorist -propaganda-the-paris-attack-and-social-media.

28 J. M. Berger and Jonathon Morgan, "The ISIS Twitter Census: Defining and Describing the Population of ISIS Supporters on Twitter," Brookings, March 2015, https://www.brookings.edu /wp-content/uploads/2016/06/isis_twitter_census_berger_morgan.pdf; "Combating Violent Extremism," *Twitter Blog*, February 5, 2016, https://blog.twitter.com/official/en_us/a/2016/combating -violent-extremism.html.

29 Jenna McLaughlin, "Twitter Is Not at War with ISIS. Here's Why," *Mother Jones*, November 18, 2014, https://www.motherjones.com/politics/2014/11/twitter-isis-war-ban-speech.

30 Julia Greenberg, "Why Facebook and Twitter Can't Just Wipe Out ISIS Online," *Wired*, November 21, 2015, https://www.wired.com/2015/11/facebook-and-twitter-face-tough-choices-as -isis-exploits-social-media.

31 Caleb Garling, "Twitter C.E.O. Dick Costolo on Receiving Death Threats from ISIS," *Vanity Fair*, October 9, 2014, https://www.vanityfair.com/news/tech/2014/10/twitter-ceo-death-threats-isis.

32 Tobias Salinger, "ISIS Supporters Celebrate Paris Attacks on Twitter with Hateful Hashtag 'Paris Is Burning': Reports," *New York Daily News*, November 14, 2015, https://www.nydailynews .com/2015/11/14/isis-supporters-celebrate-paris-attacks-on-twitter-with-hateful-hashtag-paris -is-burning-reports.

33 Nabeelah Jaffer, "The Secret World of Isis Brides: 'U Dnt Hav 2 Pay 4 ANYTHING If u r Wife of a Martyr,'" *The Guardian*, June 24, 2015, https://www.theguardian.com/world/2015/jun/24 /isis-brides-secret-world-jihad-western-women-syria.

34 Rita Katz, "The State Department's Twitter War with ISIS Is Embarrassing," *Time*, September 16, 2014, https://time.com/3387065/isis-twitter-war-state-department.

35 This campaign of the Center for Strategic Counterterrorism Communications began at the end of 2013, with an affiliated YouTube channel and Facebook page launching in summer of 2014. Alberto M. Fernandez, "Here to Stay and Growing: Combating ISIS Propaganda Networks," Brookings, October 2015, https://www.brookings.edu/wp-content/uploads/2016/06/is-propaganda _web_english.pdf.

36 Jeff Giesea, "It's Time to Embrace Memetic Warfare," *Defence Strategic Communications* 1, no. 1 (March 1, 2016): 67–75, https://doi.org/10.30966/2018.riga.1.4.

37 Berger, "The Evolution of Terrorist Propaganda."

38 DiResta and Goldstein, "Full-Spectrum Propaganda in the Social Media Era."

39 Marc Wortman, "The Fake British Radio Show That Helped Defeat the Nazis," *Smithsonian Magazine,* February 28, 2017, https://www.smithsonianmag.com/history/fake-british-radio-show-helped-defeat-nazis-180962320.

40 Ibid.

41 Rid, *Active Measures,* 12.

42 US Department of State, *Active Measures: A Report on the Substance and Process of Anti-U.S. Disinformation and Propaganda Campaigns,* Institute of World Politics, August 1986, https://www.iwp.edu/wp-content/uploads/2019/05/Soviet-Active-Measures-Substance-and-Process-of-Anti-US-Disinformation-August-1986.pdf.

43 Peter Steiner, "Nobody Knows You're a Dog" [cartoon], *New Yorker,* July 1993.

44 The Senate Intelligence Committee bipartisan leadership jointly invited several researchers to pull together teams and examine the data sets. We were each unaware of the composition of other teams, to ensure that the work was done independently in light of the sensitive political nature of the election-related aspect of the material. The work was not a paid consulting engagement but rather a technical advisory relationship. The findings of the reports subsequently informed the Senate Intelligence Committee's own four-part report investigating Russian interference into the 2016 election. The announcement of our work can be at "New Reports Shed Light on Internet Research Agency's Social Media Tactics," US Senate Select Committee on Intelligence, December 17, 2018, https://www.intelligence.senate.gov/press/new-reports-shed-light-internet-research-agency%E2%80%99s-social-media-tactics. For the second volume of the report, in which the majority of it appears, see "Report of the Select Committee on Intelligence, United States Senate, on Russian Active Measures Campaigns and Interference in the 2016 U.S. Election, Volume 2: Russia's Use of Social Media with Additional Views," US Senate Select Committee on Intelligence, https://www.intelligence.senate.gov/sites/default/files/documents/Report_Volume2.pdf.

45 The cooking forum poster, "Alice Norton," an "assistant cook" whose profile said she lived in New York, claimed her family had been poisoned by the turkey and her son was hospitalized. This message reached Twitter within a few hours, via nearly one hundred IRA-affiliated Twitter accounts that linked to the post and to a Wikipedia page that had just been created, called "2015 New York Poisoned Turkey Incident." Wikipedia volunteers quickly took the page down for violating policies, but that same day a news story was posted on the domain ProudtobeBlack.com, a URL registered only a month prior, claiming that two hundred New Yorkers were hospitalized due to poisoned Walmart turkey supplied by Koch's Farm and that their tip came through "our trusted sources in NYPD." The claims were investigated by the Department of Health and Mental Hygiene, which had no records of any food poisoning episodes, and an executive at Koch Turkey Farm explained that they don't even sell turkeys to Walmart. Rob Barry, "Russian Trolls Tweeted Disinformation Long Before U.S. Election," *Wall Street Journal,* February 20, 2018, https://www.wsj.com/graphics/russian-trolls-tweeted-disinformation-long-before-u-s-election.

46 Darren L. Linvill and Patrick L. Warren, "Troll Factories: Manufacturing Specialized Disinformation on Twitter," *Political Communication* 37, no. 4 (February 5, 2020): 447–67, https://doi.org/10.1080/10584609.2020.1718257.

47 Deen Freelon et al., "Black Trolls Matter: Racial and Ideological Asymmetries in Social Media Disinformation," *Social Science Computer Review* 40, no. 3 (April 7, 2020): 560–578, https://doi.org/10.1177/0894439320914853.

48 Black women, frequent targets of online trolling, had begun to talk about accounts that attempted to manipulate the Black community, particularly around the time of Gamergate. They used the hashtag *#YourSlipIsShowing* to call attention to provocateurs that they suspected to be racist trolls from 4chan (later 8chan); subsequent research into IRA data suggested that some of the activity was additionally boosted, and joined, by Russian trolls who took advantage of real racial tension and shifting norms around online harassment. See, for example, comments by analyst Shireen Mitchell in this *New York Times* analysis of Russian troll messaging around the Women's March: Ellen Berry, "How Russian Trolls Helped Keep the Women's March Out of Lock Step," *New York Times,* September 18, 2022, https://www.nytimes.com/2022/09/18/us/womens-march-russia-trump.html; for coverage of online impersonation strategies targeting

Black women, see Morgan Jerkins, "Black or Bot? The Long, Sordid History of Co-opting Blackness Online," *Mother Jones*, September-October 2022, https://www.motherjones.com/media/2022/09/disinformation-russia-trolls-bots-black-culture-blackness-ukraine-twitter.

49 Renée DiResta et al., "The Tactics and Tropes of the Internet Research Agency," *U.S. Senate Documents*, October 2019, https://digitalcommons.unl.edu/senatedocs/2.

50 Ben Popken, "Russian Trolls Duped Global Media and Nearly 40 Celebrities," *NBC News*, November 3, 2017, https://www.nbcnews.com/tech/social-media/trump-other-politicians-celebs-shared-boosted-russian-troll-tweets-n817036.

51 Digital Forensic Research lab investigation into the troll account @TEN_GOP: Ben Nimmo, "How a Russian Troll Fooled America," *Medium*, November 14, 2017, https://medium.com/dfrlab/how-a-russian-troll-fooled-america-80452a4806d1.

52 DiResta et al., "The Tactics and Tropes of the Internet Research Agency."

53 Ibid.

54 Punctuation is presented as in the original content; it is not mistyped.

55 Chris Joyner, "Watchdog: Russian Trolls Meddled at Stone Mountain Protests," *Atlanta Journal-Constitution*, March 15, 2018, https://www.ajc.com/news/state--regional-govt--politics/watchdog-russian-trolls-meddled-stone-mountain-protests/SQMhxrKgxVbsQ2ISIbyukN.

56 Todd J. Gillman, "Russian Trolls Orchestrated 2016 Clash at Houston Islamic Center, New Senate Intel Report Recalls," *Dallas Morning News*, October 8, 2019, https://www.dallasnews.com/news/politics/2019/10/08/russian-trolls-orchestrated-2016-clash-houston-islamic-center-senate-intel-report-says.

57 Renée DiResta, Shelby Grossman, and Alexandra Siegel, "In-House vs. Outsourced Trolls: How Digital Mercenaries Shape State Influence Strategies," *Political Communication* 39, no. 2 (2022): 222–253, https://doi.org/10.1080/10584609.2021.1994065.

58 "Heart of Texas" Facebook page post from February 2, 2016. It received 822 likes, 242 shares, and 509 comments.

59 DiResta and Goldstein, "Full-Spectrum Propaganda in the Social Media Era"; S. Bradshaw and P. Howard, "Troops, Trolls and Troublemakers: A Global Inventory of Organized Social Media Manipulation," Working Paper no. 2017.12, Computational Propaganda Research Project, 2017, https://ora.ox.ac.uk/objects/uuid:cef7e8d9-27bf-4ea5-9fd6-855209b3e1f6.

60 Catherine Bennette, "The Pro-Russian Propaganda Hiding in Your TikTok Feed," *The Observers*, January 10, 2021, https://observers.france24.com/en/tv-shows/truth-or-fake/20211001-the-pro-russian-propaganda-hiding-in-your-tiktok-feed.

61 Gary King, Jennifer Pan, and Margaret E. Roberts, "How the Chinese Government Fabricates Social Media Posts for Strategic Distraction, Not Engaged Argument," *American Political Science Review* 111, no. 3 (2017): 484–501, https://doi.org/10.1017/S0003055417000144.

62 Ben Nimmo, "How MH17 Gave Birth to the Modern Russian Spin Machine," *Foreign Policy*, September 29, 2016, https://foreignpolicy.com/2016/09/29/how-mh17-gave-birth-to-the-modern-russian-spin-machine-putin-ukraine.

63 Joel Gunter and Olga Robinson, "Sergei Skripal and the Russian Disinformation Game," *BBC*, September 9, 2018, https://www.bbc.com/news/world-europe-45454142; Joby Warrick and Anton Troianovski, "How a Powerful Russian Propaganda Machine Chips Away at Western Notions of Truth," *Washington Post*, December 10, 2018, https://www.washingtonpost.com/graphics/2018/world/national-security/russian-propaganda-skripal-salisbury.

64 Shelby Grossman et al., "Blame It on Iran, Qatar, and Turkey: An Analysis of a Twitter and Facebook Operation Linked to Egypt, the UAE, and Saudi Arabia," Stanford Internet Observatory, April 2, 2020, https://fsi-live.s3.us-west-1.amazonaws.com/s3fs-public/20200402_blame_it_on_iran_qatar_and_turkey_v2_0.pdf.

65 Hadeel Al Sayegh, "Saudi's Kingdom Holding Company to Maintain Twitter Stake," *Reuters*, October 28, 2022, https://www.reuters.com/markets/deals/saudis-kingdom-holding-company-maintain-twitter-stake-2022-10-28.

66 Katie Benner et al., "Saudis' Image Makers: A Troll Army and a Twitter Insider," *New York Times*, October 20, 2018, https://www.nytimes.com/2018/10/20/us/politics/saudi-image-campaign-twitter.html; Kevin Collier, "Former Twitter Employee Sentenced to More Than Three Years in Prison

for Spying for Saudi Arabia," *NBC News*, December 14, 2022, https://www.nbcnews.com/tech/security/former-twitter-employee-sentenced-three-years-prison-spying-saudi-arab-rcna61384.

67   For example, the Russian newspaper *RIA FAN*, owned by Yevgeny Prigozhin, for quite some time was publishing articles that quoted fake people—troll accounts offering "man-on-the-street" commentary—run by other entities tied to Prigozhin. This embedding of inauthentic accounts became something of a lead-generation tool for the discovery of new networks of troll accounts. Renée DiResta et al., "In Bed with Embeds: How a Network Tied to IRA Operations Created Fake 'Man on the Street' Content Embedded in News Articles," Stanford Internet Observatory Cyber Policy Center, December 2, 2021, https://cyber.fsi.stanford.edu/io/publication/bed-embeds.

68   This is the title of Pomerantsev's 2014 memoir about his time in Russia: Peter Pomerantsev, *Nothing Is True and Everything Is Possible: The Surreal Heart of the New Russia* (New York: Public Affairs, 2014).

69   Ryan Ho Kilpatrick, "'An Eye For an Eye': Hong Kong Protests Get Figurehead in Woman Injured by Police," *The Guardian*, August 16, 2019, https://www.theguardian.com/world/2019/aug/16/an-eye-for-an-eye-hong-kong-protests-get-figurehead-in-woman-injured-by-police.

70   Renée DiResta et al., "Telling China's Story: The Chinese Communist Party's Campaign to Shape Global Narratives," Stanford Internet Observatory, July 20, 2020, https://fsi.stanford.edu/publication/telling-chinas-story.

71   Jessica Brandt and Bret Schafer, "How China's 'Wolf Warrior' Diplomats Use and Abuse Twitter," Brookings, October 28, 2020, https://www.brookings.edu/articles/how-chinas-wolf-warrior-diplomats-use-and-abuse-twitter.

72   Erika Kinetz, "Army of Fake Fans Boosts China's Wolf Warriors on Social Media," *Sydney Morning Herald*, May 13, 2021, https://www.smh.com.au/world/asia/army-of-fake-fans-boosts-china-s-wolf-warriors-on-social-media-20210513-p57rfo.html.

73   A passage in the book *LikeWar* summarizes the phenomenon of dubious followers on Chinese state media accounts: "In 2016, internet users had a collective chuckle when People's Daily, the main Chinese propaganda outlet, launched a Facebook page that swiftly attracted 18 million 'likes,' despite Facebook being banned in China. This included more than a million 'fans' in Myanmar (out of the then 7 million Facebook users in that country), who instantly decided to 'like' China." A high follower count is perceived as a way to establish credibility by signaling to potential readers that the content has many other existing readers, which is required for making a dent in the crowded social media ecosystem. P. W. Singer and Emerson T. Brooking, *LikeWar: The Weaponization of Social Media* (Boston: Eamon Dolan/Houghton Mifflin Harcourt, 2018), 139.

74   Renée DiResta, Josh A. Goldstein, and Shelby Grossman, "Middle East Influence Operations: Observations Across Social Media Takedowns," Project on Middle East Political Science, August 2021, https://pomeps.org/middle-east-influence-operations-observations-across-social-media-takedowns.

75   Nicolas Six, "TikTok Used to Promote Russian Mercenary Group Wagner," *Le Monde*, December 1, 2022, https://www.lemonde.fr/en/pixels/article/2022/12/01/tiktok-used-to-promote-russian-mercenary-group-wagner_6006282_13.html.

76   Morgan Meaker, "How Ukraine Is Winning the Propaganda War," *Wired*, May 13, 2022, https://www.wired.co.uk/article/ukraine-propaganda-war.

77   Valerie Hopkins, "In Video a Defiant Zelensky Says, 'We Are Here,'" *New York Times*, February 25, 2022, https://www.nytimes.com/2022/02/25/world/europe/zelensky-speech-video.html.

78   Steve Inskeep and Odette Yousef, "Russia Claims U.S. Labs Across Ukraine Are Secretly Developing Biological Weapons," *NPR*, March 22, 2022, https://www.npr.org/2022/03/22/1087991730/russia-claims-u-s-labs-across-ukraine-are-secretly-developing-biological-weapons.

79   Feng Qingyin, "US Owes World an Explanation on Bio-Labs," *Global Times*, March 10, 2022, https://www.globaltimes.cn/page/202203/1254588.shtml.

80   Hua Chunying (@SpokespersonCHN), "US' Bio-Web," Twitter, March 17, 2022, 3:25 a.m., https://twitter.com/SpokespersonCHN/status/1504358120461635587?s=20.

81   Deng Zijun, "What Is the US Hiding in the Biolabs Discovered in Ukraine?," *Global Times*, March 17, 2022, https://www.globaltimes.cn/page/202203/1255164.shtml.

82 Linda Qiu, "Theory About U.S.-Funded Bioweapons Labs in Ukraine Is Unfounded," *New York Times*, March 11, 2022, https://www.nytimes.com/2022/03/11/us/politics/us-bioweapons -ukraine-misinformation.html.

83 Mara Hvistendahl and Alexey Kovalev, "Hacked Russian Files Reveal Propaganda Agreement with China," *The Intercept*, December 30, 2022, https://theintercept.com/2022/12/30 /russia-china-news-media-agreement.

84 Zeba Siddiqui and Christopher Bing, "Latin American Election Influence Operation Linked to Miami Marketing Firm," *Reuters*, May 4, 2023, https://www.reuters.com/world/americas /latin-american-election-influence-operation-linked-miami-marketing-firm-2023-05-04.

85 News Wires, "Israeli Firm 'Boasted' of Meddling in More Than 30 Elections Worldwide," *France 24*, January 15, 2023, https://www.france24.com/en/technology/20230215-israeli-firm-boasted -of-meddling-in-more-than-30-elections-worldwide.

86 Maurice Jakesch et al., "Trend Alert: A Cross-Platform Organization Manipulated Twitter Trends in the Indian General Election," *Proceedings of the ACM on Human-Computer Interaction* 5, no. CSCW2 (October 18, 2021): 1–19, https://doi.org/10.1145/3479523.

87 Pranav Dixit, "Modi's Political Party Creates Abusive Social Media Campaigns and Breeds Internet Trolls, Claims New Book," *BuzzFeed News*, December 27, 2016, https://www.buzzfeednews .com/article/pranavdixit/bjp-trolled-indians; Karnika Kohli, "Congress vs BJP: The Curious Case of Trolls and Politics," *Times of India*, October 11, 2013, https://timesofindia.indiatimes .com/india/congress-vs-bjp-the-curious-case-of-trolls-and-politics/articleshow/23970818.cms.

88 Samuel Woolley, *Manufacturing Consensus: Understanding Propaganda in the Era of Automation and Anonymity* (New Haven, CT: Yale University Press, 2023), 33.

89 Nathaniel Gleicher, "Removing Coordinated Inauthentic Behavior and Spam from India and Pakistan," Meta, April 1, 2019, https://about.fb.com/news/2019/04/cib-and-spam-from-india-pakistan.

90 Woolley, *Manufacturing Consensus*, 35.

91 Zoya Mateen, "Jack Dorsey: India Threatened to Shut Twitter and Raid Employees," *BBC*, June 13, 2023, https://www.bbc.com/news/world-asia-india-65886825.

92 Julia C. Wong and Hannah Ellis-Petersen, "Facebook Planned to Remove Fake Accounts in India—Until It Realized a BJP Politician Was Involved," *The Guardian*, April 15, 2021, https:// www.theguardian.com/technology/2021/apr/15/facebook-india-bjp-fake-accounts; Newley Purnell and Jeff Horwitz, "Facebook's Hate-Speech Rules Collide with Indian Politics," *Wall Street Journal*, August 14, 2020, https://www.wsj.com/articles/facebook-hate-speech-india-politics-muslim -hindu-modi-zuckerberg-11597423346.

93 Think of the GAN process as a pair of AI artists working against each other. One AI, called the "generator," tries to create something that looks real, like a lifelike photo of a person. The other AI, called the "discriminator," tries to tell if what the generator made is real or fake. They keep playing this game, with the generator getting better at making things and the discriminator getting better at spotting fakes. This competition makes the generator improve until it can create things that are so realistic, it's hard to tell they're not real. Jason Brownlee, "A Gentle Introduction to Generative Adversarial Networks (GANs)," Machine Learning Mastery, June 17, 2019, https://machinelearningmastery.com/what-are-generative-adversarial-networks-gans.

94 Shannon Bond, "AI-Generated Fake Faces Have Become a Hallmark of Online Influence Operations," *NPR*, December 15, 2022, https://www.npr.org/2022/12/15/1143114122/ai-generated -fake-faces-have-become-a-hallmark-of-online-influence-operations; Sophie J. Nightingale and Hany Farid, "AI-Synthesized Faces Are Indistinguishable from Real Faces and More Trustworthy," *PNAS* 119, no. 8 (2022): 1–3, https://doi.org/10.1073/pnas.2120481119.

95 Josh A. Goldstein and Renée DiResta, "Research Note: This Salesperson Does Not Exist: How Tactics from Political Influence Operations on Social Media Are Deployed for Commercial Lead Generation," *HKS Misinformation Review*, September 15, 2022, https://misinforeview.hks.harvard .edu/article/research-note-this-salesperson-does-not-exist-how-tactics-from-political-influence -operations-on-social-media-are-deployed-for-commercial-lead-generation.

96 Shivansh Mundra et al., "New Approaches for Detecting AI-Generated Profile Photos," LinkedIn Engineering, June 20, 2023, https://engineering.linkedin.com/blog/2023/new-approaches-for -detecting-ai-generated-profile-photos.

97 Cade Metz, "Meet GPT-3. It Has Learned to Code (and Blog and Argue)," *New York Times*, November 24, 2020, https://www.nytimes.com/2020/11/24/science/artificial-intelligence-ai-gpt3 .html.

98 DiResta, Grossman, and Siegel, "In-House vs. Outsourced Trolls."

99 Jeffrey St. Clair and Joshua Frank, "Go Ask Alice: The Curious Case of 'Alice Donovan.'" *CounterPunch*, December 25, 2017, https://www.counterpunch.org/2017/12/25/go-ask-alice-the-curious -case-of-alice-donovan-2.

100 Kris McGuffie and Alex Newhouse, "The Radicalization Risks of GPT-3 and Advanced Neural Language Models," Middlebury Institute of International Studies, September 9, 2020, https:// www.middlebury.edu/institute/sites/www.middlebury.edu.institute/files/2020-09/gpt3-article .pdf.

101 Josh A. Goldstein et al., "Generative Language Models and Automated Influence Operations: Emerging Threats and Potential Mitigations," arXiv, January 10, 2023, https://arxiv.org/abs/2301 .04246.

102 Emilio Ferrara, "Social Bot Detection in the Age of ChatGPT: Challenges and Opportunities," *First Monday* 28, no. 6 (June 5, 2023), https://doi.org/10.5210/fm.v28i6.13185; Kai-Cheng Yang and Filippo Menczer, "Anatomy of an AI-Powered Malicious Social Botnet," *arXiv* (July 2023): 1–27, https://doi.org/10.48550/arXiv.2307.16336.

103 Philip Marcelo, "FACT FOCUS: Fake Image of Pentagon Explosion Briefly Sends Jitters Through Stock Market," *AP News*, May 23, 2023, https://apnews.com/article/pentagon-explosion -misinformation-stock-market-ai-96f534c790872fde67012ee81b5ed6a4.

104 Blue checkmarks had once been awarded by Twitter to notable accounts, including news organizations and prominent people who had verified their identity. Following Elon Musk's acquisition of Twitter, most legacy accounts lost their checks, and the verification symbol became available to any account willing to pay for an $8/month subscription to Twitter (without any actual verification). There were multiple instances of accounts paying to impersonate others within the first few days of the program.

105 Joseph Menn, "Viral Pentagon Explosion Hoax Took Off from Pro-Russian Accounts," *Washington Post*, June 10, 2023, https://www.washingtonpost.com/technology/2023/06/09/viral-hoax -pentagon-twitter.

106 In 2018, researchers observing the growing sophistication of generative AI capabilities argued that the mere existence of the technology (then still difficult for most people to access) would exacerbate the growing crisis of trust. Creating convincing faked video or audio was not the only potential risk, we argued—rather, the existence of the technology itself could be used to impugn reality. Law professors Danielle Citron and Robert Chesney subsequently termed this the *liar's dividend*, describing ways in which a person—particularly a politician—could deny that a real event had happened by claiming that the evidence had actually been generated by AI. See Charlie Warzel, "Believable: The Terrifying Future of Fake News," *BuzzFeed News*, February 12, 2018, https://www.buzzfeednews.com/article/charliewarzel/the-terrifying-future-of-fake-news; Robert Chesney and Danielle Keats Citron, "Deep Fakes: A Looming Challenge for Privacy, Democracy, and National Security," *California Law Review* 107, no. 6 (2019): 1753-1820, https:// doi.org/10.15779/Z38RV0D15J.

107 Casey Tolan et al., "Slain Hamas Militants' Body Camera Videos Show the Preparation and Tactics Behind Their Terror Attack on Israel," *CNN*, October 26, 2023, https://edition.cnn.com /interactive/2023/middleeast/hamas-attack-body-cam-videos-invs-dg.

108 Miles Klee, "Verified Hate Speech Accounts Are Pivoting to Palestine for Clout and Cash," *Rolling Stone*, November 1, 2023, https://www.rollingstone.com/politics/politics-features/twitter -hate-speech-accounts-palestine-clout-1234867382.

109 Kevin Liptak, "White House Says Biden's Remark on Photos of Children Was Intended to 'Underscore the Utter Depravity' of Hamas Attack," *CNN*, October 12, 2023, https://www.cnn .com/2023/10/12/politics/joe-biden-photos-children-hamas-israel/index.html.

110 Alice Speri, "'Beheaded Babies' Report Spread Wide and Fast—but Israel Military Won't Confirm It," *The Intercept*, October 11, 2023, https://theintercept.com/2023/10/11/israel-hamas -disinformation.

111 Tiffany Hsu and Stuart A. Thompson, "A.I. Muddies Israel-Hamas War in Unexpected Way," *New York Times*, October 28, 2023, https://www.nytimes.com/2023/10/28/business/media/ai-muddies-israel-hamas-war-in-unexpected-way.html.

112 Christopher Mims, "Is Anything Still True? On the Internet, No One Knows Anymore," *Wall Street Journal*, November 10, 2023, https://www.wsj.com/tech/ai/deepfake-video-is-anything-still-true-on-the-internet-89843150.

113 Requirements and means of verification vary by country; see "About Ads About Social Issues, Elections or Politics," Meta Business Help Center, accessed December 19, 2023, https://www.facebook.com/business/help/167836590566506?id=288762101909005.

114 "Inauthentic Behaviour," Meta Transparency Center, accessed December 19, 2023, https://transparency.fb.com/en-gb/policies/community-standards/inauthentic-behavior.

115 Cory Dunton, "Get Helpful Context with About This Image," *Google Blog*, May 10, 2023, https://blog.google/products/search/about-this-image-google-search.

116 Samantha Bradshaw, Renée DiResta, and Christopher Giles, "How Unmoderated Platforms Became the Frontline for Russian Propaganda," *Lawfare*, August 17, 2022, https://www.lawfaremedia.org/article/how-unmoderated-platforms-became-frontline-russian-propaganda-0.

117 Interestingly, as Twitter has undergone a change of ownership and fired most of its integrity teams, it is not pursuing investigations into foreign influence operations as thoroughly as it once did.

118 Three Kid Rock pages on Gettr, Gab, and Truth Social had nearly identical bios and were likely from the same user. Graphika and the Stanford Internet Observatory, "Suspected Russian Actors Leverage Alternative Tech Platforms in Continued Effort to Covertly Influence Right-Wing U.S. Audiences," *Graphika*, December 13, 2022; Donald J. Trump (@donaldjtrumpjr), "Yup," Instagram, June 15, 2022, https://www.instagram.com/p/Ce1j3F2u5nY.

119 Trump, "Yup."

120 Vittoria Elliott, "Telegram's Bans on Extremist Channels Aren't Really Bans," *Wired*, November 28, 2023, https://www.wired.com/story/telegram-hamas-channels-deplatform.

121 Marianna Spring, "Marianna Vyshemirsky: 'My Picture Was Used to Spread Lies About the War,'" *BBC*, May 17, 2022, https://www.bbc.com/news/blogs-trending-61412773.

122 Maayan Lubell, "Exclusive: Facebook Removes More Russia Posts Claiming Children's Hospital Bombing a Hoax," *Reuters*, March 16, 2022, https://www.reuters.com/world/europe/exclusive-facebook-removes-more-russia-posts-claiming-childrens-hospital-bombing-2022-03-16.

123 See, for example, this collaboration between CNN and Clemson University investigating a Russian troll factory in Ghana: Clarissa Ward, "Inside a Russian Troll Factory in Ghana," *CNN*, March 12, 2020, https://edition.cnn.com/videos/world/2020/03/12/russian-trolls-ghana-ward-pkg-vpx.cnn.

124 Miles Klee, "Twitter Fires Election Integrity Team Ahead of 2024 Elections," *Rolling Stone*, September 27, 2023, https://www.rollingstone.com/culture/culture-news/twitter-elon-musk-fires-safety-team-2024-elections-1234832199.

125 Kate Starbird, Ahmer Arif, and Tom Wilson, "Disinformation as Collaborative Work," *Proceedings of the ACM on Human-Computer Interaction* 3, no. CSCW (November 7, 2019): 1–26, https://doi.org/10.1145/3359229.

126 Samantha Bradshaw, Renée DiResta, and Carly Miller, "Playing Both Sides: Russian State-Backed Media Coverage of the #BlackLivesMatter Movement," *International Journal of Press/Politics*, February 28, 2022, https://doi.org/10.1177/19401612221082052.

127 Stanford Internet Observatory Team, "Digital Street Conflict," Stanford Internet Observatory Cyber Policy Center, June 3, 2020, https://cyber.fsi.stanford.edu/io/news/digital-street-conflict.

128 Amanda Seitz, Eric Tucker, and Mike Catalini, "How China's TikTok, Facebook Influencers Push Propaganda," *AP News*, March 30, 2022, https://apnews.com/article/china-tiktok-facebook-influencers-propaganda-81388bca676c560e02a1b493ea9d6760.

129 Vincent Ni, "China Hires Western TikTokers to Polish Its Image During 2022 Winter Olympics," *The Guardian*, January 22, 2022, https://www.theguardian.com/world/2022/jan/22/china-hires-western-tiktokers-to-polish-its-image-during-2022-winter-olympics.

130 David Gilbert, "Russian TikTok Influencers Are Being Paid to Spread Kremlin Propaganda," *Vice*, March 11, 2022, https://www.vice.com/en/article/epxken/russian-tiktok-influencers-paid -propaganda.

131 See, for example, Henry John Farrell and Bruce Schneier, "Common-Knowledge Attacks on Democracy," *SSRN Electronic Journal*, November 17, 2018, https://doi.org/10.2139/ssrn.3273111: "Election security does not simply involve physical infrastructure, such as ballots and polling booths. It also involves roughly consensual expectations about how the system works, who won and who lost, and so on. If an attacker does not penetrate the physical election infrastructure, but does successfully subvert the shared expectations around the election, she can nevertheless succeed."

132 See Yochai Benkler, "The Danger of Overstating the Impact of Information Operations," *Lawfare*, October 23, 2020, https://www.lawfaremedia.org/article/danger-overstating-impact -information-operations: "If the objective of the campaign is to sow doubt and confusion, to make Americans believe that we have been infiltrated and that Russia is an all-powerful actor messing with our democracy, then overstating the importance of the campaign simply reinforces and executes the Russian plan."

133 Josh A. Goldstein and Renée DiResta, "Foreign Influence Operations and the 2020 Election: Framing the Debate," *Lawfare*, October 23, 2020, https://www.lawfaremedia.org/article/foreign -influence-operations-and-2020-election-framing-debate.

134 The US District Court for the District of Columbia, "Indictment Criminal No. (18 U.S.C. §§ 2,371, 1349, 1028A)," US Department of Justice, February 16, 2018, https://www.justice.gov /opa/press-release/file/1035562/download.

135 Gregory Eady et al., "Exposure to the Russian Internet Research Agency Foreign Influence Campaign on Twitter in the 2016 US Election and Its Relationship to Attitudes and Voting Behavior," *Nature Communications* 14, no. 62 (2023): 1–11, https://doi.org/10.1038/s41467-022 -35576-9.

136 Marshall Cohen, "Access Hollywood, Russian Hacking and the Podesta Emails: One Year Later," *CNN*, October 7, 2017, https://www.cnn.com/2017/10/07/politics/one-year-access -hollywood-russia-podesta-email/index.html.

137 "Launching the SIO Virality Project," Stanford Internet Observatory Cyber Policy Center, May 21, 2020, https://cyber.fsi.stanford.edu/io/news/launching-sio-virality-project.

138 "Iran Leader Refuses US Help; Cites Coronavirus Conspiracy Theory," *Al Jazeera*, March 23, 2020, https://www.aljazeera.com/news/2020/3/23/iran-leader-refuses-us-help-cites-coronavirus -conspiracy-theory.

139 Shelby Grossman, "Virality Project: Saudi Arabia State Media and COVID-19," Stanford Internet Observatory Cyber Policy Center, June 24, 2020, https://cyber.fsi.stanford.edu/io/news /saudi-arabia-state-media-and-covid-19.

140 Maggie Michael, "Yemen's Rebels Crack Down as COVID-19 and Rumors Spread," *AP News*, June 9, 2020, https://apnews.com/article/united-nations-health-yemen-ap-top-news-virus-outbreak -677a1fc12d864cd37eea57e5f71614a2.

141 Daniel Bush, "Virality Project (Russia): Penguins and Protests," Stanford Internet Observatory Cyber Policy Center, June 9, 2020, https://cyber.fsi.stanford.edu/io/news/penguins-and-protests -rt-and-coronavirus-pandemic.

142 DiResta et al., "Telling China's Story."

143 John Dotson, "The CCP's New Leading Small Group for Countering the Coronavirus Epidemic—and the Mysterious Absence of Xi Jinping," Jamestown Foundation, February 5, 2020, https://jamestown.org/program/the-ccps-new-leading-small-group-for-countering-the-coronavirus -epidemic-and-the-mysterious-absence-of-xi-jinping.

144 Vanessa Molter and Renée DiResta, "Pandemics & Propaganda: How Chinese State Media Creates and Propagates CCP Coronavirus Narratives," *Misinformation Review*, June 8, 2020, https://misinforeview.hks.harvard.edu/article/pandemics-propaganda-how-chinese-state-media -creates-and-propagates-ccp-coronavirus-narratives.

145 Paul Mozur et al., "China Uses YouTube Influencers to Spread Propaganda," *New York Times*, December 31, 2021. https://www.nytimes.com/interactive/2021/12/13/technology/china-propaganda -youtube-influencers.html.

146 Renée DiResta, "For China, the 'USA Virus' Is a Geopolitical Ploy," *The Atlantic*, April 11, 2020, https://www.theatlantic.com/ideas/archive/2020/04/chinas-covid-19-conspiracy-theories /609772.

147 Lijian Zhao (@zlj517), "CDC was caught on the spot," Twitter, March 12, 2020, 10:37 a.m., https://twitter.com/zlj517/status/1238111898828066823.

148 DiResta, "For China, the 'USA Virus' Is a Geopolitical Ploy."

149 Bret Schafer and Raymond Serrato, "Reply All: Inauthenticity and Coordinated Replying in Pro-Chinese Communist Party Twitter Networks," Institute for Strategic Dialogue, August 6, 2020, https://www.isdglobal.org/isd-publications/reply-all-inauthenticity-and-coordinated-replying -in-pro-chinese-communist-party-twitter-networks; Brandy and Schafer, "How China's 'Wolf Warrior' Diplomats Use and Abuse Twitter."

150 Renée DiResta et al., "Sockpuppets Spin COVID Yarns: An Analysis of PRC-Attributed June 2020 Twitter Takedown," Stanford Internet Observatory, June 11, 2020, https://fsi.stanford.edu /publication/june-2020-prc-takedown.

151 Josh Lederman, "U.S. Insisting That the U.N. Call Out Chinese Origins of Coronavirus," *NBC News*, March 25, 2020, https://www.nbcnews.com/politics/national-security/u-s-insisting -u-n-call-out-chinese-origins-coronavirus-n1169111.

152 Nathaniel Gleicher, "Labeling State-Controlled Media on Facebook," Meta, June 4, 2020, https://about.fb.com/news/2020/06/labeling-state-controlled-media; "New Labels for Government and State-Affiliated Media Accounts," Twitter, August 6, 2020, https://blog.twitter.com /en_us/topics/product/2020/new-labels-for-government-and-state-affiliated-media-accounts.

CHAPTER 7: VIRUSES, VACCINES, AND VIRALITY

1 Jennifer Kasten, "What Judy Mikovits Gets Wrong," *Medpage Today*, May 12, 2020, https:// www.medpagetoday.com/infectiousdisease/generalinfectiousdisease/86461.

2 Sheera Frenkel, Ben Decker, and Davey Alba, "How the 'Plandemic' Movie and Its Falsehoods Spread Widely Online," *New York Times*, May 21, 2020, https://www.nytimes.com/2020/05/20 /technology/plandemic-movie-youtube-facebook-coronavirus.html.

3 Angelo Fichera et al., "The Falsehoods of the 'Plandemic' Video," FactCheck.org, May 8, 2020, https://www.factcheck.org/2020/05/the-falsehoods-of-the-plandemic-video.

4 See Jon Cohen, "Controversial CFS Researcher Arrested and Jailed," *Science*, November 19, 2011, https://www.science.org/content/article/controversial-cfs-researcher-arrested-and-jailed. Charges were later dropped.

5 Jon Cohen, "In a Rare Move, Science Without Authors' Consent Retracts Paper That Tied Mouse Virus to Chronic Fatigue Syndrome," *Science*, December 22, 2011, https://www.science.org/content /article/updated-rare-move-science-without-authors-consent-retracts-paper-tied-mouse-virus.

6 Stuart J. D. Neil and Edward M Campbell, "Fake Science: XMRV, COVID-19, and the Toxic Legacy of Dr. Judy Mikovits," *AIDS Research and Human Retroviruses* 36, no. 7 (July 2020): 545–549.

7 Martin Enserink and Jon Cohen, "Fact-Checking Judy Mikovits, the Controversial Virologist Attacking Anthony Fauci in a Viral Conspiracy Video," *Science*, May 8, 2020, https:// www.science.org/content/article/fact-checking-judy-mikovits-controversial-virologist-attacking -anthony-fauci-viral.

8 Josh Rottenberg and Stacy Perman, "Meet the Ojai Dad Who Made the Most Notorious Piece of Coronavirus Disinformation Yet," *Los Angeles Times*, May 13, 2020, https://www.latimes .com/entertainment-arts/movies/story/2020-05-13/plandemic-coronavirus-documentary-director -mikki-willis-mikovits.

9 "Infodemic," WHO, https://www.who.int/health-topics/infodemic.

10 "Launching the Virality Project," Stanford Internet Observatory Cyber Policy Center, https:// cyber.fsi.stanford.edu/content/virality-project.

11 Katherine Schaeffer, "Nearly Three-in-Ten Americans Believe COVID-19 Was Made in a Lab," Pew Research, April 8, 2020, https://www.pewresearch.org/short-reads/2020/04/08/nearly-three -in-ten-americans-believe-covid-19-was-made-in-a-lab; Aaron Blake, "How the Covid Lab Leak Became the American Public's Predominant Theory," *Washington Post*, March 16, 2023, https:// www.washingtonpost.com/politics/2023/03/16/lab-leak-theory-polling.

12 Blake, "How the Covid Lab Leak Became the American Public's Predominant Theory."

13 Leana S. Wen, "How to Investigate the Lab-Leak Theory Without Inflaming Anti-Asian Hate," *Washington Post*, June 1, 2021, https://www.washingtonpost.com/opinions/2021/06/01/we-need -investigate-lab-leak-theory-without-inflaming-anti-asian-hate.

14 Meta's moderation policy on the lab leak hypothesis shifted over time. The date of the origin of the policy is elusive, but by May 2021, they had begun to step back from moderating origin claims. See Elizabeth Culliford, "Facebook No Longer Banning Posts Calling the Coronavirus 'Man-Made,'" *Reuters*, May 27, 2021, https://www.reuters.com/world/china/facebook-no-longer -banning-posts-calling-coronavirus-man-made-2021-05-27.

15 Early in the pandemic, as there was significant concern about transmission even outdoors, authorities made decisions about what could stay open and what had to close, about the kinds of gatherings that were approved and the kinds that were not. While some of these choices could be explained by public health officials simply not knowing where the lines should have been at that point, there was also what could be read as ideological bias to some of the policies (attending outdoor mass protests related to racism in the summer of 2020 was declared reasonable even as attending outdoor church services was banned in many locales). This seeming hypocrisy was quickly seized upon by partisan influencers and media, who saw an opportunity to reinforce ideological divides around "woke" capture of public health officials and institutions who were more concerned about looking antiracist or not offending China than undertaking a clear-eyed assessment of the facts and risks.

16 Roxanne Khamsi, "Coronavirus Is Bad. Comparing It to the Flu Is Worse," *Wired*, February 8, 2020, https://www.wired.com/story/coronavirus-is-bad-comparing-it-to-the-flu-is-worse.

17 Avery Hartmans, "Silicon Valley VC Firm Andreessen Horowitz Is Asking Visitors to Avoid Handshakes Due to the Coronavirus Outbreak," *Business Insider*, February 7, 2020, https:// www.businessinsider.com/andreessen-horowitz-coronavirus-fears-handshake-ban-2020-2.

18 Balaji (@balajis), "The Wuhan mayor is being pressed to resign after approving a group dinner with 40,000 people, knowing that a deadly virus was on the loose…," Twitter, February 6, 2020, https://twitter.com/balajis/status/1225178842580619265.

19 See, for example, the March update note on this *BuzzFeed* article: Dan Vergano, "Here's What We Do and Don't Know About the Deadly Coronavirus Outbreak," *BuzzFeed News*, January 28, 2020, https://www.buzzfeednews.com/article/danvergano/coronavirus-cases-deaths-flu.

20 Balaji (@balajis), "Don't let these wokes rewrite history," X, April 25, 2021, 9:48 p.m., https://x .com/balajis/status/1386391617167183872.

21 T. A. Frank, "'The Coronavirus Crisis Was Built for Insurgent Information': Why Some Early MAGA Adopters Went Against Trump's Virus Doctrine," *Vanity Fair*, March 23, 2020, https://www.vanity fair.com/news/2020/03/why-some-early-maga-adopters-went-against-trumps-virus-doctrine.

22 Zeynep Tufekci, "Why Telling People They Don't Need to Mask Backfired," *New York Times*, March 17, 2020, https://www.nytimes.com/2020/03/17/opinion/coronavirus-face-masks.html.

23 Kerrington Powell and Vinay Prasad, "The Noble Lies of COVID-19," *Slate*, July 28, 2021, https://slate.com/technology/2021/07/noble-lies-covid-fauci-cdc-masks.html.

24 Lucy Tompkins et al., "Entering Uncharted Territory, the U.S. Counts 500,000 Covid-Related Deaths," *New York Times*, February 22, 2021, https://www.nytimes.com/2021/02/22/us/us -covid-deaths-half-a-million.html.

25 Renée DiResta and Isabella Garcia-Camargo, "Virality Project (US): Marketing Meets Misinformation," Stanford Internet Observatory, Freeman University Spogli Institute for International Studies, May 26, 2020, https://fsi.stanford.edu/news/manufacturing-influence-0.

26 Andrei Makhovsky, "Nobody Will Die From Coronavirus in Belarus, Says President," *Reuters*, April 13, 2020, https://www.reuters.com/article/us-health-coronavirus-belarus/nobody-will-die -from-coronavirus-in-belarus-says-president-idUSKCN21V1PK.

27 Jason Burke, "Tanzania's Covid-Denying President, John Magufuli, Dies Aged 61," *The Guardian*, March 18, 2021, https://www.theguardian.com/world/2021/mar/17/tanzanias-president-john -magufuli-dies-aged-61.

28 Tom Nichols, *The Death of Expertise: The Campaign Against Established Knowledge and Why It Matters* (New York: Oxford University Press, 2017), 29–30.

29 Hugo Mercier, *Not Born Yesterday: The Science of Who We Trust and What We Believe* (Princeton, NJ: Princeton University Press, 2020), 222.

30 Brian Kennedy, Alec Tyson, and Cary Funk, "Americans' Trust in Scientists, Other Groups Declines," Pew Research Center, February 15, 2022, https://www.pewresearch.org/science/2022 /02/15/americans-trust-in-scientists-other-groups-declines.

31 Daniel A. Cox et al., "America's Crisis of Confidence: Rising Mistrust, Conspiracies, and Vaccine Hesitancy After COVID-19: Findings from the May 2023 American Perspectives Survey," American Survey Center, September 28, 2023, https://www.americansurveycenter.org/research /americas-crisis-of-confidence-rising-mistrust-conspiracies-and-vaccine-hesitancy-after -covid-19.

32 Ashley Kirzinger et al., "The COVID-19 Pandemic: Insights from Three Years of KFF Polling," KFF, March 7, 2023, https://www.kff.org/coronavirus-covid-19/poll-finding/the-covid-19-pandemic -insights-from-three-years-of-kff-polling.

33 *2022 Edelman Trust Barometer* [Research Report] (Edelman Trust Institute, 2022), https:// www.edelman.com/sites/g/files/aatuss191/files/2022-01/Trust%2022_Top10.pdf.

34 *2022 Edelman Trust Barometer: Global Report* [Research Report] (Edelman Trust Institute, 2022), https://www.edelman.com/sites/g/files/aatuss191/files/2022-01/2022%20Edelman%20 Trust%20Barometer%20FINAL_Jan25.pdf.

35 "2023 Edelman Trust Barometer: Navigating a Polarized World," Edelman, https://www.edelman .com/trust/2023/trust-barometer.

36 Jonathan Haidt, "Why the Past 10 Years of American Life Have Been Uniquely Stupid," *The Atlantic*, April 11, 2022, https://www.theatlantic.com/magazine/archive/2022/05/social-media -democracy-trust-babel/629369.

37 Tim Miller, "President Candace," *The Bulwark*, July 18, 2023, https://plus.thebulwark.com/p /president-candace-owens.

38 Mercier, *Not Born Yesterday*, 225–247.

39 Rottenberg and Perman, "Meet the Ojai Dad."

40 This is where Willis's editing skills are most apparent; Mikovits had done dozens of interviews with conspiracy theorist YouTube channels in the weeks leading up to Plandemic. They got some attention within the communities but were not breakout successes because she often rambled and relied on scientific jargon. *Plandemic*, by contrast, skillfully worked around the speaker's tendency toward convoluted explanations.

41 "#1263—Renée DiResta," *The Joe Rogan Experience*, Spotify, March 2019, https://open.spotify .com/episode/5VX7FJGIYr1eKSEagOeb22.

42 Todd Spangler, "Joe Rogan Tries to Clarify Controversial Comments About COVID Vaccines," *Reuters*, April 30, 2021, https://www.reuters.com/article/variety/joe-rogan-tries-to-clarify-controversial -comments-about-covid-vaccines-idINL4N2MM5PH.

43 E. J. Dickson, "How Joe Rogan Became a Cheerleader for Ivermectin," *Rolling Stone*, September 2, 2021, https://www.rollingstone.com/culture/culture-features/joe-rogan-covid19-misinformation -ivermectin-spotify-podcast-1219976.

44 Diane Mapes, "Spinning Science: Overhyped Headlines, Snarled Statistics Lead Readers Astray," *Fred Hutch Cancer Center, Hutch News Stories*, February 13, 2020, https://www.fredhutch.org /en/news/center-news/2020/02/spinning-science-overhyped-headlines-snarled-statistics-lead -readers-astray.html.

45 Naomi Klein, *Doppelganger: A Trip into the Mirror World* (New York: Farrar, Straus and Giroux, 2023), 106–107.

46 Sheera Frenkel, "The Most Influential Spreader of Coronavirus Misinformation Online," *New York Times*, July 24, 2021, https://www.nytimes.com/2021/07/24/technology/joseph-mercola -coronavirus-misinformation-online.html.

47 Jon D. Lee, *An Epidemic of Rumors: How Stories Shape Our Perceptions of Disease* (Boulder: University Press of Colorado and Utah State University Press, 2014), 59.

48 Tara Haelle, "This Is the Moment the Anti-vaccine Movement Has Been Waiting For," *New York Times*, August 31, 2021, https://www.nytimes.com/2021/08/31/opinion/anti-vaccine-movement .html.

49 Renée DiResta, "Anti-vaxxers Think This Is Their Moment," *The Atlantic*, December 20, 2020, https://www.theatlantic.com/ideas/archive/2020/12/campaign-against-vaccines-already-under-way/617443.

50 Brandy Zadrozny, "Parents Are Poisoning Their Children with Bleach to 'Cure' Autism. These Moms Are Trying to Stop It," *NBC News*, May 21, 2019, https://www.nbcnews.com/tech/internet/moms-go-undercover-fight-fake-autism-cures-private-facebook-groups-n1007871.

51 Renée DiResta and Claire Wardle, "Online Misinformation About Vaccines" (paper contributed to "Meeting the Challenge of Vaccination Hesitancy," Sabin-Aspen Vaccine Science & Policy Group, May 2020, https://www.sabin.org/app/uploads/2022/04/Sabin-Aspen-report-2020_Meeting-the-Challenge-of-Vaccine-Hesitancy.pdf).

52 Julia Carrie Wong, "How Facebook and YouTube Help Spread Anti-vaxxer Propaganda," *The Guardian*, February 1, 2019, https://www.theguardian.com/media/2019/feb/01/facebook-youtube-anti-vaccination-misinformation-social-media; Jessica Glenza, "Majority of Anti-vaxx Ads on Facebook Are Funded by Just Two Organizations," *The Guardian*, November 14, 2019, https://www.theguardian.com/technology/2019/nov/13/majority-antivaxx-vaccine-ads-facebook-funded-by-two-organizations-study.

53 WHO, *Measles Outbreak in the Pacific—Situation Report No. 9: Joint WHO/UNICEF Measles Outbreak Response and Preparedness in the Pacific*, World Health Organization, 2019, https://www.who.int/docs/default-source/wpro---documents/dps/outbreaks-and-emergencies/measles-2019/measles-pacific-who-unicef-sitrep-20200103.pdf.

54 Erin Schumaker, "Low Vaccination Rate and Deadly Medical Mistake Led to Samoa Measles Outbreak: Health Experts," *ABC News*, November 27, 2019, https://abcnews.go.com/Health/low-vaccination-rate-deadly-medical-mistake-led-samoa/story?id=67317110.

55 Renée DiResta, *On Virality: How the Anti-vaccine Movement Influences Public Discourse Through Online Activism* (The Lancet and Financial Times Commission Report), July 15, 2020, https://www.governinghealthfutures2030.org/wp-content/uploads/2021/10/072020_Renee-DiResta_On-virality-How-the-antivaccine-movement-influences-public-discourse-through-online-activism.pdf.

56 The outbreak in Brooklyn began in September 2018 and lasted through July 2019. See Jane R. Zucker et al., "Consequences of Undervaccination—Measles Outbreak, New York City, 2018–2019," *New England Journal of Medicine* 382, no. 11 (March 2020): 1009–1017, https://doi.org/10.1056/NEJMoa1912514.

57 "Combatting Vaccine Misinformation," Meta Newsroom, Meta, March 7, 2019, https://about.fb.com/news/2019/03/combatting-vaccine-misinformation.

58 Erin Schumaker, "Anti-vaccine Leaders Targeting Minority Becomes Growing Concern at NYC Forum," *ABC News*, November 10, 2019, https://abcnews.go.com/Health/rfk-jrs-york-city-vaccine-forum-highlights-concerns/story?id=66158336.

59 DiResta and Garcia-Camargo, "Virality Project (US)."

60 Renée Diresta and Gilad Lotan, "Anti-vaxxers Are Using Twitter to Manipulate a Vaccine Bill," *Wired*, June 8, 2015, https://www.wired.com/2015/06/antivaxxers-influencing-legislation.

61 The Virality Project, "Memes, Magnets and Microchips: Narrative Dynamics Around COVID-19 Vaccines," Stanford Digital Repository, February 24, 2022, https://doi.org/10.25740/mx395xj8490.

62 There is a case study of our joint effort here: Hussain S. Lalani et al., "Addressing Viral Medical Rumors and False or Misleading Information," *Annals of Internal Medicine*, August 2023, https://doi.org/10.7326/M23-1218.

63 Anna Kata, "Anti-vaccine Activists, Web 2.0, and the Postmodern Paradigm—an Overview of Tactics and Tropes Used Online by the Anti-vaccination Movement," PubMed, December 13, 2011, https://pubmed.ncbi.nlm.nih.gov/22172504.

64 William Rowley, *Cow-Pox Inoculation: No Security Against Small-Pox Infection* (London: J. Barfield, 1805), 11.

65 Richard B. Gibbs, letter reproduced in *Human Nature: A Monthly Journal of Zoistic Science*, June 1867, 176, in archive of the International Association for the Preservation of Spiritualist and Occult Periodicals, http://iapsop.com/archive/materials/human_nature/human_nature_v1_n3_june_1867

.pdf. Although this letter comes from Richard B. Gibbs, the detail about the syphilitic family is something that Gibbs quotes from a "Dr. Smedley, of Matlock Bank Hydropathic Establishment."

66 Francis T. Bond, "The Vaccination Problem," *British Medical Journal* 2, no. 1929 (1897): 1828.

67 Tara C. Smith, "Vaccine Rejection and Hesitancy: A Review and Call to Action," PubMed, July 18, 2017, https://pubmed.ncbi.nlm.nih.gov/28948177.

68 Micah Lee, "Network of Right-Wing Health Care Providers Is Making Millions Off Hydroxy-chloroquine and Ivermectin, Hacked Data Reveals," *The Intercept*, September 28, 2021, https://theintercept.com/2021/09/28/covid-telehealth-hydroxychloroquine-ivermectin-hacked/.

69 Richard M. Carpiano et al., "Confronting the Evolution and Expansion of Anti-vaccine Activism in the USA in the COVID-19 Era," *Lancet* 401 (2023): 967–970.

70 Renée DiResta, "The Anti-vaccine Influencers Who Are Merely Asking Questions," *The Atlantic*, April 24, 2021, https://www.theatlantic.com/ideas/archive/2021/04/influencers-who-keep-stoking-fears-about-vaccines/618687.

71 Nicki Minaj (@NICKIMINAJ), "My cousin in Trinidad won't get the vaccine cuz his friend got it & became impotent...," Twitter, September 13, 2021, https://twitter.com/NICKIMINAJ/status/1437532566945341441.

72 Grant Rindner, "Nicki Minaj's Cousin's Friend's Balls, Explained," *GQ Magazine*, September 16, 2021, https://www.gq.com/story/nicki-minaj-vaccine-twitter-met-gala-2021.

73 Robyn Dixon, "Want to Skip the Vaccine in Russia? You Could be Suspended from Work," *Washington Post*, July 28, 2021, https://www.washingtonpost.com/world/europe/russia-vaccine-rules-putin/2021/07/27/640ea8b6-ebff-11eb-a2ba-3be31d349258_story.html; Daria Litvinova, "Russia Mandates Vaccinations for Some as Virus Cases Surge," *AP News*, June 25, 2021, https://apnews.com/article/europe-russia-health-coronavirus-pandemic-business-42d0c14f054537 1e16a360b677cb4c38.

74 Michael R. Gordon and Dustin Volz, "Russian Disinformation Campaign Aims to Undermine Confidence in Pfizer, Other Covid-19 Vaccines, U.S. Officials Say," *Wall Street Journal*, March 7, 2021, https://www.wsj.com/articles/russian-disinformation-campaign-aims-to-undermine-confidence-in-pfizer-other-covid-19-vaccines-u-s-officials-say-11615129200.

75 Reuters Fact Check, "Fact Check—Chimpanzee Adenovirus Vector in the AstraZeneca COVID-19 Vaccine Does Not Cause Monkeypox," *Reuters*, May 24, 2022, https://www.reuters.com/article/factcheck-health-monkeypox/fact-check-chimpanzee-adenovirus-vector-in-the-astrazeneca-covid-19-vaccine-does-not-cause-monkeypox-idUSL2N2XG0W1.

76 Manveen Rana and Sean O'Neill, "Russians Spread Fake News over Oxford Coronavirus Vaccine," *The Times*, October 16, 2020, Internet Archive, https://web.archive.org/web/20201021023753/https://www.thetimes.co.uk/article/russians-spread-fake-news-over-oxford-coronavirus-vaccine-2nzpk8vrq.

77 Charlie Haynes and Flora Carmichael, "The YouTubers Who Blew the Whistle on an Anti-vax Plot," *BBC News*, July 25, 2021, https://www.bbc.com/news/blogs-trending-57928647.

78 "July 2021 Coordinated Inauthentic Behavior Report," Meta, August 10, 2021, https://about.fb.com/news/2021/08/july-2021-coordinated-inauthentic-behavior-report.

79 Adam Satariano and Davey Alba, "Burning Cell Towers, out of Baseless Fear They Spread the Virus," *New York Times*, April 10, 2020, https://www.nytimes.com/2020/04/10/technology/coronavirus-5g-uk.html.

80 Kelvin Chan, Beatrice Dupuy, and Arijeta Lajka, "Conspiracy Theorists Burn 5G Towers Claiming Link to Virus," *AP News*, April 21, 2020, https://apnews.com/article/health-ap-top-news-wireless-technology-international-news-virus-outbreak-4ac3679b6f39e8bd2561c1c8eeafd855.

81 Jeff Horwitz, *Broken Code: Inside Facebook and the Fight to Expose Its Harmful Secrets* (New York: Knopf Doubleday Publishing Group, 2023), 177.

82 Camille Caldera, "Fact Check: Nurse Who Fainted After COVID-19 Vaccination Is Alive and Well," *USA Today*, December 23, 2020, https://www.usatoday.com/story/news/factcheck/2020/12/23/fact-check-nurse-who-fainted-after-being-vaccinated-alive/4024424001.

83 Brandy Zadrozny, "Conspiracy Theorists Made Tiffany Dover into an Anti-vaccine Icon. She's Finally Ready to Talk About It," *NBC News*, April 10, 2023, https://www.nbcnews.com/tech/misinformation/tiffany-dover-conspiracy-theorists-silence-rcna69401.

84 The Virality Project, "Memes, Magnets and Microchips," 50–52.

85 "Table 4. CICP Claims Compensated (Fiscal Years 2010–2023)," US Health Resources and Services Administration, Countermeasures Injury Compensation Program, https://www.hrsa.gov/cicp/cicp-data/table-4.

86 "The Joe Rogan & Dr. Peter Mccullough Interview," ZDOGGMD, December 17, 2021, https://zdoggmd.com/peter-mccullough.

87 "Joe Rogan Interview with Peter McCullough Contains Multiple False and Unsubstantiated Claims About the COVID-19 Pandemic and Vaccines," Health Feedback, https://healthfeedback.org/claimreview/joe-rogan-interview-with-peter-mccullough-contains-multiple-false-and-unsubstantiated-claims-about-the-covid-19-pandemic-and-vaccines.

88 Bruce Y. Lee, "Have More Athletes Died Suddenly Since Covid-19 Vaccines Arrived? Such Claims Lack Evidence," Forbes, January 14, 2023, https://www.forbes.com/sites/brucelee/2023/01/14/no-evidence-of-more-athletes-having-died-suddenly-despite-covid-19-vaccine-claims/?sh=22d1dc2875c2.

89 Ali Swenson and Angelo Fichera, "'Died Suddenly' Posts Twist Tragedies to Push Vaccine Lies," AP News, February 4, 2023, https://apnews.com/article/vaccine-died-suddenly-misinformation-a8e3a80a015ba9bf78b6bd4f3c271f58.

90 Angelo Fichera, "Claims Baselessly Link COVID Vaccines to Athlete Deaths," AP News, January 9, 2023, https://apnews.com/article/fact-check-covid-vaccines-athlete-deaths-1500-989195878254.

91 Ibid.

92 "Crazy, Disturbing Damar Hamlin Conspiracy Theory Emerges," NBC Sports, January 25, 2023, https://www.nbcsports.com/nfl/profootballtalk/rumor-mill/news/crazy-disturbing-damar-hamlin-conspiracy-theory-emerges.

93 McCullough was suspended from Twitter in July 2021 on his account @cov19treatments. While he was able to start another account (@p_mcculloughmd) in November of that year, he was upset that Twitter would not give it Verified status. He, along with several other physicians suspended for COVID-19 misinformation, sued Twitter in June 2022, claiming that Twitter violated its Covid-19 misinformation guidelines by suspending the doctors' accounts because "none of these physicians posted false or misleading information, nor did they receive five strikes before suspension." The lawsuit was tossed out on Strategic Lawsuit Against Public Participation (SLAPP) grounds, with the court reaffirming Twitter's right to carry the content it saw fit. See Robert W. Malone, MD et al. v. Twitter Inc. et al., CGC-22-600397 (Cal. Super. Ct. Jun. 27, 2022), https://docs.reclaimthenet.org/Malone-et-al-vs-Twitter-rtn-87.pdf.

94 "Re: Notice of Recommended Disciplinary Sanction," addressed to Dr. McCullough, from the American Board of Internal Medicine (ABIM), signed by Furman S. McDonald, chair of Credentials and Certification Committee, ABIM ID: 136084, October 18, 2022, accessed on DocumentCloud database, https://www.documentcloud.org/documents/23242430-abim-decision-on-mccullough.

95 Horwitz, Broken Code, 178–179.

96 Klein, Doppelganger, 110.

97 Derek Thompson, "The Pandemic's Wrongest Man," The Atlantic, April 1, 2021, https://www.theatlantic.com/ideas/archive/2021/04/pandemics-wrongest-man/618475.

98 "Leaderboard: Top Politics publications," Substack, https://substack.com/leaderboard/politics.

99 Naomi Nix, Cat Zakrzewski, and Joseph Menn, "Misinformation Research Is Buckling Under GOP Legal Attacks," Washington Post, September 23, 2023, https://www.washingtonpost.com/technology/2023/09/23/online-misinformation-jim-jordan.

100 Charles Silver and David A. Hyman, "COVID-19: A Case Study of Government Failure," Pandemics and Policy Series, Cato Institute, September 15, 2020, https://www.cato.org/pandemics-policy/covid-19-case-study-government-failure.

101 Eric Reinhart, "Why U.S. Pandemic Management Has Failed: Lack of Attention to America's Epidemic Engines," STAT, October 5, 2021, https://www.statnews.com/2021/10/05/jails-prisons-schools-nursing-homes-america-epidemic-engines; Eric Lipton et al., "The C.D.C. Waited 'Its Entire Existence for This Moment.' What Went Wrong?," New York Times, June 3, 2020, https://

www.nytimes.com/2020/06/03/us/cdc-coronavirus.html; Derek Thompson, "Why America's Institutions Are Failing," *The Atlantic*, June 16, 2020, https://www.theatlantic.com/ideas /archive/2020/06/why-americas-institutions-are-failing/613078; Erika Edwards, "How the CDC's Communication Failures During Covid Tarnished the Agency," *NBC News*, October 1, 2022, https://www.nbcnews.com/health/health-news/cdcs-communication-failures-covid-tarnished -agency-rcna46425; "First Lessons from Government Evaluations of COVID-19 Responses: A Synthesis," *OECD*, January 21, 2022, https://www.oecd.org/coronavirus/policy-responses/first -lessons-from-government-evaluations-of-covid-19-responses-a-synthesis-483507d6; Eleanor Schiff and Daniel J. Mallinson, "Trumping the Centers for Disease Control: A Case Comparison of the CDC's Response to COVID-19, H1N1, and Ebola," *Administration & Society* 55, no. 1 (2023): 158–183, https://doi.org/10.1177/00953997221112308; Sudip Parikh, "Why We Must Rebuild Trust in Science," Pew, February 9, 2021, https://www.pewtrusts.org/en/trend/archive /winter-2021/why-we-must-rebuild-trust-in-science.

102 Catalina Jaramillo, "It's Not News, nor 'Scandalous,' That Pfizer Trial Didn't Test Transmission," FactCheck.org, October 18, 2022, https://www.factcheck.org/2022/10/scicheck-its-not-news -nor-scandalous-that-pfizer-trial-didnt-test-transmission.

103 Reuters Fact Check, "Preventing Transmission Never Required for COVID Vaccines' Initial Approval; Pfizer Vax Did Reduce Transmission of Early Variants," *Reuters*, October 14, 2022, https://www.reuters.com/article/factcheck-pfizer-vaccine-transmission/fact-check-preventing -transmission-never-required-for-covid-vaccines-initial-approval-pfizer-vax-did-reduce-transmission -of-early-variants-idUSL1N31F20E.

104 Susanna Naggie et al., "Effect of Ivermectin vs Placebo on Time to Sustained Recovery in Outpatients with Mild to Moderate COVID-19: A Randomized Clinical Trial," *JAMA* 328, no. 16 (2022): 1595–1603, https://jamanetwork.com/journals/jama/fullarticle/2797483; Kirsten Bibbins-Domingo and Preeti N. Malani, "At a Higher Dose and Longer Duration, Ivermectin Still Not Effective Against COVID-19," *JAMA* 329, no. 11 (2023): 897–898, https://jamanetwork .com/journals/jama/fullarticle/2801828; Maria Popp et al., "Ivermectin for Preventing and Treating COVID-19," Cochrane Library, July 28, 2021, https://www.cochranelibrary.com/cdsr /doi/10.1002/14651858.CD015017.pub2/full.

105 "Claim by Steve Kirsch That the Amish Don't Experience Autism, Cancer, or High COVID-19 Mortality Because They Don't Vaccinate Is Baseless," Health Feedback, https://healthfeedback .org/claimreview/claim-steve-kirsch-amish-dont-experience-autism-cancer-high-covid-19 -mortality-because-they-dont-vaccinate-baseless.

106 "Twitter Files," Wikipedia, last modified November 15, 2023, http://en.wikipedia, https:// en.wikipedia.org/wiki/Twitter_Files.

107 Matt Taibbi (@mtaibbi), "This is a devastating email. Here is Stanford's Virality project—which partners with multiple state agencies—recommending against 'stories of true vaccine side effects' and...," Twitter, March 10, 2023, Internet Archive, https://web.archive.org/web/20230310151556 /https://twitter.com/mtaibbi/status/1633955467968802816.

108 Mikki Willis, "Is Your Immune System at the Mercy of...Whatever's Next?," Plandemic Series, https://plandemicseries.com/Fierce-Immunity.

109 Siva Vaidhyanathan, *Antisocial Media: How Facebook Disconnects Us and Undermines Democracy* (Oxford: Oxford University Press, 2018), p. 15.

110 Jonathan Rauch, *The Constitution of Knowledge: A Defense of Truth* (Washington, DC: Brookings Institution Press, 2021), 234.

111 Sheryl Gay Stolberg and Benjamin Mueller, "Lab Leak or Not? How Politics Shaped the Battle over Covid's Origin," *New York Times*, March 19, 2023, https://www.nytimes.com/2023/03/19 /us/politics/covid-origins-lab-leak-politics.html.

112 Neil Jay Sehgal et al., "The Association Between COVID-19 Mortality and the County-Level Partisan Divide in the United States," *HealthAffairs* 41, no. 6 (June 2022), https://www.healthaffairs .org/doi/abs/10.1377/hlthaff.2022.00085; David Ovalle, "Vaccine Politics May Be to Blame for GOP Excess Deaths, Study Finds," *Washington Post*, July 24, 2023, https://www.washingtonpost .com/health/2023/07/24/covid-vaccines-republicans-deaths.

113 Klein, *Doppelganger*,101.

114 Moises Velasquez-Manoff, "The Anti-vaccine Movement's New Frontier," *New York Times*, May 25, 2022, https://www.nytimes.com/2022/05/25/magazine/anti-vaccine-movement.html.

115 Benjamin Bratton, *The Revenge of the Real: Politics for a Post-pandemic World* (London: Verso, 2021), 11.

CHAPTER 8: THE FANTASY INDUSTRIAL COMPLEX

1 Mike Benz (@MikeBenzCyber), "It's true. When I ran cyber at State, we leaned heavily on SpaceX for all things satellite-related. Always had a seat at the table," Twitter, July 29, 2023, 9:33 p.m., https://web.archive.org/web/20230907145812/https://twitter.com/MikeBenzCyber/status/1685403088075853824.

2 Benz describes himself in myriad ways depending on the interview. His official State Department employment page indicates a November 2020 appointment (see "Michael A. Benz," US Department of State, November 24, 2020, https://2017-2021.state.gov/biographies/michael-a-benz), and his prior stint as a speechwriter for Secretary Carson is confirmed at "Assistant Secretary for Public Affairs (HUD) Employee Salaries 2019," OpenPayrolls, accessed September 25, 2023, https://openpayrolls.com/federal/united-states-department-of-housing-and-urban-development/2019-assistant-secretary-for-public-affairs. In other biographies he has been identified as a diplomat (see "Mike Benz," Townhall, n.d., Internet Archive, https://web.archive.org/web/20220530091853/https://townhall.com/columnists/mikebenz). In one interview, he puts the dates of his employment as "Fall 2020 to January 2021" and alludes to speechwriting for President Trump as well (see Abhinandan Mishra, "Anti-India Cabal in US State Department Manipulated Online Discourse on PM Modi: Ex US Diplomat," *Sunday Guardian* (India), updated February 5, 2023, Internet Archive, https://web.archive.org/web/20230206060214/https://sundayguardianlive.com/news/anti-india-cabal-us-state-department-manipulated-online-discourse-pm-modi). In another interview, he laid out his responsibilities for his few months at the State Department: "I was the deputy assistant secretary for International Communications and Information Technology, which is a long way of saying I ran the big tech portfolio for the State Department in the Economic Bureau. I had three divisions under me. One was on security defending IT as it relates to low earth satellites and SpaceX and subsea cables and fiber optics. Another was our U.S. tech policy vis-a-vis countries on a one-off basis. The third division was multilateral affairs, which is basically the private sector" (see "Unraveling the Web of Internet Freedom: A Candid Conversation with Mike Benz, Former Diplomat Turned Digital Freedom Advocate," *Federal Newswire*, April 23, 2023, Internet Archive, https://web.archive.org/web/20230419170152/https://thefederalnewswire.com/stories/641707686-weekend-interview-mike-benz).

3 See Mike Benz, "'Department of Homeland Censorship': How DHS Seized Power over Online Speech," August 27, 2022, Internet Archive, https://web.archive.org/web/20230517184202/https://foundationforfreedomonline.com/department-of-homeland-censorship-how-dhs-seized-power-over-online-speech; additionally articulated on Twitter in many threads, e.g., Mike Benz (@MikeBenzCyber), "Chris Krebs, the DHS director at CISA who deputized EIP and Atlantic Council to censor 22 million tweets during the 2020 election cycle, even gave the opening remarks at the Atlantic Council tell-all about how they colluded to silence conservatives," Twitter, December 23, 2022, 5:35 p.m., Internet Archive, https://web.archive.org/web/20230906174807/https://twitter.com/MikeBenzCyber/status/1606342725975961600.

4 Center for an Informed Public, Digital Forensic Research Lab, Graphika, and Stanford Internet Observatory, "The Long Fuse: Misinformation and the 2020 Election," Stanford Digital Repository: Election Integrity Partnership, March 3, 2021, https://purl.stanford.edu/tr171zs0069.

5 Mishra, "Anti-India Cabal in US State Department Manipulated Online Discourse."

6 Benz uses this metaphor repeatedly to capture attention from credulous audiences on Twitter (see Mike Benz [@MikeBenzCyber], "Would love to explain the AI censorship death star superweapon to @joerogan," Twitter, July 1, 2023, 8:35 p.m., Internet Archive, https://web.archive.org/web/20230906192037/https://twitter.com/MikeBenzCyber/status/1675347554895302657), often with accompanying footage of himself discussing the concept. For a summary of one such video, see Melissa Fine, "Elon Musk 'Picked a Fight with America' Say Critics, 'He Has

No Idea the DARPA Rattlesnake He Just Stepped On,'" *BizPac Review*, July 3, 2023, Internet Archive, https://web.archive.org/web/20230711021158/https://www.bizpacreview.com/2023/07/03/elon-musk-picked-a-fight-with-america-say-critics-he-has-no-idea-the-darpa-rattlesnake-he-just-stepped-on-1373855.

7 Stanford's portion of this $3 million award was $748,437 over five years. For details, see "$2.25 Million in National Science Foundation Funding Will Support Center for an Informed Public's Rapid-Response Research of Mis- and Disinformation," University of Washington Center for an Informed Public, August 15, 2021, https://www.cip.uw.edu/2021/08/15/national-science-foundation-uw-cip-misinformation-rapid-response-research.

8 The project was first announced at Jason Foster, "My New Project: Empower Oversight: Because That's What Whistleblowers Do," *Stubborn Things*, July 2, 2021, https://jasonfoster.substack.com/p/my-new-project. In 2022, Mike Benz's Foundation for Freedom Online website acknowledged Empower Oversight in its footer; see "Protecting Digital Liberties, Educating about Censorship, Promoting Online Freedom," Foundation for Freedom Online, Internet Archive, https://web.archive.org/web/20220829203730/https://www.foundationforfreedomonline.com.

9 Robert Faturechi, "A Partisan Combatant, a Remorseful Blogger: The Senate Staffer Behind the Attack on the Trump-Russia Investigation," *ProPublica*, March 28, 2018, https://www.propublica.org/article/jason-foster-the-senate-staffer-behind-the-attack-on-the-trump-russia-investigation.

10 "Mission," Empower Oversight Whistleblowers & Research, accessed September 23, 2023, Internet Archive, https://web.archive.org/web/20230809021038/https://empowr.us/mission.

11 "Disinfo Dictionary: Benz, Mike," *Tablet*, March 27, 2023, https://www.tabletmag.com/sections/news/articles/disinformation-dictionary#benz.

12 Greg Piper, "Stanford Accused of Rebooting CIA Mind-Control Project with 'News Source Trustworthiness Ratings,'" Just the News, updated August 25, 2023, Internet Archive, https://web.archive.org/web/20230825102917/https://justthenews.com/accountability/watchdogs/stanford-accused-rebooting-cia-mind-control-project-news-source.

13 Jeff Cercone, "Partnership Targeted Election Misinformation, Not Conservatives," PolitiFact, October 11, 2022, https://www.politifact.com/factchecks/2022/oct/11/instagram-posts/partnership-targeted-election-misinformation-not-c.

14 Benz, "Department of Homeland Censorship.'"

15 See Harry G. Frankfurt, *On Bullshit* (Princeton, NJ: Princeton University Press, 2005). A liar attempts to conceal their deception; a bullshitter simply does not care about the truth.

16 There is an online adage known as Brandolini's law, or the bullshit asymmetry principle: "The amount of energy needed to refute bullshit is an order of magnitude bigger than that needed to produce it." See Alberto Brandolini (@ziobrando), "The bullshit asimmetry: the amount of energy needed to refute bullshit is an order of magnitude bigger than to produce it," Twitter, January 10, 2013, 11:29 p.m., https://twitter.com/ziobrando/status/289635060758507521.

17 "A Statement from the Election Integrity Partnership," Election Integrity Partnership, October 5, 2022, https://www.eipartnership.net/blog/a-statement-from-the-election-integrity-partnership.

18 John Suler, "The Online Disinhibition Effect," *CyberPsychology & Behavior* 7, no. 3 (2004): 321–326, https://doi.org/10.1089/1094931041291295.

19 Jeremy Frimer et al., "Incivility Is Rising Among American Politicians on Twitter," *Social Psychological and Personality Science* 14, no. 2 (March 2023): 259–269, https://doi.org/10.1177/19485506221083811.

20 Sandra González-Bailón and Yphtach Lelkes, "Do Social Media Undermine Social Cohesion? A Critical Review," *Social Issues and Policy Review* 17, no. 1 (January 2023): 155–180, https://doi.org/10.1111/sipr.12091.

21 Brandy Zadrozny, "House GOP Candidate Known for QAnon Support Was 'Correspondent' for Conspiracy Website," *NBC News*, April 14, 2020, https://www.nbcnews.com/tech/tech-news/georgia-congressional-candidate-s-writings-highlight-qanon-support-n1236724.

22 Paul LeBlanc, "Video Surfaces of Marjorie Taylor Greene Confronting Parkland Shooting Survivor with Baseless Claims," *CNN*, updated January 28, 2021, https://www.cnn.com/2021/01/27/politics/marjorie-taylor-greene-david-hogg-video/index.html.

23 Steven W. Webster, Adam N. Glynn, and Matthew P. Motta, "Partisan Schadenfreude and Candidate Cruelty," *Political Psychology*, August 23, 2023, https://doi.org/10.1111/pops.12922.

24 Yoel Roth, "Trump Attacked Me. Then Musk Did. It Wasn't an Accident," *New York Times*, September 18, 2023, https://www.nytimes.com/2023/09/18/opinion/trump-elon-musk-twitter.html.

25 Sara Dorn, "Marjorie Taylor Greene Assails Ex-Twitter Execs for Banning Her Account—Accuses One of Endorsing Child Sexualization," *Forbes*, February 8, 2023, https://www.forbes.com/sites/saradorn/2023/02/08/marjorie-taylor-greene-assails-ex-twitter-execs-for-banning-her-account-accuses-yoel-roth-of-endorsing-child-sexualization/?sh=47cdc9153848.

26 Russell Muirhead and Nancy L. Rosenblum, *A Lot of People Are Saying: The New Conpiracism and the Assault on Democracy* (Princeton, NJ: Princeton University Press, 2019), 56.

27 Adrian Blanco and Amy Gardner, "Where Republican Election Deniers Are on the Ballot Near You," *Washington Post*, updated November 8, 2022, https://www.washingtonpost.com/elections/interactive/2022/election-deniers-running-for-office-elections-2022.

28 Karen Yourish, Larry Buchanan, and Denise Lu, "The 147 Republicans Who Voted to Overturn Election Results," *New York Times*, updated January 7, 2021, https://www.nytimes.com/interactive/2021/01/07/us/elections/electoral-college-biden-objectors.html.

29 Greta Bedekovics and Ashleigh Maciolek, "Election Deniers Lost Key Races for Federal and State Offices in the 2022 Midterm Elections," Center for American Progress, November 22, 2022, https://www.americanprogress.org/article/election-deniers-lost-key-races-for-federal-and-state-offices-in-the-2022-midterm-elections.

30 Elizabeth Dwoskin and Jeremy B. Merrill, "Trump's 'Big Lie' Fueled a New Generation of Social Media Influencers," *Washington Post*, September 20, 2022, https://www.washingtonpost.com/technology/2022/09/20/social-media-influencers-election-fraud.

31 Elizabeth Dwoskin (@lizzadwoskin), "NEW: Been working for months on this data project w/@jeremybmerrill. The 'big lie' wasn't just a plan to overturn the election. It was massive clout-building exercise that spawned a generation of influencers," Twitter, September 20, 2022, 7:20 a.m., https://twitter.com/lizzadwoskin/status/1572229291496308737?s=20.

32 Jesse Singal, "Teen Fiction Twitter Is Eating Its Young," *Reason*, June 2019, https://reason.com/2019/05/05/teen-fiction-twitter-is-eating-its-young; Katy Waldman, "In Y.A., Where Is the Line Between Criticism and Cancel Culture?," *New Yorker*, March 21, 2019, https://www.newyorker.com/books/under-review/in-ya-where-is-the-line-between-criticism-and-cancel-culture.

33 Nick Popli, "How M&M's Became the Latest Flash Point in the Culture Wars," *Time*, January 23, 2023, https://time.com/6249551/m-m-candy-mascots-culture-wars.

34 Tyler Kingkade et al., "How an Urban Myth About Litter Boxes in Schools Became a GOP Talking Point," *NBC News*, October 14, 2022, https://www.nbcnews.com/tech/misinformation/urban-myth-litter-boxes-schools-became-gop-talking-point-rcna51439.

35 Many, many things attributed to Mark Twain on the internet were not actually said by Mark Twain.

36 Venkatesh Rao, "The Internet of Beefs," *Ribbonfarm*, January 16, 2020, https://www.ribbonfarm.com/2020/01/16/the-internet-of-beefs.

37 Petter Törnberg, "How Digital Media Drive Affective Polarization Through Partisan Sorting," *Proceedings of the National Academy of Sciences* 119, no. 42 (October 2022), https://www.pnas.org/doi/10.1073/pnas.2207159119.

38 University of Amsterdam, "Social Media Polarizes Politics for a Different Reason Than You Might Think," Phys.org, October 12, 2022, https://phys.org/news/2022-10-social-media-polarizes-politics.html.

39 Victoria A. Parker et al., "The Ties That Blind: Misperceptions of the Opponent Fringe and the Miscalibration of Political Contempt," *PsyArXiv*, October 1, 2021, https://doi:10.31234/osf.io/cr23g.

40 Ruby Edlin and Lawrence Norden, "Poll of Election Officials Shows High Turnover amid Safety Threats and Political Interference," Brennan Center for Justice, April 25, 2023, https://www.brennancenter.org/our-work/analysis-opinion/poll-election-officials-shows-high-turnover-amid-safety-threats-and.

41 Jim Hoft, "What's Up, Ruby?...BREAKING: Crooked Operative Filmed Pulling Out Suitcases of Ballots in Georgia IS IDENTIFIED," *Gateway Pundit*, December 3, 2020, Internet Archive,

https://web.archive.org/web/20201204030147/https://www.thegatewaypundit.com/2020/12
/ruby-breaking-crooked-democrat-filmed-pulling-suitcases-ballots-georgia-identified. Rudy Giuliani, who had served as Trump's personal lawyer, participated in defaming the women, who
were awarded $148 million in damages in a defamation case against him. Eileen Sullivan, "Jury
Orders Giuliani to Pay $148 Million to Election Workers He Defamed," *New York Times*, De-
cember 15, 2023, https://www.nytimes.com/2023/12/15/us/politics/rudy-giuliani-defamation
-trial-damages.html.

42 Anita Snow, "Armed Groups Can Monitor Arizona Ballot Drop Boxes, Federal Judge Rules,"
PBS NewsHour, October 28, 2022, https://www.pbs.org/newshour/politics/armed-group-can
-monitor-arizona-ballot-drop-boxes-federal-judge-rules.

43 Melody Gutierrez, "Anti-vaccine Activists, Mask Opponents Target Public Health Officials—
at Their Homes," *Los Angeles Times*, June 18, 2020, https://www.latimes.com/california/story
/2020-06-18/anti-mask-protesters-target-county-health-officers; Stephanie Lai, "Dozens Protest
Outside of Home of L.A. County's Public Health Director," *Los Angeles Times*, November 29,
2020, https://www.latimes.com/california/story/2020-11-29/dozens-protest-outside-of-la-health
-director-barbara-ferrers-echo-park-home.

44 Anna Maria Barry-Jester et al., "Pandemic Backlash Jeopardizes Public Health Powers, Leaders," *KFF Health News*, December 15, 2020, https://kffhealthnews.org/news/article/pandemic
-backlash-jeopardizes-public-health-powers-leaders.

45 Prof. Peter Hotez, MD, PhD (@PeterHotez), "Spotify Has Stopped Even Sort of Trying to Stem
Joe Rogan's Vaccine Misinformation. It's really true @annamerlan just awful," Twitter, June 17,
2023, 7:05 a.m., https://twitter.com/PeterHotez/status/1670040001751445504.

46 Peter Hotez, "Vaccine Scientist Speaks Out on Harassment After Joe Rogan Challenged Him,"
interview by Erin Burnett posted to YouTube by CNN, June 22, 2023, at 5:49, https://www
.youtube.com/watch?v=nGlE4f5P5oI.

47 Joe Rogan (@joerogan), "Peter, if you claim what RFKjr is saying is 'misinformation' I am offering you $100,000.00 to the charity of your choice if you're willing to debate him on my
show with no time limit," Twitter, June 17, 2023, 3:27 p.m., https://twitter.com/joerogan
/status/1670196590928068609.

48 Elon Musk (@elonmusk), "He's afraid of a public debate, because he knows he's wrong," Twitter,
June 17, 2023, 4:58 p.m., https://twitter.com/elonmusk/status/1670219488485154816.

49 Follower counts as of June 18, 2023.

50 Keren Landman, "Joe Rogan Wants a 'Debate' on Vaccine Science. Don't Give It to Him,"
Vox, June 22, 2023, vox.com/2023/6/22/23768539/rogan-rfk-hotez-debate-vaccine-deniers
-better.

51 Jeremy Littau, "Social Media Has Collapsed Good Debate," *The Atlantic*, June 24, 2023, https://
www.theatlantic.com/technology/archive/2023/06/joe-rogan-rfk-jr-interview-debate/674515.

52 Mark Norris, "Vaccine Expert Dr. Peter Hotez Harassed Outside Houston Home After
Weekend of Online Attacks," Texas Public Radio, June 19, 2023, https://www.tpr.org/public
-health/2023-06-19/vaccine-expert-dr-peter-hotez-harassed-outside-houston-home-after-weekend
-of-online-attacks.

53 For multiple perspectives see Jeremy Littau, "Social Media Has Collapsed Good Debate," *Atlantic*, June 24, 2023, https://www.theatlantic.com/technology/archive/2023/06/joe-rogan-rfk
-jr-interview-debate/674515, and Mike Solana, "Debatable Tactics," Pirate Wires, June 19, 2023,
https://www.piratewires.com/p/pirate-wires-rogans-debatable-tactic.

54 Anna Merlan, "Meet the New, Dangerous Fringe of the Anti-vaccination Movement," *Jezebel*,
June 29, 2015, https://jezebel.com/meet-the-new-dangerous-fringe-of-the-anti-vaccination-171
3438567.

55 This opinion has since become far more visible and even mainstream, with parents advocating for ballot measures to ensure that curriculum choices are restored. Mike Ege, "California
Math Wars: San Franciscans Demand Return of 8th Grade Algebra," *San Francisco Standard*,
November 13, 2023, https://sfstandard.com/2023/11/13/california-math-wars-san-franciscans
-demand-8th-grade-algebra.

56 Parker et al., "The Ties That Blind."

57 Anthony Adragna, Daniella Diaz, and Jennifer Scholtes, "Multiple Members Are Detailing Death Threats and Other Intimidation They've Faced for Opposing Jim Jordan's Speakership Bid," *Politico*, October 19, 2023, https://www.politico.com/live-updates/2023/10/19/congress/speaker-race-threats-house-00122416.

58 Roth would be targeted by a mob himself shortly after, in December 2022, when Elon Musk baselessly made allegations suggesting that he condoned child sexualization online. He wrote about the experience in Yoel Roth, "I Was the Head of Trust and Safety at Twitter. This Is What Could Become of It," *New York Times*, November 18, 2022, https://www.nytimes.com/2022/11/18/opinion/twitter-yoel-roth-elon-musk.html.

59 Renée DiResta et al., "Assessing Inauthentic Networks Commenting on the US Midterms," Election Integrity Partnership, November 1, 2022, https://www.eipartnership.net/blog/inauthentic-foreign-networks.

60 Jack Posobiec (@JackPosobiec), profile page, Twitter, November 2, 2022, Internet Archive, https://web.archive.org/web/20221102055859/https://twitter.com/JackPosobiec.

61 P. W. Singer and Emerson T. Brooking, *LikeWar: The Weaponization of Social Media* (Boston: Eamon Dolan/Houghton Mifflin Harcourt, 2018), 129.

62 Jack Posobiec (@JackPosobiec), "The 'independent analysts' citied by Twitter's Head of Safety and Integrity were behind censoring the Hunter Biden laptop in 2020", Twitter, November 2, 2022, archived at https://web.archive.org/web/20221102194354/https://twitter.com/JackPosobiec/status/1587836232582692871.

63 Renée DiResta, "The Twitter Files Are a Missed Opportunity," *The Atlantic*, December 15, 2022, https://www.theatlantic.com/ideas/archive/2022/12/twitter-files-content-moderation-transparency/672468.

64 Devin Coldewey, "Deconstructing 'The Twitter Files,'" *TechCrunch*, January 13, 2023, https://techcrunch.com/2023/01/13/deconstructing-the-twitter-files.

65 Novelist Michael Crichton coined a phrase to describe the phenomenon of trusting a source in one area while forgetting its unreliability in another: Gell-Mann Amnesia. "You open the newspaper to an article on some subject you know well... You read the article and see the journalist has absolutely no understanding of either the facts or the issues. Often, the article is so wrong it actually presents the story backward—reversing cause and effect. I call these the 'wet streets cause rain' stories. Paper's full of them. In any case, you read with exasperation or amusement the multiple errors in a story, and then turn the page to national or international affairs, and read as if the rest of the newspaper was somehow more accurate about far-off Palestine than it was about the story you just read. You turn the page, and forget what you know." Michael Crichton, "Why Speculate?" (speech, International Leadership Forum, La Jolla, California, April 26, 2002), Michael Crichton, Internet Archive, http://web.archive.org/web/20070714204136/http://www.michaelcrichton.net/speech-whyspeculate.html.

66 Robert Collier, "Venezuelan Politics Suit Bay Area Activists' Talents / Locals Help Build Chavez's Image, Provide Polling Data," *SFGATE*, August 21, 2004, https://www.sfgate.com/politics/article/Venezuelan-politics-suit-Bay-Area-activists-2700433.php.

67 Michael Shellenberger (@shellenberger), "46. The FBI's influence campaign may have been helped by the fact that it was paying Twitter millions of dollars for its staff time," Twitter, December 19, 2022, 10:36 a.m., Internet Archive, https://web.archive.org/web/20230916181050/https://twitter.com/shellenberger/status/1604908670063906817.

68 Oliver Darcy, "Elon Musk Claims the FBI Paid Twitter to 'Censor Info from the Public.' Here's What the Twitter Files Actually Show," *CNN*, December 20, 2022, https://www.cnn.com/2022/12/20/media/elon-musk-fbi-twitter-reliable-sources/index.html.

69 Steve Nelson, "House GOP Wants FBI's Twitter Censorship, Reimbursement Records," House of Representatives Judiciary Committee, December 23, 2022, https://judiciary.house.gov/media/in-the-news/house-gop-wants-fbis-twitter-censorship-reimbursement-records.

70 D'Angelo Gore, "FBI Reimbursed Twitter for Providing User Information," FactCheck.org, February 6, 2023, https://www.factcheck.org/2023/02/fbi-reimbursed-twitter-for-providing-user-information.

71 Renée DiResta, "Fiction vs Reality: My Texts with Michael Shellenberger," *Renee's Substack*, March 31, 2023, https://reneediresta.substack.com/p/fiction-vs-reality-my-texts-with; Sam Harris,

"Social Media & Public Trust: A Conversation with Bari Weiss, Michael Shellenberger, and Renée DiResta," video posted to YouTube by Sam Harris, February 1, 2023, 1:08:52, https://www.youtube.com/watch?v=tVeL5HX4uDY.

72 Bari Weiss (@bariweiss), "THREAD: THE TWITTER FILES PART TWO. TWITTER'S SE-CRET BLACKLISTS," Twitter, December 28, 2022, 4:15 p.m., https://twitter.com/bariweiss/status/1601007575633305600.

73 "Libs of TikTok," Wikipedia, last modified September 25, 2023, 4:56 p.m., https://en.wikipedia.org/wiki/Libs_of_TikTok.

74 See notes 46–48 in Chapter 5 for a collection of research discussing conservative content performance on social media.

75 "Terms of Service," InfoWars, accessed December 19, 2023, Internet Archive, https://web.archive.org/web/20231205213951/https://www.infowars.com/terms-of-service.

76 Trash Discourse (@ThaWoodChipper), "Breaking: FBI releases Cyber Plan w/ @kyleseraphin @americamission_," Twitter Spaces, March 2, 2023, 8:59 a.m., Internet Archive, https://web.archive.org/web/20230324011816/https://twitter.com/ThaWoodChipper/status/1631338520697802752?s=20. Create audio archive.

77 "Hearing on the Weaponization of the Federal Government, Before the Select Subcommittee on the Weaponization of the Federal Government," 118th Congress, US House of Representatives Committee Repository, March 9, 2023, https://docs.house.gov/Committee/Calendar/ByEvent.aspx?EventID=115442.

78 Andrea Bernstein, "Republican Rep. Jim Jordan Issues Sweeping Information Requests to Universities Researching Disinformation," *ProPublica*, March 22, 2023, https://www.propublica.org/article/jim-jordan-disinformation-subpoena-universities.

79 Jim Jordan refused to cooperate with the House Select Committee to Investigate the January 6th Attack on the United States Capitol, commenting, "This request is far outside the bounds of any legitimate inquiry, violates core constitutional principles and would serve to further erode legislative norms." He subsequently defied a subpoena from the committee, writing, "Public statements by members of the Select Committee indicate that it seeks to use its subpoena authority for improper motives and for the self-aggrandizement of its members." See Luke Broadwater, "Jim Jordan Refuses to Cooperate with Jan. 6 Panel," *New York Times*, updated October 13, 2023, https://www.nytimes.com/2022/01/09/us/politics/jim-jordan-jan-6-panel.html; Rep. Jim Jordan (@Jim_Jordan), "Response to the January 6th Committee," Twitter, May 25, 2022, 4:00 p.m., https://twitter.com/Jim_Jordan/status/1529598191854923776/photo/3.

80 Rep. Dan Bishop (@RepDanBishop), "To be sure, @MikeBenzCyber and @FFO_Freedom have made themselves indispensable in bringing to light the largest government censorship scheme in US history," Twitter, May 11, 2023, 8:38 a.m., Internet Archive, https://web.archive.org/web/20230920235530/https://twitter.com/RepDanBishop/status/1656760668911988774.

81 Michael Shellenberger, "'The Most Dangerous People in America Right Now,'" *Public* (blog), March 23, 2023, Internet Archive, https://web.archive.org/web/20230323150149/https://public.substack.com/p/the-most-dangerous-people-in-america; Michael Shellenberger, "Why Renee DiResta Leads the Censorship Industry," *Public* (blog), April 3, 2023, Internet Archive, https://web.archive.org/web/20230403185119/https://public.substack.com/p/why-renee-diresta-leads-the-censorship.

82 America First Legal, "Jill Hines & Jim Hoft v. Alex Stamos, et al.," blog post at https://aflegal.org/litigation/jill-hines-jim-hoft-v-alex-stamos-et-al. A copy of the lawsuit can be found at https://dockets.justia.com/docket/louisiana/lawdce/3:2023cv00571/199277.

83 Mike Masnick, "The Good, the Bad, and the Incredibly Ugly in the Court Ruling Regarding Government Contacts with Social Media," *Techdirt*, July 6, 2023, https://www.techdirt.com/2023/07/06/the-good-the-bad-and-the-incredibly-ugly-in-the-court-ruling-regarding-government-contacts-with-social-media.

84 "Stanford University Files Amicus Brief in Missouri v. Biden Appeal," press release, Stanford University Freeman Spogli Institute for International Studies, July 28, 2023, https://fsi.stanford.edu/news/stanford-university-files-amicus-brief-missouri-v-biden-appeal; *Missouri v. Biden*, 3:22-CV-01213 (W.D. La. Mar. 20, 2023).

85 Kate Starbird, "Addressing Falsehoods and the Manipulated Narrative of House Judiciary Committee Majority Document: 'The Weaponization of CISA: How a 'Cybersecurity' Agency Colluded with Big Tech and 'Disinformation' Partners to Censor Americans,'" University of Washington Center for an Informed Public, August 23, 2023, https://www.cip.uw.edu/2023/08/23/starbird-house-judiciary-committee-report.

86 Jonathan Blitzer, "Jim Jordan's Conspiratorial Quest for Power: How the Ohio Republican Built an Insurgent Bid for Speaker on the Lies of Donald Trump," *New Yorker*, October 21, 2023, https://www.newyorker.com/magazine/2023/10/30/jim-jordans-conspiratorial-quest-for-power.

87 Steven Lee Myers and Sheera Frenkel, "G.O.P. Targets Researchers Who Study Disinformation Ahead of 2024 Election," *New York Times*, June 19, 2023, https://www.nytimes.com/2023/06/19/technology/gop-disinformation-researchers-2024-election.html.

88 Naomi Oreskes and Erik M. Conway, *Merchants of Doubt: How a Handful of Scientists Obscured the Truth on Issues from Tobacco Smoke to Global Warming* (New York: Bloomsbury Press, 2010), 34.

89 Michael E. Mann, *The Hockey Stick and the Climate Wars: Dispatches from the Front Lines* (New York: Columbia University Press, 2012), 61.

90 Ibid., 200.

91 Post from Medhi Hasan documenting this interaction is at Mehdi Hasan (@mehdirhasan), "Me: 'It's just error after error, Matt?' @mtaibbi: 'Well, that is an error.' Watch me confront Matt Taibbi with multiple, unacknowledged, and glaring mistakes in his Twitter Files reporting…," Twitter, April 6, 2023, Internet Archive, https://web.archive.org/web/20230407052848/https://twitter.com/mehdirhasan/status/1644064242419617803. Media summary with embedded video can be found here: Justin Baragona, "MSNBC Host Makes Matt Taibbi Squirm over His 'Twitter Files' Errors," *Daily Beast*, April 6, 2023, https://www.thedailybeast.com/msnbc-host-mehdi-hasan-makes-matt-taibbi-squirm-over-his-twitter-files-errors.

92 Brandy Zadrozny, "Michael Benz, a Conservative Crusader Against Online Censorship, Appears to Have a Secret History as an Alt-Right Persona," *NBC News*, October 6, 2023, https://www.nbcnews.com/tech/internet/michael-benz-rising-voice-conservative-criticism-online-censorship-rcna119213.

93 Richard Spencer (@RichardBSpencer), "The notion that 'frame game' was engaged in 'deradicalization' is absurd. Though he obviously was trying to channel the AltRight in a certain direction for an outside player," Twitter, October 6, 2023, 8:04 p.m., Internet Archive, https://web.archive.org/web/20231009184131/https://twitter.com/RichardBSpencer/status/1710491232487854111.

94 Excerpted from a thread that Frame Game (sometimes "framegames") posted to Twitter and then archived to his Steemit blog. The post appears with the title "Thread 1: A Jewish Perspective on Jewish Influence" and the following description: "Below is a repost of my viral Twitter thread with over 5 million total impressions over the course of a week. With Twitter's speech bonfire fully underway, this thread is being archived here in eternity's bosom. It is reproduced with no edits, and was bound by Twitter's 140 character limit at the time of its writing, in August 2017." See framegames, "THREAD 1: A Jewish Perspective on Jewish Influence," steemit, https://web.archive.org/web/20231007003239/https://steemit.com/blog/@framegames/thread-1-a-jewish-perspective-on-jewish-influence-on-the-west.

95 We were sued in May 2023 in Texas as "de facto government agents" by the "New Civil Liberties Alliance" on behalf of activists alleging they were injured by their COVID-19 vaccines. See *Dressen v. Flaherty*, "Complaint for Declaratory and Injunctive Relief," 3:23-cv-00155 (S.D. Tex. 2023), https://nclalegal.org/wp-content/uploads/2023/05/Dressen-Complaint-Filed-5.22.23.pdf.

96 Naomi Nix and Cat Zakrzewski, "U.S. Stops Helping Big Tech Spot Foreign Meddling Amid GOP Legal Threats," *Washington Post*, November 30, 2023, https://www.washingtonpost.com/technology/2023/11/30/biden-foreign-disinformation-social-media-election-interference/.

97 Darius Tahir, "The NIH halts a research project. Is it self-censorship?," CBS News, August 5, 2023, https://www.cbsnews.com/news/nih-halts-research-project-is-it-self-censorship/.

98 Zach Greenberg, "Chilling open records request targets University of Washington faculty, threatens academic freedom," *The FIRE newsdesk*, November 15, 2022, https://www.thefire.org

/news/chilling-open-records-request-targets-university-washington-faculty-threatens-acade
mic-freedom.

99 Russell Muirhead and Nancy L. Rosenblum, *A Lot of People Are Saying: The New Conpiracism and the Assault on Democracy* (Princeton, NJ: Princeton University Press, 2019), 9.

CHAPTER 9: THE PATH FORWARD

1 Alan Brinkley, *Voices of Protest: Huey Long, Father Coughlin and the Great Depression* (New York: Vintage Books, 1983), 97.

2 Ibid., 143.

3 Forrest Davis, "Father Coughlin," *The Atlantic*, December 1935, https://www.theatlantic.com /magazine/archive/1935/12/father-coughlin/652107.

4 Clyde Haberman, "Today in History: The Father Coughlin Story," *PBS*, March 9, 2022, https:// www.pbs.org/wnet/exploring-hate/2022/03/09/today-in-history-the-father-coughlin-story.

5 Thomas Doherty, "The Deplatforming of Father Coughlin," *Slate*, January 21, 2021, https:// slate.com/technology/2021/01/father-coughlin-deplatforming-radio-social-media.html.

6 Tianyi Wang, "Media, Pulpit, and Populist Persuasion: Evidence from Father Coughlin," *American Economic Review* 111, no. 9 (2021): 3064–3092, https://doi.org/10.1257/aer.20200513.

7 "Father Coughlin Blames Jews for Nazi Violence," History Unfolded: US Newspapers and the Holocaust, https://newspapers.ushmm.org/events/father-coughlin-blames-jews-for-nazi-violence.

8 Davis, "Father Coughlin."

9 Doherty, "The Deplatforming."

10 Diane Cypkin, "A Rhetorical Critical Analysis of Father Coughlin's Radio Broadcast, November 20, 1938, or Call It What You Will...It's Still Anti-Semitism!," *Journal of Radio Studies* 4, no. 1 (1997): 134–150, https://doi.org/10.1080/19376529709391688.

11 "Father Coughlin Blames Jews," History Unfolded.

12 Bill Kovarik, "That Time Private US Media Companies Stepped in to Silence the Falsehoods and Incitements of a Major Public Figure...in 1938," *The Conversation*, January 15, 2021, https:// theconversation.com/that-time-private-us-media-companies-stepped-in-to-silence-the-falsehoods -and-incitements-of-a-major-public-figure-in-1938-153157.

13 "Priest Won't Meet WMCA Conditions," *New York Times*, November 27, 1938, 42, https:// timesmachine.nytimes.com/timesmachine/1938/11/27/99571181.html?pageNumber=42#.

14 Kovarik, "That Time Private US Media Companies."

15 Doherty, "The Deplatforming."

16 Otto D. Tolischus, "Germany to Keep Dieckhoff at Home," *New York Times*, November 27, 1938, 46, https://timesmachine.nytimes.com/timesmachine/1938/11/27/99571225.html.

17 Kovarik, "That Time Private US Media Companies."

18 "6,000 Here Cheer Coughlin's Name," *New York Times*, December 19, 1938, 6, https://timesmachine .nytimes.com/timesmachine/1938/12/16/98873857.html#.

19 "Fewer Coughlin Pickets; Protest at Radio Station over Ban Is Repeated," *New York Times*, December 26, 1938, 27, https://www.nytimes.com/1938/12/26/archives/fewer-coughlin-pickets -protest-at-radio-station-over-ban-is.html; "WMCA Picketing Limited; Confined by Police to Broadway Side of Building," *New York Times*, June 19, 1939, 8, https://www.nytimes.com/1939 /06/19/archives/wmca-picketing-limited-confined-by-police-to-broadway-side-of.html.

20 David Goodman, "Before Hate Speech: Charles Coughlin, Free Speech and Listeners' Rights," *Patterns of Prejudice* 49, no. 3 (2015): 199–224, https://doi.org/10.1080/0031322X.2015.10 48972.

21 "Coughlin Copies Goebbels Speech," *Daily Clarion-Ledger*, December 31, 1938, 1, published on-line at Newspapers.com, September 23, 2018, https://www.newspapers.com/article/23966340.

22 "Coughlin Supports Christian Front; While Not a Member, 'I Do Not Disassociate Myself from Movement,' Priest Says," *New York Times*, January 22, 1940, 1, https://www.nytimes.com /1940/01/22/archives/coughlin-supports-christian-front-while-not-a-member-i-do-not.html.

23 The FBI raid of the headquarters of the Christian Front led to the arrest of seventeen men who came to be called the "Brooklyn Boys." However, sixteen of the seventeen were found not guilty. See Andrew Lapin, "Ep. 7: Sedition," *Radioactive: The Father Coughlin Story*, March 9, 2022,

https://www.pbs.org/wnet/exploring-hate/2022/03/09/ep-7-sedition; J. P. O'Malley, "FBI Files Shine Light on Homegrown Nazi Plot to Overthrow US Government During WWII," *Times of Israel*, January 28, 2022, https://www.timesofisrael.com/fbi-files-shine-light-on-homegrown -nazi-plot-to-overthrow-us-government-during-wwii; Editors of Encyclopaedia Britannica, "Christian Front," *Britannica*, n.d., https://www.britannica.com/topic/Christian-Front.

24 Kovarik, "That Time Private US Media Companies."

25 "Father Coughlin Blames Jews," History Unfolded.

26 Stewart M. Hoover and Douglas K. Wagner, "History and Policy in American Broadcast Treat-ment of Religion," *Media, Culture and Society* 19, no. 1 (January 1997): 7–27, published online at Religion Online, https://www.religion-online.org/article/history-and-policy-in-american -broadcast-treatment-of-religion.

27 Ibid.

28 In 1949, the FCC implemented the Fairness Doctrine, which aimed to regulate public discourse on controversial topics in broadcast media by requiring equal time for balanced opposing view-points. This rule itself sparked controversy due to its vague criteria for what qualified as a view-point requiring equal debate. In 1987, under President Ronald Reagan, the FCC repealed the Fairness Doctrine, citing its stifling impact on free speech.

29 Kate Klonick, "The New Governors: The People, Rules, and Processes Governing Online Speech," *Harvard Law Review* 131, no. 6 (April 2018): 1598–1670.

30 Christopher St. Aubin and Jacob Liedke, "Most Americans Favor Restrictions on False Informa-tion, Violent Content Online," Pew Research Center, July 20, 2023, https://www.pewresearch .org/short-reads/2023/07/20/most-americans-favor-restrictions-on-false-information-violent -content-online.

31 Daphne Keller, "Lawful but Awful? Control over Legal Speech by Platforms, Governments, and Internet Users," *University of Chicago Law Review Online*, June 28, 2022, https://lawreviewblog .uchicago.edu/2022/06/28/keller-control-over-speech.

32 Renée DiResta, "The Digital Maginot Line," *Ribbonfarm*, November 28, 2018, https://www .ribbonfarm.com/2018/11/28/the-digital-maginot-line.

33 Giuseppe Russo et al., "Spillover of Antisocial Behavior from Fringe Platforms: The Unintended Consequences of Community Banning," *Proceedings of the International AAAI Conference on Web and Social Media ICWSM* 16 (2023): 742–753, https://doi.org/10.48550/arXiv.2209.09803.

34 Jeff Kosseff, *Liar in a Crowded Theater: Freedom of Speech in a World of Misinformation* (Balti-more: Johns Hopkins University Press, 2023).

35 Jeremy Boreing (@JeremyDBoreing), "Twitter canceled a deal with @realdailywire to pre-miere What is a Woman?...," Twitter, June 1, 2023, Internet Archive, https://web.archive.org /web/20230601142311/https://twitter.com/JeremyDBoreing/status/1664255321630552065.

36 Some of Twitter's policies regularly intersected with active fronts in the culture war, turning the policies themselves into a matter of controversy as well as an opportunity to capture atten-tion. For example, it had a long-standing rule that prohibited harassing *individual* transgender users (such as by referring to them with prior names or pronouns) while still allowing criticism of trans-related policies and laws or identity politics writ large. This attempt to minimize the harassment of individual users, however, was often framed as inherently anticonservative; some argued that it forced conservatives to use pronouns that they disagreed with, which impinged upon their freedom of speech. The targets of the speech, however, were also users who wanted to express themselves on Twitter as well. As with many moderation decisions, calls sometimes hinged on whether individual moderators felt that a word or phrase was harassment, merely offensive, or an overreaction by the reportee. More importantly, however, the policy became a source of secondary attention-capture for clout and profit, as those who alleged that they were moderated unfairly—or felt they went unheard—subsequently commanded attention cycles highlighting the incidents.

37 Jeremy Boreing (@JeremyDBoreing), "I appreciate the reply. We posted the two clips flagged by Twitter and they were indeed labeled 'hateful conduct' and the share functions were dis-abled on the...," Twitter, Juny 1, 2023, https://twitter.com/JeremyDBoreing/status/16643327 65226057730?s=20.

38 Daysia Tolentino and David Ingram, "Musk's response to an anti-trans video sparks 24 hours of chaos at Twitter," *NBC News*, June 3, 2023, https://www.nbcnews.com/tech/social-media/musk-elon-twitter-ella-irwin-trans-video-what-is-a-woman-stream-rcna87429.

39 Robert B. Cialdini, *Influence: Science and Practice*, 5th ed. (1984; reis., Boston: Pearson, 2009), 210–211.

40 "Community Principles," TikTok, last updated March 2023, https://www.tiktok.com/community-guidelines/en/community-principles.

41 "Ensuring Respect for Free Expression, Through Independent Judgement," Oversight Board, https://www.oversightboard.com.

42 For example, Twitter and Facebook have programs to ensure that moderation actions against high-profile users are checked by multiple reviewers, including at times the executive team. Preliminary indications from some of our data in the 2020 election suggested that lower-follower accounts were actioned for election misinformation even as influencers with far more reach did not appear to be. This is perhaps a natural defensive stance for Big Tech platforms, but it preferentially favors those with large audiences or offline power. Renée DiResta and Matt Debutts, "'Newsworthiness,' Trump, and the Facebook Oversight Board," *Columbia Journalism Review*, April 26, 2021, https://www.cjr.org/the_new_gatekeepers/facebook-oversight-board-2.php.

43 For a nuanced explanation of how content moderation work is done and the mental health impacts it has, see Casey Newton, "The Trauma Floor: The Secret Lives of Facebook Moderators in America," *The Verge*, February 25, 2019, https://www.theverge.com/2019/2/25/18229714/cognizant-facebook-content-moderator-interviews-trauma-working-conditions-arizona.

44 "Singapore Tightens the Reins on Extreme Social Media Content," *Japan Times*, November 12, 2022, https://www.japantimes.co.jp/life/2022/11/12/general/social-media-content-law-singapore.

45 Yashraj Sharma, "Twitter Accused of Censorship in India as It Blocks Modi Critics," *The Guardian*, April 5, 2023, https://www.theguardian.com/world/2023/apr/05/twitter-accused-of-censorship-in-india-as-it-blocks-modi-critics-elon-musk.

46 Charlie Savage, "Trump's Order Targeting Social Media Sites, Explained," *New York Times*, May 28, 2020, https://www.nytimes.com/2020/05/28/us/politics/trump-twitter-explained.html.

47 David Shepardson, "Biden Revokes Trump Order That Sought to Limit Social Media Firms' Protections," *Reuters*, May 17, 2021, https://www.reuters.com/technology/biden-revokes-trump-order-that-sought-limit-social-media-firms-protections-2021-05-15.

48 Fletcher Schoen and Christopher J. Lamb, "Deception, Disinformation, and Strategic Communications: How One Interagency Group Made a Major Difference," Institute for National Strategic Studies, June 1, 2012, https://inss.ndu.edu/Media/News/Article/693590/deception-disinformation-and-strategic-communications-how-one-interagency-group.

49 Fred Barbash, "U.S. Ties 'Klan' Olympic Hate Mail to KGB," *Washington Post*, August 7, 1984, https://www.washingtonpost.com/archive/politics/1984/08/07/us-ties-klan-olympic-hate-mail-to-kgb/80918fe8-fcf0-46cf-bb58-726ee46d8ce9.

50 Michael Dhunjishah, "Countering Propaganda and Disinformation: Bring Back the Active Measures Working Group?," *War Room*, July 7, 2017, https://warroom.armywarcollege.edu/articles/countering-propaganda-disinformation-bring-back-active-measures-working-group.

51 Knight First Amendment Institute at Columbia University, https://knightcolumbia.org/blog/channel/jawboning.

52 Will Oremus with David DiMolfetta, "Disinfo Researchers Are Under Pressure from the Right. They're Starting to Push Back," *Washington Post*, August 3, 2023, https://www.washingtonpost.com/politics/2023/08/03/disinfo-researchers-are-under-pressure-right-theyre-starting-push-back.

53 Mike Masnick, "5th Circuit Cleans Up District Court's Silly Jawboning Ruling About the Biden Admin, Trims It Down to More Accurately Reflect the 1st Amendment," *Techdirt*, September 11, 2023, https://www.techdirt.com/2023/09/11/5th-circuit-cleans-up-district-courts-silly-jawboning-ruling-about-the-biden-admin-trims-it-down-to-more-accurately-reflect-the-1st-amendment.

54 Stanford University filed an amicus brief with the Supreme Court, as we had with the Fifth Circuit, fact-checking the claims about us and our work. That can be found at http://www.supremecourt.gov/DocketPDF/23/23-411/294255/20231226143930837_Murthy%20v.%20Missouri%20--%20SCOTUS%20Amicus%20FINAL.pdf.

55 Yoel Roth, "Getting the Facts Straight: Some Observations on the Fifth Circuit Ruling in Missouri v. Biden," *Jawboning* (blog), Knight First Amendment Institute at Columbia University, September 27, 2023, https://knightcolumbia.org/blog/getting-the-facts-straight-some-observations-on-the-fifth-circuit-ruling-in-missouri-v-biden-1.

56 *State of Missouri, et al. v. Joseph R. Biden Jr., et al.,* 3:22-CV-01213 (W.D. La. Jul. 4, 2023), https://ago.mo.gov/wp-content/uploads/missouri-v-biden-ruling.pdf.

57 Robby Soave, "Inside the Facebook Files: Emails Reveal the CDC's Role in Silencing COVID-19 Dissent," *Reason*, January 19, 2023, https://reason.com/2023/01/19/facebook-files-emails-cdc-covid-vaccines-censorship.

58 For coverage of the controversy, see David Ingram, "Elon Musk's Twitter Faces Censorship Allegations in India Free Speech Battle," *NBC News*, January 25, 2023, https://www.nbcnews.com/tech/social-media/modi-twitter-bbc-musk-elon-documentary-watch-video-rcna67497. Also see Lumen's post about Twitter ceasing contributions: Lumen (@lumendatabase), "As of April 15th, 2023, Twitter has not submitted copies of any of the takedown notices it receives to Lumen…" Twitter, April 27, 2023, 4:25 p.m., https://twitter.com/lumendatabase/status/1651578251599310849.

59 Herbert A. Simon, "Designing Organizations for an Information-Rich World," in M. Greenberger (ed.), *Computers, Communications, and the Public Interest* (Baltimore: Johns Hopkins Press, 1971).

60 Renée DiResta, "How Online Mobs Act like Flocks of Birds," *NOEMA*, November 3, 2022, https://www.noemamag.com/how-online-mobs-act-like-flocks-of-birds.

61 Kaitlyn Tiffany, "Very, Very Few People Are Falling Down the YouTube Rabbit Hole," *The Atlantic*, August 30, 2023, https://www.theatlantic.com/technology/archive/2023/08/youtube-rabbit-holes-american-politics/675186.

62 Sandra González-Bailón et al., "Asymmetric Ideological Segregation in Exposure to Political News on Facebook," *Science* 381, no. 6656 (July 2023): 392–398, https://doi.org/10.1126/science.ade7138.

63 Kai Kupferschmidt, "Does Social Media Polarize Voters? Unprecedented Experiments on Facebook Users Reveal Surprises," *Science*, July 27, 2023, https://www.science.org/content/article/does-social-media-polarize-voters-unprecedented-experiments-facebook-users-reveal; Brendan Nyhan et al., "Like-Minded Sources on Facebook Are Prevalent but Not Polarizing," *Nature* 620 (July 2023): 137–144, https://www.nature.com/articles/s41586-023-06795-x.

64 Justin Hendrix and Paul M. Barrett, "The Meta Studies: Nuanced Findings, Corporate Spin, and Media Oversimplification," *Tech Policy Press*, August 2, 2023, https://www.techpolicy.press/the-meta-studies-nuanced-findings-corporate-spin-and-media-oversimplification.

65 Aviv Ovadya and Luke Thorburn, "Bridging Systems: Open Problems for Countering Destructive Divisiveness Across Ranking, Recommenders, and Governance," Knight First Amendment Institute at Columbia University, October 26, 2023, https://knightcolumbia.org/content/bridging-systems.

66 Tom Cunningham, "Ranking by Engagement," *Tom Cunningham*, May 8, 2023, https://tecunningham.github.io/posts/2023-04-28-ranking-by-engagement.html; "Ranking by Engagement," Integrity Institute, May 8, 2023, https://integrityinstitute.org/blog/ranking-by-engagement.

67 Jonathan Stray, "Designing Recommender Systems to Depolarize," *First Monday* 27, no. 5 (2022), https://doi.org/10.5210/fm.v27i5.12604.

68 For example, studies suggest that platforms play a role in driving people to untrustworthy websites and that Facebook played a smaller role in 2020 than in 2016. Ryan C. Moore, Ross Dahlke, and Jeffrey T. Hancock, "Exposure to Untrustworthy Websites in the 2020 US Election," *Nature Human Behaviour* 7 (2023): 1096–1105, https://www.nature.com/articles/s41562-023-01564-2.

69 Gordon Pennycook and David G. Rand, "Fighting Misinformation on Social Media Using Crowdsourced Judgements of News Source Quality," *Proceedings of the National Academy of Sciences* 116, no. 7 (January 28, 2019): 2521–2526, https://doi.org/10.1073/pnas.1806781116.

70 Eric Jaffe, "The 'Contagion' of Social Networks," *Los Angeles Times*, September 13, 2010, https://www.latimes.com/archives/la-xpm-2010-sep-13-la-he-social-networks-health-20100913-story.html.

71 Eli Pariser and Talia Stroud's nonprofit organization New_ Public maintains a Substack with research into how norms shape digital spaces. See, for example, "Understanding How Norms

Shape Digital Spaces," *New_ Public*, Substack, December 10, 2023, https://newpublic.substack.com/p/understanding-how-norms-shape-digital.

72 Philip Bump, "From the Election to the Riot, Nearly a Third of Facebook's Top Link Posts Were from Right-Wing Media," *Washington Post*, January 12, 2021, https://www.washingtonpost.com/politics/2021/01/12/election-riot-nearly-third-facebooks-top-link-posts-were-right-wing-media.

73 Renée DiResta, "Free Speech Is Not the Same as Free Reach," *Wired*, August 30, 2018, https://www.wired.com/story/free-speech-is-not-the-same-as-free-reach.

74 "Freedom of Speech, Not Reach: An Update on Our Enforcement Philosophy," *Twitter Blog*, April 17, 2023, https://blog.twitter.com/en_us/topics/product/2023/freedom-of-speech-not-reach-an-update-on-our-enforcement-philosophy.

75 Di Zhao, Pouriya, and Auro, "Twitter: The Algorithm," GitHub repository, 2023, https://github.com/twitter/the-algorithm.

76 Ragul Bharvaga et al., "Gobo: A System for Exploring User Control of Invisible Algorithms in Social Media," *CSCW* (2019): 151–155, https://doi.org/10.1145/3311957.3359452.

77 Francis Fukuyama et al., "Report of the Working Group on Platform Scale," Stanford Internet Observatory Cyber Policy Center, November 17, 2020, https://cyber.fsi.stanford.edu/publication/report-working-group-platform-scale.

78 Ethan Zuckerman and Chand Rajendra-Nicolucci, "From Community Governance to Customer Service and Back Again: Re-examining Pre-web Models of Online Governance to Address Platforms' Crisis of Legitimacy," *Social Media and Society* 9, no. 3 (July-September 2023): 1–12, https://doi.org/10.1177/20563051231196864.

79 Tobias Rose-Stockwell, *Outrage Machine: How Tech Amplifies Discontent, Disrupts Democracy—and What We Can Do About It* (London: Piatkus, 2023), also summarized in brief essay form in Tobias Rose-Stockwell, "Facebook's Problems Can Be Solved with Design," *Quartz*, April 30, 2018, https://qz.com/1264547/facebooks-problems-can-be-solved-with-design.

80 James Vincent, "Twitter Is Bringing Its 'Read Before You Retweet' Prompt to All Users," *The Verge*, September 25, 2020, https://www.theverge.com/2020/9/25/21455635/twitter-read-before-you-tweet-article-prompt-rolling-out-globally-soon.

81 Avie Schneider and Scott Horsley, "How Stock Market Circuit Breakers Work," *NPR*, March 9, 2020, https://www.npr.org/2020/03/09/813682567/how-stock-market-circuit-breakers-work.

82 Renée DiResta and Tobias Rose-Stockwell, "How to Stop Misinformation Before It Gets Shared," *Wired*, March 26, 2021, https://www.wired.com/story/how-to-stop-misinformation-before-it-gets-shared.

83 Renée DiResta, "Elon Musk Is Fighting for Attention, Not Free Speech," *The Atlantic*, April 14, 2022, https://www.theatlantic.com/ideas/archive/2022/04/elon-musk-buy-twitter-free-speech/629571.

84 For more suggestions on friction, see Ellen P. Goodman and Karen Kornbluh, "Social Media Platforms Need to Flatten the Curve of Dangerous Misinformation," *Slate*, August 21, 2020, https://slate.com/technology/2020/08/facebook-twitter-youtube-misinformation-virality-speed-bump.html; Ellen P. Goodman, "Digital Information Fidelity and Friction," Knight First Amendment Institute at Columbia University, February 26, 2020, https://knightcolumbia.org/content/digital-fidelity-and-friction; Brett M. Frischmann and Susan Benesch, "Friction-in-Design Regulation as 21st Century Time, Place, and Manner Restriction," *Yale Journal of Law and Technology* 25 (August 2023): 377–447, https://dx.doi.org/10.2139/ssrn.4178647. Also see the library of design interventions broached by user experience (UX) researchers that can be found at the Integrity Institute's website at https://integrityinstitute.org.

85 St. Aubin and Liedke, "Most Americans Favor."

86 For an in-depth examination of these volunteer moderators as a civic labor force in online governance, see J. Nathan Matias, "The Civic Labor of Volunteer Moderators Online," *Social Media + Society*, April 4, 2019, https://journals.sagepub.com/doi/full/10.1177/2056305119836778.

87 Spandana Singh, "Everything in Moderation: An Analysis of How Internet Platforms Are Using Artificial Intelligence to Moderate User-Generated Content," *New American*, July 22, 2019, https://www.newamerica.org/oti/reports/everything-moderation-analysis-how-internet-platforms-are-using-artificial-intelligence-moderate-user-generated-content.

88 "Topologies and Tribulations of Gettr: A Month in the Life of a New Alt-Network," Stanford Internet Observatory Cyber Policy Center, August 12, 2021, https://cyber.fsi.stanford.edu/io /news/topologies-and-tribulations-gettr.

89 David Thiel and Miles McCain, "Gabufacturing Dissent: An In-Depth Analysis of Gab," Stanford Digital Repository, June 1, 2022, https://doi.org/10.25740/ns280ry2029.

90 Asawin Suebsaeng and Adam Rawnsley, "A Pro-Trump Social Network Wants to Corner the Anti-vax 'Jizz Market,'" *Rolling Stone*, March 16, 2023, https://www.rollingstone.com/politics /politics-features/covid-vaccines-infertility-antivax-gettr-social-media-1234697898.

91 Jay Caspian Kang, "What Bluesky Tells Us About the Future of Social Media," *New Yorker*, May 12, 2023, https://www.newyorker.com/news/our-columnists/what-bluesky-tells-us-about-the -future-of-social-media.

92 Alex Heath, "This Is What Instagram's Upcoming Twitter Competitor Looks Like," *The Verge*, June 8, 2023, https://www.theverge.com/2023/6/8/23754304/instagram-meta-twitter-competitor -threads-activitypub.

93 DiResta, "How Online Mobs Act."

94 Joseph B. Bak-Coleman et al., "Stewardship of Global Collective Behavior," *Proceedings of the National Academy of Sciences*, June 21, 2021, https://www.pnas.org/doi/10.1073/pnas.2025 764118.

95 Marcus Aurelius, *Meditations*, trans. Martin Hammond (London: Penguin Books, 2006).

96 Anya Schiffrin, "Fighting Disinformation with Media Literacy—in 1939," *Columbia Journalism Review*, October 10, 2018, https://www.cjr.org/innovations/institute-propaganda-analysis.php.

97 Institute for Propaganda Analysis, *Propaganda, How to Recognize It and Deal with It* (New York: Institute for Propaganda Analysis, 1938), 2.

98 Alfred McClung Lee and Elizabeth Briant Lee, *The Fine Art of Propaganda: A Study of Father Coughlin's Speeches* (New York: Harcourt, Brace and Company, 1939). The ABCs of propaganda were "ASCERTAIN the conflict element in the propaganda you are analyzing. BEHOLD your own reaction to this conflict element. CONCERN yourself with today's propaganda associated with today's conflicts. DOUBT that your opinions are 'your very own.' EVALUATE, therefore, with the greatest care, your own propagandas. FIND THE FACTS before you come to any conclusion. GUARD always, finally, against omnibus words."

99 The "Tricks of the Trade" were articulated in Chapter 3 of *The Fine Art of Propaganda*. I have selected the most appropriate modern emojis available, but here note the original pictographs chosen: Name Calling was symbolized by "the ancient sign of condemnation used by the Vestal Virgins in the Roman Coliseum, a thumb turned down"; Glittering Generality was symbolized by "a glittering gem that may or may not have its apparent value"; Transfer was symbolized by a mask of the style worn by ancient Greek and Roman actors; Testimonial was symbolized by a seal and ribbons, the "stamp of authority"; Plain Folks was symbolized by an old shoe (period slang for an old friend); Card Stacking was symbolized by an ace of spades, "a card traditionally used to signify treachery"; and Band Wagon was symbolized by a bandmaster's hat and baton.

100 Anya Schiffrin, "Fighting Disinformation in the 1930s: Clyde Miller and the Institute for Propaganda Analysis," *International Journal of Communication* 16 (2022): 3715–3741.

101 Philipp Markolin, "Distort, Discredit, Dismiss: The Manipulation Playbook of Anti-science Actors, Part 2," *The Protagonist Future?*, May 15, 2023, https://protagonistfuture.substack.com/p /distort-discredit-dismiss.

102 Stephan Lewandowsky, Ronald E. Robertson, and Renée DiResta, "Challenges in Understanding Human-Algorithm Entanglement During Online Information Consumption," *Perspectives on Psychological Science*, July 10, 2023, https://doi.org/10.1177/17456916231180809.

103 For a full discussion of recent studies examining intervention and responses to political rumors, see Adam J. Berinsky, *Political Rumors: Why We Accept Misinformation and How to Fight It* (Princeton, NJ: Princeton University Press, 2023).

104 Lisa Belkin, "Procter & Gamble Fights Satan Story," *New York Times*, April 18, 1985, https:// www.nytimes.com/1985/04/18/garden/procter-gamble-fights-satan-story.html.

105 Robert Skvarla, "When 1980s Satanic Panic Targeted Procter & Gamble," *Atlas Obscura*, July 13, 2017, https://www.atlasobscura.com/articles/procter-gamble-satan-conspiracy-theory.

106 See Jean-Noël Kapferer, *Rumors: Uses, Interpretations and Images* (New Brunswick, NJ: Transaction Publishers, 2013), chap. 7–8.

107 Laura Blumenfeld, "Procter Gamble's Devil of a Problem," *Washington Post*, July 15, 1991, https://www.washingtonpost.com/archive/lifestyle/1991/07/15/procter-gambles-devil-of-a-problem/36f27641-e679-40f4-ac02-9d12c59a2f3b.

108 Kapferer, *Rumors*, 235.

109 Jessica Contrera, "A QAnon Con: How the Viral Wayfair Sex Trafficking Lie Hurt Real Kids," *Washington Post*, December 16, 2021, https://www.washingtonpost.com/dc-md-va/interactive/2021/wayfair-qanon-sex-trafficking-conspiracy.

110 Kate Starbird et al., "What Makes an Election Rumor Go Viral? Look at These 10 Factors," Neiman Lab, October 25, 2022, https://www.niemanlab.org/2022/10/election-rumors-gone-viral.

111 Stephanie Saul, "Looking, Very Closely, for Voter Fraud," *New York Times*, September 16, 2012, https://www.nytimes.com/2012/09/17/us/politics/groups-like-true-the-vote-are-looking-very-closely-for-voter-fraud.html.

112 As writer Robert Tracinski points out, secret conspiracies and cabals are a staple of Hollywood, so we perhaps shouldn't be surprised when people think that's how our political system works. For more on the connection between entertainment tropes and those that appear in political conspiracy theories, see Robert Tracinski, "The Paranoid Style in American Entertainment," *The UnPopulist*, June 1, 2023, https://www.theunpopulist.net/p/the-paranoid-style-in-american-entertainment.

113 Reuters Staff, "Evidence Disproves Claims of Italian Conspiracy to Meddle in U.S. Election (Known as #ItalyGate)," *Reuters*, January 15, 2021, https://www.reuters.com/article/uk-fact-check-debunking-italy-gate-idUSKBN29K2N8.

114 Jigsaw, "7 Insights from Interviewing Conspiracy Theory Believers," *Medium*, March 17, 2021, https://medium.com/jigsaw/7-insights-from-interviewing-conspiracy-theory-believers-c475005f8598; Renée DiResta and Beth Goldberg, "'Prebunking' Health Misinformation Tropes Can Stop Their Spread," *Wired*, August 28, 2021, https://www.wired.com/story/prebunking-health-misinformation-tropes-can-stop-their-spread.

115 Garret Morrow et al., "The Emerging Science of Content Labeling: Contextualizing Social Media Content Moderation," *Journal of the Association for Information Science and Technology* 73, no. 10 (2022): 1365–1386, https://doi.org/10.1002/asi.24637.

116 Zeve Sanderson et al., "Twitter Flagged Donald Trump's Tweets with Election Misinformation: They Continued to Spread Both on and off the Platform," *Harvard Misinformation Review*, August 24, 2021, https://misinforeview.hks.harvard.edu/article/twitter-flagged-donald-trumps-tweets-with-election-misinformation-they-continued-to-spread-both-on-and-off-the-platform.

117 Stephan Lewandowsky and Sander van der Linden, "Countering Misinformation and Fake News Through Inoculation and Prebunking," *European Review of Social Psychology* 32, no. 2 (2021): 348–384, https://doi.org/10.1080/10463283.2021.1876983.

118 A channel of experimental intervention content created by Google Jigsaw can be found here: Info Interventions, YouTube Channel, https://www.youtube.com/channel/UCiov-3rtgg9Nl_ezyWyOHpQ.

119 Josh Compton, Ben Jackson, and James A. Dimmock, "Persuading Others to Avoid Persuasion: Inoculation Theory and Resistant Health Attitudes," *Frontiers in Psychology* 7, article 122 (2016): 1–9, https://doi.org/10.3389/fpsyg.2016.00122.

120 "Happy Ending," TV Tropes, https://tvtropes.org/pmwiki/pmwiki.php/Main/HappyEnding.

121 Ryan Schocket, "This Woman Tweeted About Having Coffee Every Day with Her Husband—the Internet Tore Her Apart," *BuzzFeed*, October 24, 2022, https://www.buzzfeed.com/ryanschocket2/woman-backlash-for-coffee-husband-tweet.

122 Ezra Klein, "Elon Musk Got Twitter Because He Gets Twitter," *New York Times*, April 27, 2022, https://www.nytimes.com/2022/04/27/opinion/elon-musk-twitter.html.

123 Chris Bail, *Breaking the Social Media Prism: How to Make Our Platforms Less Polarizing* (Princeton, NJ: Princeton University Press, 2021), 101–107.

124 The Climate Science Legal Defense Fund (https://www.csldf.org) offers legal support and educational information to the field and works to ensure that scientists "can conduct, publish, and

discuss their research and advocate for science without the threat of political harassment, censorship, or legal intimidation." For more information, see the fund's website. Physicians started the group Shots Heard Round the World (https://shotsheard.org) to offer support and collective response to medical professionals targeted by anti-vaccine activists.

125 Renée DiResta, "Virus Experts Aren't Getting the Message Out," *The Atlantic*, May 6, 2020, https://www.theatlantic.com/ideas/archive/2020/05/health-experts-dont-understand-how -information-moves/611218.

126 Naomi Oreskes and Erik M. Conway, *Merchants of Doubt: How a Handful of Scientists Obscured the Truth on Issues from Tobacco Smoke to Global Warming* (New York: Bloomsbury Publishing, 2010), 263–265.

127 Lauren Kinkade, "5 Good—and Often Funny—Government Social Media Accounts," *Governing*, December 4, 2022, https://www.governing.com/community/5-good-and-often-funny -government-social-media-accounts.

128 Jaber F. Gubrium and James A. Holstein, *Analyzing Narrative Reality* (Thousand Oaks, CA: Sage Publications, 2009), 211.

129 Taylor Lorenz, "To Fight Vaccine Lies, Authorities Recruit an 'Influencer Army,'" *New York Times*, August 1, 2021, https://www.nytimes.com/2021/08/01/technology/vaccine-lies-influencer -army.html.

Index

RENÉE DIRESTA is the technical research manager at the Stanford Internet Observatory, a cross-disciplinary program of research, teaching, and policy engagement for the study of abuse in information technologies. She studies how information spreads in the digital age, examining how rumors and propaganda proliferate and how emerging technologies reshape the playing field. She has analyzed geopolitical campaigns created by foreign powers such as Russia, China, and Iran; voting-related rumors that led to the January 6 insurrection; and domestic influencers pushing health misinformation and conspiracy theories. She is a contributor at *The Atlantic* and *Wired*. Her bylined writing has appeared in *Foreign Affairs*, *Columbia Journalism Review*, *New York Times*, *Washington Post*, *Yale Review*, *The Guardian*, *POLITICO*, *Slate*, and *Noema*, as well as many academic journals.

PublicAffairs is a publishing house founded in 1997. It is a tribute to the standards, values, and flair of three persons who have served as mentors to countless reporters, writers, editors, and book people of all kinds, including me.

I. F. STONE, proprietor of *I. F. Stone's Weekly*, combined a commitment to the First Amendment with entrepreneurial zeal and reporting skill and became one of the great independent journalists in American history. At the age of eighty, Izzy published *The Trial of Socrates*, which was a national bestseller. He wrote the book after he taught himself ancient Greek.

BENJAMIN C. BRADLEE was for nearly thirty years the charismatic editorial leader of *The Washington Post*. It was Ben who gave the *Post* the range and courage to pursue such historic issues as Watergate. He supported his reporters with a tenacity that made them fearless and it is no accident that so many became authors of influential, best-selling books.

ROBERT L. BERNSTEIN, the chief executive of Random House for more than a quarter century, guided one of the nation's premier publishing houses. Bob was personally responsible for many books of political dissent and argument that challenged tyranny around the globe. He is also the founder and longtime chair of Human Rights Watch, one of the most respected human rights organizations in the world.

. . .

For fifty years, the banner of Public Affairs Press was carried by its owner Morris B. Schnapper, who published Gandhi, Nasser, Toynbee, Truman, and about 1,500 other authors. In 1983, Schnapper was described by *The Washington Post* as "a redoubtable gadfly." His legacy will endure in the books to come.

Peter Osnos, *Founder*